The Law of Contract

Raymond J. Friel

BCL (NUI), LM (Exeter), Barrister at Law
Lecturer in Law, University of Limerick

THE ROUND HALL PRESS

This book was typeset by
Gilbert Gough Typesetting, Dublin, for
THE ROUND HALL PRESS
Kill Lane, Blackrock, Co. Dublin, Ireland
and in North America for
THE ROUND HALL PRESS
c/o International Specialized Book Services
5804 NE Hassalo Street, Portland, OR 97213

A catalogue record for this title
is available from the British Library.

ISBN 1-85800-054-8 hbk
1-85800-066-1 pbk

Printed in Ireland
by Colour Books Ltd

Dedicated to my wife, Majella
and my children, Kevin, Kelly and Brandon

Preface

It is not often that a preface forms an integral part of a text, yet, in writing this book, I have been left with little choice. The reason for this is twofold. First, the area of contract law is already well served by major legal writers, both here and in England. Any new text requires an explanation as to how it proposes to assist our legal understanding of the contractual relationship. Secondly, and of no less significance, this text is sufficiently different from the standard format that we have become familiar with in this jurisdiction; accordingly, some justification of the route chosen by this author is needed. In a limited way this preface attempts to answer those two issues, and in doing so, hopefully, leads to a fuller understanding of the text that will follow it.

First, the law of contract is generously blessed with many excellent treatises on the subject. It is true to say that without these fine contributions, our understanding of the contractual relationship would be greatly impaired. Yet, understanding does not stand still: a time may come when it is right to look again at such an area as contract. Most of the major works in contract, both here and in England, have a long tradition. Whilst benefiting from this longevity, they also suffer somewhat from it. Longevity has led to an evolution of analysis rather than a revolution. This is not necessarily a criticism, the refinement of thought is to be encouraged. It does, however, illustrate that there is space for a fresh approach which, lacking the luxury of such an evolutionary development, is forced to return to first principles. In such manner does legal thought grow. It is not for one moment suggested that new analyses are to be accepted uncritically. The benefit is in advancing new theories, even if, ultimately, they are rejected. In that sense, this text aims to achieve just that: the advancement of new approaches to old problems. It is for the reader to make use of them as appropriate. It is also hoped to avoid the pitfall, too often suffered by the more innovative works on contract, of being so revolutionary in analysis as to be inaccessible to the average lawyer or law student. It does not advance legal theory if a text is confined to the upper shelves of the Law Library, to be used only by a few legal theorists. A balance must be achieved.

The second issue posed above is, in some ways, resolved by the answer to the first issue. This text is different from the standard Irish work. Usually, an Irish textbook will follow the approach adopted in England, and then add Irish variations through local case law. In a number of situations, these Irish cases will be pale reflections of their English counterparts. Indeed, in many instances, there will be attempts to stretch our case law to fit the English principle, even though the similarity is quite tenuous. This is not meant in a critical sense. It merely reflects the reality.

The common law system, wherever situated, depends on the availability of disputes that must be resolved. It is in the judicial resolution of disputes that a corpus, or body, of precedent is built up to give a complete picture of the law. There is no luxury which is comparable to that in the civil law systems of reference to a Code, designed to resolve every conceivable dispute. In a jurisdiction the size of our nearest neighbour, this poses few difficulties. Their legal history is a long, continuous stream. For much of its existence, this legal history has been a shared stream between both ourselves and the British, a stream which many Irish lawyers helped shape. It has not been such a shared stream for nearly eighty years. Their concerns are no longer ours. Yet we continue to assume that they are.

Given a population of under four million, it follows that many principles of law have yet to come before the courts for adjudication. The Supreme Court of this State has made it abundantly clear that English Law does not operate as precedent in this jurisdiction. The inescapable conclusion is that there is a vast corpus of law that remains to be expressed by the courts. For too long, it has been the custom to blindly follow English precedent. It is a core belief of this text that, given the unenumerated Irish common law due to the paucity of case law, it is perfectly legitimate to call upon precedent, not only from England, but from other common law jurisdictions, in particular the United States, Australia and Canada. The obstacles to access have been eradicated in the electronic age. Moreover, much of the analysis of US, Canadian and Australian courts is to be preferred over that espoused in English courts. It should also be possible for Irish courts to adopt these different approaches, given that, in the absence of real Irish authority in so many areas of contract, the shape of our common law still remains open. The text, therefore, remains an open conceptual analysis of many areas of contract, drawing upon not merely the usual line of English authority and Irish observance, but also upon the diversity of the common law as operated in the jurisdictions outlined above. Attempts have also been made to reflect the ever closer European Union and the need to create a European legal ethos if we are to play a full role in the integration process.

But the text aims at more than just this. It aims to advance debate on the general reform of contract. Even where a line of English authority has been adopted in this jurisdiction, reference is made to the approach in other jurisdictions, and these alternative approaches treated with as much validity as those currently accepted. All case law, from whatever jurisdiction and despite not being precedent, operates as a signpost. To take only one direction and then refuse to investigate different directions later, may not always be a wise choice. The design of the text is to show as many signposts as possible within the common law systems, even if at the end the author has chosen, for purposes of clarity, to elect for one approach.

One point not touched upon so far has been the scope of contract as a field of analysis. Here, again, the text has taken a singular approach. If one can be forgiven for using a negative approach, it is best to define the scope of contract by stating that which is excluded. Contracts concerning the relationship of employer/employee are not dealt with to any great extent for a number of reasons which effectively preclude their use as analogous logic for extrapolating general principles of contract law. Perhaps the employer/employee relationship was founded on the concepts of contract, but, just as contract was founded on the concepts of tort, employment contracts have long outgrown their origin. Employment law is heavily controlled by legislation, human rights provisions, industrial relations policy, economic policy and so forth. Its regulation extends far beyond the individual relationship involved, but represents the relationship between society, capital and government. The underlying policy rationale differs significantly from that of contract and these issues are better dealt with in dedicated works.

A similar point must be made with respect to contracts of insurance, for, unlike South Africa, these contracts continue to be regarded as a species apart from general contracts. Whether this is right or wrong is debatable, but the fact remains that such contracts are decided on different policy grounds: their use as signposts in terms of general contractual analysis is to be regarded with caution.

Finally, a text serves the purpose not merely of exposition of the law but also as a vehicle for reform. The text goes some way to achieving this. It does not follow that the reader is expected to accept all the propositions uncritically. On the contrary, it will have served its purpose if it spurs discussion, negative as well as positive. The footnoting is designed to permit the more adventurous researcher the opportunity to delve deeper into the critical issues involved.

I turn to thank all those people without whom this work would not have been published. First and foremost, my widow, or at least that what she must have often thought she was whilst I was writing this text, Majella. Without her inspirational views and discussion and her enthusiasm to finish the project I doubt if I would have had the endurance to ever finish. This has truly been a joint enterprise. To my youngest son, Brandon, whose arrival during this period, and his urgent need for feeding at 2am and 6am, involved him in deep discussion of issues in contract law that will assure him a maladjusted adulthood. To Mary O'Brien, secretary of the Law Department at the University of Limerick who can be summed in one word: irreplaceable! To my colleagues at the Department of Law, in particular Professor Henry Ellis (Head of Department) and Paul McCutcheon for their encouragement, and to Eoin Quill and Michael Mee for incessant conversations on contract. I also thank those students who, during the last six years, have added to my understanding of this fascinating area. And a word of special thanks to the publishers, in particular, Michael Adams and Eilis Maguire, whose patience and tolerance with my foibles is greatly appreciated. In the end however, there is no one to blame for any errors or omissions other than myself and whilst the above mentioned people have a right to share in any credit that might be given towards this text (though not the royalties!), I alone stand responsible for its shortcomings. Given the comments made earlier I have stated the law as I believe it to be this 1st day of June 1995.

RJF

Department of Law,
University of Limerick.

Contents

ENFORCEABLE CONTRACTS

VITIATION OF THE CONTRACT

POLICY RESTRAINTS ON CERTAIN CONTRACTS

DISCHARGE OF THE CONTRACT

REMEDIES FOR BREACH

ASSIGNMENT OF RIGHTS

Table of Cases

Table of Statutes

3. STATUTORY INSTRUMENTS

4. UNITED KINGDOM STATUTES

5. EUROPEAN REGULATIONS

6. AMERICAN STATUTES AND MATERIALS

7. INTERNATIONAL LAW STATUTES

1.00

Introduction

The law of contract concerns voluntary relationships between two or more people.[1] The structure and analysis of this area of law familiar to us today was shaped largely in the 18th century.[2] It has often been said that unless we learn the lessons of history we are doomed to repeat the mistakes of the past. Certainly, a grasp of the history of contract law is very helpful for understanding the present-day rules governing what has become a core subject in legal education within every common law system.

The origin of contract law lies in the law of tort,[3] its evolution in the works of free marketeers like Adam Smith,[4] and its future in the regulatory aspects of modern economics.[5] What follows is a short history of the law of contract; the reader is encouraged to examine the many more detailed works on this subject.[6]

---

1   As examples of how varied the concept of contract can be, examine the following representative possibilities: Murdoch, *Dictionary of Irish Law*, defines a contract as a legally binding agreement; contrast this with *Ballentine's Law Dictionary* which states: 'A term which is simple in its superficial aspect but actually difficult of succinct definition, since nothing less than the whole body of applicable precedent will suffice for the purpose of definition. *Williston, Contracts*, 3rd ed., s. 1 summarily defined as an agreement upon sufficient consideration to do or refrain from doing, a particular lawful thing. 17 Am J2d Contr. s. 1'; 1 Williston, *Contracts*, s. 1 which states: 'A contract is a promise or set of promises, for breach of which the law gives a remedy, or the performance of which the law in some way recognizes as a duty'; or the more modern formulation of Macneil, *The New Social Contract*, 4 (1980): 'The relations among parties to the process of projecting exchange into the future'.

2   See, particularly, Baker, *An Introduction to English Legal History* (1990); Atiyah, *The Rise and Fall of Freedom of Contract* (1979).

3   The law of tort concerns the imposition of a legal relationship between the plaintiff and defendant because it is just to do so; for example if X, while driving his car knocks Y down, the law of tort will impose a relationship between X and Y requiring X to compensate Y for the injuries suffered. Unlike a contract, the relationship between X and Y is not voluntary. For a detailed work on the law of tort, see McMahon and Binchy, *Irish Law of Torts*, 2nd ed. (1990); for a discussion of the historical use of the law of tort in the development of the law of contract, see the writ of assumpsit, 1.04.

4   For a fuller discussion, see chapter 2.

5   Chapter 2.

6   In particular, Simpson, *A History of the Common Law of Contract* (1975); Farnsworth, 'The Past of Promise: An Historical Introduction to Contract', 69 *Columbia Law Review*, 576.

1.01 THE COMMON LAW

Curiously, although contract law is now seen as a bedrock of the modern legal system, originally it fell outside the ambit of the common law courts.[7] Initially, those courts dealt only with issues that arose between the Crown and its subjects, declining jurisdiction unless there was a royal interest in the action.[8] Thus, around the 12th century disputes of a contractual nature between citizens were dealt with through other dispute-resolution mechanisms, of which the common law was only one.[9] Even where the common law courts accepted jurisdiction over a contractual agreement; the common law was not necessarily the best mechanism for resolving such disputes: often the common law courts were inaccesible and expensive when compared with the alternatives.[10]

The growth of the common law is the story of an emerging monopoly, a dispute-resolution system that would eventually conquer its competitors. It should not be forgotten that the basic reason behind this emerging monopoly was simply the search by the courts for increased revenues to satisfy an ever-growing army of adherents, employees, functionaries and philosophers: the more jurisdiction the common law had, the greater its revenues from court and counsel fees.[11] It was some time before another legal system would emerge to effectively challenge the inexorable growth in the common law's jurisdiction. During this period, the common law would steamroll over all its competitors, taking jurisdiction over actions as it saw fit. The area of contractual relationships was ripe for the taking, but this did not happen as easily as might have been expected.

---

7   The common law courts were those established by the King and which travelled the length and breadth of England dispensing the King's justice. This was said to be 'common' to all the people of England. Since these courts were established by the King, their primary jurisdiction was restricted to issues which concerned the King. As was said in Glanvill X 18, 'It is not the custom of the court of the Lord King to protect private agreements' (1180), quoted in Cheshire, Fifoot and Furmston, *The Law of Contract*, 12th ed. (1993), p. 1.

8   Baker, op. cit..

9   Other typical examples of dispute resolution included Church courts, manor courts, university courts and so forth. Remember England was a polyglot society drawing on Celtic, Norman, Roman and Germanic influences. Popular methods of dispute resolution would have included ancient religious rites as well as sheer force of arms!

10 The limited causes of action and the undesirability of the primary common law remedy (damages) in many instances forced people to alternative methods.

11 A legacy of this is to be found in the excessively long formulation of legal documents, born in a time when lawyers were paid by the word and therefore the longer it took to say something, the higher the level of fees earned. Today, although fees are calculated differently, documents remain verbose both by tradition and experience of court interpretation of documents.

1.02 CONTRACTS UNDER SEAL

The first type of contract action that the common law would absorb was the formal 'contract under seal';[12] such written agreements under seal became known as 'covenants'. The reason that covenants were absorbed quickly into the common law was because the common law was based on feudal concepts which placed great emphasis on formality as a sign of seriousness. However, since only the rich could read and write, or at least were in a position to afford to employ those who could, the extension of this jurisdiction was limited to the upper echelons of society. These covenants developed separately from contracts which were not made under seal, and therefore do not form part of the general law of contract which concerns us in this text.[13]

Informal contracts not made under seal remained unenforceable in the common law courts for some time. Initially, the courts may have been quite happy not to extend their jurisdiction. Written documents, used mostly by the upper echelons of society, were of necessity both limited in number and lucrative in value. Aggrieved people of the upper classes could afford to pay for the privilege of using the common law courts. Moroever, an unplanned extension of the courts' jurisdiction to informal contracts would have certain drawbacks; in particular, the number of potential claimants would be relatively large while their individual wealth would be limited.

1.03 INFORMAL CONTRACTS: DEBT SUR CONTRACT AND DETINUE

However, after the common law courts absorbed covenants, it emerged that, for one reason or another, few people, even among the wealthy, used covenants.[14] Far from being overwhelmed in terms of work, the common law courts were still short of revenues, so they felt it necessary to extend their jurisdiction by taking jurisdiction over informal contracts.

12   A seal was a small blob of red wax applied to the document and into which a ring would be impressed. Such rings often bore the form of the family crest. However, a ring was not necessary, and a fingernail would suffice. Today the sealing wax has been replaced by a red self-adhesive sticker: cf. Hazeltine, 'The Formal Contract of Early English Law', 10 *Columbia Law Review* 608.

13   For a brief discussion of contracts under seal see chapter 7 on Consideration, below at page 82.

14   The reason for this is unclear. Instead, penal bonds were used whereby X would covenant to pay Y £200 if he failed to pay on an informal agreement the original sum £50. A breach of the informal agreement would render X liable to the penalty covenant; the aim presumably was to act *in terrorem*, that is, to terrorise the party against whom such a draconian convenant would be enforced. The difficulty was that the penal bond could be rendered useless if lost, or somehow defaced (say, by the seal coming off). Moreover, if the debtor failed to have the bond defaced or destroyed upon satisfaction of the informal agreement, the creditor could still enforce the bond. These bonds fell into disuse with the advent of equity's view of penalty clauses, discussed in chapter 25.

The existing actions of *debt sur contract*[15] and *detinue*[16] offered limited appeal to a claimant. Under these forms of action, the claimant could sue for the debt, that is the amount due, under the contract. These actions offered an attractive solution to informal contract enforcement, but they could only be used to enforce the debt arising from a contract: they were not available where a promise to perform something under the contract had not been complied with, since no debt could have arisen.[17] But by far the biggest drawback to using these forms of action was that they involved 'trial by compurgation', or 'waging the law', whereby the defendant had to swear on oath that the debt was not owed, and then produce eleven other people who would similarly swear as to the facts of the case. If the defendant could persuade eleven others to swear in such manner, the plaintiff would lose and the debt would not be enforced. If the defendant could not find eleven such people, then the plaintiff would win and the debt would have to be paid. Not many litigants found security in this form of resolution, since it was common to pay people to 'wage the law' on one's behalf. It was at this point that the common law found its growth severely impeded by one single competitor which it was never to defeat but with which it was ultimately to form a market-splitting agreement: equity.

1.04 ASSUMPSIT

Dissatisfaction with the common law forced many to resort to the Lord Chancellor in search of a more suitable response.[18] The Lord Chancellor, dispensing his judgments in the courts of equity, became a formidable 'competitor', and it soon became apparent that a large area of jurisdiction was being lost to the common law. This was particularly so in the field of informal contracts. Accordingly, the action of assumpsit was taken off the shelf and modified to

15 An action enabling a claimant to recover money owing to him on foot of a contractual agreement.
16 An action to enabling a claimant to recover goods of his wrongfully detained by another.
17 Suppose X agreed to sell his horse to Y for £500. If X gives Y the horse but does not receive the £500, then X can sue for the amount owing either as a debt sur contract or under detinue. But if Y refuses to take the horse and failed to proceed with the contract, Y could not sue to enforce the contract, since no debt or detinue had arisen.
18 Since the common law courts dispensed the King's justice, a claimant who was unhappy with a decision of the common law court could make a direct appeal to the King. When this occurred, the King would delegate the task of adjudication to his chief clerical officer, the Lord Chancellor, since the Lord Chancellor was the keeper of the King's conscience. It is from the Lord Chancellor that the legal system of equity developed. Equity and the common law were 'fused' in the Judicature Act 1877 after competing with each other for centuries. They are now adminstered in the unified court structure that we have today. Equity acts as a 'gloss' on the common law, seeking to complete the common law, and avoids direct disputes with the common law rules, where possible. Where the two conflict, equity prevails. For a fuller discussion of equity, see Keane, *Equity and Trusts in the Republic of Ireland* (1988).

assist the common law in expanding its jurisdiction over contractual relationships. Assumpsit was a writ form of action[19] used in the prosecution of tortious actions. It had numerous advantages, notably the flexibility of the writ which enabled it to be modified as required. Moreover, the trial of the action was by way of jury, and the remedy available to the litigant was damages.[20] The action on contract was now framed as one of tort. Thus, in *Skyrne v. Butolf* [21] a doctor promised to cure ringworm in return for a sum of money. The money was paid, but the ringworm was not cured. The real action was for breach of contract. The writ, however, was formulated in tort along the lines that the doctor had carried out his responsibilities with malfeasance, that is, he had carried out the task incorrectly. The disadvantage of the writ of assumpsit was that no action would be sustainable for non-feasance, that is, a failure to do that which was promised.[22] This extension to non-feasance occurred in *Pickering v. Thurgood*,[23] creating the true breach-of-contract action used today.

1.05 PROMISE OR CONTRACT?

The cumulative effect of these cases was that an action lay for breach of a promise. The courts, however, were not prepared to enforce promises without limitation. They required an underlying cause of the contract, the motivating factor or, as it is commonly referred to today, the 'consideration' for the contract.[24] From a line of cases which determined what was an enforceable motivation and what was not, the common law developed the doctrine of 'consideration' (discussed more fully later).[25] 'Consideration' became a requirement for all contracts not under seal. Consideration did not receive universal acceptance, and some argued that contracts which had been reduced to writing and signed did not require 'consideration'. Firstly, because, such a contract had a valid and enforceable motivation (the parties had reduced it to writing) and, secondly, the absence of a seal was an irrelevancy as society moved away from the formalism of the feudal era.[26] However, in *Rann v.*

---

19 The writ was a formal written document through which legal cases commenced. They were very precise and technical and fell into established categories. If the facts of a legal dispute could not be brought within the precedent of an existing writ, access to the court was not possible.
20 Damages is the primary common law remedy. It is the payment of a monetary sum to the injured party to compensate for any harm or injury suffered.
21 2 Ric 2 (Ames Series) 223.
22 *Watton v. Brinth*, YB 2 Hen 4, fo 3, pl 9.
23 93 YB Sel Soc 4 (1533).
24 *Joscelin v. Shelton* (1557) 3 Leon 4, Benl 57, Moo KB 51; McGovern, 'Contract in Medieval England: The necessity for quid pro quo and a sum certain', 13 *Am J Leg. Hist.*
25 *Stone v. Wythipol* (1588) Cro Eliz 126, 78 ER 383.
26 See the judgment of Lord Mansfield in *Pilans v. Van Mierop* (1765) 3 Burr 1663.

Hughes[27] that approach was finally rejected. Despite its tortured evolution, history and application, 'consideration' remains firmly rooted in our legal system.[28]

Finally, it should be remembered that the common law's rivalry with equity had not been totally successful. Equity remained a strong competitor of the common law and its impact on contract has been significant.[29] This is particularly so in terms of the remedies available in a contract action and the interpretation of some contractual terms.[30]

1.06 MODERN DEVELOPMENTS

By the 19th century, contract law had come into its own in the complex world of Industrial Revolution England. A notion of individual freedom and rational behaviour gained prominence. Today's contract law is heavily influenced by such notions. In *Printing and Numerical Registering v. Sampson* it was said that:

> If there is one thing more than another which public policy requires it is that men of full age and competent understanding shall have the utmost liberty in contracting and that their contracts, when entered into freely and voluntarily, shall be held sacred and shall be enforced by the Courts of Justice.[31]

The classical analysis of offer and acceptance rests upon the simplistic notion of two people of equal status meeting each other to arrange mutually agreeable terms. Neither side has the advantage, and either party can walk away from the potential contract without fear. The result is an agreement with which the courts will seldom interfere. At the time the theory of contract being agreement between people of equal status became dominant, the legislature was clearly interfering with contracts, protecting the parties to a contract and regulating such arrangements.[32] It can only have done so on the grounds that the idealistic picture painted by the courts was not true: people seldom meet equally. Also

---

27 (1778) 7 Term Rep 350; likewise Lord Mansfield's other attack on consideration, namely its extension to cover moral obligation, was rejected in *Eastwood v. Kenyon* (1840) 11 Ad & El 438; see generally chapter 7 for a fuller treatment of consideration.
28 See, generally, Fried, *Contract as Promise* (1981); Holmes, *The Common Law* (1898).
29 See chapter 16 on Mistake; chapter 17 on Misrepresentation; chapter 26 on Equitable Remedies to mention a few.
30 See, generally, chapter 14 on Exclusion Clauses; chapter 25 on Remedies at Common Law.
31 LR 19 Eq 462.
32 Witness the Sale of Goods Act 1893.

questionable is the extent to which influences from civil law systems came to mould traditional common law thinking through writers such as Powell, Chitty, Pollock and Anson.[33]

In the next chapter, the underlying theories behind contractual relationships are explored, particularly the concept of mutual assent.

---

33 In particular the work of Pothier, *Treatise on the Law of Obligations*, translated into English in 1806.

2.00

Contract Theory

2.01 WHAT IS A CONTRACT?

Any major work on contract must begin with a definition of the term 'contract'.[1] In legal terms a contract almost always presupposes an *enforceable* contract, that is, a contract enforceable by an action through the courts. Thus, a contract differs from a promise: although a promise may exhibit all the signs of a contract and be subject to similar analysis, it does not form part of contract law since it is of itself unenforceable.[2] But even within this general understanding there is no standardised definition of contract. The US Restatement, Contract defines it as:

> a promise or a set of promises for the breach of which the law gives a remedy, or the performance of which the law in some ways recognises as a duty.[3]

This requires an agreed definition of a 'promise', and the Restatement goes on to give just that:

> a manifestation of intention to act or refrain from acting in a specified way, so made as to justify a promise in understanding that a commitment has been made.[4]

---

1   See chapter 1, fn. 1.
2   Typically, promises such as gifts etc. fail to have the necessary consideration required for enforcement; see chapter 7; cf. Fried, *Contract as Promise*, op. cit., whose basic thrust is that 'promise' is the moral bedrock of contract law.
3   Restatement, Second, Contract, s. 1, based on Williston: see chapter 1, fn. 1. A Restatement is a general statement of legal principle in a given field of law, drawn up by members of the legal profession using existing case law but advocating reform where necessary. It is not binding on any court, but it has been instrumental in the development of US law. *Ballantine's Law Dictionary*, op. cit., defined it as: 'a statement of rules of law in certain subjects adopted and promulgated by the American Law Institute, the statement of a rule being entitled to weigh as a product of expert opinion and as the expression of the law by the legal profession. *Poretta v. Superior Dowel*, Co 153 Mo 308, A 2d 361, 71 ALR 2d 989'. (The American Law Institute, or ALI, is an association of legal academics and practitioners from all over the US). There is no comparable concept in Ireland.
4   Restatement, Second, Contract, s. 2(1).

Moreover, the courts have held that contracts which are wholly in the future can be enforced. It is not merely that one party has performed his or her promise and the other is remiss. In the US case of *Bolin Farms v. American Cotton Shippers Association*[5] the court accepted that a future promise to buy in exchange for a future promise to sell could be an enforceable contract. The case typified a number of actions around the mid-1970s, whereby farmers with cotton crops just planted sold forward contracts[6] on their harvest at the prevailing prices (around 30 cents a pound). At harvest time, when the contracts were to come into operation, cotton had become scarce and now sold at 80 cents a pound. Attempts by the farmers to ignore the forward contracts were, of course, unsuccessful. Curiously, it was taken for granted that people could be bound by a future promise of their intention.

Treitel has defined a contract as:

> an agreement giving rise to obligations which are enforced or recognised by law.[7]

In many ways this definition is clearer than the Restatement, although it begs the question of what constitutes an agreement. Agreement presupposes that there are at least two parties[8] and that the parties have expressed the desire to be bound by their intention to pursue a certain course of action. But beyond that, one is forced (if relying upon Treitel's definition) to investigate what attributes of an agreement render it a contract. We find that it is a contract when it exhibits characteristics which render it amenable to the judicial process.

For example, in the US case of *Trustees of Dartmouth College v. Woodward*[9] the provision of the American Constitution to the effect that no State shall pass any law impairing the obligations of contracts[10] was held to apply to a royal charter granted by George III. This would come within Treitel's definition in the loosest sense. Yet it would not constitute the ordinary legal understanding

---

5   370 F. Supp 1353 (WD La 1974); the case is by no means a startling precedent but is used for illustrative purposes only; cf. Treitel, op. cit., p. 1.
6   A forward contract is a contract where the parties agree to buy and sell a particular item for a given price at a given time in the future. Normally the item is not in existence at the time the contract is made; for example, a farmer enters into a forward contract on 1 January to sell his crop for £300 per tonne when it is harvested in August.
7   Treitel, op. cit., p. 1.
8   Despite the colloquialism of making an agreement with oneself, it is clear that, in general, agreement normally involves two or more people: cf. *Eastman v. Wright*, 6 Pick 316 (Mass 1828): 'It is a first principle that in whatever different capacities a person may act, he can never contract with himself, nor maintain an action against himself. He can in no form be both obligor and obligee.'
9   17 US (4 Wheat) 518 (1819).
10 Constitution of the United States of America, Art. 1, s. 10.

of the term.[11] By contrast, in *Rajah v. Royal College of Surgeons*[12] Keane J held that the charter given to the Royal College of Surgeons in Dublin was a private contract and therefore not amenable to judicial review.

Pollock defined a contract as:

> a promise or set of promises which the law will enforce. The specific mark of a contract is the creation of a right not to a thing but to another man's conduct in the future.[13]

This definition is helpful in that it focusses on the personal relationship in the contract—on the fact that it is an agreement between people which shapes their future. Often contracts are seen as affecting things or services; in reality a contract attempts to regulate a relationship, reflecting a diversity that is all too often misunderstood, for, as Corbin points out,

> no definition can ever be the only 'correct' definition. It is a matter of usage and convenience. Usages differ but convenience requires that the usage should be conscious.[14]

It may well be that an all-embracing definition of the term 'contract' is unnecessary. Once something is classified as a contract, it is subject to the close analytical scrutiny that follows in this work when something adverse happens to the relationship between the parties. It will be identified as a contract by compliance with well established rules of 'offer', 'acceptance', 'consideration' and so forth. However, the attempt to define the term in advance is by no means futile, because it does help us understand why we enforce some agreements and not others. It is to this theoretical understanding of contract that we now turn.

2.02 SOME COMMON ELEMENTS AND THEORIES

It is clear from the foregoing that two features are common to any contract:

- plurality of parties and

- an agreement concerning a future course of action.

---

11   Certainly, Farnsworth, op. cit., p. 3 argues that the case is unusual and does not fit well with the modern American understanding of the term 'contract' since it was wholly executory and therefore not a contract at all. It could be implied into the college's royal charter that there was a promise not to alter it in the future, but this may stretch things too far since the charter could have been revoked in its entirety.
12   [1994] 1 ILRM 233.
13   Pollock, *Contracts*, op. cit., p. 1.
14   Corbín, op. cit., p. 5, fn. 2.

Yet, if that were all, a gift would be a contract, since it involves at least two parties and is an agreement to, say, transfer property at some time in the future. But the law of gifts is not the law of contract. What distinguishes those transactions which we deem to be contracts from those which we deem to be gifts? Firstly, a gift is unilateral in that one party is the sole motivator.[15] Contracts, as we understand them, are bargained-for exchanges: there is in a very real sense a promise made in exchange for another thing or promise. There is a mutuality in the transaction (clearly identified by Adam Smith).[16]

The bargained-for exchange   In Adam Smith's model of contract, an exchange is an economic transaction in which both parties seek to maximise their advantage. Smith's model of contract imposes a rational and commercial basis to the contract transaction. Contract serves economics by permitting the transfer of goods and services at the highest value through a cost-effective and efficient distribution system.[17] Contract becomes the medium through which the free market operates. It follows that where a free market does not exist, the need for contract law should also disappear, but this is clearly not so. In the early days of the Soviet Union, Lenin believed that contracts could be replaced by administrative norms. This followed logically from the dissolution of capitalism: the end of capitalism meant the abolition of the marketplace; the production, supply and distribution of goods and services would occur by central regulation. Yet in 1921 Lenin was forced to admit defeat and re-introduce contract law along traditional lines.[18] It must be, therefore, that contract survives even where the economic norms of capitalism have been removed and that, accordingly, contract law does not exclusively serve economic requirements. However, it is true to say that economic realities have shaped our application of contract law, for, as it has been said,

> the primitive state of eighteenth century American contract law is underscored by the surprising fact that some American courts did not enforce executory contracts where there had been no part performance. The pressure to enforce such contracts would not be great in a pre-market economy where contracts for future delivery were rare.[19]

---

15   Finding a phrase to describe the equally complex notion of a gift is impossible. The term used here, motivator, may appear to exclude situations where the gift is in fact motivated by a third person or indeed by the actions of the beneficiaries themselves. But the gift is unilateral; the law gives no other person a right to pursue or compel the motivator to act.

16   Smith, *An Inquiry into the Nature and Causes of the Wealth of Nations*, p. 19: 'never talk of their own necessities but of their disadvantages', with regard to contractual relationships.

17   See, generally, Posner, *Economic Analysis of Law*, 3rd ed.

18   In general, see La Fave (ed.), *Law in the Soviet Society*, particularly pages 128-9.

19   Horwitz, 'The Historical Foundations of Modern Contract Law', 89 *Harvard LR* 929.

It is clear that a principal reason for enforcing entirely executory contracts[20] is founded upon modern market conditions, but this does not lead to the conclusion that the enforcement of such promises would not have come in the absence of the market.[21] Moreover, the bargain theory presupposes that all actions are pursued on an economically rational basis; yet, many transactions are pursued for other reasons, and a contract will be enforced by the courts even if it does not work to the advantage of both parties, provided that it had been freely entered into.[22]

Reliance   If the bargain theory does not give us a generalised rationale for the enforcement of contracts, are there any alternative theories? The notion of 'reliance' seems to provide an unlikely substitute. Reliance occurs where X has expectations created by a promise given by Y, a promise which X has acted upon. Contracts are not enforced merely because an expectation is created and subsequently relied upon. Certainly, it is true to say that the courts have increasingly come to enforce contracts without consideration on the basis of reliance.[23] However, the evolution of reliance in contract law has been too erratic and too recent to give credence to the claim that it forms a basis of contract theory.[24] Further, it would be difficult in this situation to distinguish the law of gifts from that of contract, since reliance is often present in donative (that is, gift) transactions.

Individualism   The enforcement of the free actions of men lies close to the heart of many contract theorists. Heavily influenced by mainland European thinkers,[25] this rationale for contract was particularly strengthened by the works of Pollock. While closely allied to the economic rationale of Adam Smith mentioned earlier, the theory of individualism in contract is taken to a higher

---

20   Executory contracts are those which are to take place entirely in the future, that is, neither party to the contract has at the time of the agreement performed any element of the obligations under the contract.

21   Simpson, 'The Horowitz Thesis and the History of Contracts', 46 *University of Chicago Law Rev* 533.

22   The law will uphold a contract where X sells a house to Y for £5,000, even though the house might be worth £50,000, provided it is satisfied that X has freely chosen to enter into such an agreement. No attempt is made to examine the wisdom of such a contract. See chapter 7 on Consideration.

23   See chapter 8 on Enforcement without Consideration; it is more accurate to view such decisions as a response to the sometimes harsh operation of the doctrine of consideration. It does not indicate any generalised theory of reliance.

24   But see Atiyah, *The Rise and Fall of Freedom of Contract*, op. cit., who argues that reliance is the dominating force behind contract. His historical analysis of reliance in contract is overstated. It may be that it is Atiyah's writings that have brought the reliance concept to greater prominence in modern times, a concept that will be an important feature of the future development of contract law.

25   Pothier, op. cit.; *Cox v. Troy* (1822) 5 B & Ald 474, 480 (Pothier was regarded by Best J as the highest authority next to a decision of a court in England) UCC, s. 2-302.

philosophical plane by removing the need for a market. Indeed, greater emphasis is placed on enforcement of a common course of action arrived at by consent between two or more people: a meeting of minds; the contract is once again the expression of the human relationship, the enforcement of a common purpose. However, this cannot really be separated from the earlier bargain theory, because, in the absence of an economic element, a common agreement to give a gift would also be a contract. Moreover, such a rationale presupposes that the parties are equally met; yet contracts are enforced everyday where the inequality between the parties is strikingly obvious. A meeting of minds can occur only in an artificial reality where all parties possess equivalent strengths and weaknesses. This would render the market element of the theory redundant, because the bargain theory requires a maximisation of the relative needs and strengths of both parties (thus signalling that they are unequal). Further, in ideal situations such freedom of contract could not be fettered or in any way interfered with, since to do so would restrict the freedom of the individual. In practice, however, such regulation is commonplace; both the legislature and the courts constantly intervene where the parties are not equally met in terms of bargaining power. This inequality of bargaining power has been recognised in the United States[26] and certainly hinted at in a number of English judgments.[27] Essential services monopolies and multinational corporations which use the 'standard form contracts'[28] are instances of contracting only on given terms. This method of contracting denies the freedom to negotiate the contract to one of the parties in the transaction. If X wishes to avail of an electricity supply, he is not able to alter the standard terms and conditions of supply offered by the electricity company. Similarly, if X wishes to buy a Ford product, he is unable to negotiate the terms of the sale, other than perhaps the price, and even that negotiation is to an extent illusory.[29] Mutual assent is a fiction that has long since passed from commercial or everyday reality, if it ever really existed. The instances where such freedom remains are so few as to be considered virtually insignificant and certainly not sufficient to base a theory of contract.[30]

26   UCC, s. 2-302.
27   *Schroeder Music Publishing v. Macaulay* [1974] 3 All ER 616, but see *McCord v. ESB* [1980] ILRM 153.
28   The standard form contract is a pre-printed contract which is not open to negotiation by the party seeking to avail of the goods or services on offer from the supplier.
29   The car dealer may seem to be offering a discount, but this has already, presumably, been incorporated into the original cost. The important point is that X cannot say, 'Extend the warranty', or otherwise vary the terms of the contract, since such modern contracts are offered on a 'take it or leave it' basis. In France these are termed 'contrats d'ahesion': see Nichols, *French Law of Contract*.
30   For a different view see Braucher, 'Freedom of Contract and the Second Restatement', 78 *Yale Law Journal* 598: 'the effort to restate the law of contracts in modern terms highlights the resilence of private autonomy in an era of expanding government activity. . . . Freedom of contract, refined and redefined in response to social change, has power it always had.'

2.03 CONTRACT OR CONTRACTS

Given that it is virtually impossible to find a rationale for contract that satisfies the multifaceted nature of the beast, perhaps there should be nominate contracts just as there are general principles of criminal law and nominate crimes of special application. A nominate contract would be a contract that concerns a particular transaction. Thus, there could be a law of contracts-for-sale which would govern all contracts which sought to transfer ownership in property. Similarly, there could be a law for contracts-for-hire or -lease and so on. This view has some merit, and in Roman law contracts were defined as real,[31] consensual[32] or innominate.[33] However, in *Cehave NV v. Bremer Handell-gesellschaft MbH*[34] the issue was laid to rest when Roskill LJ stated:

> It is desirable that the same legal principles should apply to law of contracts as a whole and that different legal principles should not apply to different branches of that law.[35]

However, this is not entirely self-evident. Certain contracts have become so specialised that it is inappropriate to analyse them in depth in a general work on contract. Contracts of employment and contracts of insurance are examples of such specialised contracts. While some of the general contractual principles apply to these transactions, fuller discussion is best left to the specialised works available. There is undoubtedly a general theory of contractual analysis which applies to all contracts and the concept of nominate contracts is not unjustified as an analysis of certain transactions.[36] It has been suggested that the reluctance to accept nominate contracts may stem from the rivalry between Harvard and Yale Law Schools.[37] However, modern statutory intervention normally con-

---

31 Such contracts were dependent upon delivery and could not be applied to a pure exchange of promises.

32 Such contracts could be used to enforce an exchange of promises yet to be executed but confined to sale, hire, partnership and mandate transactions.

33 Innominate contracts were never required by classical Roman philosophy. They emerged by the 6th century in response to political needs of the time. They required a quid pro quo to be enforceable and one side had to have completed performance. There is some support for the view that this quid pro quo was the precursor to consideration in the common law. It should be noted that the 'stipulation' was another method of enforcement which required a formal ritual to make the promise binding.

34 [1975] 3 All ER 739.

35 Op. cit., at 756.

36 See Chitty, op. cit.; vol. 2 deals with Special Contracts.

37 Taken from Cheshire, *Fifoot and Furmston*, op. cit., p. 24, fn. 17: 'In his entertaining book, *The Death of Contract*, Professor Grant Gilmore argues that in Americal law, general contract theory was an invention of the Harvard Law School. Professor Gilmore held a chair at Yale.' The motivation for this was the statement in Gilmore's work that 'the idea that there was such a thing as a general law—or theory—of contract seems never to have occurred to the legal mind until Langdell [Harvard] stumbled across' (at

fines itself to nominate contracts: for example, contracts for the sale of goods are the subject of special statutory regime.[38]

2.04 REFORM OF CONTRACTS

The debate rages on as to the theory underlying contract law. Modern jurists and philosophers continue to explore the relationship between tort and contract;[39] others concentrate on the economic analysis of the subject.[40] Yet it was Sir Henry Maine who declared that

> the movement of the progressive societies has hitherto been a movement from Status to Contract.[41]

And it is true that contract law is intertwined with the growth of a more personalised democracy. Where status as a landowner or hereditary birthright once held pride of place, contract law facilitated the growth of individual freedom which expanded upwards into the democratic institutions.[42] Contract law was primarily developed by the judiciary and is therefore to an extent an unwieldy body of jurisprudence not always accessible to lawyer or layman. In the United States, the American Law Institute,[43] concerning itself not with theory but with the need to make the law accessible, produced the Restatement, Contract, assisted by some of the great contract law jurists of the time.[44] It was finally promulgated in 1932. A revised form of this—Restatement, Second, Contract—was completed in 1981. A Restatement consists of principles of law derived primarily from the case law of the fifty states in the United States. In some ways it is similar to a statute in terms of layout, but it is not enacted and does not carry the force of law. Neither does a Restatement operate as precedent. It aims to state a rational corpus of law with respect to a given area of the law. The Restatements draw on existing case law but are not governed by them, and

---

p. 6). However, Farnsworth, op. cit., is of the opinion the current obsession with contractual theory owes more to Gilmore than to Langdell.

38 Sale of Goods and Supply of Services Act 1980.
39 Coleman, *Risks and Wrongs*.
40 Posner, *Economic Analysis of Law*; Collins, *Law of Contract* (2nd ed.), pp. 1-39; Coleman, *Risks and Wrongs*.
41 Maine, *Ancient Law*, p. 170.
42 Witness, for example, the move away from giving the right to vote based on one's property holdings, the traditional example of democracy by virtue of status.
43 The American Law Institute (ALI) is an association of academic lawyers, members of the judiciary and practitioners of law.
44 Willinston was the 'reporter' charged with responsibility of preparing drafts of the Restatement to the ALI for consideration; Corbin acted as 'special adviser and reporter' for the provisions on Remedies in Contract. All drafts were debated and approved by the ALI.

some departures have occurred in a desire to complete a logical law of contract.[45] The Restatements are supplemented by commentaries and examples as to the impact of the rules.[46] The American courts have found them most useful as persuasive authority. There are those, of course, who take issue with the emphasis in the Restatements upon what the law of contract is rather than what it should be;[47] however, the drawbacks of Restatements have been exaggerated.[48]

Restatements have enabled the courts to push the boundaries of the law further than they would otherwise have reached. A jurisdiction of the size of Ireland simply does not have the volume of case law from which to develop a coherent and independent corpus of jurisprudence. One method of overcoming this difficulty would be to draw up Restatements of the law in a number of areas. A Restatement, particularly of the law of contracts, would not merely be an exposition of existing Irish case law but would draw upon precedents from as vast a source as possible. It would be an ideal instrument to enable the judiciary in Ireland to make full use of their freedom to depart from the doctrine of precedent as enunciated in the mid-1960s.[49] Many benefits can accrue from reasoned argument not subject to the expediencies of decision-making in a practical dispute. This is particularly true in Ireland, where the resources are not in place to give the judiciary the luxury of sufficient time and resources fully to deliberate their judgments. It would give a direction as to the law in a case which has previously has been the subject of litigation. Such a Restatement is to be preferred to the continual reliance on English case law.

Throughout this text reference is made, where appropriate, to the American Restatements. The reader is advised to note that these Restatements are used in the context of illustration and comparison for the purposes of analysis; they do not represent a binding source of authority for the courts.

45 S. 90 Promissory Estoppel.
46 The first Restatement was designed to be supplemented by a series of individual treatises on various areas, but this was abandoned.
47 Writers such as Gilmore, op. cit.; MacNeil, *The New Social Contract*; Unger, 'The Critical Law Studies Movement', 89 *Harvard Law Rev* 1685; Atiyah, op. cit.
48 Clark, 'Restatement of the Law of Contracts', 42 *Yale Law Journal* 643, 655: 'A Restatement then can have no other authority than as the product of men learned in the subject who have studied and deliberated over it. It needs no other and what could be higher?'
49 *The State (Quinn) v. Ryan* [1965] IR 110; Byrne and McCutcheon, *The Irish Legal System* (2nd ed.), p. 118 et seq.

3.00

Offer

3.01 INTRODUCTION

The formation of a contract is traditionally divided into two principal elements: *offer* and *acceptance*. Together these form a concluded contract, provided there is no intervening disability such as lack of capacity[1] or formalities.[2] A concluded contract will only be enforced in a court if it has 'consideration'. Consideration is that element of a contract which binds the parties in a legal sense; it normally takes the form of the 'price' of the contract. It is dealt with in chapter 7.

Offer and *acceptance* are the terms used by lawyers to analyse either the subjective meeting of minds of the parties or the objective manifestation of mutual assent,[3] necessary for the formation of a contract. They are artificial divisions in one entire process that does not easily lend itself to such structures. Nonetheless, as tools for critical analysis they remain unsurpassed. Simply put, a contract can be expressed algebraically as

$$O + A = Ag$$
$$Ag + Co = EC$$

where O = offer, A = acceptance, Ag = agreement, Co = consideration and EC = enforceable contract.

This formulation presupposes at least two parties—that is, one party who makes an offer, which is then accepted by another party to form a contract. One difficulty that remains is whether offer and acceptance are to be determined

---

1 Capacity concerns limitations placed on persons which protect them from entering into legally binding contracts because society feels that they are unable to give a true consent to the contract; for example, children, lunatics etc.; see chapter 5 for a fuller discussion.
2 Some contracts must conform to certain procedural requirements, such as that they must be in writing, signed and so forth. These requirements are known as 'formalities' and are dealt with in chapter 10.
3 Whether the concepts of offer and acceptance are viewed as the intention of those who underake the act in question or whether a third party looking on would view them as an offer or acceptance does not affect that the analysis of the transaction occurs by way of labels of offer and acceptance. A full discussion of this issue takes place in chapters 1 and 2.

objectively or subjectively; this difficulty runs through virtually all contractual analysis. On the one hand, a contract is supposed to be a relationship between two or more parties and their *subjective* intention should take precedence. On the other, because a contract fulfils a social role[4] it must be the subject of social norms and an *objective* analysis is required. While the courts use either theory when it is convenient, it is objective intention which is dominant. We turn then to examine the elements in the formation of a contract beginning with, in this chapter, the Offer.

3.02 AN OFFER DEFINED

What constitutes an offer? Curiously, the definition of the basic starting-point for any contract is in fact far from clear.[5] Many definitions have been attempted and each carries an element of difficulty.[6] One possibility is that an offer is a promise to do or to refrain from doing some specified thing in the future.[7] Of course, this begs the question as to what constitutes a promise. One definition of a promise is that it is

> a manifestation of intent to act or refrain from acting in a specified way, so made as to justify a [person] in understanding that a commitment has been made.[8]

This, to an extent, merely repeats the concept of offer outlined earlier, but it does add one important new element, namely, commitment. We shall see later that this can be quite useful, but that it too suffers from difficulties.[9] If the above definition is correct, it would, for example, imply not merely the making of an

---

4   A contract performs a social role since it regulates commercial activity and private dealings; therefore, society has an interest in ensuring that such contracts are monitored and not used unfairly against the disadvantaged.

5   See Farnsworth, op. cit., p. 135 et seq.; Calamari and Perillo, op. cit., p. 31 et seq.; Treitel, op. cit., p. 8 et seq.; Cheshire, Fifoot and Furmston, op. cit., p. 28 et seq.; *Adams v. Lindsell* (1818) 1 B&D Ald 681; Anson, *Principles of the English Law of Contract*, 2nd. ed., p. 15 et seq.; See also a fuller discussion of the relatively recent historical development of the concept of offer and acceptance in the 19th century in chapter 1.

6   *New Zealand Shipping Company v. Satterthwaite* [1975] AC 154, 167 *per* Wilberforce J: 'English Law having committed itself to a rather technical and schematic doctrine, in application takes a practical approach, often at the cost of forcing the facts to fit uneasily into the marked slots of offer, acceptance and consideration'; see chapter 2 for a discussion of the overlap between offer, acceptance and consideration; Llewellyn, 'On Our Case Law of Contract: Offer and Acceptance' I and II, 48 *Yale LJ1*, 779.

7   Calamari and Perillo, op. cit., p. 31.

8   Restatement, Second, Contracts, s. 2; *Day v. Amex Inc*, 701 F 2d 1258.

9   See the executed contract example discussed supra; moreover, the concept of the promise as being integral to the contract has been seriously questioned by its omission from the Restatement, Second, which concerns itself with a willingness to enter into a bargain which invites acceptance. This replaces the use of 'promise' terminology found

offer but also a completed contract since the commitment is intended to be entered into irrespective of the actions of the person to whom it was addressed (the 'promisee' in legal terms). This clearly is not so, but it does raise a far more fundamental issue: it may well be unsatisfactory to define, or attempt to define, the offer in exclusive terms, independent of other factors. In truth, as mentioned earlier, these terms—offer, acceptance and so forth—are convenient tools of legal analysis but not an end in themselves.[10] It may well be impossible to define offer satisfactorily in isolation from its natural partner, acceptance.[11] Perhaps the best way to put it is that an offer empowers the person to whom it was addressed to create a contract by acceptance.[12]

Such an approach would certainly go a long way in resolving the executed contract of sale. An executed contract of sale occurs where the parties have arranged their affairs so that there is nothing to perform. For example, X and Y meet, and X says to Y, 'You may keep the book that I lent you if you pay me £50.' Such a situation would not fall within the concept of a promise as outlined earlier, since X is making the offer without any promise. If Y promises to pay the sum involved, it is Y who is making the promise, even though he is accepting X's offer. Of course, if Y hands the money over immediately, then even Y has made no promise, but it cannot be suggested that no contract has been formed. A superior method of analysing the concept of an offer is to determine it by way of agreement, namely, that a contract is a bargain made by the parties, determined as a question of fact and to be found in their language or by implication from other circumstances. The difficulty here is that while this helps with respect to what constitutes a contract, it does not move us any further along the analysis of the individual elements of such a contract.

If it is necessary to have a standard definition of contract, the preferred definition would be a

> a willingness to contract on certain terms made with the intention that it shall become binding as soon as it is accepted by the person to whom it is addressed.[13]

This is not an entirely satisfactory definition, but it is the best available.

in the first Restatement, and is further in accord with the UCC which talks of bargain and agreement: see Mooney, 'Old Kontract Principles and Karls New Kode', 11 *Vill.L.Rev* 213; Barndt, 'The Possible Words of promise', 45 *Tex.L.Rev* 44; Fried, *Contract as Promise*, op. cit.

10   Farnsworth, op. cit., p. 112 et seq. terms the entire operation the 'bargaining process' and see chapter 2 for a fuller discussion of the issues of external manifestation of agreement.

11   Restatement, Second, Contracts, s. 22, Comment a. (possible to have a completed contract even though one is unable to pinpoint the separate occurrence of an offer and its acceptance); *New Zealand Shipping Co. v. Satterthwaite* [1975] AC 154, 167.

12   *Storer v. Manchester CC* [1974] 1 WLR 1403; *League Gen Ins Co. v. Tvedt*, 317 NW 2d 40 (1982).

13   Treitel, op. cit., p. 8.

3.03 TO WHOM MAY AN OFFER BE MADE?

As a general rule, no restriction is placed on the person, or persons, to whom an offer may be made. We shall see later that a contract will only be enforced between certain persons (under the concept of 'capacity' some people are prevented from entering into contracts because they lack the requisite ability to give their consent—for example, because they are too young, or are of unsound mind etc.: see chapter 5) but this does not operate to prevent an offer being made to any person.[14] This is so even if an offer is made to one who does not have the requisite capacity.[15] The outcome of such an offer may have no legal effect, but it is a valid offer. An offer can be made to more than one person, even to persons not known by the person making the offer. I can, therefore, make an offer in the abstract: it does not have to be aimed at any particular individual. The most common example of this would be the reward situation, where the offeror promises to reward a person who finds some lost article or animal.

Thus, in *Carlill v. Carbolic Smokeball Co.*[16] the defendants had advertised the effectiveness of their product, a smokeball designed to prevent those who followed the recommended instructions from contracting the influenza virus. At the time of this case, influenza was a menacing disease which often proved fatal. So confident were the defendants in their product that they promised to pay the then princely sum of £100 to those who purchased their product, took it as prescribed but still contracted the influenza. The plaintiff, Mrs Carlill, having read the advertisement, purchased the item, took it as prescribed but nonetheless caught the influenza virus. She sought to claim the £100 according to the terms of the advertisement. This is a case we shall refer to extensively on the issue of formation of the contract, but at this point one interesting defence, among many pleaded by the company, was that the advertisement could not have constituted an offer since it was not addressed to any person in particular; in fact, it could be said to be an offer made to the world, or, at the very least, readers of the paper in question. This, the defendants claimed, was too uncertain to find that an offer had been made. In effect they were claiming that an offer had to have a restricted mailing list. In finding for the plaintiff, the court dismissed this defence, as well as the other defences raised by the company. It held that there was nothing inherently wrong with an offer made to the world at large. A contract only occurs with that portion of the world that decides to

14 Capacity limits a person's ability to accept an offer, not to receive one; the issue is discussed in fuller detail in chapter 5.

15 An offer can be made to a group of people even if among that group there are those who by virtue of a lack of capacity could not accept it. Similarly, an offer made to one individual is not invalidated simply because the offeree has no capacity to accept (though such an exchange is of little concern to the lawyer).

16 [1892] 2 QB 484; [1893] 1 QB 256; see also *Kennedy v. London Express Newspapers* [1931] IR 532 (an offer of insurance to daily purchasers of the Express Newspapers was accepted by plaintiff's purchase in Ireland).

accept such an offer. If the offeror is willing to assume to himself the risk as to how many persons accept the offer, then so be it. Thus, an offer can be made to one or more people who may be both unknown and indeterminate.

The case in question posed another issue which we shall now examine: to what extent must the offeror intend to make an offer? It was clear from the facts of this case that the company were genuinely surprised that the plaintiff had treated the advertisement as a serious offer, since they intended it be an advertising promotion. How did the court deal with the argument that the advertisement was not intended to be an offer and certainly not intended to be taken seriously?

3.04 INTENTION TO OFFER

To what extent must an offeror intend to make an offer?[17] In *Carlill*[18] we have seen that the offeror did not intend to make an offer but was engaged in what could be described as advertising hype, that is, making claims for his product not seriously intended to be taken for real. Many advertisments do just that—the car that promises to attract highly desirable members of the opposite sex, or, in these more environmentally conscious days, the car that promises to protect the bunny rabbits and trees on the planet. In essence this is what the Carbolic Smokeball Company was doing—making exorbitant claims for its product which could not be accepted as serious by the people reading such advertisments. This argument had received a welcome in the courts prior to this case. By and large advertisements are not intended to create offers, even where the advertisment contains no greater claim than the price of the product or its specification.[19] Thus, an advertisment contained in a newspaper or brochure is not normally an offer which can be accepted; it is regarded as an invitation to treat,[20] that is, an offer to receive offers—a lure, the fly on the end of the fishing

17 See Treitel, op. cit., p. 8-9; Calamari and Perillo, op. cit., p. 25-31. Farnsworth, op.. cit., p. 137.

18 [1892] 2 QB 484; [1893] 1 QB 256.

19 *Schenectady Stove Co. v. Holbrook*, 101 NY 45, 4 NE 4 (1885) (catalogue was not an offer); *Ward v. Johnson*, 209 Mass. 89, 95 NE 290 (1911) (circular not an offer) *Fisher v. Bell* [1960] 3 All ER, 731 (display of goods with price tag is not an offer); *Partridge v. Crittendon* [1968] 1 WLR 1204 (advertisement in newspaper not an offer for sale). Note that Treitel, op. cit., p. 13 differentiates between advertisements of bilateral contracts which are never offers and unilateral contracts, such as *Carlill* or the reward posters which will be offers. This goes too far. Some bilateral advertisments may be intended to be offers and if so intended there should be no reason to deny them effectiveness. The issue must be decided case by case, looking at the objective intention of the offeror, discussed supra. As Farnsworth, op. cit., points out at p. 138, the usefulness of precedents in this sphere must be marginal.

20 The term 'invitation to treat' is a term of art and therefore has no technical meaning ascribed to its actual words but is a shorthand way of stating that the element of a transaction was an invitation to receive offers. This does mean that there are other statements outside of offers or invitations to treat; these are discussed later.

line. It baits the addressee to make an offer which the seller is free to accept or reject. There are advantages to this approach. If an advertisment were an offer, what would be the situation where the price of the product was misprinted for one reason or another?[21]

In *Carlill* the court reminded us that it was not the nature of the act in question that was crucial, but the intent behind this act. In this case, the defendants had gone to considerable lengths to bring about a belief in the mind of the person reading the advertisment that it was intended as an offer—not just the usual advertising hype. Thus, they placed a sum of money on deposit in a special account with a named bank from which the £100 was to be paid. They detailed, in considerable depth, the conditions to be satisfied before claiming the £100, and so on. All of these actions led to the objective belief that the defendants intended to make a serious offer. The court had to choose between objective belief or subjective belief.[22] They opted for objective belief by asking would a third party looking on at the events in question to come to the conclusion that the offeror intended to make an offer, irrespective of the actual intention of the offeror. Thus, if X jokingly offers to sell his favourite car for 50p, no offer has come into existence provided an objective third party would conclude that X did not intend to make such an offer. On the other hand, if X jokingly makes an offer that a third party would consider serious, then an acceptance will be binding even if X did not intend to be so bound. Again the same principles would apply if X had made the statements due to the fact that he were vexed, angry or excited. It also stands to reason that Y may have personal knowledge that no offer has been made, even though, from an objective viewpoint, it may appear that a serious offer has been made: for example, Y may know that the offer

---

21   If an advertisement is an offer, then the offeror will be bound by the terms of the offer and accordingly the offer can be accepted as presented even if it contains a mistake not due to any fault of the offeror, such as a printer's error on price. At first glance it may appear correct to deny advertisments the effect of being an offer save in rare circumstances, but this would overlook a number of factors. Firstly, it is the offeror who chooses the medium and, since he has taken the advantages that the medium can offer, why should the law protect him from its disadvantages? Secondly, the offeror could avoid this danger by inserting in the advertisement a statement that errors and omissions are excepted. Finally, any error caused by the negligence of another could be recovered under the law of tort from the person who carries the blame for the error.

22   *Hotchkiss v. National City Bank*, 200 Fed. 287, 293 (SDNY 1911): 'A contract has, strictly speaking, nothing to do with the personal or individual intent of the parties. A contract is an obligation attached by mere force of law to certain acts of the parties, usually words, which ordinarily accompany and represent a known intent.' This sums up the objective approach and should be contrasted with Williston, 'Mutual Assent in the Formation of Contracts' in *Selected Readings on the Law of Contracts* 119 (1931) which finds expression within a 'meeting of minds' theory outlined in Chapter 2; see also Whittier, 'The Restatement of Contracts and Mutual Assent' 17 *Calif.L.Rev* 441 ('To act intentionally is not to desire the consequences of that intention', at 447-448).

concerns something which has been a matter of jocularity between the parties for some time previous.[23]

This 'objective test' is not without difficulties and, although it has held sway for some time, new approaches are beginning to emerge which may cast some doubt on it.[24] The problem about the objective test of determining if an offer has been made is that it does not fit well within the traditional concept of contract as being a meeting of minds discussed earlier.[25] For a meeting of minds approach to succeed, it would require a subjective test, enquiring into the mental state of the offeror to see whether an offer was intended. Such an approach has considerable merit and is the dominant thought behind French jurisprudence.[26] The disadvantage is that it removes the addressee of the offer from the equation, yet the impact of the statements on the person to whom they are aimed is of the utmost importance. The best solution would be to retain the current objective test and seriously question whether the meeting-of-minds theory of contract holds sway in the modern commercial world, or indeed whether it ever did.[27]

3.05 OFFERS DISTINGUISHED

It has been shown that the crucial element in the formation of an offer is the intention of the offeror, ascertained objectively. It follows that we can determine, in advance, situations where the courts will hold that something is not an offer but an invitation to treat. However, an individual may act so as to convert into an offer what would objectively be regarded as an invitation to treat. Thus, in *Carlill* it was held that while the objective view that an advertisment does not ordinarily constitute an offer, was reversed by objective acts of the defendant to make an offer, evidenced by the great lengths that the defendants went to show earnest good faith.

The principle underlying advertisments underlies many other everyday realities. For example, a kitchen showroom may attractively display its products to the best advantage, placing pleasing combinations of woods and appliances for people to browse through. Yet the displays themselves are not meant to be sold; they are indicative of the style that the purchaser can have. Much will

---

23 *Smith v. Richardson*, 31 Ky LR 1082; *Higgins v. Lessig*, 49 IllApp 459 (1893) (words not an offer because offeror was over excited and could not be taken seriously); *Keller v. Holderman*, 11 Mich 248 (1863) (whole matter was a frolic).
24 See chapter 2.
25 See chapter 1.
26 Chloros, 'Comparative aspects of the intention to create legal relations in contract', 33 *Tul L Rev*, 607; even with the subjective test, some external manifestation is required. Thus in practice the difference may not be as great as the theory would suggest.
27 The concept of freedom to contract and a true meeting of minds may be valid if society conducts business on a one-to-one basis but with companies it is not possible to discover the thoughts of a company. Further, how can an individual alter corporate contracts?; see chapters 1 and 2.

depend on the purchaser's individual kitchen, the sort of remedial work necessary to install the units, and so forth. It will also depend on the availability of the supplier to install the units. The seller may choose to proceed with one customer and not another, if, say, one of the customer's request is uneconomical. The purpose is to maximise the number of offers received and yet retain overall control as to which offers to accept. This also finds expression in advertisements, and also in modern retailing with the self-service store. Most modern stores arrange themselves in an appealing and exciting way, encouraging one to enter, browse and ultimately purchase. In such a situation, where the items are displayed with a price sticker the intention must be they are to be sold—but who offers and who accepts?

In *Boots Cash Chemist v. Pharmaceutical Society of Great Britain*[28] the defendants introduced a novel way of selling goods for that time—the self serve concept where the goods were displayed on the shelves with prices attached. Customers walked around the store, selecting their requirements before approaching the centralised cash point of sale, where they proceeded to pay for their purchases. The goods in question were, however, subject to statutory regulation which prevented their *offer for sale* other than by a qualified chemist.[29] At the centralised cash point of sale, a qualified chemist was present but not at the locations where the items in question were displayed. The plaintiffs argued that the display of the goods in question constituted an offer for sale and that, in the absence of a qualified chemist, the defendants were in breach of the law. This argument was rejected; it was held that the display of the goods was an invitation to treat which resulted in the customer's proceeding to the centralised cash point of sale, at which stage the customer made an offer with respect to those goods he tendered before the cashier. The defendants were free to accept or reject the offer, at which point a qualified chemist was present. This approach has been followed in Ireland in *Minister of Industry and Commerce v. Pim*,[30] where in similar circumstances the display of a suit in a window which carried the credit terms for purchase, but not the corresponding cash price, was held not to be in violation of the statutory bar on offering goods for sale on credit in such a manner.[31] The display was merely an invitation to treat which invited offers to be made by the general public.

Is there any sound policy reasoning behind this approach? It might be argued that to regard advertisements or displayed items as offers would be inappropriate because no reference is made to the quantity of goods on offer and an offer cannot be made where the quantity is left uncertain.[32] This is somewhat

---

28 [1953] 1 QB 401. The case is not helpful in determining when the acceptance is made by the store, see chapter 4.
29 Pharmacy and Poisons Act 1933, s. 18(1).
30 [1966] IR 154.
31 Hire Purchase Act 1946.
32 See Calamari and Perillo, op. cit., p. 33 et seq.

fallacious. On this approach, *Carlill* should have gone the way of the defendants since it was not possible to predict with certainty the number of people who would accept the offer.[33] Likewise, such reasoning may be countered by the inference that the reasonable man would presume that the items were offered on the basis of reasonable quantity, on a first-come, first-served basis. This would be the case in advertments. With respect to the display of goods, the items are obviously available only to the quantity displayed and no more.[34] For goods on display, it might be argued that since a store owner has the right to eject any customer or have him removed,[35] no offer can be made where the offeror can prevent a person from accepting it. This again poses difficulties in that it mixes questions of land law and contract law; just because I can restrict access to my property, surely this does not affect whether I have made an offer or not. The two issues are distinct: one concerns whom I wish to allow onto private property; the other is supposed to be a question of objective intention. Can it be seriously argued that a third person looking at a display or advert does not believe that the intention is to offer the goods for sale? The issue is in fact one of policy rather than rationale.[36]

The instance of the bus which trundles along its route day after day is illustrative in this connection. Is the bus making an offer by stopping at the various points, an offer which is accepted as soon as you board the bus; or is it an invitation to treat — the passenger offering himself to the conductor to be taken someplace and the conductor being free to accept or reject? In *Wilkie v. London Passenger Transport Board*[37] Lord Greene proposed that the contract was concluded as soon as the intending passenger set foot on the bus since this is the act of acceptance.[38] The view more consistent with earlier case law is that the opposite is true, that is, that the passenger makes an offer when he gets on the bus, an offer which the driver or conductor is free to accept or reject. The interesting point here is that even at relatively high levels of jurisprudence, there remains a surprising degree of confusion. If it is a policy-based decision that advertments and displays are invitations to treat, it follows that, likewise, bus

---

33   It might be argued that, in *Carlill*, the potential number of people who could accept could be estimated at a maximum of the number of units of the smokeball sold during the period in question and thus was not uncertain as to quantity. This is too far to have to go to make the proposition workable. The defendants clearly did not envisage doing this, nor presumably did any plaintiff, actual or potential.

34   It surely could not be beyond the law to imply into offers of a self-service nature that the items are on offer to that limited extent they are displayed.

35   Certainly this was advanced in *Boots Cash Chemist* and it does state a well settled principle of land law that the owner or occupier of property has absolute control over who may come onto the property. This is not lost in a retail shop situation.

36   It is policy because to elect that the display of goods is either an offer or an invitation to treat is perfectly reasonable, both having advantages and drawbacks and both valid choices which the courts arbitrate.

37   [1947] 1 All ER 258.

38   [1947] 1 All ER 258 (obiter).

routes etc. are also invitations to treat. The aim of the bus in plying these routes is similar in character to an advertisment: it seeks to attract people to the service being offered, but it makes no promise that the service will always be available.[39] Of course, there would be nothing to prevent a counter argument that the policy rationale behind these earlier cases has disappeared and therefore the policy should be reversed. This is the situation in France where the display of goods is considered to be a conditional offer subject to the right of the offeror to refuse an unreasonable acceptance.[40] In the United States, *Giant Food Inc. v. Washington Coca Cola Bottling Co.*[41] has resulted in a ruling that the display of goods in a supermarket constitutes an offer; this overturns the traditional concept in US law (which had followed the principle outlined in the *Boots* case).

The difficulties with respect to mistakes in advertisments or labels can be overcome by the so-called 'Printer's Ink' statutes, which make misleading and false advertising an offence.[42] Moreover, even in the absence of a corresponding Uniform Deceptive Trade Practices Act[43] in Ireland, it is likely that a person here who advertises goods and services with no intention of selling them as advertised, might be guilty of an offence.[44]

As discussed earlier, even if the act in question falls within one of the currently recognised instances of an invitation to treat, it may be that the intention of the person making this act will be sufficient to transform an invitation to treat into an offer. Suppose, for example, I advertise on Monday

---

39   It might be arguable that different rules should apply with respect to public services and those operated by private individuals. A public service is not an invitation to treat since it operates irrespective of offers and therefore a public bus service is in fact an offer since it is mandated by law. Different considerations apply to a privately operated service. Note that in *Wilson v. Belfast Corporation* a newspaper report of an offer by the Corporation to pay half the wages of employees who enlisted in the Great War was held not to be an offer since the Corporation did not intend to conduct its affairs in this manner; therefore if they had, it would have been an offer; see *Billings v. Arnott* (1945) 80 ILTR 50.

40   Nicholas, *French Law of Contract*, op. cit. p. 59 et seq.; Chloros, 'Comparative aspects of the intention to create legal relations in contract', 33 *Tul L Rev* 607; Schlesinger, *Formation of Contracts: A Study of the Common Core of Legal Systems*, pp. 364-365.

41   273 Md 593, 332 A 2d 1 (1975); *Lasky v. Economy Grocery Stores* 65 NE 2d 305, 163 ALR 235 (1946) (Massachusetts Supreme Court held that display of goods on a shelf is an offer); *Sancho Lopez v. Fedor Food Corp.*, 211 NYS 2d 953 (1961) (New York Court held that display of goods an offer); in both *Lasky* and *Sancho Lopez*, the action concerned an exploding bottle which injured the customer. If the display was an offer, then it might have been accepted by the store owner bringing a contract into existence and yielding strict liability for the customer's injuries rather than leaving the customer to rely on an action of negligence in tort.

42   See *McKinney's New York Personal Law*, s. 190.20 as an example.

43   Dole, 'Merchant and Consumer Protection: The Uniform Deceptive Trade Practices Act', 76 *Yale LJ* 485. The Uniform Act condemns advertising goods with no intention of selling them or of selling them in any reasonable quantity unless so limited expressly in the advertisement.

44   It might also fall foul of the Advertising Standards Authority.

that I will sell for £1 a 54' colour TV valued at £1,500 to the first person through the door of my store on the following Saturday. I see X camping outside my store waiting for the sale to begin, and I enjoy the increased publicity this is bringing my store. On Saturday, just before I open, I peer out the window at X, unkempt, unshaved and unwashed, almost collapsing from starvation. I then proceed to place a sign saying the sale has been cancelled. Has X any rights? In theory the answer is no, since my promotion was an invitation to treat which I withdrew before any offer was made. Even if I allowed X enter and make an offer, I could still refuse to accept it. In the US case of *Lefkowitz v. Great Minneapolis Surplus Store*[45] a similar fact situation arose and the court held that the store owner had made an offer which the plaintiff had accepted by being the first to present himself with the requisite $1. Calamari and Perillo make much of the fact that the case concerned the sale of a single item. They argue that the judgment might have been different if more than one item had been on offer, since it would be unclear as to how many units would be available to each customer.[46] This cannot be. In the absence of any restriction on quantity, it is safe to assume that the first purchaser could buy the entire available stock. The offeror has made his offer free of restrictions and thus subject to such risk. According to the Restatement, Second, the case revolved around the inclusion of the words: FIRST COME FIRST SERVED.[47] These constituted a promise which would normally be missing from an ordinary advertisment. But this too fails to satisfy the issues raised, because we have already seen that a promise is not necessary to the making of an offer. The case requires a court to examine the intention of the person involved as to whether a third party would view that an offer was intended.

One further point in the example outlined at the start of the preceding paragraph would be where the store owner does not withdraw the offer but refuses, on sound principles of land law, to refuse entry to a person of such unkempt and untidy appearance. Thus, even though the offer is not revoked, it cannot be accepted by the person most deserving of it. Such conflicts of principle are interesting and would probably require resolution on equitable grounds.

If we accept that, in modern conditions, the display of items constitutes an offer to sell, this can only be so where the offer is sufficiently certain as to the terms on which it is being made. The ordinary display situation will make it clear that the quantity displayed is available at the price displayed. Likewise an advertisement implies that the items are on offer for the stated price to the extent that they are available. But there will be many situations where actions do not go beyond an outward appearance of inviting interest. A general advertisement proclaiming the immense value of a brand of motor cars, which contains no information other than a general price 'from £10,000', never constitutes an

45   251 Minn 188, 86 NW 2d 689 (1957).
46   Calamari and Perillo, op. cit., p. 37.

47   Restatement, Second, Contracts, s. 26, ill.1.

offer, because its terms are too vague in that they are not capable of being accepted but must be further elucidated through negotiation.[48] It is the lack of certainty in displays or advertisments that is the crucial element in denying them the characteristics of an offer.

3.06 STATEMENTS THAT ARE NEITHER OFFERS NOR INVITATIONS TO TREAT

Some statements cannot be categorised as offers or invitations to treat, because they do not contain the requisite elements for either. All that is important to the law of contract is whether the statement constitutes an offer, the rest being effectively disregarded. But for the purposes of analysis one has to distinguish invitations to treat which invite the making of offers from statements that do not. The reason for this is that a response to an invitation to treat is more likely to be regarded as an offer which can in turn be accepted. However, if the statement is not an invitation to treat, then the response to the statement will usually be regarded as an invitation to treat, thus delaying or preventing a contract from arising.

Statements of intention   Statements of intention, opinion, hopes or expectations constitute neither offers nor invitations to treat. In the American case of *Anderson v. Backlund*[49] a tenant farmer was behind in his rent to the landlord. After explaining the reason for the arrears, the landlord advised to the tenant purchase more cattle. The tenant worried that he might be overstocked with respect to the amount of water available but was assured by the landlord to '[n]ever mind about the water, John, I will see there will be plenty of water because it never failed in Minnesota yet.' The tenant then purchased over 100 cattle but unfortunately the rains did fail in Minnesota that year, causing extensive loss to the tenant. The statement of the landlord could not be considered an offer but a statement of opinion, presumably on the basis that the events outlined were out of his control.[50] It might have been different if the landlord had said that he would make good any loss suffered by the tenant arising from water shortage.[51]

Thus, in *Harvey v. Facey*,[52] in response to a question, 'What is the lowest cash price you would accept for a property?' the reply was 'Lowest cash price £900'. It was held that the reply was not an offer but a statement of intention or opinion to which the inquirer could not signal his acceptance. Likewise, a

48   See chapter 2.
49   159 Minn 423, 199 NW 90 (1924).
50   Yet there will be situations where a valid contract will be created over an event which is out of the control of both parties: lack of control is one issue only.
51   Restatement, Second, Contracts, s. 2, Comment d.
52   [1893] AC 552.

statement that 'I am going to sell my car for £10,000' is not an offer, since it constitutes a statement of future action. It is not intended to be something which can be accepted. In the American case of *Owen v. Tunison*,[53] in response to an inquiry as to whether the defendant would accept $6,000 for his store, he replied, 'It would not be possible for me to sell it unless I was to receive $16,000 cash.' It was held that this reply was not an offer which could be accepted by the defendant and, contrary to the judgment, it is difficult to see how it could even be classified as an invitation to treat. It was nothing more than a statement of opinion in response to a hypothetical question. The corollary is also true and perhaps more illustrative of the point. The plaintiff's initial statement, 'Will you sell your store for $6,000?', could not constitute an offer since it merely inquired as to a factual situation.

Letter of intent   Business transactions are often completed by way of so-called 'letters of intent'. These do not constitute offers. It must be realised that the label is not of crucial importance; what matters is the substance of the transaction. Labelling the item as a letter of intent cannot alter the substantive reality that it is in fact an offer capable of acceptance.[54] Policy statements must also be distinguished so that in the American case of *Beverage Distributors v. Olympia Brewing Co.*[55] it was held that the following statement did not constitute a promise: 'it is our intention that if they show the ability and application required to make the business successful under reasonable direction of our organisation, they shall have a reasonable amount of the new common stock, which will be issued exclusively to members of our organisation.' It constituted a statement of policy and was thus not capable of acceptance.

Estimates   A slightly more difficult situation arises with the concept of the estimate given by workmen, (or indeed professionals such as lawyers or accountants) as to the anticipated cost of work to be done for a client. It is obvious that no one believes the estimate to be calculated with scientific exactitude; it is more of an approximate figure. A figure sometimes said to be in the 'neighbourhood' of the final outcome.[56] But if the exact figure is not binding, to what extent is the 'neighbourhood' binding? And who judges what the neighbourhood is, if it is binding? The answers to these questions are far from clear. In the United States some cases have used the concept of equitable estoppel if the plaintiff can be reasonably shown to have relied upon the near accuracy of the estimate and if the defendant who gave the estimate was an

53   131 Me 42, 15 A 926 (1932).
54   *California Food Service Corp v. Great Am. Ins.*, 128 Cal Rptr 67 (1982).
55   440 F 2d 21 (1971); *Tansey v. College of Occupational Therapists* unreported, High Court, Murphy J 1986 (information pack to student did not constitute an offer but was merely designed to convey information).
56   *United States v. Briggs Manufacturing*, 460 F 2d 1195; note that the decision was based on equitable principles; see infra.

expert.[57] Whether such cases could be used in this jurisdiction remains to be seen. Moreover, many industry specific voluntary codes of practice require accredited professionals to honour quotes so given.

Quotes What of the situation where someone quotes the price of an item? In *Fairmount Glass Works v. Grunden-Martin Woodenware*[58] (the so-called *Mason green jar* case) the defendant, in response to an inquiry for the price of 1,000 Mason green jars, replied with specific details of price and terms in a document that was headed a 'quote'. This is similar to the case of *Harvey v. Facey* mentioned above, and one would have expected that the quote was not an offer but a statement of fact or intention at worst, an invitation to treat at best. Nonetheless, the court held that the quote was in fact an offer. Crucial to the decision appears to be the fact that it was in response to an inquiry that sought an offer; that it was detailed in its terms and conditions; and that it required 'immediate acceptance'. In *Harvey*, the two latter factors were clearly absent: there was insufficient detailing of the terms and conditions on which the defendant was offering the property for sale, and it did not invite an acceptance (as had been the situation with the *Mason green jar* case). The detail required of an offer is probably not determinate, provided the offer is certain to the extent of what is being negotiated. With real property, such as land, this requires many details, but for personal property it usually requires few details. A quote or other similar action will constitute an offer when it invites acceptance: in a sense it then fulfils the definition of an offer outlined earlier.

3.07 SOME SPECIAL SITUATIONS

Two situations give rise to special consideration—the auction and the tender. As a general rule both are governed by the same principles, and there is no particular logic behind those principles. In an auction, the bids constitute the offers, which are accepted by the fall of the hammer whereby the items are 'knocked down', so to speak.[59] Putting the item up for auction constitutes an invitation to treat; the offers received may be accepted or rejected. The last offer has the effect of terminating the previous lower bid; that is, a bid by X of £10 will terminate the earlier bid by Y of £8. Such offers are rejected by withdrawing the items from the auction, normally because they have failed to reach the 'reserve price', that is, a minimum price set by the seller below which he will not proceed. Occasionally, in an effort to secure as much interest in an item as possible, auctions are advertised as being held 'without reserve'. The addition of these two words significantly alters the position. Once an auction is to be

57   *Dennington Partridge v. Mingus*, 179 NW 2d 748.
58   106 Ky 659, 51 SW 196 (1899).
59   Sale of Goods Act (1893), s. 58(2).

held 'without reserve' and the auction has begun, the item in question must be sold to the highest bidder, no matter how low that bid may be.[60] It is not possible to withdraw the item in question.

Advertising an auction, either with or without reserve, involves no guarantee that the auction will be held, and a prospective bidder can claim no compensation if he has travelled at great expense to attend an auction only to discover that it has been cancelled, perhaps because the items in question have been sold prior to the auction.[61]

Tenders are little more than written auctions where people are invited to tender an offer to undertake some work or purchase some goods. Each tender received offers to contract at a given price which the person who seeks the tender is free to accept or reject. Like bids in an auction, the tender constitutes an offer and the person who places the tender is free to accept any or none. If the tender is advertised with the stipulation that it will go to the highest or lowest bidder depending on the circumstances, this operates along the lines of an auction without reserve and in receiving tenders one is obligated to accept the highest or lowest offer, as the case may be.[62] This opens up the potential, as exposed in *Harvela Investments v. Royal Trust of Canada*,[63] to the so-called 'referential bid'.[64] Here the first defendant had accepted a tender made by the second defendant which offered to pay $101,000 more than the highest offer received in the tender process. The plaintiffs had placed the highest fixed bid. The first defendant had rejected the bid as it could not be the highest bid, given the existence of the referential bid offered by the second defendant. The House of Lords held against the referential bid as being an invalid bid, presumably on the grounds that otherwise future tendering could consist of nothing but referential bids and therefore there would be no real offer to base such referential bids on. This argument, while possible, is unlikely. It is more probable that many people will have a limit beyond which they will not go; that is, few bidders have a blank cheque policy. If such a bidder is willing effectively to pay any price which is asked, why should he be prevented from so doing and why should the acceptor be so prevented from accepting a bid that is clearly to his advantage? Moreover, an acceptor can negative the chances of obtaining only referential bids, and thereby having nothing to refer those bids to, by expressly excluding such bids in the terms of the tender. If he does not do so, it is at his own peril. The *Harvela* case while representing present law, must be of doubtful logic.

---

60   *Tully v. Irish Land Commission* (1961) 97 ILTR 174. It is presumed that damages are awarded against the auctioneer who withdraws the item, although he is normally indemnified by the true owner of the item. The calculation of such damages is unclear; see *Warlow v. Harrison* (1859) 1 E&E 309.

61   *Harris v. Nickerson* (1873) LR 8 QB 286.

62   Clark, op. cit., p. 9;. 1 Corbin, s. 46.

63   [1986] AC 207.

64   A referential bid is one made with reference to the other offers or bids received; for example, '£100 more than any bid received.'.

It is interesting to note that the *Harvela* case concerned a tender given to a select few parties and was not of general circulation. People were specifically invited to give bids. In other jurisdictions, there have been cases where on similar facts tenders of that sort have been held to be offers.[65]

3.08 TERMINATION OF OFFERS

Any offer may be terminated before it has been accepted. Once an offer has been accepted, it cannot be terminated since a completed contract has come into existence. It thus becomes important to know when an effective acceptance has occurred; this will be examined in the next chapter.[66] At this point, we will study the actions that affect the existence of an offer and the ability of the offeror to withdraw same.

Rejection   An offer may be terminated by rejection. Once an offer has been made, a refusal to accept brings it to an end. There are a number of possibilities. First, the offer is rejected by express words or conduct. This poses no difficulties: X offers to sell Y his car for £5,000; Y refuses this offer but later, having thought about it and discussed it with his bank manager, returns to X, saying he is willing to proceed. Y's first refusal operates to cancel X's original offer. Y's subsequent statement constitutes an offer which X is free to accept or reject.[67] This is so even if the item in question is still in X's possession, that is, if it has not been sold to a third party. The only difficulty arises where Y replies to X's original offer in a way that is not clear as to whether it is a rejection of that offer or an inquiry for further details. Thus, in *Stevenson, Jacques & Co v. McLean,*[68] a telegram asking whether delivery might take place over a period of four months was held not to be a rejection of the original offer but merely an inquiry.

An offer may be rejected by implied words or conduct; for example, X does

---

65   *Ron Engineering Construction Eastern Ltd v. Ontario* (1981) 119 DLR (3d) 267; *Martselos Services Ltd v. Arctic College* (1994) 111 DLR (4th) 65; *Harvela* may be explicable on the basis that the tender was addressed to two parties only to determine which of them would pay the highest price and permitting a referential bid would have defeated that purpose; see also *Blackpool and Fylde Aero Club v. Blackpool Borough Council* [1990] 3 All ER 25 (tender sent to invited participants to be received in a special envelope and before a certain time, tender lodged within time but due to fault of the offeror it was not collected until after the deadline had expired and was not considered. *Held* that the offeror was contractually bound to consider the tender as the terms of the offer were binding).

66   See page 39, infra.

67   *Tinn v. Hoffman & Co.* (1873) 29 LT 271; *Hyde v. Wrench* (1840) 3 Beav 334 (counter offer has same effect as rejection); see fn. 4 below; Restatement, Second, Contracts, s. 39, Comment a.

68   (1880) 5 QBD 346.

not reject the original offer but in fact makes a 'counter offer'.[69] Thus, X offers to sell the vehicle for £5,000, to which Y replies, 'I'll give you £4,500.' This is a counter offer, and, although the original offer has not been expressly rejected, Y's response effectively rejects and destroys the original offer. This shall be looked at in in greater detail in the chapter on Acceptance. It is interesting to note that, with a slight variation (Y says, 'Will you take £4,500?'), such a response may be construed as an inquiry leaving the original offer intact and capable of acceptance. Furthermore there is some American authority that a counter offer may not destroy an original offer if certain words are used, for example, 'keeping the offer under advisement'.[70]

Finally it is important to note that a rejection of an offer is not valid until it is received by the offeror.[71] If an acceptance of the offer is received before the rejection, then a completed contract comes into effect.

Revocation   Can the offeror revoke the offer? There is no reason why the offeror should not be able to do so, provided that such revocation occurs before acceptance. It is important to remember that revocation of an offer is not effective until it is received.[72] It is therefore vital to determine at what stage an acceptance occurs, particularly where an acceptance can occur before it is received by the offeror,[73] for this may well result in a completed contract having come into existence unknown to the offeror, and in a vain attempt to revoke his offer, which has already been accepted.[74]

Must the revocation of the offer be communicated to the offeree? In *Dickinson v. Dodds*,[75] Dodds offered to sell his property to Dickinson. He stated that this offer would remain open until a given date in the future. One day before the deadline, Dickinson was approached by a stranger who claimed the property had been sold to a third party, a person called Allen. Dickinson nonetheless subsequently purported to accept the offer, ignoring the knowledge gained from the stranger. Dickinson was unsuccessful in forcing the transaction to proceed. The revocation had been reasonably communicated to Dickinson and was

---

69   *Hyde v. Wrench* (1840) 3 Beav 334 (X offered his farm to Y for £1,000. Y offered £950, which was rejected. The subsequent attempt by Y to accept the offer of £1,000 was held ineffective).

70   Restatement Second, Contracts, s. 39, ill. 3; *Radford & Guise v. Practical Premium Co.*, 125 Ark 199.

71   See Treitel, op. cit., p. 42-43; Restatement, Second, Contracts, s. 40.

72   *Walker v. Glass* [1979] NI 129 (revocation of the offer effective when made prior to the act of acceptance — in this case the payment of a deposit — despite offeror being advised of offeree's intention to accept the offer); *Byrne v. Tienhoven* (1880) 5 CPD 344; revocation does not occur merely by the offeror acting inconsistent with the existence of an offer: *Adams v. Lindsell*, 1 B & Ald 681.

73   Under the 'postal rule' an acceptance sent by the post is valid once it has been posted. It does not have to received.

74   See the postal rule outlined in chapter 4 on Acceptance.

75   (1876) 2 ChD 463.

therefore valid. The subsequent attempt to accept the offer was invalid as the offer was no longer in existence. There are difficulties with this approach, since it removes the necessity for the offeror to make any attempt to convey the revocation.[76] Is an offeree bound by information he overhears from others that the offer has been revoked, perhaps by way of its being accepted by a third party? What if offeree X hears that the offeror has made a new offer to a third party, offeree Y? Does that implicitly revoke the offer made to offeree X? Or would it only work with respect to offeree X and not offeree Y, who would be entitled to assume that the offeror has put himself at peril by having more than one offer current with respect to the same item?[77] It is unfortunate that the case causes more unnecessary confusion in this regard; the better view would be to render such indirect revocation ineffective. There are sound jurisprudential reasons for requiring the revocation of an offer to come exclusively from the offeror and not to permit the actions of the offeree to determine revocation. Indirect revocation should not be confused with attempted revocation.[78] Attempted revocation is effective if the offeree becomes aware of it. Attempted revocation is an attempt by the offeror to revoke the offer which has not yet succeeded because, say, the offeror cannot locate the offeree. If the offeree subsequently hears that the offeror is looking all over town for him to revoke the offer, then the offer is revoked from the time the offeree became aware of that fact. Indirect revocation would occur if the offeror sold the item in question to another person, without attempting to revoke the offer to the original offeree. In that situation, *Dickinson* would support the view that revocation takes place if the offeree becomes aware of the revocation, by whatever means, including his own efforts. This is a poor decision.[79]

One final point in *Dickinson* is that the offeror promised to keep the offer open for a given amount of time. In contract we are not concerned with the enforcement of promises. This promise was not enforceable as it does not satisfy the full requirements of a contract; notably, no consideration had been given for the promise to render it enforceable in a court. For a further and fuller discussion of this issue, see the chapter on Consideration.[80]

How may an offer made to a number of unidentifiable people (such as an advertisement), be revoked? The revocation notice should take the same form as the offer. To be effective the notice of the revocation should be for the same duration and with the same prominence as the offer.[81] If this is not possible, then the revocation must occur by the best means possible, given the facts of

---

76 1 Corbin, s. 40; Treitel, op. cit., pp. 41-42; Calamari and Perillo, op. cit., pp. 97-98.

77 Restatment, Second, Contracts, s.40; Calamari and Perillo, op. cit., p. 98.

78 For a fuller discussion of the concept, see Calamari and Perillo, op. cit., pp. 96-98.

79 This directly conflicts with the earlier made point that merely acting inconsistent with the offer does not revoke it.

80 Chapter 7.

81 Restatement, Second, Contracts, s. 43; *Shuey v. U.S.* 92 US (2 Otto) 73, 23 L Ed 697 (1875).

the case.[82] Even where the offer is made to persons unknown, if the offeror is aware of the identity of one or more of the offerees, then revocation should be communicated directly to them.[83]

Unilateral offers cannot be revoked once acceptance commences, even though it is not complete.[84] A unilateral offer invites acceptance by perform-ance, the most typical example being the reward cases—notices attached to lamp-posts stating, 'Find my Dog. Reward £50'. No one expects notification of acceptance of such an offer; acceptance is intimately bound up with the performance of the offer. If I offer you £5,000 if you eat 500 pizzas I cannot wait until you are on Pizza No. 498 before whispering in your ear: 'I've changed my mind, the offer is revoked!' Such revocation is ineffective. Compare this to the situation where I say that if you eat 500 pizzas tomorrow at 12 noon, I will give you £5,000. Of course, this can be revoked at any time prior to 12 noon tomorrow but not thereafter, because acceptance will have commenced even though you may not have completed the acceptance.[85]

Lapse of time   An offer cannot remain open indefinitely. We have already seen that where an offer is stated to be open for a given amount of time this is not binding. The offer may be revoked prior to the stated time.[86] However, if the offer is not revoked, it expires once the deadline has passed.[87]

Where no deadline is given during which acceptance must occur, an offer remains open for a reasonable amount of time. What is reasonable depends entirely upon the circumstances of the offer. Thus in *Ramsgate Victoria Hotel*

---

82   Williston, s. 59A.
83   Restatement, Second, Contracts, s. 46, ill. 1.
84   *Daulia v. Four Millbank Nominees* [1978] Ch 231; traditionally common law views an offer to a unilateral contract as revocable up until the point acceptance is completed. This is consistent with general principles but its application would be unjust. An offer to a unilateral contract becomes irrevocable once the task of acceptance has begun. Accordingly the offeree is not bound to complete the contract just because he has commenced its acceptance but the offer is now incapable of revocation; see Restatement, Second, Contracts, s. 45.
85   This requires distinguishing between commencement and preparation of the acceptance; see *Bretz v. Union Cent Life Ins Co.*, 134 Ohio St. 171, 16 NE 2d 272 (1938), Restatement, Second Contracts, s. 45, Comment f.
86   *Dooley v. Egan* (1938) 72 ILTR 155 (immediate acceptance could be required failing which the offer lapsed); *Parkgrange Investments v. Shandon Park Mills*, unreported, High Court, 2 May 1991, Carroll J: 'a purchaser who does not accept a contract as proffered runs the risk that his counter offer will not be accepted. A purchaser who ignores a time limit for accepting an offer runs the risk that it will lapse.'
87   This follows logically. An offer that carries with it a notice of its expiration cannot be valid beyond it. There is, of course, some difficulty with when the time is to run from, for, as Williston (1 s. 53A) and Corbin (1 S.35) point out, this can be ambiguous: for example, an offer, stated to last for eight days, is sent on the 1st of the month but is not received until the 4th of the month; from which date is time to run? The issue is resolved if the offer is phrased as eight days 'from the date hereof'.

v. Montefiore[88] a delay from June to November was considered to be too long and resulted in the offer lapsing. In *Loring v. City of Boston*[89] a reward which was not claimed until four years after it had been advertised was held to have lapsed due to passage of time. Likewise, telephone or oral communication invites an immediate response which does not last beyond the communication in question.[90] An offer made by airmail or fax requires a response in similar fashion and so forth.[91]

In addition to calculating the time for which the offer is open, what is the effect of a late acceptance, that is, one received after the expiry of the specified date or a time calculated to be reasonable? One view is that the offeror can waive the lateness of the acceptance and accept it without notifying the person who sent the acceptance.[92] This would appear to be the least preferred view,[93] though the criticisms are somewhat overstated.[94] The so-called 'late acceptance is in reality a new offer which must be accepted in the usual manner. This is the approach adopted by the Restatement, Second,[95] but the difficulties of such a rigid approach have been considerable.[96] There seems no reason why a late acceptance cannot operate as a valid acceptance, at the option of the offeror. If the offeror chooses to accept a late acceptance, and the offeree has sent a late acceptance aware that it might not qualify, both parties have acted at their peril: why should the law deny them their wishes if it is to both parties' satisfaction?

Death or incapacity   Curiously, the effect of death on an offer is far from clear. It is important to remember that we are concerned with a death which occurs prior to the acceptance of the offer. If a death occurs after the acceptance of the offer, then the enforcement will depend on the nature of the contract, that is, whether it can be performed from the estate of the deceased person or whether it is a personal obligation which is frustrated by death.

Notice of the death of the offeror to the offeree constitutes a revocation of the offer.[97] What is the situation where the offeree is unaware of the offeror's

---

88   (1866) LR 1 Exch 109.
89   7 Metcalf 409 (1844).
90   For a fuller discussion of these issues see chapter 4 on Acceptance.
91   *Entores v. Miles Far East Corp.* [1955] 2 QB 327
92   1 Williston, s. 92.
93   Restatement, Second, Contracts, s. 70, Comment a.
94   The argument runs that it violates a basic principle of contract law, namely, the communication of acceptance (1 Williston, s. 92) but with respect the communication of acceptance is aimed at protecting the offeror and if he elects to drop this protection, then so be it. The only manner in which it can be unwittingly lost is in the postal rule situation, but even there the offeror, having utilised the medium of the mail, does so at his own peril and cannot subsequently resile from its disadvantages.
95   To the extent that the Restatement in fact resolves the issue at all, see Restatement, Second, Contracts, s. 70, Comment b.
96   *Santa Monica Unified School Dist. v. Persh*, 5 Cal App 3d 945, 85 Cal Rptr 463 (1970).
97   *In re Whelan* [1897] 1 IR 575; *Coulthart v. Clementson* (1879) 5 QBD 42.

death? In *Bradbury v. Morgan*[98] the deceased had written to the plaintiffs seeking that they extend credit to X which would be guaranteed by the deceased. The plaintiffs extended credit and were unaware of the subsequent death of the deceased. They subsequently sought to enforce the guarantee against the defendants, the deceased's estate. Channell B was of the opinion

> In the case of a contract death does not in general operate as a revocation, but only in exceptional cases and this is not within them.[99]

This case concerned a completed contract, after which death had occurred. It was enforceable because it could be satisfied out of the deceased's estate. The majority view in the United States is that the death of the offeror revokes the offer even if the offeree was unaware of this death,[100] but this has been described as a 'frequently criticised relic of the subjective theory'.[101] The minority view would be that if the offeree is unaware of the offeror's death, then the offer is not revoked. The latter view is preferable. Where the offeree is aware of the offeror's death, no acceptance occurs, because the offer is revoked by the act of death. If the offeree is unaware of the offeror's death, then the offer is not revoked and may be accepted. The enforcement of the completed contract will, however, depend on the nature of the contract. A personal contract is not enforceable, whereas a non-personal contract is.[102] A personal contract is one which requires the offeror to do something personal, such as to sing or write a book. The offeror's obligation cannot be satsified from his estate. A non-personal contract can be satisfied from the estate of the offeror if it requires the payment of money or the transfer of property. The distinction may seem academic, but there will be instances when it is important to discover whether a contract has been entered into, even if it is unenforceable.[103]

The death of the offeree is a different matter. An offer, even one made to the world at large, is made on the assumption that it is to living people and that it is not made to dead people.[104] Accordingly, the offer would lapse with the death

---

98 (1862) 1 H&C 249.
99 Channell B, fn. 32, op. cit., p. 475.
100 Restatement, Second, Contracts, s. 48, Comment a.
101 Oliphant, 'Duration and Termination of an Offer', 18 *Mich L Rev* 201; Calamari and Perillo, op. cit., p. 95.
102 The 'estate' of a deceased person is the sum total of the assets held by the deceased at the moment of his death.
103 For example, it may well be that on one fact situation if a contract has been completed then it may be performed out of the estate of the deceased offeror, whereas if it was merely an offer, then the death of the offeror may terminate the offer, even if a concluded contract could have been enforced against the deceased's estate.
104 *Reynolds v. Atherton* (1921) 125 LT 690: 'It would be more accurate to say that the offer having been made to a living person who ceases to be a living person before the offer is accepted, there is no longer an offer at all. The offer is not intended to be made to a dead person or to his executors, and the offer ceases to be an offer capable of acceptance' *per* Warrington LJ at p. 695; see also Calamari and Perillo, op. cit., pp. 95-96.

of the offeree; this occurred in *In re Irvine*,[105] where an acceptance posted by the son of the offeree after his death was held to be invalid.

One final point is that an offeror may suffer from a lack of capacity which occurs subsequent to the offer being made; for example, X makes an offer and is subsequently declared insane.[106] This should be treated identically to the effect of death on the offeror. As to what constitutes incapacity, see a detailed exposition in the chapter on Capacity.

105 [1928] 3 DLR 268.
106 Restatement, Second, Contracts, s. 48, Comment b.; Calamari and Perillo, op. cit., p. 95.

4.00

Acceptance

4.01 INTRODUCTION

We have already seen how an offer is best defined in terms of something which can be accepted. It might be thought, therefore, that an 'acceptance' can be defined with relative ease, yet the same difficulties that arise with the concept of the offer arise here as well. Many of the difficulties stem from an analysis of a single transaction into artificial segments such as offer and acceptance. One thing is clear: an acceptance concludes the formation of a contract. Note that an acceptance does not affect the validity or enforcement of a contract, but only its formation. A contract is formed once an offer has been accepted, but there are many reasons why that contract may not be enforced.[1]

Moreover, it should be remembered that a valid acceptance results in the end of the offer: once accepted, an offer cannot be revoked or altered in any way. The offer, which, prior to acceptance, had an independent existence, now survives only as an element of the entire contract.

What then, defines an acceptance? Corbin states that it is

> a voluntary act of the offeree whereby he exercises the power conferred upon him by the offer and thereby creates the set of legal relations called a contract.[2]

This definition is of limited usefulness, because we must first satisfy ourselves that an offer has been made. Indeed, an acceptance is really a response to an offer, a response which completes a contract. Prolonged analysis of the acceptance merely results in a circular argument. Offer and acceptance are the two sides of the same coin, they are natural partners. In defining offer in the preceding chapter, many of the difficulties outlined are applicable also to acceptance.

---

1   Lack of capacity of any party, see chapter 5; lack of formalities, chapter 6; lack of consideration, chapter 7.
2   Corbin, 'Offer and Acceptance and some of the Resulting Legal Relations', 26 *Yale Law Journal* 169, 199.

4.02 WHO MAY ACCEPT?

The person to whom an offer is addressed is the only person who can accept that offer, and is known as the offeree. Therefore, an offer cannot be accepted by someone other than the offeree. This highlights the extraordinary power that the offeror has in determining the extent to which he is willing to enter into a contractual agreement. There is no right in the offeree to transfer the power of acceptance;[3] however, once the acceptance is complete and a contract has come into existence, it is possible that contractual rights can be assigned (we shall discuss this later).[4]

For example: X and Y are discussing the sale of X's car to Y. X says, 'I will sell it to you for £5,000.' It is not open to a passer-by, Z, to interject and say, 'I'll take it at that price.' X's offer was made to Y alone. X addressed no offer to Z. The same would be true where Y had rejected X's offer before Z's interjection.[5]

An offer can be made to anyone and in any form. Thus, offers to the entire world have been held valid. But how is the identity of the offeree to be ascertained? If the offeree is specified by the offeror, there will seldom be any difficulty. A problem arises in the interpretation of an offer which involves more than one specific offeree. For example, suppose X makes an offer to Y and Z: must both Y and Z accept, or is it sufficient for Y alone to accept? In American law, all the offerees must accept.[6] This is normally the case in Ireland as well, but it is more accurate to say that such situations are a question of fact to be determined by a court on a case by case basis. The proper construction placed on the wording of the offer, as to whom the offeree is supposed to be, is the meaning that the reasonable man would take from the offer.

The same holds true where the identity of the offeree is not specified in the offer, that is, the identity is to be determined by using the reasonable man test:[7] who in the opinion of the reasonable man would be the intended addressees of the offer in question? This is a determination which will change from circumstance to circumstance.[8]

3   Restatement, Second, Contracts, s. 52; Wagner, 'How and by Whom may an offer be accepted', 11 *Vill.L.Rev* 95.

4   See chapter 28 ibid.

5   *Apostolic Revival Tabernacle v. Febel Inc.*, 131 Ill App 579, 266 NE 2d 545.

6   *Meister v. Arden-Mayfair Inc*, 276 Or 517, 555 P 2d 923 (1976).

7   Restatement, Second, Contracts, s. 29

8   In *Carlill v. Carbolic Smokeball Co.*, op. cit., the offer could be accepted by any number of persons who knew of the offer, whereas an offer of a reward for finding a lost kitten will only be capable of acceptance by one person. Yet both are unilateral offers made to the public, see 1 Williston ss. 32, 33A. One interesting point is the situation where a reward is offered for information leading to the conviction of certain criminals. More than one person may accept such an offer, yet it cannot be the belief of a reasonable man that the offer was to pay the reward to every one who offers the information. There is some merit in dividing the reward between those who gave the information, see 1 Corbin, op. cit., s. 64.

One final point is the problem raised by Calamari and Perillo,[9] where an offer is made to a person or corporation trading under a business name and where the ownership subsequently changes hands. Suppose X is trading under the name 'Acme Supply' and receives an offer from Y. Before the offer is accepted, Z buys X out and then purports to accept the offer made by Y. Can Z do this? Remember, unlike a company, a business name has no legal status and is not an entity *per se*. Under principles of company law, a change in ownership of a company will not affect any of its legal responsibilities: the company is liable on its own account.[10] What, then, is the answer to the problem of the business name? Calamari and Perillo seem unsure and suggest that it may, ultimately, be a question of fact to be determined from all the surrounding circumstances. The best advice is preventative in nature: namely, offers should not be made to business names, but only to individuals or companies.

4.03 INTENTION TO ACCEPT

Must the offeree intend to accept the offer? Theoretically, the answer is yes. However, there are a number of difficulties with this simplistic response. First, we must distinguish forcefully between offers made in bilateral and unilateral contracts, since they yield different consequences. *Bilateral* contracts are addressed to specified individuals and create a contract once accepted, even though the object of that contract has not been performed. *Unilateral* contracts are, in general, addressed to a wider audience and are not accepted until performance has begun.

Intent versus motive   As a general rule, no acceptance is valid unless made with intent to accept the offer.[11] This pre-supposes that the offeree had knowledge of the offer.[12] This is certainly the view taken by the major English treatises on contract. This requirement for intent to accept an offer is based on the agreement theory of contract which requires that an acceptance is given in exchange for an offer.[13] It is important not to confuse intent with motive. The law seldom concerns itself with the motives of individuals, which are too varied

---

9   Calamari and Perillo, op. cit., p. 77 et seq. The facts are loosely based on *Boulton v. Jones*, 157 Eng Rep 232 (Ex 1857)
10   See chapter 5 on Capacity to Contract.
11   1, Williston ss. 66, 67; *Parkgrange Investments v. Shandon Park Mills*, unreported, High Court, May 1991, Carroll J.
12   *Tracomin SA v. Anton C. Nielsen* [1984] 2 Lloyds Rep 195; note that once knowledge of the offer is present, the presumption is the offeree intends to accept the offer. This presumption is rebuttable by evidence to the contrary.
13   *R. v. Clarke* (1927) 40 CLR 227, see Treitel, op. cit., p. 34 et seq; Cheshire, Fifoot and Furmston, op. cit., p. 54 et seq; but cf. *Gibbons v. Proctor* (1891) 64 LT 594 (information was given by plaintiff before he was aware of the reward. Held that he was entitled to the reward).

to be discernible.[14] Thus, in *Williams v. Carwardine*[15] a statement leading to the conviction of certain criminals for which there was a reward, was held to be an acceptance of the reward offer. The person making the statement knew of the reward, but was motivated by the fact that she thought she was near death and wanted to repent for her sins before departing this life. It was held that she could recover the reward which had been offered. This case can be contrasted, irreconcilably, with the leading Australian case of *R. v. Clarke,*[16] where a suspect, knowing there was a reward for the conviction of the perpetrators of a crime of which he was suspected, gave information leading to the conviction of the real criminals. His motive was to clear his name. He claimed the reward but failed in his action on the basis that he had not given the information in exchange for the offer but had acted for his own reasons.

Subjective v objective intent   The cases illustrate two different approaches to the theory of contract law. *Carwardine* represents an objective theory, whereas *Clarke* represents a subjective theory. *Carwardine* can be rationalised on the basis that intent is that which may be objectively verified, that is, the making of a statement leading to the conviction of the criminals. Presumably intent can only be negated by evidence that the acceptance of the offer was involuntary—for example, where the information was given as a result of police interrogation. It is not the case that a person who, as a result of police questions, gives information which leads to the conviction of some criminal is entitled to a reward, unless that person has voluntarily given the information to the police on his own initiative. In the absence of factors which negate intent, the motive of the act, be it revenge or repentance, does not invalidate the acceptance. This approach is the better proposition of the two cases. *Clarke* has been justified on a number of grounds in Carter and Harland.[17] They suggest two possibilities. The first is that Clarke had not brought himself within the confines of the reward offer. However, this is doubtful on the facts of the case; nor did the court feel it necessary to deal with it to any great extent in the judgement.[18] The second possibility is that *Carwardine* and *Clarke* are reconcilable and that the difference is one of evidence. The evidence in *Carwardine's* case was that she intended to accept the offer, whereas the evidence in *Clarke* was that there was

14   'For the Devil himself knows not the intent of a man': Anon (1478) YB 17 Edw IV Pasch. fl-pl.2. cited in Fifoot, *History and Sources of the Common Law*, p. 253.
15   (1833) 5 C & P 566, 4 B&Ad 621.
16   (1927) 40 CLR 228.
17   Carter and Harland, op. cit., p. 54 et seq. Note that in America, *Simmons v. US*, 308 F 2d 160 is authority for the proposition that it is sufficient if the actions of the offeree were in some part caused by the offer, even if only to a minor extent.
18   The evidence of the plaintiff did not lead to the arrest of one of the convicted murderers. The arrest of that murderer occurred before the information was given. Moreover, the information led to the conviction of persons who committed one of the two murders only. The argument is that this 'acceptance' did not sufficiently correspond with the offer of the reward.

no motivation other than self-preservation and a corresponding lack of intent to accept. This proposition, that the cases are reconcilable, relies on the Australian approach of a subjective theory of contract which is not applicable here.

However, a word of warning about the rule may be appropriate at this stage. In coming to the proposition that no acceptance is valid without intent, and therefore knowledge of the offer, the authorities have relied almost exclusively on cases involving unilateral offers, and notably the so-called reward cases.[19] There is a certain logic to this theory. A unilateral offer cannot be accepted without intent, since there is no evidence available to prove an exchange of offer and acceptance.[20] Yet reward cases involve elements of public policy that confuse the issues involved, and it may be that to draw a generalised analysis from them is misleading.[21] Moreover, in bilateral contracts this requirement of knowledge of the offer does not apply. There may be situations where the general rule and the objective theory of contract are not reconcilable.

In the case of bilateral contracts, we have already seen that the objective theory is currently dominant. It will therefore come as no surprise to discover that the subjective intent of the offeree is irrelevant in determining whether an acceptance has been made, provided there is sufficient objective evidence proving that an acceptance has been effected. In short, no intention would seem to be necessary for the acceptance of a bilateral offer.[22] Using Calamari and Perillo's rather extreme example,[23] suppose X sends an offer to Y in the post of which Y is totally unaware. This is received but left unopened by Y. If, for unknown reasons, Y scribbles a note, saying, 'I accept', and posts same, then a completed contract has come into existence, since there is objective evidence of both offer and acceptance. It is not the purview of the courts to examine the reasons for such bargains. It is clear from the above that knowledge of the offer is not a prerequisite to acceptance of a bilateral offer.[24] How, then, can this be 'squared' with the earlier rule which stated that an acceptance had to be made

---

19 *Glover v. Jewish War Veterans* 68 A 2d 233; *Fitch v. Snedaker*, 38 NY 248; *Upton RDC v. Powell* [1942] 1 All ER 220.

20 It is not always clear why this should be. Suppose X is a wealthy man who wishes from idle curiosity to see the fastest possible time it will take to swim from a buoy to the shore. He posts a notice to the effect that the fastest person will win £10,000. Let us further assume that at the very time the swim is to take place, Y, fleeing from a boat moored at the buoy, jumps into the water and proceeds to swim to shore in the fastest time. Why should Y be refused the reward due to lack of knowledge? The Restatement, Second, s. 23, Comment (c) ill. 2 expressly rejects this proposition but makes an exception for standing governmental reward in ill. 3 of the Comment. The differentiation is based on the fact that the climate required for governmental actions differ from private concerns but it is hard to see exactly why.

21 Restatement, Second, Contracts, s 23 Comment (c); Calamari and Perillo, op. cit., p. 69 et seq.

22 *Nationwide Resources Corp v. Massabni*, 134 Ariz. 557, 658 P. 2d 210 (1982).

23 Op. cit., p. 73-74.

24 Restatement, Second, Contracts, s. 23 Comment b.

with intent and therefore knowledge?[25] It cannot be that a unilateral offer requires knowledge to be accepted, but a bilateral offer does not. The more rational logic is that applicable to bilateral contracts and it should be extended to cover unilateral offers. It seems that the Restatement has erred in its approach.

Thankfully the sort of situation described in the example rarely occurs in real life. The subjective intention of the offeree is irrelevant in determining whether a valid acceptance has been made;[26] only objective intention is required. In a bilateral offer, that may mean that knowledge of the offer is not necessary, whereas in unilateral offers knowledge of the offer is normally required before the act of performance can be said to be an objective acceptance.[27] Government rewards are a special form of unilateral offer and should not require knowledge of the offer before a valid acceptance occurs since public policy is best served by fostering the supply of information to law enforcement agencies.[28]

4.04 ACTS OF ACCEPTANCE

We have discussed the necessary element of intent that is required before an acceptance can be made. We have seen that the next requirement is to determine if sufficient acts have occurred before the acceptance can be regarded as valid, bringing a binding contract into existence. It is also important to bear in mind that the relevance of finding out when sufficient acts of acceptance have occured is crucial in determining at what stage a completed contract has come into existence and, accordingly, upon what terms. In practice, finding sufficient acts of acceptance is by far the most important element of a contract. Parties to a prospective contract may continue to negotiate long after a legally binding contract has come into existence, and the terms and conditions of the contract may, as far as the parties are concerned, be a matter of dispute but may, by operation of contract law principles, have been settled by them some time earlier and sometimes much to their astonishment. Nor should it be forgotten that in the modern commercial world negotiations take place against a backdrop of the 'battle of the forms'. In this situation each side to the prospective contract claims

25 For some curious logic see Restatement, Second, s. 23, Comment d ill. 6 with its subjective assent manifested with objective evidence.
26 Cf. *Parkgrange Investments v. Shandon Park Mills*, unreptorted, High Court, 2 May 1991, Carroll J. In this case the defendant signed the draft agreement in order to establish tax liability, but before deciding to accept the offer. Carroll J held no contract had come into existence as there was no intention to accept.
27 The requisite intention is to accept the offer, not perform the requested act. It is not possible to accept if the existence of an offer is not known (though the offeror could waive such a requirement). It is, however, possible to accept an offer the terms of which are unknown. Thus I cannot, in the example referred to in footnote 20, participate in the race if I am unaware of the existence of the offer. If I know that there was some offer extant but am unaware what the prize is or the route to be taken, I can still validly accept.
28 In reality as the Restatement suggest this is a non-contractual obligation on the part of the State.

to enter into the contract on their standard terms and conditions. It is the document which a court holds to be an acceptance which determines which of the forms will win the battle.[29]

In analysing an act of acceptance it is convenient to distinguish them into three principal categories: express acceptance, acceptance by conduct and acceptance by silence. We now turn to deal with each one in more detail.

Express acceptance By this we mean an oral or written acceptance of an offer; for example, a letter or a telephone conversation responding positively to an offer. Again, an express acceptance must be differentiated from a counter offer. Thus, an act which appears to be an acceptance may be interpreted by the court as a counter offer and constitute a rejection of the offer. The effect such a counter offer has on the original offer is discussed fully in chapter 4. An acceptance must accept the offer exactly; it cannot vary or alter the terms of the offer in any way whatsoever.[30] Any change purported to be made by the acceptance to the terms of the offer, no matter how minute, will render the purported acceptance invalid. Indeed, it may even terminate the offer unless the alteration can be construed as an inquiry only.[31] In determining what constitutes an acceptance, care should be taken not to confuse a subsequent memorandum or record of the contract (which may inaccurately describe the contract) with the actual act of acceptance.[32]

There are exceptions to the rule that an express acceptance must correspond exactly with the offer. For example, a valid acceptance can still occur where the acceptance asks for a variation in the terms of the offer but makes it clear that even if such variation is refused, the offer is still accepted on the original terms.[33] A new term in the acceptance, which is of benefit to the offeror, can be adopted

---

29 *Butler Machine Tool v. Ex-Cell-O Corp* [1979] 1 WLR 401; *Chichester Joinery v. Mowlem* (1987) 42 Build LR 100; *Unidare v. Scott* [1991] 2 IR 88 for an objective view of contract.

30 *Tansey v. College of Occupational Therapists*, unreported, High Court, 27 August 1986: 'it is difficult to conceive of an acceptance which would itself prescribe conditions. Ordinarily a communication in the course of negotiations leading to a contract which contains conditions not previously agreed by the party to whom the communication is addressed will fall to be treated as a new or counter-offer rather than an acceptance' *per* Murphy J; *Hyde v. Wrench* (1840) 3 Beav 334.

31 *Stevenson v. McLean* (1880) 5 QB 346 (a request for information concerning an extension in delivery times was held not to be a counter offer).

32 *Monaghan County Council v. Vaughan* [1948] IR 306; *Irish Life Assurance Co. v. Dublin Land Securities* [1989] IR 253 (on appeal Supreme Court decided on different issues); note that this concept was used in the earlier decisions concerning 'subject to contract', see *Park Hall School v. Overend* [1987] IR 1, subsequently overturned; it does mean that a ticket given after an agreement has been concluded cannot form part of the contract unless the writing is required as a formality before enforcement is possible; see chapter 6 generally.

33 Restatement, Second, Contracts s. 39 ill 3; *Radford and Guise v. Practical Premium Co.*, 125 Ark 199; *Brangier v Rosenthal*, 337 F 2d 952, 954: '[the] assent being clear

by the offeror without rendering the acceptance invalid.[34] The correct interpretation, however, of the insertion of a new term in the acceptance which is of benefit to the offeror, is to regard the acceptance as a new offer which the original offeror then accepts by way of conduct. Finally, any new term in the acceptance which would in any event have arisen by virtue of law can be disregarded: for example, an acceptance that incorporates the provisions of the Sale of Goods and Supply of Services Act 1980 does not become invalid merely because such incorporation was not outlined in the original offer, since these terms would be incorporated into the contract automatically by operation of the statute.

One further point worth making about express acceptances is the harshness of the requirement that the acceptance be of the exact offer only, particularly since failure to do this renders the entire acceptance invalid and terminates the original offer. In the United States, the injustice of an enthusiastic application of this requirement of exact acceptance[35] has led to an alteration under the UCC, s. 2-207. According to this provision, an acceptance which purports to vary the terms of the offer is valid, unless the said acceptance expressly makes the acceptance conditional upon assent to the altered terms. The question then arises as to what consititutes the terms of the contract: the original offer or the varied terms of acceptance. The UCC stipulates that for merchants (non-consumers) the varied terms shall take precedence unless:

(a) the offer expressly excluded such variation in the acceptance, and

(b) the variation materially alters the offer or

(c) notification of objection has been made by the offeror within a reasonable time from receipt of the acceptance.

For others (principally consumers), the position is that the variation constitutes a proposal to amend the offer which if not accepted by the offeror is not valid. Therefore, in contracts between non consumers, such varied terms form part of the contract unless they contravene one of the three grounds. For all other contracts, the varied terms do not form part of the contract unless expressly adopted.[36]

and unqualified, the requests, inquiries and mild grumblings which accompanied it did not convert it into a counter offer'.

34   *Quadling v. Robinson* (1967) 137 CLR 192 (a promise to pay purchase price earlier than requested in the offer did not invalidate acceptance); what constitutes an advantage? In *Nelson Equipment Co. v. Harner*, 230 P 2d 188 an earlier delivery date was held not to be an advantage to the offeror unless it could be shown that the earlier delivery had been requested; where the term is neutral to the offeror, it constitutes a valid acceptance: *Domb v. Isoz* [1980].

35   Termed in that jurisdiction as the 'mirror image' rule or 'ribbon matching'; *Dorton v. Collins & Aikman Corp*, 453 F 2d 1161 (1972).

36   For a fuller discussion see generally Calamari and Perillo, op. cit., p 102 et seq.; note

The aim of the UCC was to deal with the growing phenomenon of the battle of the forms referred to earlier.[37] This battle has protagonists that are not particularly just or honourable. A simple policy choice is required, favouring either the offeror or the offeree. The UCC has attempted to resolve this issue, and while it is true that the statute has been described as 'a murky piece of prose . . . not too happily drafted',[38] it is far superior to the situation on this side of the Atlantic. In the UK, and presumably in Ireland, the 'last shot' rule[39] has effectively created a battle of the forms that cannot be lost but also one that cannot be won.[40] The result is that it is more likely that the parties will be held not to have entered any contract at all.

Acceptance by conduct In some senses, this is another version of express acceptance with the expression taking the form of action or conduct.[41] In fact, many contracts in every day life are accepted by conduct only. We have shown that a display of goods in a supermarket is an invitation to treat which, when an item is picked up and presented to the cashier, constitutes an offer made by the customer with respect to that item. The cashier then accepts the offer, but he or she does so by conduct, that is, she rings up the correct amount on the cash till and seeks your money. At best she may engage in idle conversation about the weather; at worst she will ignore your contemptible existence but at no stage will she expressly accept your offer.[42] Yet the transaction is valid. Acceptance has occurred by conduct.

It is useful, however, to divide the situation into unilateral and bilateral contracts. Unilateral contracts almost automatically imply that they are accepted by conduct,[43] such as finding either the lost kitten or the criminal, etc. The only way to accept unilateral contracts is to undertake performance of the requested task. For a bilateral contract, acceptance by conduct is less frequent, since the parties will normally have some express evidence of acceptance, such as a handshake or conversation or scribbled notes (what is normally missing will be an official record of the agreement). In legal terms, this sort of thing constitutes

that judicial analysis of these provisions has led to some difficulties that might not be readily apparent from the brief synopsis given, see *Roto Lith v. FP Bartlett*, 297 F 2d 497 (1962).

37 Calamri and Perillo, op. cit., p. 102, Macauley, 'Non-Contractual Relations in Business: A preliminary study', 28 *Am Soc Rev* 55.

38 Calamari and Perillo, op. cit., p 111, fn 46, 47.

39 *Butler Machine Tool Co. v. Ex-Cell-O Corp* [1979] 1 All ER 965; *BRS v. Arthur Crutchley* [1967] 2 All ER 285.

40 Treitel, op. cit., p. 20.

41 *Brogden v. Metropolitan Rly Co.* (1877) 2 App Cas 666; *Wettern Electric v. Welsh Development Agency* [1983] QB 796.

42 Restatement, Second, Contracts, s. 4 ill 2.

43 *Billings v. Arnott* (1945) 80 ILTR 50 (offer to pay half wages of employees who joined the army was accepted by employee joining the army); *Carlill v. Carbolic Smokeball Co.* [1893] 1 QB 256; *Brennan v. Lockyer* [1932] IR 100.

an express acceptance, not an acceptance by conduct. Acceptance by conduct in its purest form is best evidenced in the case of *Wettern Electric v. Welsh Development Agency*.[44] Here the plaintiff began to perform work according to the terms of a letter of offer sent by the defendants but to which the plaintiff had made no reply. The defendant did not object to the work having commenced until some time later, when they denied that any contract had arisen since the plaintiff had not expressly accepted the offer. The court held that a contract had come into existence, the plaintiff having accepted the offer by conduct. Such reasoning is not free from difficulty. First, the judgment appears to assume that the offeror has knowledge of the conduct of the offeree so as to be in a position to assent to the conduct. It is not clear why this should be so. If the offer has not been terminated and is still in existence, then it can be accepted at any stage by the offeree, and there are many situations where knowledge of the acceptance is not necessary on the part of the offeror, save where the offer expressly requires that such knowledge be given to the offeror. An acceptance by conduct is effective only from the time the offeror became aware of the conduct, but the offeree runs a considerable risk that before the offeror becomes aware of the acceptance, the offer will be terminated. In such a situation, the conduct is not an acceptance since the offer lapses.[45] For example, suppose on the 1st of the month X offers a contract to Y to build a house for £50,000. Y does not respond to X, yet on the 15th Y commences to build the house. X becomes aware of it on the 20th. The contract will come into existence on the 20th. For the period from the 15th to the 20th, Y was at risk that the offer by X might have been revoked or in some other way terminated and that his 'acceptance' was invalid. But as long as the offer is still extant, the contract comes into existence as soon as the acceptance is known by the offeror. This, of course, raises new problems as to how the offeror should have obtained this knowledge of the acceptance by conduct: directly or by third parties? This is discussed below in the next section.

The offer must also be relatively exact in terms of detail. In the supermarket case, referred to at the beginning of the section, it was easy to find an acceptance, since the item is clearly priced and the terms and conditions limited. But let us return to the transaction at the cash till. Suppose that when looking at your prospective purchase the cashier can find either no price or an incorrect price. When the correct price is discovered, you will be asked if that is OK before the transaction is proceeded with. This reveals a difficulty with acceptance by conduct, though not an insurmountable one, as Clarke believes.[46] The offer which it is being purported to accept must be sufficiently clear so as to enable the terms of the contract to be determined by the courts. If the offer is too vague, it stands to reason that it cannot be accepted by conduct. In our example of house builders X and Y, such conduct could not constitute an acceptance, since it was

44   [1983] 796.
45   *McEvoy v. Moore* (1902) 36 ILTR 99.
46   Clark, op. cit., p. 10 et seq.

unclear what type of house was to be built, how many bedrooms, wood or concrete, one or two storeys, etc., etc. But what do we really mean when we say the offer is too vague? We mean that the negotiations of the contract have not finished; one of the parties has 'jumped the gun', mistakenly believing that the contract was concluded. When the transaction is looked at in the cold light of day by a court, it is clear that the situation is ambiguous: the absence of any express acceptance indicates an absent of contract. It is all a question of timing; if the offeree accepts by conduct too early, then no contract arises because there is in effect no real offer to accept;[47] but if the offeree waits until a stage during the negotiations where it is possible to hold that an offer is extant, then a contract will arise.

Finally, we turn to discuss the concept of 'dominion' as a method of acceptance by conduct. *Dominion* relates to goods offered to the recipient and which the recipient treats as having been accepted,[48] for example, goods sent on approval which are not returned but are used by the recipient in a manner consistent with the creation of a binding contract. We are concerned here not with unsolicited goods (which are the subject of legislation)[49] but with goods sought by the offeree and which are now being used in a manner that can objectively be determined to result in the exclusion of the rights of the original offeror. Such acts of dominion result in actions both in contract[50] and tort.[51] In tort, the action is for conversion, in contract, the action is for non payment of the relevant items. An act of dominion in the case of solicited goods results in a binding contract, breach of which is enforceable in the courts. For an action to lie in contract the act of dominion must not be wrongful.[52] If the dominion is wrongful, that is not in accord with the terms of the offer, the action is one exclusively in tort for conversion. Where the dominion is lawful, a litigant may elect to proceed with either action.[53]

---

47 *Parkgrange Investments v. Shandon Park Mills*, unreported, High Court, 2 May 1991, Carroll J (signature on a draft agreement did not constitute an acceptance as it was only signed as a preparatory measure to obtain tax clearance before deciding to enter the contract or not).

48 Sometimes known as inertia selling; see generally Restatement, Second, Contracts, s. 69.

49 Sale of Goods and Supply of Services Act 1980, s. 47; at common law the recipient of unsolicited goods was a bailee of those goods.

50 *Raible v. Puerto Rico Industrial Development Co.*, 392 F 2d 424 1968.

51 The doctrine of conversion is an action in tort taken against a defendant who has appropriated goods for his own use but which belong to the plaintiff, see McMahon and Binchy, *Irish Law of Torts*, 2nd ed. (1990) p. 354 et seq.

52 Restatement, Second, Contracts, s. 69, Comment e.

53 To give an example, X delivers a car to Y to test drive before making a decision to buy it. Y sells the vehicle, he has exercised dominion over the car but it is wrongful and therefore X's action lies in tort for conversion. Suppose Y simply does not return the car, Y exercises dominion over it and can be sued by X in both tort for conversion or contract in that Y has accepted the offer outstanding by his act of dominion.

Acceptance by silence   As a general rule, a 'party cannot by the wording of his offer turn the absence of a communication into an acceptance and compel the recipient of his offer to remain silent at his peril'.[54] Likewise, it would also be unacceptable if the offer were to deem acceptance on the happening of a certain event over which the offeree had no control (I offer you my car for £5,000, which I will deem you to have accepted if the sun rises tomorrow). This is effectively an attempt to obtain an acceptance by silence and is thus treated similarly.

This rule received judicial approval in *Felthouse v. Bindley*, a case concerning a letter sent by the plaintiff offering to buy a horse, which, *inter alia*, stated 'If I hear no more about him, I shall consider the horse mine'. The horse was mistakenly sold by an auctioneer acting on behalf of the offeree. The plaintiff sued the auctioneer in conversion, claiming that a contract had come into existence despite the silence of the offeree. The court rejected the claim; silence could not operate to impose a contract between the offeror and the offeree. The case is open to some criticism on its own facts, but the principle enunciated seems correct. In *Russell & Baird v. Hoban*[56] the plaintiff sent a sale note offering to supply certain material with a condition that, if the sale note were kept three days beyond the date of the note, it would be held to have been accepted by the defendant. Ronan J had no difficulty in disposing with the case, stating that 'no man can impose such conditions upon another'.

A number of points need to be made about the general rule before discussing the exceptions. First, an offer cannot take away the right of the offeree to expressly refuse the offer. At worst it merely attempts to place a duty upon the offeree expressly to reject the offer or else fall liable to the contract (though the offeree can never in these circumstances have such a positive duty imposed upon him or her). Thus, in the earlier example of deemed acceptance on the occurrence of the sun rising, the offeree can of course expressly reject the offer, though is not required to do so.

Secondly, where the offeree does remain silent, such silence can be ambiguous: has the offeree accepted the offer or is she just relying on the common law to avoid a contract coming into effect?[57] Can the offeror deny the contract by saying that all was silence from the offeree? The argument has some merit: since the contract could not be imposed by silence, why can the offeree take advantage of the silence to constitute a valid acceptance? The reason is simple: the offeror exposes himself to this risk by framing the offer in the manner he chose. Silence was what he requested, and the result is that the silence has left him in an uncertain position. This is to be expected if the law is to discourage such questionable tactics on the part of the offeror. The determination of whether the

54   Clark (US), op. cit., ss. 31, 32; *The Leonidas D* [1983] 3 All ER 737.
55   (1882) 11 CBNS 869.
56   [1922] 2 IR 159.
57   Restatement, Contract, s. 72(1) b; Calamari and Perillo, op. cit., p. 84.

offer was accepted in such a situation is found by an investigation into the subjective intent of the offeree.[58]

We turn now to the *exceptions to the general rule*. First, both parties can agree that silence will constitute assent to the contract, as, for example, where the offer is replied to in terms such as 'If you hear no more from me by Friday, you may assume that I have accepted the offer'.[59] Here the offeree has voluntarily assumed the risk of acceptance by way of silence, and the law will not stand in the way of enforcement of such a contract. A variation on this arises where the need for express communication of the acceptance is dispensed with due to a course of past dealings between the parties, such that there is a legitimate expectation that silence indicates acceptance.[60] The test to be applied is that of the reasonable man, that is, whether a reasonable person in the shoes of the offeror would have believed that a contract had come into existence.

Further, there is the concept of *implied in fact contracts for services*.[61] This doctrine applies only to the provision of services which, by their nature, cannot be returned once given. Suppose, for example, that X's vehicle has broken down on the side of the road and he is approached by Y, a passer-by who happens to be a mechanic. Y commences to fix the vehicle. Has a contract come into existence between X and Y? The better view would be that where an offeree accepts services offered with a reasonable opportunity to reject them and with reason to believe that they are offered with the expectation of compensation, then a completed acceptance has occurred.[62] There are two key issues in the above example. First, had X a reasonable opportunity to reject the offer? If X had left the vehicle unattended and gone in search of help, returning to find Y working on the vehicle, then the services rendered during X's absence would fall outside this doctrine since X had no reasonable opportunity to reject them. If, on the other hand, X, on his return, watches as Y sets to work, he had an opportunity to reject the actions of Y and his silence must be taken as acceptance. Secondly, would a reasonable man have concluded that the actions of Y were gratuitous? If so, there was no offer to accept on the part of X.[63] This is a question of fact to be determined from the totality of the circumstances. It is true to say that, within family relationships, it will be harder to prove that there was an expectation of compensation than it will be between unconnected

---

58 Restatement, Contracts, s. 72(1) (b); Restatements, Second, Contracts, s. 69(1) b.

59 *Attorney Grievance Commission v. McIntire*, 405, A 2d 273 (1979); 1 Williston s. 91C.

60 *Rust v. Abbey Life Insurance* [1979] 2 Lloyds Rep 334; 1 Corbin s. 75; Restatement, Second, Contracts, s. 69(1) c Comment d; *Hobbs v. Massoit Whip Co.*, 33 NE 495 (1893); there is little doubt that such implied acceptance by previous dealings is more common in the United States than in England.

61 Calamari and Perillo, op. cit., p 83 et seq; see also Dell, 'Principle against Unjust Enrichment', (1993) 15 *DULJ* 27 and Chapter 26.

62 Restatement, Second, Contracts, s. 72(1) a; *Spencer v. Spencer*, 63 NE 947 (1902).

63 *Lirtzman v. Fuqua Industries*, 677 F 2d 548 (1982).

persons,[64] but this is a presumption that can be rebutted and the cases are best decided on a case by case approach.

Finally, what appears to be silence may in fact be considered by the court to constitute acceptance by conduct. In *Rust v. Abbey Life Ins. Co.*[65] the court held, *obiter*, that even if a policy document sent by the defendant constituted a counter offer,[66] the said counter offer had been accepted by the plaintiff (since he remained silent for seven months before returning the policy and seeking repayment of the money). Although the judgment refers to conduct, it is clear that this was a case of silence.

4.05 COMMUNICATION OF ACCEPTANCE

The mere fact that an act of acceptance has occurred is not sufficient.[67] This act of acceptance must be communicated to the offeror.[68] An acceptance is valid only when it is received by the person making the offer. In *Parkgrange Investments v. Shandon Park Mills*[69] Carroll J held that a contract for sale, which the defendant had signed as a preparatory measure to obtain a certificate of tax clearance in the event that the sale should proceed, did not constitute an acceptance, since it was at all times held by the defendant's solicitor and was never communicated to the plaintiff. The plaintiff became aware of its existence from the protracted correspondence arising from the negotiations, and obtained the document upon an order for discovery made during the action. But the defendant did not intend it to form an acceptance, and it's non-delivery to the plaintiff proved fatal. It is worth pointing out that the defendant signed the document against legal advice.

Such a rule is far from academic interest only. First, it means that an acceptance can be retracted at any stage prior to its being received by the offeror. The example given in the classical works is of X and Y standing on either side of a canal. X shouts an offer over to Y, and, while Y thinks on it and begins to reply with an acceptance shouted back across the canal, his words are drowned out by the roar of an overhead plane.[70] No contract has been concluded since X did not receive the acceptance. Y must again shout a reply which will be heard by X, though in the meantime Y may have changed his mind and may now turn on his heel and walk away. Secondly, a contract is governed by the laws of the

64   *Worley v. Worley*, 388 So 2d 502 (1980); *McKeon v. Van Slyck*, 233 NY 392 (1918).
65   [1979] 2 Lloyds Rep 334.
66   The court eventually declined to regard the document as a counter offer.
67   *Powell v. Lee* (1908) 99 LT 284; *Robophone Facilities v. Blank* [1966] 3 All ER 128; *Batt v. Onslow* (1892) 13 LR Eq 79.
68   Save where silence is deemed to be an act of acceptance: communication of silence would be impossible.
69   Unreported, High Court, 2 May 1991.
70   *Miles Far East Corp v. Entores* [1955] 2 All ER 493, 495.

jurisdiction where it has been concluded, that is, where the acceptance has been received. Thus, an offer made in London by telephone to a party in Dublin which is accepted is governed by English law since the acceptance was received in London by the offeror. This can be of crucial importance for a number of reasons, including taxation. Finally, the question of when the contract comes into existence can in some cases be vital. Once the contract is concluded, ownership in the property, which is the subject matter of the contract, passes to the purchaser. Any subsequent loss to the property is at the risk of the purchaser. This is why, traditionally, the purchaser of a house is advised to insure the property immediately upon agreeing the contract for sale, despite the fact that it may some weeks before possession is given to the purchaser.

It has been said that the reason for this rule is that it would be impossible to divine the intent of the offeree, but, as Treitel points out,[71] this would not cover the situation where the intent of the offeree could be divined with certainty,[72] as for example where the offeree has signed an acceptance which he has kept and not communicated to the offeror,[73] or where a company has recorded the acceptance of an offer to purchase shares but has not communicated same to the offeror.[74] In both examples the intent is easily proved, yet the rule would still hold that no acceptance has come into effect because it has not been communicated to the offeror.[75] A better reason might be that it would be unfair to bind the offeror without informing him; but this would not explain why an offeror will be bound by a communication sent to, say, her place of business but which is never known by the offeror.[76] In truth, the choice is one of policy. In France, some debate still arises between the proponents of the *émission* theory and the *information* theory.[77] The *émission* theory holds that no communication of the acceptance is required. This theory is favoured by the majority of French legal writers. The case law is, however, not consistent. Many cases leave it as a question of fact as to whether the parties have a contract or not. Strangely enough, some cases infer that the offer itself stipulated that a reply was necessary

71 Treitel, op. cit., p. 21 et seq.
72 It is interesting to note Treitel's view of *Powell v. Lee* (1908) 99 LT 284. He believes a communication appointing a new headmaster, conveyed in an unauthorised form (although a formal letter making the appointment had been drafted but not sent), meant that the defendant's impliedly reserved the right to reconsider his decision. As Greig and Davies point out, this is somewhat contrived.
73 *Kennedy v. Thomassen* [1929] 1 Ch 426 but cf. *Park Grange Investments*, op. cit., where this appears to have been overlooked.
74 *Best's* case (1865) 2 DJ & S 650.
75 This is different from *In re International Contract Co.* (1867) LR 3 Ch App 36 where the offeror for shares received no letter of acceptance, though the said shares had been allotted. It was held that a contract had come into existence on the basis that the offeror had attended company meetings and had received fees on the basis of his share holding. This implied an acceptance.
76 *Miles Far East Corp v. Entores* [1955] 2 QB 327.
77 See Nichols, *French Law of Contract*, op. cit., p. 72 et seq.

for an effective communication, but it is difficult to see how this is other than a back-hand justification of the *information* theory. In many ways there is little to be gained from too detailed an analysis of this problem, since all solutions carry difficulties and as long as the rule is clear, people may make arrangements on that basis.[78]

Since the policy in our legal system is to favour the offeror, it is open to the offeror to expressly dispense with such favours. So, there is nothing wrong with an offer stating that no communication of acceptance is required. If the offeror wishes to take this risk, then he does so of his own free choice. Moreover, in the case of unilateral contracts the presumption is reversed, that is, a unilateral offer impliedly dispenses with the need to communicate acceptance of the offer to the offeror.[79] Thus, a person who posts a reward for a lost kitten does not expect the neighbourhood kids to beat a path to his door informing him that they will look for the lost animal; but neither can he say to the finder that he or she never communicated acceptance of the offer and that all bets are off.

If the offeror in a unilateral offer wishes to have acceptance notified, it must be expressly requested in the offer. In the absence of any such directions in the offer, the general rule will hold true: that an acceptance must be communicated in a bilateral offer and need not in a unilateral offer.

The question then arises as to what manner the communication should take. The easiest way is to follow that which is prescribed by the offer itself.[80] Indeed, it may be that the manner prescribed is compulsory, in which case acceptance by any other means will be invalid, even if the acceptance arrives at the same time as it would have done if sent by the prescribed route.[81] Of course, it may be that the offeror will acquiesce in the alternative method of communication, but the offeree takes a risk that this will not occur. Where the offeree replies in a manner other than that requested by the offeror, then this 'acceptance' is best viewed as a counter-offer which can be accepted by conduct without any further communication between the parties.[82] It is also possible that the prescribed

---

78   *Letec Finance v. Knight* [1969] 2 NSWR 79 (finance agreement, defendant made the offer but the plaintiff was never notified of acceptance. Held no contract had come into existence. Quare: to what extent did the facts of this case (the item to be financed was faulty and had been returned) sway the court's decision? Compare with *Newlands v. Argyll General Ins Co.* (1958) 59 SR 130 (acceptance in similar circumstances valid, despite lack of communication).

79   *Carlill v. Carbolic Smokeball Co.* [1893] 1 QB 256.

80   It should be noted that in many modern transactions, it is the offeree who dictates the terms of the acceptance, *Financings Ltd v. Stimson* [1962] 1 WLR (a finance application is usually made on a form written by the offeree and which the offeror (the person seeking finance) has no power to amend. In such situations the policy objective based on the power of the offeror to make the offer in the manner he or she sees fit, is redundant.)

81   *Zinni v. Royal Lincoln-Mercury*, 406 NE 2d 212 (1980); But cf. *Tinn v. Hoffman* (1873) 29 LT 271.

82   The evidence, however, is that the courts have been willing to give a more lax

method of acceptance is not in fact compulsory but indicative,[83] for example, the wording can be construed as meaning 'as quickly as possible'. Thus a reply which arrives as quick as, if not sooner than that requested, would be sufficient.[84] For example, an offer which states that it must be accepted 'by return of post' can be validly accepted by a fax if it can be said that the offeror merely desired a quick response and was effectively limiting the time during which the offer would remain open.[85] But the wording of such an offer might, in the view of a court, not give such freedom of choice to the offeree, and instead require the offeree accept by the stated method and no other. An offeree takes a considerable risk in departing from the method of acceptance outlined in the offer.[86]

Where the offer is silent as to the method of communication of the acceptance, then the communication should be in reasonable accord with the manner in which the offer was made.[87] A word that best conjures up what is meant here is the American term 'seasonable' used in the UCC.[88] A seasonable acceptance is one which corresponds to the offer made, either expressly or by implication. Thus, an offer sent by fax would be seasonably accepted by a fax, telex or other instant communication. On the other hand, a fax sent to Australia would in all likelihood not be seasonably accepted by a surface mail letter.[89] The concept of seasonable acceptance is nonetheless fraught with conceptual difficulties. Can an offer sent by fax be seasonably accepted by a telephone call, or does it require a documentary acceptance? The answer is unclear. It is probably a question of fact to be determined at the trial of the action, since the question can only be answered in the totality of the circumstances. So long as the communication is found to be seasonable, the acceptance will be valid.[90]

---

enforcement to such clauses dictating the method of acceptance, *Tinn v. Hoffman* (1873) 29 LT 271.

83   *Kennedy v. Thomassen* [1929] 1 Ch. 426.

84   If the acceptance is somehow delayed and late in arriving, the risk the offeree has taken is that it will be repudiated; *Eliason v. Henshaw*, 4 Wheaton 225 (1819).

85   *George Hudson Holdings v. Rudder* (1973) 128 CLR 387 (requirement in the offer of acceptance by post. Held that it was not fatal when the offeree replied personally).

86   Irish courts have been quite liberal in interpretation, favouring the offeree where no harm has arisen to the offeror in the failure to comply strictly with prescribed method, reducing the risk run by the offeree: *Staunton v. Minister for Health*, unreported, High Court, 21 February 1986 (acceptance required by the offer to be by signature. Held it could be accepted by oral statement); *Walker v. Glass* [1979] NI 129.

87   *Quenerduaine v. Cole* (1883) 32 WR 185.

88   UCC s. 1-204(3)—seasonable means within the agreed time or where none is agreed within a reasonable time; s. 2-207.

89   Restatement, Second, Contracts, s. 63, 65 ill. 1 (acceptance of a telegram by mail would be effective).

90   Note in the US, differences have emerged between a seasonable acceptance undertaken in accordance with the prescribed manner of the offer (which is deemed to be effective once it has left the offeree irrespective of whether it ever arrives at it's destination) and those which are seasonable but take an alternative route than that prescribed. The latter acceptances are not effective until received by the offeror: Restatement, Second,

The whole problem of modern methods of communication has yet to be dealt with satisfactorily. In *Entores Ltd v. Miles Far East Corporation*[91] the English court held that telex communications should be treated as if the parties were in the same room as one another, and this reasoning has been approved in *Brinkibon v. Stahag Stahl*[92] with the caveat that the rule is not absolute but may have to yield where its application would lead to injustice. It is not clear, for example, what the situation would be if the telex, or fax, arrived with no one there to receive it. These are matters that will no doubt arise for adjudication at a future date. Ordinarily in conversation, if an acceptance is said but is not heard or understood, the offeree is immediately aware of this and has an opportunity to reiterate the acceptance until it is heard or understood. For example, X and Y are negotiating a contract in a crowded restaurant. As Y says that he accepts X's offer, a waiter drops a tray of plates and X cannot hear what Y has said. This will be obvious to Y who can state the acceptance again. In the modern technological forms of communication (such as faxes or E-mail), however, all the offeree can be sure of is that the acceptance has been successfully sent, but not whether anyone was there to read it.[93] The view is taken that the offeree should not be further disadvantaged, since she has no opportunity to remedy a mis-sent message. This would be in accord with the next principle which we shall discuss, the so-called *mail box* or *postal rule*.

The postal rule Perhaps the biggest single exception to the general rule that an acceptance is valid only when it is received is that of *Adams v. Lindsell*.[94] In this case the defendants wrote to the plaintiffs making an offer for the sale of wool on 2 September 1817 requiring an acceptance in the course of the post. Due to the defendant's misdirection of the letter, it did not arrive at the plaintiffs until 5 September. The plaintiffs wrote a letter of acceptance that evening which arrived at the defendants on 9 September. The defendants could have reasonably expected to receive a reply by 7 September and, having not received anything, sold the wool on 8 September to a third party. The question was: when did the contract come into existence? If the rule that the acceptance was not valid until received by the offeror, no contract arose since the offer was revoked by the

Contracts, s. 63: 'Unless the offer provides otherwise, (a) an acceptance made in a manner and by a medium invited by the offer is operative and completes the manifestation of mutual assent as soon as put out of the offeree's possession, without regard to whether it reaches the offeror . . .'; s. 67: 'Where an acceptance is seasonably dispatched but the offeree uses means of transmission not invited by the offeror . . . it is treated as operative upon dispatch if received within the time in which a properly dispatched acceptance would normally have arrived.'

91 [1955] 2 All ER 493.
92 [1982] 1 All ER 293.
93 Restatement, Second, Contracts, s. 64 deals with the telephone or other 'medium of substantially instantaneous two way communication' but this does not resolve the issues presented here.
94 (1818) 1 B&A 681.

sale of the item in question. But the court held that the acceptance occurred at the time it was posted and thus came within the control of the postal service. This was so even when the acceptance arrived late as in this case or not at all.

This unduly lenient rule in favour of the offeree is not irrational if placed in the context of its time.[95] First, in that period, all businesses kept ledgers of outgoing mail: the addressees and amount, etc. Therefore, it was relatively easy to prove that mail had been sent as distinct from proving that it had not been received. Secondly, the case is one of the earliest which looks at contract from an offer and acceptance point of view, and back in 1817 the general rule to which we referred earlier (that acceptance must be communicated) had not been laid down. Not for the first time, an exception predates the general rule! Moreover, the rule can be superseded by the offeror who can expressly stipulate the manner of acceptance and the point in time when it becomes effective. In *Holwell Securities v. Hughes*[96] the English Court of Appeal held that the wording of the offer made it clear that acceptance would not occur until it had reached the offeror, despite the transaction being conducted through the post. Thus, the rule is policy-driven on the balance of convenience which favours the offeree and which can be superseded by the express desire of the offeror. The actual case of *Adams* would probably be decided differently today in any event due to more modern methods of communication. It will be remembered that the letter of offer was late in arriving due to the offeror's misdirection of the letter, the offeree responded by return of post, since, in 1817, no quicker response would have been possible. Today, such a reply would not be seasonable, given the fact that the offer was late in arriving, confirmation of its arrival and the acceptance should in all likelihood have taken place by telephone or fax.

The net effect of the mail box rule is quite profound. Where an acceptance is made by post, it is at the point at which it comes into the hands of the postal service that a completed contract has arisen.[97] This means that both the time of the contract and the location of the contract are governed by the actions of the offeree. A letter of acceptance sent by the post from Limerick at 3.40 to an offeror in New York but which never arrives[98] at its destination creates a contract governed by Irish law as and from 3.40 on the date of posting.

There are limitations to the mail box rule.[99] It applies only where it is reasonable that the acceptance should take place via the postal system.[100] It must

---

95 Although it did not command universal acceptance when first mooted: *British and American Telegraph v. Colson* (1871) LR 6 Exch 108.

96 [1974] 1 All ER 161.

97 *Sanderson v. Cunningham* [1919] 2 IR 234 (acceptance occurred in London where the acceptance was posted).

98 *Household Fire and Carriage Accident Insurance v. Grant* (1879) 4 Ex D216.

99 *Stanhope v. Hospitals Trust (No. 2)* [1936] Ir Jur Rep 25 (will not operate where breach of international law principles involved).

100 *Henthorn v. Fraser* [1892] 2 Ch 27; *Bal v. Van Staden* [1902] TS 128 (acceptance sent

yield where its application would lead to manifest inconvenience or absurdity[101] and it is not to be applied as an absolute rule.[102] Furthermore, where the letter of acceptance has been misdirected through the negligence of the offeree (such as incorrectly addressing the letter) or of the offeror (giving an incorrect return address), the acceptance will take affect, if at all, at the time which is least favourable to the party responsible for the misdirection.[103] Finally, it must be remembered that the courts interpret at what stage an acceptance is made. Thus, what appears to be an acceptance may in fact be a counter offer and therefore not effective until it reaches the other party.

An acceptance sent through the post before notice of revocation of the offer reaches the offeree will operate to create a binding contract, even if the offeror never receives such acceptance. Thus, an acceptance to an offer sent by post on the 10th of the month creates a binding contract from that date even if a revocation of the offer is transmitted by fax later that day. The question is, however, can the letter of acceptance be revoked after posting but before arrival at the offeror? Since the acceptance occurs at posting, a completed contract should have arisen and the acceptance cannot be revoked.[104] However, there is some merit in the argument that no one is prejudiced where the acceptance is revoked before the offeror becomes aware of the acceptance and therefore no contract should come into existence.[105] Thus, if the letter of acceptance is sent on, say, the 10th of the month and later that day for some reason the offeree changes his mind and telephones the offeror saying to ignore the purported acceptance, has the offeror been adversely affected? The offeror was unaware of the existence of the acceptance until notified of its revocation. It may be in the interests of the offeror that no valid acceptance to has occurred: for example, X telephones Y, saying that Y should ignore a letter of acceptance coming in the post with respect to the shares of company X. Y thus sells the shares of company X to Z. Subsequently the shares of the company are the subject of a take-over bid and X decides that he now wants them. X claims that the letter of acceptance was complete on posting and his purported revocation is ineffective; he now sues for breach of contract. Arguably, the better view of this possibility, though there are no cases of any merit in either this jurisdiction or England, is

by post not effective when posted where there was a postal disruption known to the offeree).

101 *Holwell Securities v. Hughes*, op. cit., *per* Lawton J at 161.
102 *Tallerman v. Nathan's Merchandise (Vic)* (1957) 987 CLR 93, 111: 'a contract is not completed until acceptance of an offer is actually communicated to the offeror and a finding that a contract is completed by the posting of a letter of acceptance cannot be justified unless it is inferred that the offeror contemplated and intended his offer might be accepted by the doing of that act.'
103 Treitel, op. cit., p. 27 whilst lacking in precedent, seems to be a correct interpretation.
104 Restatement, Second, Second, s. 63, Comment c, ill 7; *Wenckheim v. Arndt* (NZ) 1 JR 73.
105 *Dick v. US*, 82 F Supp 326; 1 Corbin, s. 94.

that the acceptance is complete when posted,[106] the so called 'revocation' of the acceptance by the offeree is an attempt to discharge the contract by consent mutually. The offeror is therefore free to either reject this request and insist that the contract is performed or elect to agree that the contract is set aside.[107]

In Ireland, the Supreme Court has accepted the orthodoxy of the postal rule in *Kelly v. Cruise Catering*.[108] A contract is complete when an acceptance has been posted and therefore the country of posting will dictate the law by which the agreement is governed. However, the court also indicated that the postal rule will not be applied where an injustice would arise, and surprisingly gave an example of an injustice as being where the acceptance is lost in the post. However, the issue did not fall to be decided in the case at hand and the comment remains *obiter*. We must therefore await future developments.

Finally, the rules for international contracts for the sale of goods are governed presently by the Uniform Law on the Formation of Contracts for the International Sale of Goods. Under UFLIS an acceptance is valid only when it is communicated to the offeror,[109] when it reaches his place of business.[110] Thus no contract comes into existence if it never arrives, but it will come into existence if it merely arrives late. A revocation of an acceptance is valid if it reaches the offeror before or at the same time as the acceptance is made.[111] These rules should be borne in mind when dealing with international contracts governed by UFLIS.[112]

---

106 But cf. Treitel, op. cit., p. 27 et seq for an opposing view.
107 This election as repudiation or offer to rescind the contract is posited as a solution both in the Second Restatement (s. 63 Comment c) and the UCC (s. 2-608).
108 [1994] 2 ILRM 394.
109 Art. 6(1).
110 Art. 12(1).
111 Art. 10.
112 For a generalised discussion of these rules, see Bianca, *Commentary on International Sales Law*; Honnold, *Uniform Law for International Sales*.

5.00

Capacity to Contract

5.01 INTRODUCTION

It is a truism in the common law that the courts desire to give effect to freely entered into bargains between persons, and tend to avoid undue restrictions on this freedom of choice. Indeed, the notion of freedom receives some of its earliest and purest expressions in the economic field, and in law much of this was traditionally regulated by the law of contract. It is, therefore, not surprising that what to many might seem to be the fundamental point of departure in any survey of the law of contract (namely, who may enter into legally enforceable contracts) in fact receives little treatment in our legal system. The major works in the common law relegate the subject, if not towards the end of their discourse, at least in the latter half, to receive a merely cursory treatment.[1]

It would be wrong, however, to criticise this approach, for the truth of the matter remains that, conceptually, the capacity to contract poses few major difficulties, and while the present book breaks with the long-standing tradition of location of this topic, it does not break with the traditional approach to it. The change of location to the early part of a discourse on contract law can be justified on a number of grounds. No matter how few restrictions on the freedom to contract might be imposed by the courts, it should never be the case that the litigant can somehow be divorced from cause of action. It will be remembered that earlier the concept of contract as a relationship was mooted.[2] Since the common law revolves around the resolution of disputes rather than any grand design of conceptual theory, a fundamental feature of any analysis must be the scope of the potential litigants. Certainly, to take a logical approach to contract law, one should first enquire as to who can make a contract before explaining how.

5.02 THE GENERAL RULE

Any person can enter into a contract, but there exist situations where specific

---

1   Clark, op. cit., chapter 6; Greig and Davis, op. cit., chapter 13; Cheshire, Fifoot and Furmston, op. cit., chapter 13; Calamari and Perillo, op. cit., chapter 8; Treitel, op. cit., chapter 13.
2   See chapter 2 generally.

classes of persons are denied the right to enforce (or have enforced against them) these contracts, on the grounds of public policy. The denial can be full or it can merely involve a restriction on either enforcement of the contract or the remedies available. Before dealing with the situations where these people have restricted capacity to contract, we should first say a few words about the concept of a 'person'. By that we mean natural and legal persons. Natural persons pose no difficulty; they are ordinary human beings. Natural persons, even those with the most unnatural desires and habits, have (as far as the law is concerned) the most extensive legal powers. They have this right through the fortune of birth into the human race rather than birth into a particular political unit, creed or race. Thus, in this jurisdiction, non-citizens have the same power to contract as citizens. On the other hand, some entities can be awarded a legal personality, for example, a company. There are a number of important points to note about this acquired legal personality. First, since it has been acquired, it can be taken away: thus, a company may lose its legal personality if it does not operate in accordance with formal requirements laid down by law. Second, legal persons do not enjoy as extensive legal rights as natural persons; accordingly their ability to enter into contracts, while recognised, is more limited than that available to natural persons. More will be said on this topic below.

There are a number of organisations that fall somewhere between these two definitions and unless the law specifically grants them the right to contract, they cannot of themselves enter into contracts, and their relations with the world must arise through the agency of either a natural or legal person. That 'agency', a term used advisedly, has considerable repercussions for all parties involved; few people realise this. Indeed, since most of these organisations are in fact social and sports clubs, it is strange to think that volunteers in these organisations can find themselves saddled with more extensive liability for the actions of the group than can the controller of a business enterprise. There would seem, therefore, to be some merit in the argument that the freedom to contract should be extended beyond persons to include such organisations as do not currently fall into the rather simplistic classification adopted by the common law.

5.03 RESTRICTIONS ON CAPACITY

All persons, natural and legal, can enter into contracts. However, on the grounds of public policy, certain persons, when parties to a contract, render elements of the contract unenforceable. This is an important feature: the contract is not rendered null and void; merely, the power to enforce it, by either party, receives a limited acceptance by the court. Thus, even if one of the parties lacks capacity, it is still possible that consequences will flow from such contract which may actually bind third parties. All of the various restrictions on capacity have been imposed by the courts on the grounds of public policy, though the policy varies from one case to the next. As society changes, some of the older restrictions have been removed as unacceptable. Thus, for example, married women are now given the right to contract, a right that once was held contrary to public policy.[3] A few restrictions still remain, and it is to these which we now turn.

5.04 ALIENS

Generally speaking aliens, that, is non-resident foreign nationals, have full capacity. Enemy aliens, that is, nationals of countries with which the State is at war,[4] may not sue in the courts of the land for as long as we remain at war with them.[5] They can, however, be sued and accordingly lodge defences, counter-claims, etc. In other words, once open to legal proceedings they can avail of the full rigour of the law, but they are denied the right to initiate actions of their own accord.

Where the enemy alien is lawfully residing in the State, the ability to sue does apply, so in *Volkl v. Rotunda Hospital*[6] a resident national of the Austro-Hungarian Empire was permitted to sue the hospital for negligence. Further-more, the personal intent of the litigant is not important provided his sovereign is not at war with the State. Thus, in *Pedlar v. Johnstone*[7] the litigant, a US citizen had come to Ireland to take part in the 1916 rising, in a sense conducting his own private war. Nonetheless, that was not sufficient to remove his right to sue to enforce a claim for detinue and conversion against the police, as his sovereign was not at war with the State.

Two points of interest arise in this area: when is the State at war with another state and, since the disability only lasts for the duration of the war, is the Statute of Limitations suspended for the duration? With respect to a declaration of war, the Constitution reserves the exercise of that right to the Dáil, as it does participation in a war.[8] Thus, it is envisaged that the State may participate in a war without formally declaring one, but it would seem that, in the absence of a formal declaration, nationals of a hostile state will not be enemy aliens merely because we are participating in a war against that state. There is a growing tendency to avoid declarations of war in modern international relations which effectively means that few aliens will be barred from action.

---

3   Thus married women are now no longer under any disability to enter contracts without their husbands permission: Married Women's Status Act 1957, s. 2(1). Indeed, additional protection is given by virtue of ss. 7, 8.
4   The loyalty of the alien is not relevant, see Binchy, *Irish Conflict of Law* (1988) p. 171; see also *Pedlar v. Johnstone* [1920] 2 IR 450.
5   *Pedlar v. Johnstone* [1920] 2 IR 450.
6   [1915] 1 KB 857.
7   [1920] 2 IR 450.
8   Bunreacht na hÉireann 1937, Art. 28(3)(1); there is a clear distinction in this article between a declaration of war and participation in a war, though both require the consent of the Dáil.

With respect to the Statute of Limitations, the problem is somewhat more obtuse. Time runs irrespective of the fact that the alien is debarred from proceeding with an action, since there is no provision to prevent the statute from coming into effect in these cases. Thus, suppose A is an enemy alien who is owed money by B. A cannot sue B to enforce this debt while the war continues. Despite this, the Statute of Limitations begins to run; in six years the debt is statute barred and A cannot recover the money B owes him. However, at equity, such a defence mounted by B must receive a reluctant acceptance, at the very least. The problem is far from academic, since many wars last at least as long as the six year limitation period in question.

5.05 FOREIGN SOVEREIGNS AND THEIR REPRESENTATIVES

In the interests of international relations there has been a general tendency to confer immunity on the activities of diplomatic representatives from abroad.[9] There are a number of reasons for this. Firstly, most States desire to protect their nationals, who represent that country's interest and, since the basis of diplomacy is reciprocity, the benevolent treatment of foreign diplomats in the host country should be reciprocated by similar treatment of the host country's diplomat abroad. Furthermore, as representatives of a sovereign State, diplomats should be governed by the laws of that State and not the host country. In recent times there has been much criticism for abuses of this system, but it remains in force and in the area of contract law it confers on the foreign diplomat the ability to enter into contracts without legal obligation.[10] It is important to note that the immunity extends only to properly accredited diplomats, not merely to someone operating on the strict orders and for the sole purpose of a foreign government. Thus in *Saorstat & Continental Steamship v. De Las Morenas*[11] the defendant, a military officer in the Spanish army, sought to have proceedings against him dismissed on the basis that liability for non-performance of the contract lay properly against the Spanish State. The defendant had come to Ireland at the end of the Second World War to purchase horses for the Spanish army. He had entered into a contract with the plaintiff which he had now breached. The plaintiff proceeded against the defendant. The defendant could not (nor did he attempt) to rely on diplomatic immunity but on the related rule of sovereign immunity, which prevents a foreign sovereign from being impleaded directly

9 Diplomatic Relations and Immunities Act 1967; Vienna Convention on Diplomatic Relations (1961).
10 To the extent that a party to such a contract is not amenable to the jurisdiction of the courts unless he or she voluntarily submits to it; *National Bank v. Hunter* [1948] Ir Jur Rep 33 (failure to plead the immunity renders the defendant liable to the court's jurisdiction).
11 [1945] IR 291.

or indirectly before the courts of another State. His application was rejected because nowhere was express reference made to the State of Spain by the plaintiff. The remedy was sought against the defendant personally and could be satisfied out of the defendant's assets only. With respect, the argument of the defence carried with it more cogency and attempted to illustrate the policy decision underlying sovereign immunity. It was clear from the facts of the case that the Spanish government would be obliged to re-imburse the defendant for any loss he sustained while working on their behalf. Furthermore, the plaintiff must have been aware of the risks he took in entering into such a contract, for the booking notice was addressed to the 'Spanish Commission for the Purchase of Horses, per Col. de las Morenas'. O'Byrne J, giving the judgment, seemed to accept one could not implead a sovereign State directly or indirectly, yet confined the decision itself to the lack of direct impleading, that is, failing to name the Spanish State on the summons. Yet the facts disclose one of the clearest cases of indirect impleader and therefore one must doubt whether indirect impleader is prohibited in this jurisdiction. In his argument, O'Byrne J stated that there was no difference between the formulation of Atkin LJ in *The Cristina*[12] and that of Greene MR in *Haile Selassie v Cable and Wireless*,[13] but Atkin talked about the '. . . courts of a country will not implead a foreign sovereign, that is they will not by their process make him against his will a party to legal proceedings.'[14] On the surface this concerns only direct impleader and would justify the decision in *De Las Marenas*. The Greene MR formulation effectively extends the concept beyond that to include situations where the sovereign is not directly mentioned in the summons but the net effect is as if it were. Thus the court could have held that the *Haile Selassie* judgment was of dubious legal value or it could have accepted that it modified *The Cristina*. To state they were the same was fallacious, and to give the decision given required disapproval of the Greene formulation, which was not forthcoming.

Few of the difficulties have been removed by the Diplomatic Relations and Immunities Act 1967. In giving effect to the provisions of the 1963 Vienna Convention on Consular Relations, the Act removes immunity from action where the official is acting on behalf of the foreign sovereign in a contract where he did not expressly or impliedly contract as agent of that foreign sovereign.[15] In other words, knowledge by the other party can affect the diplomat's immunity. But this Act applies only to consular officials or employees. The defendant was neither. Further, the case concerned sovereign immunity on an indirect basis. Binchy points out that indirect impleader can arise by a number of means; most revolve around the second limb of the Atkin approach and to that extent concern ownership or possession of assets over which a judgment is sought. If

12   [1938] AC 485.
13   [1939] 1 Ch 182.
14   [1938] AC 485, 490.
15   Diplomatic Relations and immunities Act 1967 s. 6(1), 2nd Schedule; Art 43(2)(a) 1967 Vienna Convention, Art. 43(2)(a) 1967.

that is so, the concept of indirect impleader should receive a restricted application. There is support for that view arising out of recent English decisions, decisions that reverse earlier beliefs as to the common law in this area.[16] In *Trendtex Trading Corp v. Central Bank*[17] the Court of Appeal refused immunity for purely commercial transactions. Yet *De Las Morenas* could not be said to be a purely commercial transaction. The *Trendtex* case concerned state trading companies who engage in commercial activities, for example, nationalised industries in the freight transportation field. This seems sensible. Where a foreign State engages in a commercial activity, there is no policy ground that can justify placing such transactions above the national court. But the defendant in the case at hand was not engaged in a commercial activity. In certain respects the better analogy is with the case of *The Eolo*,[18] which concerned the requisitioning of a ship by a foreign sovereign (the Italian government) who was paying for the privilege of such requisitioning. The case is authority for the fact that the ship was accordingly conferred with the privilege of immunity. Yet the foreign sovereign was not directly named in the proceedings nor did it interfere with the foreign sovereign's ownership or possession of the property that was the subject of the action. In the *Eolo* the ship was neither under the ownership of or in the possession of the foreign sovereign but was clearly under its control. A successful action against the ship would result in loss for the foreign sovereign in much the same way as in the *De Las Morenas* case.

5.06 CONVICTS

The Forfeiture Act 1870 still has force in this jurisdiction, save to the limited extent that it has been repealed. It may also be the subject of constitutional attack. However, in the absence of such constitutional scrutiny, s. 8 of the Act remains in force and prevents a convict from entering into any express or implied contract. The Act, presumably, is designed to reinforce the policy goals of incarceration, that is, the removal of as many rights as possible.[19] It does not affect contracts entered into before a person becomes a convict because becoming a convict is one of the permitted disabilities listed in the Statute of Limitations that stops time from running.[20] In *O'Connor v. Coleman*[21] a solicitor was barred from recovering legal expenses from a convicted person.

---

16 *Kahan v. Pakistan Federation* [1951] 2 KB 1003.
17 [1977] QB 529 [1977] QB 529; see *Government of Canada v. EAT and Burke* [1992] ILRM 325 (Sovereign immunity did not apply to commercial transactions. Thus an award for wrongful dismissal could be made against the Canadian Embassy); *McElhinny v. Secretary of State for*

Northern Ireland [1994] 2 ILRM 115 (applied the principle in *Government of Canada v. EAT and Burke*, op. cit., outside of employment law): see Heffernan (1992) 14 *DULJ* 160.
18 [1918] 2 IR 78.
19 2 Williston s. 272.
20 Statute of Limitations 1957 s. 48(1) (c).
21 (1947) 81 ILTR 42.

One becomes a convict on being found guilty of treason or a felony and being sentenced to death or penal servitude.[22]

5.07 INTOXICATION

Contracts entered into between parties, one of whom is so intoxicated that he is unable to comprehend what he is doing, must be divided into two classifications: contracts for necessities and all other contracts. A contract for necessities involves those items that one would reasonably expect to be required by virtue of the human condition. It finds a somewhat unsatisfactory statutory definition in the Sale of Goods Act 1983 as 'goods suitable to the condition in life. . . .'[23] What constitutes necessities is a question of law for the court to decide; more will be said on the matter later with respect to contracts involving minors.

A contract, concerning necessities, entered into by a party so intoxicated that he cannot comprehend what he is undertaking, places that party under the same obligation to pay a reasonable price for those necessities as applies to minors and insane people.

Where the contract does not concern necessities, the intoxicated party will not be liable if the intoxication was such that he was unable to comprehend the nature of what he was doing and the other party was aware of the intoxication at the time the contract was made. In that event, a voidable contract is created. The intoxicated party may elect to repudiate the voidable contract or he may elect to affirm the contract, at his option, once the intoxication has been removed.[24] Such affirmation is to be by express word, deed, or by conduct or performance.[25]

There is thus a double requirement:

> sufficient intoxication to remove comprehension from the person and knowledge of that intoxication by the other party.[26]

Both requirements are far from clear. The requirement of a degree of intoxication that removes comprehension envisages a large number of situations where a person may imbibe so that he may be more reckless in his dealings than he would be in the cold light of day. This is not say that he would have lost all comprehension of what he was doing. Certainly the law gives little sympathy[27]

22 Forfeiture Act 1870, s. 6; Murdoch, *Dictionary of Irish Law*.
23 Sale of Goods Act 1893, s. 2.
24 *Matthews v. Baxter* (1873) LR 8 Ex 132.
25 Failure to repudiate a contract, immediately after the intoxication has passed, may prove fatal to the claimant: *Bawell Grain Co v. Ross* (1917) 37 DLR 620.
26 *Core v. Gibson* (1843) 13 M&W 623, unreported, High Court, 24 June 1976.
27 *Cook v. Bagnell Timber Co.*, 94 SW 695 (1906) (there was a minority view in this case that intoxication is never a defence in itself).

to those who have taken more alcohol than they should; but the nature of alcohol, like most narcotics, is that self-control tends to be lost, even though the drinker is aware of what is happening. There are many examples of cases where a person will do something when drunk that he would not be prepared to contemplate if sober. Moreover, agreement can be easier to secure in a relaxed and convivial atmosphere, and it is usual that many business dealings are lubricated with not inconsiderable amounts of alcohol. In *White v. McCooey*[28] the court refused to uphold a contract where the intoxication did not remove comprehension: the contract was rejected on the grounds of unconscionability. This seems palpably correct, although it does leave open considerable latitude to the court, making it difficult to predict the outcome of a case in advance.

The requirement that the other party be aware of the intoxication will normally be easy to prove.[29] Smell of alcohol to the breath, staggering, slurring of words: these will normally be self-evident to any on-looker. But the contract may in fact be negotiated over the phone (or in some other manner) whereby it would be unreasonable for the other party to be aware of the intoxication. Nonetheless, an enforceable contract comes into existence. It should be noted that all that is required is that the party is aware of the intoxication. There is no requirement that he be aware of the extent of the intoxication, that is, whether it removes comprehension or not.[30] Parties who enter into contracts with people who are intoxicated do so at their own peril. A contract cannot be enforced because one party says, 'I knew he was drunk but not to the extent that he had no comprehension of what he was doing.'

The correct sequence is:

(a) determine if the sober party knew of the other party's intoxication.

If yes, then,

(b) enquire if the intoxicated party was intoxicated to the extent that he lost comprehension.

If the intoxicated party did not comprehend what he was doing, then

a voidable contract occurs.

If the intoxicated party knew what he was doing, then, an enforceable contract arises (unless the court, using its inherent equitable jurisidiction, determines it to be unconscionable and sets it aside on the basis of unconscionability).[31]

---

28 Unreported, High Court, 24 June 1976.
29 2 Williston, s. 259.
30 Restatement, Second, Contracts, s. 16.
31 *Blomley v. Ryan* (1956) 99 CLR 362; *Grealish v. Murphy* [1946] IR 35; *McCrystal v. O'Kane* [1986] NI 123; *White v. McCooey*, unreported, High Court, 24 June 1976.

5.08 INSANE PEOPLE

Much of what has been said about drunkards with respect to capacity applies also to people who are insane.[32] A contract made with an insane person is valid unless the other party knew of the insanity.[33] The principal difference is that insanity, unlike drunkenness, normally lasts longer and therefore the party is usually under a disability to contract for a longer period of time. Moreover, the question of knowledge of the insanity by the other party will be more difficult to establish. Some people who are legally insane may appear normal.[34] Additionally, the insanity must be of type to remove knowledge from the person as to what he is doing. Again, this may not always be the case, though a court is unlikely to impose a contract on a person who has been judged insane even if he knew the nature of his act. Of course, during a temporary bout of lucidity an insane person may enter into an enforceable contract, and that contract is enforceable even if the insanity were to return.[35] The onus of proof rests with the person alleging the disability, in this case the insane person.[36]

In the case of necessities, the position is identical with that of drunkards and minors: unless it can be shown that the litigant intended to set himself up as a benefactor, such a contract is enforceable.

5.09 BODIES CORPORATE

Unlike natural persons, bodies corporate are not imbued with absolute powers. Bodies corporate cannot commit rape or be sentenced to jail; this is a direct consequence of their very nature. Moreover, just as human beings can produce a document that entitles them to claim human heritage, namely, their birth certificate, so too can bodies corporate produce documentary proof of their legal person status. Unlike their human counterparts, this documentary evidence is considerably more detailed; it is within these papers that the very life of the body corporate is to be found, detailing what it can and cannot do.

The most numerous example of bodies corporate are those incorporated

---

32 Modern terminology now uses phrases like mental patient, persons of unsound mind and so forth. The phrases are not defined but for a definition of a mental disorder, see Mental Health Act 1983 s. 1 (England).

33 *Imperial Loan Co v. Stone* [1892] 1 QB 599; it may seem strange that a person whose mind is unbalanced will be the subject of a contract, but it involves a balancing of competing policy rights: *Hart v. O'Connor* [1985] 3 WLR 214 (this case suggests that unconcscionability may offer a better solution than capacity to resolve this issue); *Hassard v. Smith* (1872) Ir 6 Eq 429 (there is a wider view of 'fair and bona fide' in transactions with insane people).

34 It is for this reason, to ensure commercial certainty, that the validity of such contracts are upheld: *Beverly's* case (1603) 4 Co Rep 123b.

35 *Hall v. Warren* (1809) 9 Ves 605.

36 *In're K.* [1988] Ch 310.

under the Companies Acts 1963-1990. These are limited liability companies which have been 'born' by compliance with certain statutory requirements concerning their formation. For such corporations, their 'birth certificate' is made of a number of documents: the articles[37] and memorandum of association[38] and their certificate of incorporation.[39] The cumulative effect of these documents is not merely to give legal life to such creations but to regulate the activities that they may engage in and the powers they may exercise in order to achieve these objectives. The most important document from the point of view of contract is, of course, the memorandum of association, which empowers the company to pursue a particular course of action[40] and grants it the necessary powers such as raising finance, buying land and so forth. However, a company has no independent life of its own but must live, almost vicariously, through humans in the form of a board of directors. These people are given powers to bind the company in its dealings with other individuals or companies, but that power, unlike a human person's, is not absolute. Instead, it is limited by the requirement that the power must be granted by the memorandum in pursuit of an object of the company and exercised by an officer of the company so authorised by the articles of association.[41] For example, a company may be given the power to borrow money, but that power may available only for the attainment of the objects of the company, which may be, for example, to build houses. Moreover, the power may only be exercisable by the chairman of the company's board of directors. Thus, if the managing director borrowed money to finance an oil exploration venture, it is clear that the company is acting outside of its abilities at several levels. The transaction would be termed *ultra vires*.[42] The question to be asked is, to what extent does this transaction bind either the company or the party who supplied the loan, that is, the third party.

The question of whether the transaction binds either the company or the party who supplied the loan is made more difficult once it is appreciated that the company presents no such limitation to the public when it is doing business. It would not be practical to expect every party dealing with a company to investigate the various documents before agreeing to anything, yet the law presumes this through the doctrine of constructive notice,[43] which states that

---

37 Companies Act, 1963, s. 11; Keane, *Company Law in the Republic of Ireland*, 2nd ed. (1992) pp. 61-67.
38 Companies Act, 1963, s. 5; Keane, op. cit., pp 49-60.
39 Companies Act 1963, s. 18.
40 Companies Act 1963, s.6(1)(c).
41 For the liability of a company for the actions of its officers, the rule is that provided the officer of the company acted with ostensible authority, an internal irregularity will not deprive the third party of enforceable rights against the company, though the company may of course claim against the officer of the company in default: *British Bank v. Turquand* (1856) 6 E&B 327; *Ulster Investment Bank v. Euro Estates* [1982] ILRM 57.
42 *Ashburn Railway Carriage v. Riche* (1875) LR 7 HL 653; *In re Jon Beauforte (London) Ltd* [1953] Ch 131.
43 Company documents are public documents open for inspection: Companies Act s. 370.

one will be deemed to have knowledge of that which one ought to have knowledge of. The documents of a company are open to inspection; therefore, the party should have availed himself of the ability to examine the import of these documents to ensure the company is not acting *ultra vires*. Indeed, a company is required by law to advertise that it is in fact a company;[44] therefore, it is not unreasonable to saddle the party dealing with the company with liability when he was aware of the dangers and should have been more mindful of them. Where the company does not advertise itself as being a company, it would, of course, be wrong to saddle such a party with liability.

Such a doctrine is so harsh[45] that it would be difficult to implement fully. It has, in fact, been abrogated in a large number of situations,[46] most recently as a result of our membership of the European Union.[47] The move has been away from dealing with the issue as a problem for the company and, instead, looking at the unfairness of its application to third parties who deal with a company innocently. Thus, simply put, a company that acts *ultra vires* will be liable in contract to the extent that it will not infringe on third-party rights where it would be unreasonable to so do and the third party is dealing in good faith. Moreover, the so-called internal management rule in *Turquand's* case will bind a company where an officer of that company acts with ostensible authority. Beyond that, it is outside the scope of the mandate of this text to further elucidate the area, one of the most complex in company law; the reader is directed to several excellent texts in this area, notably Keane, *Company Law in the Republic of Ireland*, Ussher, *Company Law in Ireland* and Forde, *Company Law*.

---

44 Companies Act 1963, s. 114 as amended by Companies Act 1982, s. 15.

45 Cohen Committee, Cmd 6659 (1945); Jenkins Committee, Cmd 1249 (1962); note also *In re PMPA Garage (Longmile) Ltd (No. 2)* [1992] ILRM 349 (restitution and estoppel may be available for acts *ultra vires* the company); see McCann (1992) *ILT* 79 and O'Dell (1992) 14 *DULJ* 123.

46 *Bell Houses v. City Wall Properties* [1966] 2 QB 656; *Martin v. Irish Industrial Benefit Society* (1960) Ir Jur Rep 42; Companies Act 1963. s. 8(1): 'Any act or thing done by a company which if the company had been empowered to do the same would have been lawfully and effectively done, shall, notwithstanding that the company had no power to do such act or thing, be effective in favour of any person relying on such act or thing who is not shown to have been actually aware at the time when he so relied thereon, that such act or thing was not within the powers of the company . . .'; *Northern Bank Finance v. Quinn*, unreported, High Court, 8 November 1979.

47 European Communities (Companies) Regulation 1973, Art 6: In favour of any person dealing with a company in good faith, any transaction entered into by an organ of the company, being its board of directors or any person registered under these regulations as a person authorised to bind the company, shall be deemed to be within the capacity of the company and any limitation of the powers of that board or person whether imposed by the memorandum or articles of association or otherwise may not be relied upon as against any person so dealing with the company.

5.10 INFANTS

The courts have always been mindful of the need to protect those who are incapable of exercising a full and free consent in the formation of a contract by virtue of their age; this now has legislative expression. In this jurisdiction the relevant age, referred to as the 'age of majority', where an individual is no longer required to be so protected is 18[48] or, if he or she is under 18, then from such time as he or she has been or is married.[49] The reduction in the age of majority from 21 is in accordance with general trends world-wide.[50] Thus, contracts with infants or minors under 18 years of age if unmarried, or with minors under 16 years of age if previously or presently married, are subject to certain protections afforded by both the common law and the Infants Relief Act 1874.

The general rule is that a contract made with an infant is voidable at the infant's option.[51] Statutory provisions[52] have, however, restored the old common law rule that contracts with infants were void since the infant could not give the requisite consent to form a contract.[53]

As an exception to this rule some contracts are considered to be valid where the subject matter of the contract is considered a 'necessary'. We have already seen how the Sale of Goods Act 1893, s. 2 defines a necessity;[54] a large body of case law has in fact developed which classifies items as either 'necessities'[55] or not.[56] It would appear that a feature common to 'necessities' is their use to satisfy a basic requirement of human life, including sustenance, clothing,

48 Age of Majority Act 1985, s. 2(1).
49 Id.; marriage under the age of 16 is void unless the prior permission of the President of the High Court is obtained: Marriages Act 1972, s. 1(1), the effective date for this is 1 January 1975; it overturns common law distinction of marriage for boys of 14, girls 12.
50 *Report on the Age of Majority, the Age for Marriage and some connected Subjects* (1977) LRC 2; *Report of the Committee on the Age of Majority*, Cmd 3342 (1969).
51 This would appear to be the US position and represents a more logical development of existing law: Restatement, Second, Contracts, s. 14.
52 Infant Relief Act 1874, discussed below. For example, inter-firm relationships often occur through the medium of contract; *Breedlove v. Freudenstein*, 89 F 2d 324 (1937).
53 *Henry v. Root*, 33 NY 526 (1865).
54 Supra. 66.
55 *Chapple v. Cooper* (1844) 13 M&W 252 (contract for funeral services of spouse); *First Charter Financial Bank v. Musclow* (1974) 49 DLR (3d) 138 (vehicle, if used for work or domestic related purposes but not if used for entertainment purposes); *Hands v. Slaney* (1800) 8 TR 578 (clothing for a minor's servant); *Peters v. Fleming* (1840) 6 M&W 42 (rings and a watch chain for a rich man's son!); *Soon v. Wilson* (1962) 33 DLR (2d) 428 (books for a student); *Jenner v. Walker* (1869) 19 LT 398 (engagement ring for woman minor is to marry).
56 *Ryder v. Wombwell* (1868) LR 4 Ex 32 (jewelled cuff links; the jury had found them to be a necessity, the court overturned the jury's finding as being without supporting foundation); *Nash v. Inman* [1908] 2 KB 1 (11 fancy waistcoats since infant had enough waistcoats already); *Wharton v. Mackenzie* (1844) 5 QB 606 (*obiter*: if son of the richest man in kingdom bought a racehorse, it would not be a necessity); *Whittington v. Hill* (1619) Cro Jac 494 (tools to carry on a trade).

shelter, and so forth.[57] Beyond that, almost everything else will not be regarded as a 'necessity'. In that regard the particular use to which the items are put is important; thus, food is a necessity but supplied in abundance it may be a luxury.[58]

It is clear that only an executed contract for the supply of 'necessities' is covered by these provisions.[59] Thus, a contract to deliver 'necessities' which has not yet been performed cannot be specifically enforced by the party who is of age, and the minor is free to reject the delivery of goods or services so contracted for.[60] Moreover, the infant is liable not for the contracted price of the necessities but for the reasonable value of them.[61]

It is also firmly established that contracts of service which are beneficial to the infant are to be upheld.[62] This is so because many infants engage in apprenticeships and other training contracts which are beneficial to the infant and which an adult would not offer an infant if the contract were to be unenforceable. The contract must be shown to be beneficial in substance to the infant. Thus, in *Clements v. London and North Western Railway*[63] an infant employee contracted to relinquish protection under the Employee Liability Act 1880 in return for joining the railway scheme which fixed lower levels of compensation. Nonetheless, on the whole the infant benefited from the contract. Compare this with *De Francesco v. Barnum*:[64] a contract for service (to sing) imposed no obligation on the adult party to provide work for the infant, yet restrained the infant in a number of ways, including limiting her right to marry! However, *Cowern v. Neild*[65] illustrates that a benefit in itself is insufficient to

---

57   *Chapple v. Cooper* (1844) 13 M&W 252, 258: 'Things necessary are those without which an individual cannot reasonably exist. In the first place, food, raiment, lodging and the like. About these there is no doubt. Again as the proper cultivation of the mind is as expedient as the support of the body in, instruction in art or trade, or intellectual, moral and religious information may be a necessary also ... the assistance and attendance of others ... articles of mere luxury are always excluded though luxurious articles of utility are in some cases allowed.' (Alderson B)491 F 2d 1147 (1974).

58   A party of champagne and wild ducks were held by a jury to be necessaries for undergraduates: (1874) Hansard Vol. 219, ser 3 col. 1225, this and other jury verdicts led to a clamp down by the judiciary.

59   Sale of Goods Act 1893, s. 2: . . . at the time of the sale and delivery.

60   *Nash v. Inman* [1908] 2 KB 1; *Wallin v. Highland Park*, 102 NW 839 (1905). But cf. *Roberts v. Gray* [1913] 1 KB 520, 530: 'I am unable to appreciate why a contract which is in itself binding . . . can cease to be binding merely because it is still executory' (Hamilton LJ); *Greenspan v. Slate*, 12 NJ 426 (1953); Treitel, op. cit., p. 484 et seq argues this point of view quite strongly but it is suggested he is overborne by the authorities to the contrary on the issue.

61   Sale of Goods Act 1893, s. 2; *Nash v. Inman* [1908] 2 KB 1; *Pontypridd Union v. Drew* [1927] 1 KB 214; 2 Williston, ss. 240-244.

62   *Chaplin v. Leslie Frewin (Publishers)* [1966] Ch 71.

63   [1894] 2 QB 482.

64   (1890) 45 ChD 430.

65   [1912] 2 KB 419.

enforce the contract and that it must be part of a structured service or apprenticeship contract, though in modern times the courts have begun to appreciate that the concept of such contracts might have to be enlarged.[66]

In almost all contracts with infants, the infant does not have to repudiate the contract to escape liability. However, a number of contracts result in a permanent benefit being bestowed upon the infant subject to recurring obligations. These have received special treatment, although (as Treitel points out)[67] there is no logical reason why this should be so. However, the case law establishes that contracts concerning land,[68] company shares,[69] partnerships,[70] family settlements[71] and insurance[72] are all contracts which are voidable by the infant only if he repudiates the contract. Repudiation can occur during the infancy, but this can be withdrawn before or shortly after reaching majority.[73] No money can be recovered under such a voidable contract, so that in *Steinberg v. Scala (Leeds) Ltd*[74] the court held that where shares were allotted but repudiated when a call was made on them, there could be no return of the money first paid as there had been no total failure of consideration.[75]

Under the Infant Relief Act 1847, s.1 all contracts other than for necessities are void where the infant enters into an agreement to receive goods or a loan.[76] The Act does not work in reverse. Thus, where the infant gives a loan or supplies goods, the Act does not apply. It appears that title to goods will pass under such

---

66 *Doyle v. White City Stadium* [1935] 1 KB 110.

67 Op. cit., p 491 et seq.

68 *North Western Railway v. McMichael* (1850) 5 Ex 114; *Keteley's* case (1613) 1 Bromnl 120; *Blake v. Concannon* (1870) IR 4 CL 323 (infant was liable for rent for period of use prior to repudiation but cf. *In re Jones* (1881) 18 ChD 109: the better view is that there is no liability for past usage; see, however, the New Hampshire approach discussed later).

69 *Dublin & Wicklow Railway v. Black* (1852) 8 Ex 181; *Northern Western Railway v. McMichael* (1850) 5 Ex 114.

70 *Goode v. Harrison* (1821) 5 B&Ald 147 (infant liable for partnership losses if he fails to repudiate after reaching majority); *Lovell & Christmas v. Beauchamp* [1894] AC 607 (an infant cannot share in profits/assets of the business, unless all liabilities cleared); *Griffiths v. Delaney* (1938) 4 Ir Jur Rep 1 (not liable for debts of partnership during infancy).

71 *Duncan v. Dixon* (1890) 44 ChD 211; *Paget v. Paget* (1882) 11 LR (Ir) 26 (could repudiate as soon as discovered that she was underage at time of entering settlement, some ten years later).

72 *Stapleton v. Prudential Assurance* (1928) 62 ILTR 56 (infant cannot repudiate contract once risk has begun to run).

73 *Slator v. Trimble* (1861) 14 Ir CLR 342.

74 [1923] 2 Ch 452.

75 *Corpe v. Overton* (1833) 10 Bing 252.

76 This includes transactions derived from such contracts, *Bateman v. Kingston* (1880) 6 LR (Ir) 328 (no action on loan note used to pay for necessaries, though the note carried interest).

an arrangement even though it falls foul of the Act,[77] unless there is a complete failure of consideration.[78]

The Act states in s. 2:

> No action shall be brought whereby to charge any person upon any promise made after full age to pay any debt contracted during infancy, or upon any ratification made after full age of any promise or contract made during infancy, whether there shall or shall not be any new consideration for such promise or ratification after full age.

5.11 CONTRACTING WITH ONESELF

We have already seen that it is not possible at law to make a contract with oneself, since a contract is a two party relationship.[79] But the baldness of such a statement is not always appropriate in modern terms.[80] While it is true that a person lacks the capacity to enter into a contract with himself or herself, there may be times when to apply this rule with too much rigour would yield an injustice.[81] Thus, in *United States v. Alaska Steamship Co.*[82] a company was appointed agent for the US government and in that capacity contracted with its stevedoring division. The contract was not set aside on the company's argument that it was attempting to contract with itself. While this case may be explained on the basis of agency, there will be situations where a person acts in more than one capacity at any given time.[83] In these situations, an external manifestation of a contract might be sufficient to create a contract.

---

77   *Stocks v. Wilson* [1913] 2 KB 235; but cf. *Prokopetz v. Richardson's Marina* (1979) 93 DLR (3d) 442.
78   *Pearce v. Brain* [1929] 2 KB 310.
79   Chapter 2, Restatement, Contracts, s. 15, Comment a.
80   For example, inter-firm relationships often occur through the medium of contract; *Breedlove v. Freudenstein*, 89 F 2d (1937).
81   Restatement, Second, Contracts, s. 9, Comment a.
82   491 F 2d 1147 (1974).
83   Restatement, Second, Contract, s. 9 Comment b.

6.00

Delaying or denying a contract

6.01 INTRODUCTION

The stage has been reached whereby a contract has been formed between parties
of the requisite capacity. The next stage of the process is to determine if the
contract so formed is enforceable. But first, a few words need to be said about
delaying or denying the existence of a contract. Normally this is done because
there is something that needs to be satisfied before the contract comes into effect,
if at all. The contract is, therefore, dependent upon certain events; this can be
useful in a large number of cases. The contract has been formed, but it is put
into suspense for a period of time. It may be that the suspense will never end or
that the events hoped for will not transpire and the contract will lapse. Perhaps
the most common example of contracts which never take effect is one which
depends on one party obtaining the requisite finance for the purchase. So, if I
go into a car dealer to purchase a new vehicle, I may well make my order subject
to obtaining the requisite finance from either bank or leasing company. All other
elements of the contract are in place, but it is put into suspense depending on
the decision of the finance company. If I obtain the finance, the contract arises
automatically; nothing further need be undertaken. If I do not obtain the finance,
the contract lapses: its existence was dependent upon an event which did not
occur.

The clause can be classified as 'conditions precedent and subsequent'.

6.02 CONDITIONS PRECEDENT AND SUBSEQUENT

Conditions precedent operate to suspend the existence of any contract until such
time as a specified event has occurred.[1] Thus, in *Pym v. Campbell*[2] the contract
was not enforceable on the basis of oral evidence that it was not to have effect
until the subject matter (an invention) had been approved by a third party and
that this had never happened. In *Aberfoyle Plantations v. Cheng* the contract
was not to take effect until the vendor had obtained a renewal of the leases

---

1   *Schuler's* case [1972] 1 WLR 840, 850: 'a prerequisite to the very existence of the
    contracts.' *per* Denning MR.
2   (1856) 6 E&B 370.

involved, something which failed to happen; it was held that no contract had come into existence. Thus, until a condition precedent has been satisfied, no contract exists between the parties and, therefore, no remedy can be given under the law of contract. This approach has been criticised in the Australian High Court in *Perri v. Coolangatta Investments*.[3] In that case, the court held that it was preferable to interpret the terms of the agreement as requiring a condition precedent to performance of the contract, rather than denying that the contract had come into existence at all. This enabled the court to exercise greater latitude in adjusting the rights of the parties and ensuring that justice was done. The net effect of the Australian approach is to interpret the contract as being subject to a *condition subsequent*: the contract comes into existence but is not enforceable due to the failure of a condition.

A *condition subsequent* arises after a contract has come into existence but its full performance is subject to some condition; failure to perform that condition brings the contract to an end: rights will still exist arising from the contract that once was. In *Marten v. Whale*[4] the agreement called for the approval of title by the purchaser's solicitor, but the court ruled that this did not prevent the contract from coming into existence. Rather, the clause was a condition regulating the passing of the property. This is a *condition subsequent*. However, in reality all conditions are *conditions precedent*. The question is, precedent to what?[5] A condition can be precedent to the existence of the contract itself or precedent to its enforcement. A *condition subsequent* is a condition that is not precedent to the existence of the contract itself but precedent to the enforcement of the contract. This can lead to confusion. In *Bentworth Finance v. Lubert*[6] the delivery of a log book was held to be a condition precedent to the existence of a contract, yet, as Cheshire, Fifoot and Furmston point out, this can hardly be true as a general rule.[7] In *Myton v. Schwab-Morris*[8] a deposit appears to have been regarded as a condition precedent, this is also difficult to justify.

Conditions subsequent or precedent, referred to by Treitel as contingent conditions to distinguish them from promissory conditions,[9] must be clear and unambiguous in meaning. In *Lee Parker v. Izzet (No. 2)*[10] a condition requiring the purchaser to obtain a 'satisfactory mortgage', was held too uncertain to be enforceable. The problem word in the contract was: 'satisfactory'. The meaning of the term satisfactory is one of subjective evaluation. Had the condition, as is

3   (1982) 149 CLR 537, in particular Gibbs CJ, 542, confining the decision to its particular facts; *Property and Bloodstock v. Emerton* [1968] Ch 94.

4   [1917] 2 KB 480.

5   *Maynard v. Goode* (1926) 37 CLR 529.

6   [1967] 2 All ER 810.

7   Op. cit., p. 148.

8   [1974] 1 All ER 326

9   Op. cit., p. 58 et seq.; promissory conditions are those terms of a contract for which breach entitles repudiation and are to be distinguished from warranties, see chapter 15.

10   [1972] 2 All ER 800.

normal, been made subject to mortgage approval, it would have been valid. Moreover, neither party may attempt to prevent the condition occurring. In *Mackay v. Dick*[11] a machine was sold on condition that it could do the work involved at a specified rate in a particular location, but the purchaser refused the vendor the opportunity to put the machine to trial. The purchaser was in breach, since he had allowed no reasonable opportunity to the vendor for completion of the condition.[12] Finally, reasonable steps must be taken to ensure compliance with the condition, where the condition imposes a duty to act. Thus, in *Hargreaves Transport v. Lynch*[13] the contract contained a condition that the sale of the land would occur only after the purchaser had obtained planning permission. The court held that the purchaser was under an obligation to take reasonable steps to obtain such permission.

A contingent condition may be waived by the party for whose benefit it has been made, leaving him open to sue on foot of the contract, or, indeed, being sued.[14]

6.03 SUBJECT TO CONTRACT

Traditionally the phrase 'subject to contract' has been used in contracts for the sale of land in order to demonstrate that no enforceable agreement comes into existence until such time as a formal contract has been signed or exchanged. It is a shorthand method of describing the myriad contingent conditions that would apply in the complicated process of land transactions. The rule is well settled in England by *Tiverton Estates v. Wearwell*,[15] following a period of turbulence in the property market caused by 'gazumping'. In rising property markets, the use of the term 'subject to contract' can postpone the agreed sale, thus enabling the vendor to continue to look for a higher price for the property from another prospective purchaser, certain that the original purchaser who has committed at that stage is unlikely to withdraw. A number of English cases in the early 1970s seemed to limit the effectiveness of the phrase, but that has now been rejected by *Tiverton*.

Certain decisions in this jurisdiction appeared to question the earlier established validity of the phrase, 'subject to contract',[16] in particular *O'Flaherty v. Arvan Property*[17] and *Casey v. Intercontinental Bank*.[18] In *Kelly v. Park Hall*

11 (1881) 6 App Cas 251.
12 Treitel, op. cit., p 59 refers to *Bournemouth FC v. Manchester United FC*, Times, 22 May 1980 where, in the transfer of a football player, part of the fee was made conditional upon the player scoring 20 goals. The player was dropped before he had an opportunity to score 20 goals. A breach had occurred in not affording the player a reasonable opportunity to score the requisite goals.
13 [1969] 1 WLR 215.
14 *McKillop v. McMullan* [1979] NI 85.
15 [1975] Ch 146.
16 *Thompson v. The King* [1920] 2 IR 365.
17 Unreported, High Court, 3 November 1976.
18 [1979] IR 364.

School[19] the phrase 'subject to contract' was described as meaningless where all the terms had been agreed upon. The High Court basically refused to follow these judgments,[20] and the Supreme Court finally recanted in *Boyle and Boyle v. Lee*.[21] The phrase is now restored to its original meaning. It denies the existence of any contract until a formal contract has been signed.

A question still remains where the phrase 'subject to contract' is inserted subsequent to the concluded oral agreement. This normally occurs when professionals come into the picture after the parties themselves have negotiated the transaction. As a result of Keane J's decision in *Silver Wraith*,[22] (where he held that the parties could not seriously have intended to conclude such a complex agreement without recourse to legal and professional advice),[23] it would seem that this may no longer prove a problem.

Where the phrase 'subject to contract' is used by mistake[24] or is inconsistent with the terms of the contract,[25] it will have no effect and the contract will come into immediate effect.

6.04 INTENTION TO BE LEGALLY BOUND

A contract may, in a number of relatively limited situations, fail to be enforced even though it is correctly formed, because the parties do not intend for the agreement to be the subject of the court's jurisdiction. Since the bargain theory of contract dominates legal thought it is clear that the

> views of the parties as to what are the requirements of a contractor what contracts are enforceable without a writing and what are not, are wholly immaterial . . . the law not the parties fixes the requirements of a legal obligation.[26]

However, without further elucidation such a statement clearly goes too far.

---

19 [1979] IR 340.
20 In particular, see *Mulhall v. Haren* [1981] IR 312.
21 [1992] ILRM 65; see also Dwyer, 'Subject to Contract — a controversy unresolved?' (1993) 3 ISLR 16.
22 Unreported, High Court, 8 June 1989.
23 The case itself actually involved the phrase 'subject to a full lease being agreed'. This was indicative that the parties had not really come to an agreement. Such a finding will normally be easy to prove.
24 *Michael Richards Property v. Corporation of Wardens, Southwark* [1975]3 All ER 416.
25 *Alpenstow v. Regalian Properties* [1985] 1 WLR 721 (Held that the insertion of the term 'subject to contract' was irreconcilable with an express stipulation as to the time to execute agreement. It would probably be very difficult to find similar facts. The use of this case as a precedent is, therefore, marginal).
26 Williston, op. cit., pp. 20-21.

While it is true that the parties to a contract cannot of themselves set the legal requirements for its enforceability, certain situations are considered by the courts to be of such a special nature that, if the parties evidence an intention not to be legally bound by the agreement, the courts will honour that intention. It must be clearly stated that it does not work in reverse: the intention of the parties that the contract should be legally binding will not render enforceable a contract which lacks some legal requirment for enforcement (such as formalities or consideration).

Perhaps one of the clearest examples of where an intention not to be legally bound arises is in the family situation. A mother, who tells her six-year-old son that if he tidies his room she will buy him an ice cream the following day, has entered into a valid contract (leaving aside the issue of capacity for the moment). It can hardly be that if the mother fails to deliver on this promise, either party intends to pursue the issue through the local District Court! If we remove the lack of capacity and make the child 19 years of age, going to university, and raise the stakes from an ice cream to £100, the reason for not enforcing the contract becomes less clear. Accordingly, the courts have held that contracts between family members may be denied efficacy on the basis that the parties did not intend to be legally bound,[27] though this may be rebutted by evidence of an express intention to be so bound,[28] or an implied intention from the evidence.[29] The more distant the degree of blood relationship, the more likely the courts will infer an intention to be legally bound.[30]

In commercial contracts it is quite difficult to show that the parties' intention not to be legally bound should over-ride principles of the common law. But in *Rose and Frank v. Crompton*[31] the agreement was stated to be binding in honour only and not amenable to the jurisdiction of the courts. This was upheld by the court, but it held that contracts flowing from an agreement held to be binding

27 *Balfour v. Balfour* [1919] 2 KB 571 (agreements between husband and wife are not intended to be legally binding); *Rogers v. Smith*, unreported, Supreme Court, 16 July 1970 (promise by a mother that the cost of supporting her would be paid from her estate after her death was not enforceable since the promise was too general and plaintiff would have looked after the mother in any event); *Mackay v. Jones* (1959) 93 ILTR 117 (a promise given in expectation of a legacy was not enforceable since it was an agreement between family members).

28 *Courtney v. Courtney* (1923) 57 ILTR 42 (a separation agreement between husband and wife is valid when they are living apart); *Hynes v. Hynes*, unreported, High Court, 21 December 1984 (an agreement to transfer a business undertaking was held enforceable, despite being between brothers).

29 *Jones v. Padavatton* [1969] 1 WLR 328 (would a reasonable person looking at the agreement, and its surrounding facts, believe that it should be enforced); *Parker v. Clark* [1960] 1 All ER 93.

30 *Simpkins v. Pays* [1955] 3 All ER 10 (an informal agreement between a landlord and his lodger, to enter a weekly competition, held lodger entitled to a share of winnings, despite landlord's evidence that there was no intention to be legally bound).

31 [1923] 2 KB 261.

in honour only, could be treated as separate contracts and enforceable. Failing such express intention, it is highly unlikely that a court would refuse to enforce a contract simply on the basis of a lack of intention.[32] It is far more likely that the agreement will not be enforced, on the basis that it lacks certainty or is ambiguous: this is discussed post. The burden of rebutting the presumption of an intention to enter a legally binding agreement in a commercial contract lies with the defendant and is a difficult one to discharge.[33]

In *Kleinwort Benson v. Malaysia Mining Corporation*[34] 'letters of comfort'[35] were held by the English Court of Appeal to be governed by the exact wording of their terms, and, in the case at hand, these letters formed a statement of the then current intention of the defendants and could not be enforced as a contractual document. This overturned the decision at first instance of Hirst J, who had held that commercial agreements normally presuppose an intention to be legally bound and that letters of comfort were legally binding unless there was something that could be proved to rebut the presumption. This view, supported by the Australian courts in *Banque Brussels Lambert v. Australian National Industries*[36] seems preferable to that of the Court of Appeal. At the very least the jurisprudence on letters of comfort should not be used as a general principle.

Agreements in labour law tend, as a general rule, to be the subject of specialised rules; reference should be made to the relevant treatises on the area as to their legal enforceability.

6.05 ILLUSORY, AMBIGUOUS AND UNCERTAIN CONTRACTS

A contract which is illusory is not really a contract at all. Thus, it is not a contract

---

32   Quere, *Cadbury Ireland v. Kerry Co-op* [1982] ILRM 77 (a clause held not intended to be legally binding despite its solemnity: it was an agreement to draw up a detailed agreement, but could not be relied upon itself); *Cunard Steamship Co, Revenue Commissioners* [1931] IR 287 (a booking arrangement was held not to be binding, since it was to be followed by a subsequent contract); these cases should be treated *sui generis*.

33   *Edwards v. Skyways* [1964] 1 All ER 494 (the fact that the agreement was 'ex gratia' did not rebut the presumption of an intention to be legally bound).

34   [1989] 1 All ER 785.

35   Letters of comfort are promises made by people that they hope to keep but which they do not wish to be legally bound by: such letters are statements of intention. For example, when setting up TEAM Aer Lingus as a subsidiary of Aer Lingus, employees of Aer Lingus were persuaded to leave that company and transfer to TEAM on the basis of letters of comfort from Aer Lingus. These letters stated that if TEAM terminated their employment, the workers would be re-employed by Aer Lingus. When TEAM ran into difficulties in 1994, Aer Lingus claimed the letters had no legal effect. The issue was resolved without recourse to a court judgment.

36   Cheshire, Fifoot and Furmston, op. cit., p. 119, fn 15: unreported (1989).

to agree to do X but to excuse liability if I chose not to do X.[37] Nor is it a contract if I agree to give you X if I feel like it.[38]

Moreover, certain contracts may be too ambiguous or uncertain to be enforced. Thus, in *Central Meat Products v. Carney*[39] an agreement which failed to specify important issues of the contract, such as price variation, was held to be too uncertain to be enforced. The same is true where the agreement is ambiguous, like that in *ESB v. Newman*,[40] where a clause containing the phrase 'accounts' was ambiguous as to whether it covered ESB accounts at four different locations or an ESB account on a cumulative basis at a single location.[41] Ambiguity is likely to be resolved by the court giving an interpretation from the surrounding facts.[42] Courts will favour finding an agreement as distinct from not finding one. Where, however, this is not possible, no contract will have come into existence.[43] Agreements to agree in the future cause similar problems with respect to ambiguity and uncertainty.

---

37 *MacRobertson Miller Airlines v. Commrs of State Taxation* (1975) 133 CLR 125 (an agreement to fly from A to B contained exclusion clause for liability if airline did not in fact fly from A to B, held there could be no contract in such a situation).

38 *Provincial Bank of Ireland v. O'Donnell* (1932) 67 ILTR 142 (an agreement taking security for loans that the bank might advance, at its absolute discretion, at some time in the future was held not to be a contract as it was too uncertain).

39 (1944) 10 Ir Jur Rep 34.

40 (1933) 67 ILTR 124.

41 The latter interpretation was given in the case at hand.

42 *Hillas v. Arcos* (1932) Comm Cas 23.

43. *Scammell v. Ouston* [1941] AC 251.

7.00

Consideration

7.01 INTRODUCTION

Clearly not all contracts can be enforced in the courts. For a start, there would simply be too many for our legal system to cope with, but even more importantly, no system of law should seek to enforce a contract merely because it has satisfied the conditions outlined earlier. For example, a man and his wife agree that in future he shall go to the pub only once a week. It would be a strange world indeed if that contract were to be enforceable in a court of law, and not a little disquieting to many a husband!

For a contract to be legally binding it has to have some additional element that will enable a court to recognise its legal nature. Many different tests are used in other legal systems to check the enforceability of a contract.[1] The traditional view of the common law has been to enforce only those contracts which have, in a simplified sense, been 'paid for';[2] this is in essence an attempt

---

1   In the Roman Dutch system of South Africa they use *justa causa*, see 7.02, fn. 4; in Article 1108, French Civil Code, must have 'cause' for enforceability. This is not defined in the French Civil Code and there are two main views: Domat believes it is the *animus donandi* and Capitant views it as the determining purpose of the parties. Motive would appear to have been finally expunged as being involved, see generally Amos and Waltons, *Introduction to French Law*, p. 166 (1966); in Holland a contract is binding once an offer has been accepted, save where it operates to defraud a creditor: see *Dutch Business Law*, p. 61 (1986); in Germany there is no consideration required, see Horn, Kotz and Lesler, *German Private and Commercial Law*, p. 71 (1982); Article 1325cc of the Italian Civil Code requires 'cause' as an element to a contract, see Cantoma, *The Italian Legal System*, p. 356 et seq., (1985); in the former Soviet Union Civil Codes RSFSR (1964) Article 44 requires written proof for enforcement of contracts over a certain value. In Japan, contractual relationships do not automatically involve enforcement. In Western ideology, based on the Hebrew notion of a contract with God, contracts were used as a method of social regulation, breach of which involved considerable penalties. In Japan, as an early agrarian society, it revolved around consensus and discussion; therefore such contracts as were entered into were designed to be changed and altered with the passage of time. Nowadays, it can be difficult to assess whether any contract is in fact enforceable, but this merely echoes the entirely different approach taken to legal regulation in the Orient, see *The Japanese Legal System*, pp. 281, 308 (1976).

2   The notion of 'paid for' carries with it the element of exchange and consequently barter. The development of the common law is one centred around the practical resolution of real disputes. Accordingly, since most disputes arise in the commercial setting, it is not

by lawyers to state that something is not worth anything unless cold hard payment has been exacted for it. The term we use to describe this 'payment' is consideration.

One should always be aware, however, that payment is not the only possible test available. For example, given that contract law is based on the notion of a true meeting of minds, some systems use the concept of the parties intending to bind themselves by the contract; others use the notion of 'cause', that is, what caused the contract to be entered into in the first place.[3] We have seen earlier that, at common law, certain types of contracts which, on the surface, appear to be legitimate have not been enforced because there is a finding that the parties did not intend to be legally bound despite the presence of consideration. But the intention to be bound has never been used to enforce a contract without consideration in this jurisdiction.

These alternative tests have their advantages and the so-called doctrine of consideration has its critics;[4] indeed, our own courts have made some considerable inroads into the concept of consideration.[5] Nonetheless, consideration remains fundamental to our understanding of the law of enforceable contracts.

But consideration is not the only requirement for an enforceable contract. We will examine conditions where the need for consideration may be abrogated, and also discuss the question of who may enforce a contract (in particular, third party rights).[6] Finally we will look at certain formalities that are required in some types of contracts before they are enforceable.[7]

Contracts under Seal   Contracts made under seal are enforceable contracts and do not require consideration.[8] Contracts under seal are often referred to as 'covenants'. Although making a contract under seal is not particularly difficult, it is not the norm in the modern business world, where contracts tend to be a mixture of oral and written agreements and seldom made under seal. In the old days, the seal required a considerable degree of formality, having to conform to certain standards. Sealing a contract traditionally consisted of a blob of melted wax dropped onto the foot of the document and impressed with a family seal or, failing such seal, a thumbnail. In any event the impression in the wax was of paramount importance. Today, only companies have official seals, small presses that make an impression on documents. Individuals have substituted the wax with a small, round, plastic, self adhesive red sticker.

unnatural for the common law courts to enforce only those contracts deemed sufficiently serious. To that extent, the one unifying feature of such contracts is exchange for value; in other words, a promise must be paid for. In civil law systems, with the abstract evolution of law as a pursuit of justice, this nexus for enforceability was not immediately obvious.

3   See footnote 1.
4   See chapter 8, post.
5   See chapter 8, post.
6   See chapter 9, post.
7   See chapter 10, post.
8   1 Williston s 205; Riddell, 'The Mystery of Seal', 4 *Can Bar Rev* 156.

It should also be remembered that the enforcement of contracts made under seal arose when a considerable amount of formality attached to the affixing of a seal to a document; the signet ring normally used to impress the wax was considered a highly prized family treasure. Today such solemnity no longer exists, and this changing pattern has been recognised in America by the Uniform Commercial Code[9] which abolishes the use of a contract under seal without consideration with respect to the sale of goods.[10] Indeed, it is difficult to see why this abolition could not be usefully adopted and extended in this jurisdiction to all transactions. The ease with which it is now possible to create a contract under seal no longer ensures that the parties to the contract have displayed any greater intention to be legally bound than the parties to a written contract which is not sealed. That one requires consideration and the other does not is no longer sustainable.

Contracts not under seal   For a contract not under seal to be enforceable it must have consideration.[11] This was decided in *Eastwood v. Kenyon*,[12] which finally settled the common law requirements for enforceability.[13] In that case

----

9   The Uniform Commercial Code (UCC) is an American law, applicable to contracts for the sale of goods and other commercial transactions. It has been adopted by a majority of the states in America.

10   S. 2-203, Comment 1; see Calamri and Perillo, op. cit., pp. 301-302 for a fuller discussion of US state laws which have downgraded the importance of the seal.

11   Treitel, op. cit., p. 63 et seq.; Cheshire, Fifoot and Furmston, op. cit., p. 67 et seq.; Clark, op. cit., p. 22 et seq.; Shatwell, 1 Sydney LR 289; Sutton, *Consideration Reconsidered*, op. cit.; Hamson, 'The reform of Consideration' (1938) 54 *LQR* 233; *6th Interim Report of the Law Reform Commission*, Cmnd 5449 (1937); Atiyah, *Consideration in Contracts: A fundamental restatement* (1971).

12   (1840) 11 Ad & El 438: moral consideration was held to be insufficient to enforce a contract according to Denman LJ, rejecting an earlier stream of judgments from Mansfield LJ, see *Hawkes v. Saunders* (1782) 1 Cowp 289. Despite this, the argument that moral obligation can be used to support a contract has not entirely disappeared: see ibid., and there may be sound juristic principle for permitting such an argument; *Sharp v. Ellis* [1972] VR 137; *Rood v. Wallach*, 1904 TS 187; *Mtembu v. Webster* (1904) 21 SC 324; *Conradie v. Rossouw* 1919 AD 279; see generally Christie, *Law of Contract in South Africa* (1981); Willie and Millin's, *Mercantile Law of South Africa*, 18th ed., (1984), p. 29 et seq.; note that the South African doctrine of *justa causa* in place of consideration includes valuable consideration as understood by the Anglo-Irish system but not nominal or sham consideration, see *Kennedy v. Steenkamp*, 1936 CPD 113; for an historical analysis, see Simpson, *History of Assumpsit and the Law of Contract*, op. cit., p. 323 where he argues that the notion of moral obligation as good consideration was not an invention of Lord Mansfield but central to the early origins of the doctrine.

13   Previous cases had suggested two alternate possibilities: written contracts are enforceable without consideration since writing down a contract would be evidence of the seriousness which the parties intended (*Pilans v. Van Mierop* (1756) 3 Burr 1663), which was roundly rejected in *Rann v. Hughes* (1778) 7 Term Rep 350, or that moral obligation referred to in Footnote 1 would be sufficient. The accession of Mansfield LJ to Chief Justice of the King's Bench in 1756 ushered in an era that saw considerable questioning of the doctrine. It was not disposed of until 1840 in *Eastwood v. Kenyon*, op. cit.

an heiress received benefits from her guardian, notably an education, which she promised to repay when she came of age. She subsequently failed to honour the promise and her guardian commenced proceedings. Denam LJ, dismissing the action before him, stated that there was no valid consideration. Moral obligation was not sufficient, for once, a promise is made, there is a moral obligation to fulfil it and this moral obligation would not be acceptable to the courts as a test for enforceability.

It is useful to examine the historical accident that led to the doctrine of consideration in the common law. Useful, but it should be remembered that, whatever the accident of its birth or its tortured growth, the doctrine is firmly rooted in all the major common law systems of the world today. We shall see, when discussing the concept of promissory estoppel, that, according to at least some members of the judiciary, our growing link with the European legal system may cause a rethink on the doctrine of consideration, perhaps to the extent undertaken in South Africa where consideration was abolished in its entirety.[14]

Historically, the doctrine of consideration grew out of three different writs: *covenant, debt* and *assumpsit*. The writ of covenant was designed to enforce contracts under seal; the writ of debt designed to enforce payment of a certain sum owed as a result of performance by the claimant; and the writ of assumpsit originally lay in an action for performance that had been undertaken with misfeasance, that is, carelessly. The writ of assumpsit was subsequently extended to non-performance of what had been promised (nonfeasance). The concept of consideration came to mean a benefit to the promisor in the writ of debt and a detriment to the promisee in the writ of assumpsit. The growth of the writ of assumpsit, in place of the writ of debt, resulted in the term consideration meaning both benefit and detriment. Obviously this benefit and detriment could be best described in terms of money or money's worth, and this tied in with the concept of the writ of covenant, which made contracts under seal enforceable on the basis that the parties intended to be contractually linked because of the formality with which they had contracted. For contracts not under seal, this consideration was proof that the parties had earnestly conducted relations so as to be legally bound, and, as is well known, nothing concentrates the mind of lawyers more than dealings concerning hard currency.

7.02 DEFINITION

If a contract is a promise made by one person to another, then consideration is the price paid for this promise.[15] It further follows that this price must be in the promisor's favour, that is, the person who makes the promise (promisor) must

---

14   See Van der Merwe, et al, *Contract* (1993).
15   Pollock on Contracts, op. cit., p. 133; Williston on Contracts, op. cit., para. 100; Restatement, Contracts, para 75; *In the Matter of Deed of Trust of Owen*, 62 NC App

receive the benefit of the price and the person who accepts the promise (promisee) must pay the price for it.[16] Traditionally, the definition has been phrased in a benefit/detriment analysis; namely, consideration is the price paid (or detriment suffered) in exchange for the benefit of a promise or act. Such a definition is open to considerable criticism.[17] The need for benefit to the promisor to exist before consideration is present is not logical. If X promises to give Y his vehicle in return for Y's promise to give Z £1,000, why should such contract not be enforceable? The payment to Z may represent no benefit to X; it may in fact be a gratuitous gift on his part; but the arrangement between X and Y is surely enforceable. It cannot be that, if X gives his car to Y and Y subsequently refuses to pay the money requested to Z, X cannot enforce this agreement for want of benefit. It might be suggested, then, that even though the payment to Z is gratuitous, and of no objective benefit to X, it is of some benefit, perhaps, and could therefore be termed as 'subjective' benefit. We shall see later why such an argument is even more absurd, being little more than an attempt to undermine the true concept of consideration.

In the United States, Calamari and Perillo define 'consideration' as a legal detriment suffered by the promisee which induces, with knowledge, a promise in exchange.[18] A legal detriment is further defined as the doing of that which one is not legally obligated to do, or refraining from that which one is legally entitled to do.[19] This definition raises some interesting questions that further elucidate what we mean by consideration. The omission of any benefit analysis is to be welcomed. It does, however, raise difficulties. Firstly, the detriment is defined as that which one is not legally obligated to do; thus, if a person is under an existing obligation, the performance of that obligation may not constitute good legal detriment.[20] So, an offer to a fireman to pay him £1,000 if he does all that he can to prevent the house from being engulfed by fire is probably not

506, 303 SE 2d 351 (1983): 'consideration is the glue that binds the parties to a contract together'; *Thomas v. Thomas* (1842) 2 QB 851: 'something which is of value in the eye of the law, moving from the plaintiff'.

16   Cf. Restatement, Contracts, para. 75(2); *Cechettini v. Consumer Associates 260 Cal App 2d 295 (1968); McCellan v. McCellan*, 52 Md App 525, 451 A 2d 334 (1982); Calamari and Perillo, op. cit., p. 188: 'It is well settled in the United States that the detriment may be given by a person other than the promisee and run to a person other than the promisor.'

17   Calamari and Perillo (op. cit., p. 188) point out that since what is relevant is a legal benefit (or legal detriment) the result is the same no matter which approach that is taken. With respect, that is somewhat fallacious, for while the restriction to legal benefit may exclude the more esoteric types of subjective benefit referred to later, it does not deal with the issue of the non-esoteric benefit which is not legal, for example, the payment of money to a third party as a gratuitous gift cannot be a legal benefit (other than under an exceptionally loose interpretation which would render it similar to the current subjective benefit conundrum).

18   Calamari and Perillo, op. cit., p. 187 et seq.; *Allegheny College v. National Chautauqua County Bank of Jamestown*, 159 NE 173 (1927).

19   Calamari and Perillo, op. cit. p. 187, s. 4-2. Clark, op. cit., p. 26.

20   *Collins v. Godefrey* (1831) 1 B&Ad 950 (a promise to pay a witness for complying with

enforceable since the fireman is only doing what he is under a pre-existing obligation to do and, accordingly, he has suffered no detriment. On the other hand, if you offered him the same amount to rescue your favourite stuffed owl from the third floor of your building, this, being above and beyond the call of duty, would probably be a sufficient detriment to constitute good consideration and create an enforceable contract. We shall see later that while this is clearly the case where the legal obligation arises by way of public regulation (for example, firemen, policemen and so forth),[21] there are slight variations where it arises due to a pre-existing contract.[22]

Of course, the extent to which the party is under a pre-existing public duty may vary considerably; thus in *Ward v. Byham*[23] a couple who were living together had a child out of wedlock and therefore, by the classifications of the time, illegitimate. Subsequently, difficulties between the father and mother resulted in the mother being cast into the streets and the father keeping the child. Some time later, the mother sought return of the child and the father made her the following offer: that the child would be returned if she, the child, so chose, and in that event, the father would pay the sum of £1 per week for the child's maintenance provided that the mother proved that the child would be well looked after and happy. The mother agreed to these terms and the child chose to stay with the mother. Payments ceased after seven weeks. In an action to enforce the contract it was pleaded that no consideration had been supplied since the mother of an illegitimate child is under a statutory duty to look after her child.[24] The Court of Appeal rejected this argument, giving judgment in favour, of the mother: she had in fact provided consideration by promising to do more than she was obliged to do, namely allowing the child to choose and promising to see that she was 'happy'.[25] The case may make sense from the point of view of justice, but it does not fit in well with the doctrine of consideration unless the

a subpoena was held unenforceable); 1 Williston, Contracts, s. 132; *Salmoneron v. US*, 724 F 2d 1357 (9th Circ. 1983); *Ritchie v. White*, 225 NC 450, 35 SE 2d 414 (1945). Note in *Kerring v. Minister for Agriculture* (1989) ILRM 82 O'Hanlon J said that there might well be consideration in the strict compliance of statutory regulation. If this is so, it must be confined to facts similar to that case, that is, payment of government subvention, as distinct from obligations imposed upon citizens with no payment.

21 *England v. Davies* (1840) 11 Ad & El 856 (the plaintiff was a constable who responded to a request by the defendant for information leading to the conviction of a felon. The defendant had offered a reward for such information. Finding for the plaintiff, the court held that a constable is not bound by public duty to give individuals such information and therefore consideration was present); *Glasbrook v. Glamorgan Co. Co.* [1925] AC 270 (additional police protection during a coal mine strike was not a public duty; a contract to re-imburse the police authority for the additional protection therefore held to be valid).

22 See para. 7.05 et seq., ibid..

23 [1956] 2 All ER 318.

24 National Assistance Act 1948, s. 42: the mother of an illegitimate child is obligated to maintain it.

25 The agreement required two things of the mother: (a) proof that the child would be well

court was intimating that there was no obligation under the statute to look after the child in a manner that involved more than feeding, clothing and shelter. Moreover, the requirement that she be 'happy' is surely a type of consideration that is not quantifiable as money or money's worth, indeed it is difficult to see what detriment the mother had suffered, unless again the court was intimating that it automatically assumed that children can only be kept 'happy' by the expenditure of money additional to that which would be normal—quite amazing child psychology! More honest would be Denning's judgment where he baldly stated that such a promise would be enforceable even if nothing further were required of the mother than her statutory duty.[26] Again, while this has the advantage of honesty, it helps little in the true understanding of consideration. The case may be better confined to its family law aspect, but it is indicative of the difficulties that face any court.

The corollary is also true where the detriment suffered is that of refraining from doing that which one could legally do. Presumably it is not sufficient detriment to refrain from doing what one is not legally entitled to so do. Thus, in *Hamer v. Sidway*[27] a rich uncle, on hearing the news of his nephew's

---

looked after and happy and (b) that the child was allowed to decide for herself whether she wished to live with mother or father. What constituted happiness was not laboured by the Court, perhaps understandably so, since it is almost unattainable and may, in the end be a pursuit more than an achievable result.

26   [1956] 2 All ER 318, 319 and 498.
27   124 NY 538, 27 NE 256 (1891); *In re Wyvern Developments* [1974] 1 WLR 1097 (the benefit does not need to accrue to the promisor). This concept of forbearance arises most often in the forbearance of legal proceedings. If the proceedings are valid, then the promise to forego such proceedings will constitute consideration: *Mustang Equipment v. Welch*, 115 Ariz 206, 564 P 2d 895 (1977), Cheshire and Fifoot, op. cit., p. 79; Calamari and Perillo, op. cit., p. 201. A difficulty arises where there is an invalid basis to the proceedings: can the surrender of such the spurious proceedings constitute sufficient consideration? The modern view is to treat the surrender of such proceedings as valid consideration: *Horton v. Horton* [1961] 1 QB 215 (a husband and wife agreed to a contract for maintenance payments of £30 per month. On a true construction of the document, the husband should have deducted tax. When this was discovered, he stopped payments but was induced into entering into a new contract which provided for the payment of the £30 per month net after tax had been deducted. This new contract was valid, since the wife could have sued to rectify the agreement. Her chances of success was irrelevant, provided that she honestly believed she could succeed); see also *O'Mahoney v. Gaffney* [1980] IR 36 (a plaintiff's cause of action is discharged by a settlement agreement, even though defendant is precluded from enforcing it); *In Re Metro Investment Trust Ltd*, McWilliam J, 26/5/77 1975 No. 2741P; *Murphy v. Quality Homes*, McWilliam J, 22/6/76 1975 No. 4344P; *American Restatement of Contract*, second para. 74; 1 Williston, op. cit., para. 135B; *In re Windle*, 653 F 2d 328 (8th Circ. 1981). These proceedings cannot be vexatious or frivolous, but must be made in good faith and with an honest belief in the chance of success. No facts should be concealed which might affect the claim; *O'Donnell v. O'Sullivan*, 47 ILTR 253 (to make an agreement for a compromise there must be a reasonable claim *bona fide* intended to be pursued). Moreover, the agreement may be set aside under equity where the parties, under a

acceptance into university and hoping that the nephew should do well without distractions, offered the payment of $5,000 if the nephew refrained from partaking of the usual third-level pursuits, that is, wine, women and the horses. The nephew, an unduly studious person, agreed most readily to those terms and followed them until graduation, at which point the uncle refused to honour the contract. Understandably distressed at the items he had missed, the nephew instituted proceedings to enforce the contract; the uncle replied that the contract was unenforceable for want of consideration. The court felt otherwise inclined: the nephew had foregone what he was legally entitled to do and this constituted sufficient consideration. This case also reveals the fact that the detriment suffered does not have to be to the benefit of the person making the promise. The acts of the nephew were of little benefit to the uncle, yet the contract was valid. I may, therefore, validly conclude a contract for the sale of my car if you burn £5,000 in notes before my eyes. No one has benefited from this transaction, but legal detriment has been incurred. We shall see later, however, that when it comes to directing the benefit of the burden to someone who is not a party to the contract, the contract does exist but its enforceability by certain parties is difficult.[28] Moreover, it would appear that an agreement to refrain from doing what is illegal is not sufficient detriment: if, in the *Hamer* case, the uncle had sought the nephew to refrain from injecting heroin during his stay in college, no enforceable contract would have been created. Likewise, an agreement to refrain from committing rape or robbing banks lacks the necessary detriment to constitute consideration. Such contracts may also fall foul of the public policy provisions referred to later.[29]

Finally, the benefit/detriment definition of consideration presupposes that there is a current exchange of detriment for promise and it is not sufficient for the two to be either unconnected or, perhaps even more startlingly, to be separated by time, under a doctrine known as 'past consideration', which is discussed in fuller detail below.[30] The important issue is, of course, that the detriment and exchange constitute the one transaction. Moreover, the definition talks in terms of an exchange with knowledge. This means that again the exchange must have been induced by the detriment. It is not sufficient that the exchange occurred. The detriment must have been known by the parties to the transaction. For example, X meets Y and says, 'My friend, life has been hard on you, take the keys and logbook to my car and enjoy in good health.' Y, overcome with emotion at such generosity, replies, 'Oh great and kind friend X, I insist that you have the contents of my savings account, £300 in exchange.'

common mistake, fail to realise that a defendant has a complete defence to the plaintiff's claim: see *Magee v. Penine Insurance Co.* [1969] 2 QB 507; *Meehan v. Commodity Broking* [1985] IR 12. This is perhaps more logically analysed in terms of contracts enforceable without consideration: see chapter 8 post.

28   Cf. *Drimmie v. Davis* [1899] 1 IR 176; see chapter 9 post.
29   See chapters 19, 20 post.
30   Para 7.04 post

In dissecting that transaction, it is clear that X's offer is a gift, for it is made without the intent to induce an exchange between the parties. Y's subsequent promise is likewise a gift and not enforceable, since X has offered nothing new in the way of detriment for the gift of £300. The exchange is not bargained for. Y's promise may have been induced by X's promise, but they were not exchanged. Moreover, the exchange must be undertaken with knowledge. Thus, if A makes this gift hoping that Y will give something in return, the fact that something in return is in fact given does not make the contract enforceable, since Y was not aware of the intended exchange.

The next question that concerns us is what exactly do we mean by the term 'price'? We shall see that, in law, we mean something different from what is colloquially known as the 'price' of something.

7.03 ADEQUACY AND SUFFICIENCY

It is not the function of our legal system to investigate every bargain to ensure that a fair deal has been struck. The law is more concerned that the parties have entered into the bargain freely. It will not evaluate the bargain itself. Thus, if I sell my Rolls-Royce for £1, the law will deem the agreement to have 'adequate' consideration. 'Adequate' here is used as a term of art; such a deal may be far from adequate in the normal sense, but people are free to do as they please, and if I wish to make a fool of myself by agreeing to such a contract, then the courts will not prevent me.

The law will demand, however, that the consideration be 'sufficient'.[31] To be sufficient it must not fall into a category of consideration that the courts will not accept as making a contract enforceable. For example, if instead of the above agreement, I sell my Rolls-Royce on the condition that you remember me in your prayers at night for the next ten years, the courts will deem this to be insufficient consideration. It is interesting to note that, to a betting person, this second deal is worth considerably more than that for £1, yet it has no value to the law.

Generally, therefore, to be sufficient, the consideration must be capable of being valued in monetary terms.[32] To date it has not been possible to value the

---

31   *Ferrar v. Costello* (1841) 4 ILR 425; Treitel, op. cit.; Cheshire and Fifoot, op. cit., p. 76 et seq.; Clark, op. cit., p. 25 et seq.; *Kennedy v. Kennedy*, Ellis J, 1/12/84; *Grove White v. Wilson* [1933] IR 729 (natural love and affection between father and son is insufficient consideration); Williston op. cit., para. 101; Restatement, Contracts, para 76.

32   Of course, everything is capable of being reduced to monetary value. Prostitution values a human body in terms of cash for usage thereof, insurance policies value life in the sense of loss and tort law constantly seeks to value human suffering and misery. In other words, law (and reality) recognises that almost everything can be valued in money's worth. We must, therefore, in contract be concerned with something slightly different. It is probably objective value, what a disinterested third party might be willing to give

salvation of your soul for this purpose. Similarly the courts will not enforce a contract based upon natural love and affection[33] or moral obligation.[34] Care should be taken to question to what extent different jurisdictions will treat what is to qualify as sufficient consideration. In the Northern Ireland case of *O'Neill v. Murphy*[35] a claim that a transaction was not forced by way of duress because it was based on contract, namely, construction of buildings for a neighbouring parish in return for prayers being said for his intentions, was rejected. The court held that the prayers did not constitute sufficient consideration. The case should be treated with care because it involved an allegation of undue influence, which as discussed below may be supported by evidence showing unrealistic consideration. Moreover, the case was decided in Northern Ireland, whose judiciary may take a more secular view of things than their brethren in the Republic of Ireland. In this jurisdiction, such prayers may in fact represent good consideration, particularly if you presuppose the existence of an afterlife. Indeed, there may be something astray about a legal system that will enforce a contract for the sale of a house for the payment of 50p but will not do so for 100 Novenas said on your behalf. All but the most committed atheists must surely feel that the possibility of saving your soul is of more benefit than the 50p. That is not to denigrate the 50p consideration but to question the poor treatment of the other. Likewise, a promise to refrain from unmarried sex entered into in this jurisdiction may well not constitute valid consideration but might in the United States.[36]

Worthless consideration   In *Haigh v. Brooks*[37] the defendant received, as per his request, a worthless piece of paper in return for a promise made by him to pay £10,000. The case involved a guarantee of payment given by the defendant to the plaintiff with respect to a debt incurred by a third party. The guarantee was ineffective under law and could not operate to bind the defendant. Nonetheless, the defendant promised to pay the money for return of the worthless

money for. Thus, prayers might be excluded because a disinterested third person would be unwilling to buy them. Indeed this concept of consideration as the objective monetary value of that which is given, perhaps better explains the concept of consideration. However, it becomes more difficult to reconcile with the growing desire of the courts to recognise subjective benefit, discussed post.

33   *Bret v. JS* (1600) Cro Eliz 756.
34   *Eastwood v. Kenyon* (1840) 11 Ad & El 438.
35   [1936] NI 16.
36   This is hypothetical. Moreover, a contract to refrain from marital sex may well be invalid in this jurisdiction as being against public policy, but acceptable in the US or UK since it is the forbearance of what one is legally entitled to partake.
37   (1839) 10 Ad & El 309; *Chappell & Co. v. Nestle* [1960] AC 87 (chocolate bar wrappers which were required in part payment of a promotional offer were held to be valuable consideration, even though the company had no interest in the wrappers and threw them away once received); *Esso Petroleum v. Customs and Excise* [1976] 1 All ER 117 (World Cup Coin collection of little intrinsic value, yet held to be sufficient consideration, discussed post); *Lipkin Gorman v. Karpale* [1991] 3 WLR 10 (provision of gambling chips at casino was not consideration, they merely facilitated the game).

document. When he refused to honour this promise, the plaintiff sued him, to which he replied that the worthless scrap of paper could not constitute consideration. The court found that the defendant had bargained for the paper and accordingly would be held liable for the contract.

In the American case of *Newman and Snell's State Bank v. Hunter*,[38] a case which has been criticised, the court held that the surrender of a worthless note to the plaintiff did not constitute sufficient consideration. Here the defendant obtained the return of her deceased husband's loan note from the bank in return for her promise to pay the outstanding amount owed the bank. It is not clear how this case is reconcilable with principle; it may be true to say that it was concerned more with the vitiation of a contract for reason of circumstantial evidence of fraud.

It should be noted that the quantum of consideration present in any contract may of course give rise to an inference of undue influence or duress, topics dealt with later.[39] To this extent such contracts are valid in terms of consideration but may be set aside for want of consent free and truly given. If I have entered into a bargain to sell my house for one penny, the courts may view that fact as so unlikely as to raise an inference of dishonesty in the transaction, particularly if the purchaser is someone who exercises a degree of control over my thoughts, much as, say, a lawyer or banker might.

Sham consideration   Even where consideration does exist in the contract, can it be said that the consideration is itself only a fraud, that it is inserted into the agreement solely to give the agreement legal effect? For example, suppose we enter into an agreement where the consideration is to be £10 but where the consideration is never actually paid. This is what occurred in *Moroney v. Revenue Commissioners*[40] where a father purported to sell property to his two sons but no transfer of consideration ever took place nor was it intended to so do. In reality a gift was being made. As in *Bard v. Kent*[41] evidence was allowed to be introduced that no consideration had in fact been paid and thus it was not a binding contract but a gift.

Consideration in option contracts   *Bard v. Kent* is slightly different in that it involved an option contract, that is, a contract to keep an offer open for a given amount of time. This case concerned an offer by the lessor to extend the lease for an additional four years if the lessee would make improvements to the value of $10,000. The question was whether the offer, or more accurately, the option could be revoked for lack of consideration. We will see in a later chapter that sound policy reasons may exist for enforcing such option contracts despite the

38   243 Mich 331, 220 NW 665, 59 ALR 311 (1928).
39   *Hassard v. Smith* (1862) 6 IR Eq 429; see chapters post.
40   [1972] IR 372; see chapter post; Williston, op. cit., para. 115B.
41   19 Cal 2d 449, 122 P 2d 8 (1942).

absence of consideration, particularly in commercial transactions. In a minority of US jurisdictions[42] a fiction was indulged in to enforce the validity of such contracts and not allow the introduction of oral evidence to deny a recital[43] to the contract that such consideration had in fact been received. The reason for this is the economic utility of such contracts being enforceable, even in a non-commercial setting. In the Restatement, Second. such option contracts are enforceable despite the absence of consideration (together with contracts of guarantee)[44] provided that the option is in writing and consideration is recited therein. What is not clear is, while such options are enforceable despite the non-payment of consideration, what if the consideration constitutes something which is not acceptable, for example, natural love and affection? Since the consideration is wholly illusory in any event, why should such a contract be unenforceable for the recital of something which is not to be paid in any event. These, and related difficulties, suggest that the Restatement, Second, erred in not following the earlier Restatement, which adopted the common law position[45] and made such written offers enforceable, despite the absence of consideration, provided an intent to be legally bound is evidenced from the writing.[46] An even better solution might have been found in extending the protection afforded option contracts under the UCC so as to include those other than merchants.[47]

Token consideration   What if the amount of the consideration in no way reflects the value of what is being transacted, but its existence is designed merely to change the nature of the transaction? In this sort of situation the consideration may actually have been paid. We have said earlier that the courts will not look to the adequacy of the consideration and, while that is settled law in this jurisdiction, it does no harm to question that assumption. If the court will refuse to make a contract enforceable because a nominal consideration has not been paid, why is it willing to enforce it when such consideration has in fact been paid? If I agree to gift to you my car but for our own reasons we wish it to take the form of a contract, I may agree to sell you the vehicle for £1. If you do not

---

42   *Real Estate Co. of Pittsburgh v. Rudolph*, 301 Pa 502, 153 A 438 (1930); *Lawrence v. McCalmont*, 43 nUS (2 How,) 426, 452 11 L Ed 326 (1844); *Hubbard v. Schumaker*, 82 IllApp3d 476, 37 Ill Dec 855, 402 NE 2d 857 (1980).

43   A recital is a formal written statement, contained within a deed or document, setting forth some fact to: (a) explain the reason for the transaction, or (b) to evidence the existence of some fact, or (c) in pleading, to make a positive allegation.

44   Restatement, Contracts, para. 89B(1)(a).

45   See footnote 8 supra.

46   See also the Uniform Written Obligations Act, 9C ULA 378 (adopted 1925); 33 Purdon's Statutes Ann s 6-8 (Pennsylvania Statute adopting this Act); Hays, 'Formal Contracts and Consideration: A Legislative Program', 41 *Columbia Law Rev* 849 (this article gives a contrary view critical of this Act: intent plus formality not of themselves sufficient to enforce a contract in the absence of other factors).

47   See chapter 2, post.

give the £1, the court may hold, despite any written recital acknowledging receipt of that £1, that no consideration has been achieved. Yet if I do pay the £1, the court will enforce such contract. The difference is surely minimal and serves no useful juristic purpose. The Restatement, Second, has taken that view in contrast to the original Restatement.[48] The Restatement, Second, would take the view that this token consideration is a sham and does not constitute true consideration. The difficulty with this approach is that it forces the common law to enquire into the adequacy of the bargain. At what stage does the consideration cease to be token and become adequate. The Restatement, Second, gives no guidance. Is £100 token consideration if the value of the item is £1,000, or would it only be token if the value of the item is £10,000, or £50,000? Moreover, such an approach is inconsistent with the earlier attempt by the Restatement, Second, to permit the enforceability of option and guarantee contracts without consideration. It is suggested that the Restatement, Second, seems to be incorrect in its approach to these matters. By failing to adopt the UCC provisions (which currently apply only to merchants in contracts for the sale of goods) the Restatment, Second, has led to more confusion than any supposed gain to be had from its own version.

Illusory consideration   Another interesting possibility is that the consideration is wholly illusory. Returning to *Hamer v. Sidway* discussed above, what if the nephew who promised to refrain from wine, women and song was a mute homosexual teetotaller? Would the agreement have been enforceable in any event? Case law would suggest that such would in fact have been no consideration at all and this ties in with the concept of consideration being a detriment.[49] It is hard to see what detriment the nephew would suffer in this case. The difficulty with these cases is that they revolve around a subjective evaluation of detriment to the person. The cases really seem to have missed the real issue involved. The test is, not did the promisee suffer a subjective detriment, but did he suffer a legal detriment: that is, did he forego something that he could have

48   Restatement, Second, Contracts, para. 71 which denies the sufficiency of such consideration; Restatement, Contracts, para. 84 which states that such sham consideration is valid to make an enforceable contract; Treitel, op. cit., p. 72 points out that the distinction is a matter of common sense between that which is inadequate and that which is token. With respect, this is not so. In *Midland Bank and Trust v. Green* [1981] AC 513 the transfer of land worth £40,000 was enforceable with consideration of £500. There was evidence that the £500 was in fact paid. According to Treitel, this is, as a matter of common sense, consideration that is inadequate but not token or sham. The question that has to be posed is, using this common sense test, when would it have become token consideration, not merely inadequate consideration? At £250? £100? £50? Such an interpretation of necessity involves the Courts in making value judgments as to the adequacy of any consideration.
49   In *Arrale v. Costain Civil Engineering* [1976] 1 Lloyd's Reports 98, 106 ('no consideration to refrain from a course of conduct it was never intended to pursue'); *Colchester BC v. Smith* [1991] 2 All ER 29; cf. *Beaton v. McDivitt* (1988) 13 NSWLR 162.

availed of, even if in reality he would have no wish to do so? The corollary position illustrates this point with greater clarity. Suppose in the *Hamer* case that the nephew had already decided that he was going to work hard at college and study and therefore had decided not to partake of wine, women and song: would the contract be unenforceable because he had decided to do the item in question for other reasons? Surely not, otherwise many a contract would be overturned.[50] Can a university refuse to honour a contract with a member of faculty because he admits that as a career move he had always intended to lecture in order to hone his academic skills? Has the lecturer provided any less consideration? Such a position would be absurd. It is not possible that a promise to oneself cannot constitute good consideration. First, there would be the evidentiary burden and secondly, a promise to myself is not enforceable and therefore not binding on me. I may chose to break the promise at will. The very same promise, made to another, is quite different.

Treitel makes an interesting possibility of where X and Y enter into an agreement for the contents of a wine cellar, whatever they may be.[51] He argues that if both X and Y are aware that the cellar is in fact empty, no contract has arisen since there is no consideration. But he postulates that the same might be the case where the seller of the contents of the wine cellar is aware it is empty but the purchaser is not.[52] To examine this situation further, let us dissect the first proposition.

A promises to pay Y £5,000 for the contents of the wine cellar. If both know that the cellar is empty, then no enforceable contract comes into being, because they are attempting to use something which they know is not in existence. Suppose that unknownst to both, Z had in fact filled the cellar; would the contract be enforceable then: in other words, could A claim the contents of the cellar as a bonus? The better answer must be no, because X and Y contracted with the full knowledge that the contents of the wine cellar were not to be taken seriously. The reality of the situation cannot make or break such a contract, because the nature of the contract is understood by both parties to be an agreement for the empty contents of the wine cellar. The law will not enforce such an agreement, because it provides no consideration since the contents of an empty wine cellar are not capable of being expressed in money or money's worth. Moreover, it may be argued that the promise to pay the money was for the contents of something. Since these contents do not exist, it was not a true exchange but a gratuitous donation by X.

Suppose, however, that neither X nor Y is sure of the contents of the wine cellar; could such an agreement be enforceable? It must be accepted that there

---

50   *Brikom Investments v. Carr* [1979] QB 467 (can constitute good consideration even where other factors are responsible for the detriment).

51   Treitel, op. cit., pp. 79-81.

52   Treitel, op. cit., p. 79, fn 42 '. . . if the parties . . .', emphasis added.

is good consideration here.[53] Again the reality of the wine cellar is immaterial to such a finding. What has been bargained for is the contents of the cellar, full, empty or in between. In that sense Y suffers an objective legal detriment in that he may lose the contents of his cellar. His loss may be great or may be nothing, but it is nonetheless a legal detriment. Such contracts are entered into all the time and represent, albeit in a highly stylised manner, the ordinary vagaries of business. But the contract is binding, at least in terms of consideration.

Finally, suppose Y is aware that the cellar is empty, but this fact is unknown to A; can such a contract be enforceable, in that Y provides a legal detriment in the making of such an offer? We have seen that good consideration can be had from a worthless piece of paper, if that is what has been bargained for. And this is so even if the promisee (in this case Y) is aware that the paper is worthless and the promisor (in this case X) is not, provided that it was what he bargained for. If that is so, then in this hypothesis the agreement is binding in terms of consideration, though of course other grounds may exist for setting the contract aside (but they are not relevant here).

In summation, consideration may be more fully explicable by stating it in the following terms: it is a legal detriment that has been sought in exchange for a promise. If the promisor is aware that there is no legal detriment involved, then it is not valid consideration, but the promisee's state of mind is irrelevant, in terms of consideration in any event.[54] The real value of the legal detriment may in fact be worthless, but provided it is what has been bargained for and provided that it is a legal detriment, then it is valid.

Moreover, for taxation purposes the Revenue Commissioners have been given considerable powers to impose market values on many transactions that are the subject of tax liability, irrespective of the consideration contained within the agreement, or indeed its absence.[55]

7.04 PAST CONSIDERATION

Consideration, in order to be valid must have been agreed upon prior to the contract coming into effect, that is before a completed offer and acceptance has been made. In *Roscorla v. Thomas*[56] the purchaser agreed to buy a horse and

---

53 *Smith v. Harrison* (1857) LJ Ch. 412 ('my title [to my land] if any' was valid consideration, making a binding contract); *Brady v. Brady* [1989] AC 755 (a contract with respect to the future contents of an item could bind).

54 Of course, he will in all likelihood have exposed himself to all sorts of difficulties including fraud misrepresentation, mistake and so forth. See post.

55 See Stamp Duty Act and Capital Gains and Capital Acquisitions Acts.

56 (1842) 3 QB 234; for a discussion of past consideration see Treitel, op. cit., p. 73 et seq.; Cheshire and Fifoot, op. cit., p. 70 et seq.; Clark, op. cit., p. 27 et seq.; Much play is made on certain phrases: past, executed and executory consideration. Executory consideration is the exchange of a promise in return for a counter-promise, the entire transaction remains in futuro. Executed consideration is the exchange of a promise for

subsequent to that agreement, which was supported by consideration, the seller warranted that the said horse was free from vice. In fact the horse was unsound. The warranty as to the horse's health was unenforceable since it was not supported by consideration. The original consideration in purchasing the horse was in effect 'used up' and could not now be used to ground a second contract concerning the horse's health. It would have, of course, been different if the vendor's warranty as to the horse's health had been made prior to the completion of the contract for sale, or if the subsequent promise that the vendor made had been the subject of new consideration by the purchaser.

A more recent example involved a bank overdraft in *Provincial Bank of Ireland v. O'Donnell.*[57] In this case, a bank customer had run up a considerable sum on overdraft. The bank was quite worried about his ability to pay and, accordingly, it was agreed that his wife would sign an agreement providing security for (a) the existing overdraft accounts and (b) any future moneys that the bank might advance to her husband. The customer defaulted and the bank attempted to exercise its right to the security. The court held that the agreement in (a) as to the existing overdraft was unenforceable since it concerned past moneys, and the agreement in (b) was also unenforceable since it was too vague. Little sympathy can be had for the bank, because it could have easily created a binding contract by either getting the wife to sign a document under seal or alternatively advancing her £1 for her promise concerning the existing indebtedness of her husband. The second part of the contract need not concern us here.[58]

Past consideration should be distinguished from consideration that has not been finalised but is envisaged. There would appear to be no requirement that the amount of the consideration be specified before completion of the contract, so in *Bradford v. Roulston*[59] the plaintiff signed a document on the orders of the

---

an act and must therefore be distinguished from past consideration. In executed consideration, one must be able to prove that the promise and the act constitute a single transaction which are linked causally to each other, see *Wigan v. English and Scottish Law Life Insurance* [1909] 1 Ch 291. With respect, these distinctions do not help us understand consideration any better. It is submitted that they should be ignored. Consideration is either sufficient, or past and, therefore, insufficient. Consideration is past if it does not form part of a single transaction with the promise asserted and/or it is not causally related to said promise.

57 (1932) 67 ILTR 142; *Morgan v. Rainsford* (1845) 8 IrER 299 (a promise of payment for past improvements made to a property held to be invalid, the promise made with past consideration. A promise to pay for future improvements also held invalid as being too vague).

58 See chapters 6 post for the setting aside of a contract on the grounds of uncertainty.

59 *Lampleigh v. Braithwait* (1615) Hob 105 (help was given by plaintiff to secure prisoner's release (at the prisonser's request) was followed by a subsequent promise by the prisoner, on his release, to pay £100. *Held* this promise was enforceable, consideration was not past but uncertain as to quantum. This uncertainty was removed by the prisoner's statement); *In re Casey's Patents, Stewart v. Casey* [1892] 1 Ch 104 (consideration consisting of services rendered whilst plaintiff was manager of patent rights held to be

defendant, who subsequently made out a written promise to the plaintiff to compensate him for a certain sum. The defendant refused to pay this money on the grounds that it was unsupported by consideration, the consideration of signing the document having occurred prior to his written promise. Rejecting the defendant's argument, the court pointed out that the act was done at the insistence of the defendant and it was envisaged that some compensation would be made available to the plaintiff at the time the plaintiff was acting. It would appear therefore that, provided consideration is envisaged and that the promisor is at some disadvantage as a result of his actions, a subsequent statement as to an intention to pay some consideration is enforceable.

As Lord Scarman has observed:

> An act done before the giving of a promise to make a payment or to confer some other benefit can sometimes be consideration for the promise. The act must have been done at the promisor's request, the parties must have understood that the act was to be remunerated further by a payment or the conferment of some other benefit, and payment, or the conferment of a benefit must have been legally enforceable had it been promised in advance.[60]

Moreover, whether the requirement that present consideration should exist in all cases is doubtful. Calamari and Perillo pose the example of an offer to pay you a pension of $200 per month for forty years of faithful service. Such an offer would seem worthy of upholding but on common law principles is not enforceable.[61] In New York, the General Obligations Law (GOL) gives effect to such contracts provided that they are in writing.[62] Such statutes do not remove the need for consideration, but merely refuse to allow such contracts to be avoided due to the timing thereof. The difficulty has been that, while the GOL was designed to cover those cases where there was a pre-existing moral duty, the experience has been that the bulk of the case law has revolved around a promise to pay the existing debt of another, a quite separate issue from the case at point.[63]

valid); *In re McArdle* [1951] Ch 669 (previous work done on a house by the plaintiff could not constitute consideration sufficient to enforce a promise by the heirs of the property to repay the amount expended from the estate, even though such promise was in writing and stated the exact quantum. The work undertaken was past consideration). With respect to an infant ratifying a pre-capacity contract, see chapter 5 on Capacity; with respect to suing on foot of negotiable instruments, see chapter 26 on Remedies.

60   *Pao On v. Lau Yiu Long* [1980] AC 614,629.
61   Calamari and Perillo, op. cit., p. 191 et seq..
62   New York General Obligations Law, s. 5-1105 as amended.
63   For the purpose of the New York Statute, see 1941 *Report of the Law Revision Commission*, 345 (New York); Hays, 'Formal Contracts and Consideration: A Legislative Program', 41 *Columbia Law Rev* 849, 859; Calamari and Perillo, op. cit., p. 268 et seq.

Indeed, it may be arguable that there are cases where the exclusion of past consideration is totally inappropriate. In *Lee v. Muggerdige*[64] the court held that a contract was enforceable by virtue of its antecedent moral obligation. The judgment was overruled in most common law jurisdictions, though it has received limited acceptance.[65] Leaving aside, for the moment, the issue of pre-existing debts, the case would appear to be good authority for the situation that arises where one person has received a benefit as a result of which a promise has been made to compensate the giver of that benefit. Despite the absence of consent, where medical services are rendered to a person who is not conscious, there can be no doubt but that the value of the services so rendered may be recovered.[66] Unfortunately this only occurs in limited circumstances, and as a general rule there is no compensation for unrequested benefits. The reason for denying this 'promissory restitution'[67] is far from clear. It is certainly valid to prevent a person from being forced to pay for unrequested services, quite another not to enforce a promise freely made in return for those services. It is not being suggested that one could enforce a past promise for which the consideration was not sufficient. What we have here is a situation where the past consideration is sufficient but is excluded by virtue of its timing. In the New York section referred to earlier, it is a requirement that the past consideration would have been valid consideration, save for the time it was given or performed. Moreover, it is implicit that any such consideration must have been the subject of an express or implied exchange.

At the very least such unenforceability should not be permitted where it would lead to an injustice; this line of argument is taken by the Restatement, Second.[68] While the section may in the end raise more problems than it clarifies, it and the New York GOL mentioned earlier,[69] are serious attempts to deal with a difficult problem.

---

64 2 Taunt. 36, 128 Eng. Rep. 599 (CP 1813); 1A Corbin, op. cit., paras. 230, 231, 232: consideration was that found in the antecedent moral obligation that induced the promise, not the promise itself; Dias, 'The Unenforceable Duty', 33 *Tulane L. Rev* 473.

65 *Cotnam v. Wisdom*, 83 Ark 601, 104 SW 164 (1937); 1A Corbin, op. cit., para. 233; I Williston, op. cit., paras. 144- 147; this sort of liability may be more properly dealt with in the law of restitution, *In re Rhodes* (1890) 44 Ch D 84, *Matheson v. Smiley* (1932) 2 DLR 787; see also Chapter 26.

66 *Eastwood v. Kenyon* (1840) 11 Ad & El 438; Calamari and Perillo, op. cit., p. 247 et seq.

67 Henderson, 'Promises Grounded in the Past: the idea of unjust enrichment and the Law of Contract', 57 *Va. L Rev* 1115 (1971); Kronman & Posner, *The Economics of Contract Law* (1979); the term 'promissory restitution' has been criticised as being a contradiction in terms.

68 *Restatement, Contracts*, 2d, para. 86; for a critical analysis of the Restatement, see Braucher, 'Freedom of Contract and the Second Restatement', 78 *Yale LJ* 598 (1969).

69 See footnote 7 ibid; it is submitted that the GOL requirement that the promise be in writing is an easy way to obviate the possibilities of abuse of such a system, satisfying the stringency of the evidentiary burden that seeks to protect defendants from fraudulent litigation.

7.05 PRE-EXISTING CONTRACTUAL RELATIONSHIP

Essentially this can be divided into two situations—where the promise to perform is based on a pre-existing contractual duty between the parties, or alternatively the subject matter of the consideration concerns the performance of a contractual obligation to a third party.

The law seems to be that where the consideration involves the performance of an existing contractual duty owed to a third party it constitutes good consideration. Thus, the Privy Council in *New Zealand Shipping Co. v. Satterthwaite*,[70] better known as the *Eurymedon* case, held that the unloading of a ship, a task that was already owed to a third party, was sufficient consideration. This case follows a series of cases commencing with *Shadwell v. Shadwell*,[71] which involved a promise made by an uncle to a prospective nephew-in-law on hearing of the intended marriage between the uncle's niece and the plaintiff. The promise was to pay an annual sum of £150 until such time as the plaintiff's income from the bar exceeded 600 guineas. The marriage went ahead and some of the money was paid, though not all. On the uncle's demise, an amount remained outstanding for which the plaintiff now sought recovery from the estate of the deceased uncle. The defence argued that the plaintiff, having committed himself to marrying the niece, was under a legal obligation to do so; there could therefore be no consideration for the uncle's promise.[72] The court held that the dealings were meant to be legally binding, and it had no difficulty in finding that the consideration was sufficient. The case ignored the decision of *Jones v. Waite*,[73] a case where the consideration offered was the plaintiff's promise to pay his own debts to third parties; Lord Abinger stated:

> A man is under a moral and legal obligation to pay his just debts. It cannot therefore be stated as an abstract proposition that he suffers any legal detriment from the discharge of that duty; . . .[74]

That seems to be a correct interpretation of the law. The *Shadwell* case may be explicable under modern jurisprudence of promissory estoppel, of which more will be said later. But it cannot be seriously contended that any such detriment has been suffered by the plaintiff which would be cause of good consideration. Can I make a contract enforceable by giving you a gift and requiring you to comply with all your legal obligations? If that is so, there is a large breach in the walls of the doctrine of consideration. Yet this is what the

---

70 [1975] AC 154; for a discussion of this concept see Treitel, op. cit., p. 91 et seq.; Cheshire and Fifoot, op. cit., p. 102 et seq.; Clark, op. cit., p. 27 et seq.

71 (1860) 9 CBNS 159, 30 LJCP 145; *Saunders v. Cramer* (1842) 5 I EqR 12 (Ch).

72 At common law a promise to marry was binding and breach of which could be enforced in the courts. Such action was not removed until the Family Law Act 1981.

73 (1839) 5 Bing NC 341.

74 (1839) 5 Bing NC 341, 356.

current case law is suggesting. Such a position has not received much acceptance in the US, where, by and large, such contracts have been held to be a nullity.[75] In the Restatement, Second, such contracts are held to have sufficient consideration, though it is suggested that the benefit may be payable to the original contract holder;[76] that is, if X makes a promise to pay Z £500 for the performance of an act which Z is obligated to do under contract to Y, there may well be sufficient consideration for an enforceable contract, but the benefit, the £500 in this case, may be payable more correctly to Y, presumably on the theory that, in certain situations, Z is in fact operating as Y's agent. In truth that would appear to correctly state the logical consequence of these arrangements. In any event the *Eurymedon* would appear to represent the present law, though it must surely sit ill at ease with the general doctrine of consideration.

The most common difficulty encountered will be where the consideration is the performance of an existing contractual obligation between the parties. Once again, there are two possibilities. Firstly, the agreement may merely represent a modification of the contractual arrangement; this will be dealt with further under the concept of promissory estoppel and detrimental reliance. However, it remains possible that the parties will attempt to discharge the existing contractual obligations by the performance of part only of those obligations. Thus, for example, as in the infamous case known as *Pinnel*,[77] X owed Y a sum of money which he was unable to pay by its due date. X then offered to pay Y a portion of what he owed in return for Y's promise not to sue for the balance. This promise was forthcoming. A question arises as to why Y should agree to such a thing. In many cases it will be to Y's benefit for X to pay a portion of the money that is owed today, rather than wait until the legal process has had its way. By the end of the legal process to satisfy the full debt, one of two things are most likely to happen: other creditors will have come out of the woodwork and X's asset pool will have to be divided up among a greater number of creditors with each gaining less and/or X will have disposed of his assets to the extent that Y cannot even recover that which was offered to him before the legal process for recovery began. It can therefore make commercial sense to accept payment of less than what is owed; this is common practice, as we shall see later. In any event, in the case at bar, Y accepted the part payment and duly promised that the debt would not be pursued through the courts. In fact Y commenced proceedings for the remainder of the debt. His action was successful, for, as Lord Coke stated:

> [P]ayment of a lesser sum on the [due] day in satisfaction of a greater,

---

75   *McDevitt v. Stokes*, 174 Ky 515, 192 SW 681 (1917); *Arend v. Smith*, 151 NY 502, 45 NE 872 (1897). Note, however, that both the Restatement, Contracts and the Restatement, Second, Contracts, state that such contracts have valid consideration.

76   Restatement, Second, para. 73.

77   (1602) 5 CoRep 117a.

cannot be any satisfaction of the whole, because it appears to the judges that by no possibility, a lesser sum can be a satisfaction of to the plaintiff for a greater sum.[78]

The decision was upheld in *Foakes v. Beer*[79] and settled that the promise to pay less than what is owed cannot constitute valid consideration. The decision has been criticised,[80] but it remains, one can argue, good law and logical if consideration is to be considered a detriment. It is hard to see what detriment the debtor suffers from paying only a portion of that which is due. Of course, the situation would be different if the debtor were to promise to refrain from insolvency or bankruptcy proceedings at the behest of the creditor.[81] In that situation the debtor may in fact be suffering a legal detriment, inasmuch as that he is promising to remain outside the protection that those proceedings bring a debtor. Moreover, the problem is further resolved if the debtor promises to supply something different in return for the creditor's promise to accept part payment as discharge of the entire debt, that is, it is possible that the debtor may supply new consideration which will make the creditor's promise binding. Thus, he may offer to pay the money before the date it is due, or he may offer to discharge a debt of, say, £100 by £50 cash and a rare book. These, and other transactions, may be sufficient to prove that new consideration has been provided that will make the creditor's promise enforceable. Until the case of *D and C Builders v. Rees*[82] it had been thought that payment by way of cheque or promissory note would be sufficient to constitute new consideration.[83] In that case, Denning argued that the difference between a cheque and cash was not sufficient to constitute new consideration; this would appear to be a correct statement of law despite the earlier case law on the matter. Thus, I cannot make a promise to accept £300 in full discharge of a debt of £482 merely by paying the £300 by way of a cheque.

One would presume that if a promise to perform only part of what one is

---

78   Calamari and Perillo, op. cit., p. 211, footnote 9: 77 EngRep 237 (1602).
79   9 App Cas 605 (1884)
80   *Frye v. Hubbell*, 74 NH 358, 68 A 325 (1907); *Liebrich v. Tyler State Bank & Trust Co.*, 100 SW 2d 152 (1936); see also the Restatement, Contracts, para 73 which accepts part payment of a debt, where there are unforeseen hardships which make it more onerous than was envisaged at the time the contract was entered into, such as an economic depression.
81   *Melroy v. Kemmerer*, 218 Pa 381, 67 A 699 (1907).
82   [1966] 2 QB 617, care should be exercised with respect to this case. It is strange to see Denning LJ, who might be considered by many as a successor of the (in)famous Lord Mansfield in his desire to abolish the doctrine of consideration from the common law, reverting to a strict usage of the very same doctrine. It is clear that much of the reason for the decision revolved around the duress that the plaintiff had been placed under in accepting the part payment. For a fuller discussion of how this case might be decided today, see 7.08 post.
83   *Sibree v. Tripp* (1846) 15 M & W 23; *Goddard v. O'Brien* (1882) 9QBD 37, 822.

already under an existing contractual obligation to do is unacceptable as consideration to make a binding contract, then it would seem *a fortiori* that a promise to fulfil in full that which one is already under an existing contractual obligation to do, could, similarly, not constitute good consideration, at least not where that promise is made to the same person to whom the obligation is owed. A presumption that may not be as strong as one would have thought in the light of recent case law discussed more fully in 7.08 post. In fact, it may well be that the days of *Pinnel* and *D and C Builders* are severely numbered.

Finally, care should be taken that the rule in *Pinnel's* case applies only to a liquidated debt, that is, a debt which is ascertained as to amount and undisputed as to existence. Where the debt is in dispute either as to existence or quantum, what is the effect of the creditor accepting a certain amount that he does not consider to be sufficient? For example, X owes Y a sum of money for a completed task; X sends a cheque for £50 marked 'in full and final payment'; the cheque is received by Y, who believes the amount outstanding to be £100 but nonetheless cashes same. Does the encashment constitute an acceptance as to the quantum of the debt? It would appear to do so under the doctrine of Accord and Satisfaction.[84] Where the amount is in dispute for whatever reason, encashment or acceptance of a sum in 'full and final satisfaction' would appear to bind the parties involved, presumably because the offer of the payment in full and final satisfaction is accepted by the creditor. The difficulty remains that it may be desirable to encash such an offer without rescinding one's rights to pursue the matter further, for the very same reasons as make it expedient to accept a smaller sum in satisfaction of a larger liquidated sum. However, it would seem that the creditor writing on the cheque 'without prejudice' or 'accepted in part payment only' does not alter the conclusiveness of the encashment since the original offeror has been given no chance to accept or reject these new terms and conditions being offered by the creditor.[85]

7.06 COMPOSITION WITH CREDITORS

As pointed out earlier, the advantages of accepting only a part of what is owed by the debtor can in certain situations be compelling; but a debtor is unlikely to offer same if he is aware that the promise by the creditor to forego the full value of the debt is not enforceable. Accordingly, it is found to be useful to permit a

---

84 *Cooper v. Parker* (1885) 15 CB.
85 *Horn Waterproofing Corp v. Bushwick Iron and Steel*, 66 NY 2d 321, 497 NYS 2d 310, 488 NE 2d 56 (1985); Caraballo, 'The Tender Trap: UCC s. 1-207 and its applicability to an attempted accord and satisfaction by tendering a check in a dispute arising from a sale of goods', 11 *Seton Hall LR* 445 (1981); Calamari, 'The Check Cashing Rule', 1 *NYCLE* No. 2, p. 113; *Hastings v. Top Cut Feedlots*, 285 Or 261, 590 P 2d 1210 (1979); Rosenthal, 'Discord and Dissatisfaction: Section 1-207 of the UCC', 78 *Columbia LR* 48 (1978).

number of creditors to agree to accept a reduced payment on their debt in full satisfaction, despite the absence of any ostensible consideration, and to enforce their promise not to pursue the debtor for the balance.[86] Such arrangements are known as 'compositions with creditors'. In simple terms: composition with a single creditor is not enforceable without consideration,[87] but composition with more than one creditor is enforceable despite the absence of consideration.

Why this should be so, other than for reasons of commercial expediency, is far from clear.[88] One possible fiction is that the consideration occurs between the creditors, in that each foregoes his individual right to sue for the debt owed him in return for a similar promise made by all the creditors; but this is, of course, a theoretical nonsense. If this fiction were correct, there would still be nothing to prevent all the creditors (after receiving the part payment in full satisfaction) from agreeing to continue to pursue the balance of the debt owing, and the debtor could do little about it as he is but a beneficiary to the contract between the creditors.[89] He has suffered no detriment that would enable him to prevent their suit. The more acceptable version is to prevent breach of such agreement so as to avoid a fraud on all the parties. While weak in terms of legal theory, this version has been generally acceptable.[90] Again, the difficulty is in reconciling why such composition is valid in co-existence with the decision of *Pinnel* referred to earlier.[91] The two propositions cannot be both correct. Indeed, there is considerable argument for dealing with the matter as one of detrimental reliance, a possibility referred to later.[92]

7.07 PRE-EXISTING DUTY AND ECONOMIC DURESS

One matter that has not been directly touched upon is why the creditor is willing to accept, under any circumstances, an offer to pay less than what is owed. The natural tendency is to assume that the debtor is truly unable to meet the debt and is making an honest attempt to go some way towards meeting his lawful

---

86 For a discussion of this concept see Treitel, op. cit., p. 119 et seq.; Cheshire and Fifoot, op. cit., p. 101 et seq.; Clark, op. cit., p. 27 et seq.

87 See 7.05 supra.

88 It may well be defensible under the doctrine of promissory estoppel referred to in chapter 8, post, but its validity under a strict application of the doctrine of consideration remains doubtful. Rather than trying to force it into an uneasy relationship with consideration it would be wiser to treat this as the classic example of the application of the promissory estoppel doctrine. The same can be said of the rule in *Pinnel's* case.

89 *Boothbey v. Sowden* (1812) 3 Camp 175; *Good v. Chessman* (1831) 2 B & Ad 328; *West Yorks Darracq Agency v. Coleridge* [1911] 2 KB 326 (a composition agreement is valid even where the creditor obtains nothing)

90 *Wood v. Robarts* (1818) 1 Stark 417; *Couldry v. Bartrum* (1881) 19 ChD 394; *Cook v. Lister* (1863) 13 CBNS 543; *Hirachand Punamchand v. Temple* [1911] 2 KB 330.

91 See 7.05, supra.

92 Chapter 8, post.

obligations. But that may not always be the truth. The debtor may be using a difficulty that the creditor currently finds himself in, as, for example, where X owes Y £1,000 due by the 31st of the month. Y, however, owes Z £800 on his mortgage payment, due on the 1st of the following month. If Y defaults, he will lose his house. He is in a cash-flow shortage and needs the payment from X. If X is aware of this, he may offer to pay only £800 to Y in full and final satisfaction on the 31st of the month, or refuse to pay any sum and allow the matter to be pursued through the courts, by which time Y will have defaulted on his obligation to Z. Y may eventually recover his £1,000, but it will come a little too late. Y is being exploited by economic duress. X is using a position of advantage to avoid paying what he is legally obligated to pay. Another possibility could be that X misleads Y into believing that he cannot afford all the debt. Remember that in *D and C Builders v. Rees*[93] the offer was to accept £300 or nothing. If this does not constitute a threat, it is difficult to see what does.

In *Williams v. Roffey and Nicholls*[94] the position that consideration could be supplied in the nature of a promise to fulfil what one was legally obligated to do, namely, the performance of existing contractual duties, was upheld in a commercial setting, on the basis that such an offer may constitute a benefit to the person so agreeing, albeit a subjective benefit. In the case at bar the defendants were the main contractors to a construction project, and the plaintiffs were sub-contractors to them. It became apparent that the sub-contractors were in financial difficulty and would in all likelihood be unable to finish the project. This would result in delays for the main contractor and expose him to liquidated penalties for failing to complete on time. Accordingly, the defendants offered the plaintiffs additional sums of money if they completed the task. There was agreement on this, but subsequently the defendants refused to honour their agreement. It was held that the agreement could be enforceable. It would seem that the consideration was that the defendant was given grounds to believe that the project would not, after the payment of the additional sums, be delayed due to insolvency. Yet of course this constitutes a belief only, and it is difficult to see how this can be reconciled with the need for consideration to be capable of being valued in money or money's worth. Can it seriously be suggested that such a belief has financial value? A promise from the creditors that, if the money was paid, no insolvency proceedings would issue might be one thing; but a belief on the part of the troubled debtor that the money would 'see him right', so to

---

93 [1966] 2 QB 617.
94 [1991] 1 QB 1; the case is not easily reconcilable with the decision in cases such as *Stilk v. Myrick* (1809) 2 Camp 317 and *Harris v. Carter* (1854) 3 E & B 559 both cases which refused to hold that consideration could be found in the promise to undertake that which the plaintiff was contractually bound previously to do for the defendant. Since Purchas LJ describes *Stilk* as a pillar stone (although he goes on to point out that it might be decided differently today) it is submitted that this fuzzy reasoning by the bench has done much to damage the concept of consideration. If the verdict in *Williams* is correct, then it is on the basis of promissory estoppel and not a tortured definition of consideration.

speak, is highly questionable. It also leaves open the question of economic duress being used to alter the terms of a bargain, as we shall see later. Certainly Glidewell LJ expressly ruled out such relief where economic duress could be shown and, furthermore, he required that in practice a benefit be obtained or a disadvantage be obviated; but this is simply too impractical a test for the common law. It would seem that the only logical application of such a rule would be that, if the debtor does not subsequently become insolvent, there was a practical benefit, whereas, if he does become insolvent, then the promise is not enforceable because no practical benefit has been achieved. This merely states the facts of the case but posits no rule of general application. The principal difficulty would appear to be that it opens far too many avenues of dispute for the potential benefit recouped. It is to be hoped that subsequent cases will confine *Williams* to its peculiar facts.

However, the decision does brings this area into line with the acceptance of consideration from the performance of the obligations of a pre-existing contractual relationship to a third party. The two concepts are not dissimilar, given that in both cases the benefit is used to find consideration. Thus, consideration is the subjective benefit received by one party, rather than the objective detriment paid by the other. This reasoning, confined in the case at bar to commercial transactions, is misleading. If the test is subjective benefit received by one party, that opens the door to the admission of many forms of consideration not currently acceptable. For example, X promises to give Y £5,000 if Y says his prayers every day. This may well constitute a subjective benefit to X (Y may be his or her child whom he or she is most anxious will not burn in the flames of hell) and therefore be enforceable. It is respectfully submitted that this cannot be. In that sense the case is poor authority. Moreover, it is difficult to reconcile this case with *Pinnel's* case, and the two are inconsistent. Of course, it may be argued that *Pinnel's* case is the case that should be overturned, leaving *Williams* intact. With respect, that is not the correct solution. *Williams* is correct in result and *Pinnel* correct as to theory.

Pinnel is correct in that performance of an existing contractual duty cannot constitute sufficient consideration, but the promise made in that case may in fact be one that does not require consideration. It and *Williams* may be supportable on the grounds that such promises, as a matter of policy should be enforceable, but that policy should be based on the concept of promissory estoppel[95] and not consideration, which is clearly absent in these situations.

95   Chapter 8, post; note in *In re Selectmove* (The Times, 13 January 1994), Peter-Gibson
      LJ in the Court of Appeal gave a unanimous judgment from the three judge court and
      refused to extend the decision in *Williams v. Roffey*, saying to do so would be to throw
      away *Foakes v. Beers*, which they were not prepared to do. The case involved a
      taxpayer's agreement to pay back taxes due the Revenue in instalments. The instalments
      were late and the Revenue sued for the entire amount due. The taxpayer claimed an
      agreement between the Revenue and the taxpayer prevented this from happening (the
      case also dealt with issues of estoppel and agency). Even if the agreement had been

Moreover, the enhanced use of duress as a defence to vitiate a contractual arrangement[96] effectively means that such promises to perform part or all of a pre-existing contractual obligation may be enforceable under the concept of promissory estoppel yet the dangers referred to at the beginning of this section can be catered for by a liberal application of the duress doctrine to prevent an injustice occurring due to the enforcement of such promises.

7.08 CONSIDERATION MUST MOVE FROM THE PROMISE

Once the consideration has been deemed sufficient, there remains a further problem, traditionally classified under the above heading. Simply put, it requires that the promisee must provide the consideration before he can enforce the bargain.[97] Earlier, in discussing the definition of consideration we stated this as a *sine qua non*, so why has there been a need to repeat this rule separately? Basically this doctrine concerns contracts involving three parties; let us call them Tom, Dick and Harry. Tom agrees with Dick and Harry to convey a piece of land to Harry if Dick pays him £5,000. Why should Dick enter into such a silly bargain? Probably because Dick owes Harry the money and, rather than paying the cash to Harry, who would then pay Tom for the land, the deal can be completed in one simple transaction.

This is what happened in *McCoubray v. Thompson*[98] where X owned land that he wished to transfer to McCoubray and Thompson equally. Thompson, however, wished to have all of the land, so it was agreed between them that X would transfer the land to Thompson in consideration of Thompson's paying a sum of money to McCoubray. The land was duly transferred, but Thompson reneged his promise and failed to pay the sum of money to McCoubray. McCoubray then sued. There was an enforceable contract, since consideration was present; however, the action failed because McCoubray could not prove that he had provided any consideration with which to enforce the contract on his behalf. Of course, X could sue Thompson on his failure to honour his contractual obligations because X had supplied sufficient consideration in the form of the land. But since X was dead, there was now no one to enforce the contract. X's executors could not do so, for they would not be able to claim the expense involved as it would be of no benefit to the estate.

It should be noted, however, that not all tripartite contracts result in one of

---

correct in other ways, it failed for lack of consideration. It was not good consideration to pay that which was already obligated. Future developments are awaited with interest).
96 See chapter 18, post.
97 For a discussion of this concept see Treitel, op. cit., p. 77 et seq.; Cheshire and Fifoot, op. cit., p. 74 et seq.; Clark, op. cit., p. 29 et seq.; *Thomas v. Thomas* (1842) 2 QB 851; *Dunlop v. Selfridge* [1915] AC 847; *Pollway v. Abdullah* [1974] 1 WLR 493.
98 (1868) 2 IRCL 226.

the contractees supplying no consideration. In *Barry v. Barry*[99] the parties had a legal right under the distribution of the estate which they forewent in favour of a promise by the defendant to pay a specified sum of money. In that case the plaintiff could recover from the defendant because he had supplied some consideration. In *McEvoy v. Belfast Banking Corporation*,[100] however, a father opened an account in a bank in the joint name of his son and himself. Upon the father's death, the executors applied to the bank to have the account transferred to their names, which the bank duly did. The contents of the account were lost in a vain attempt to continue the family business. Later, the son sought the contents of the account from the bank, and the bank resisted this claim on the basis that he had supplied no consideration with respect to the opening of the account. The court rejected this and gave judgment in favour of the son. Can it be, however, that the son actually provided consideration, or is there a presumption that the opening of a joint account implies joint contributions as to its contents? The case may be valid in that sense, but it really misses the actual point in question.

The real difficulty here does not lie in the fact that the consideration has not moved from the promisee but merely that only those persons who are a party to the contract as understood by the courts will be able to enforce any obligations that arise from such a contract. In other words, a gratuitous beneficiary of a contract may not sue to enforce his rights. This does not, however, go to the substance of the contract: in none of the above cases is an argument made that no valid contract had come into existence. The issue was one of *locus standi* of the applicant claiming a benefit under the contract (this is known as 'privity' and is dealt with in some detail later).[101] This fact is often overlooked by commentators on the issue, yet it is difficult to see that this so-called requirement of consideration can be differentiated in any way from privity.[102]

7.09 SOME CONCLUSIONS

Despite its somewhat mixed reception and more than a little antipathy, the doctrine of consideration remains an integral feature of our legal system, for better or worse. For those who would favour its abolition there is much to support them, including the verdicts of several learned panels of law reform. In its defence, it has to be said that much of the difficulty surrounding the doctrine

---

99   (1891) 28 LR (Ir) 45.
100 [1935] AC 24 (Cf. SJB in 51 LQR 419 which severely criticises this particular point of the judgment); *Fleming v. Bank of New Zealand* [1900] AC 577 (a co-promisor could enforce the contract even though the other co-promisor supplied the entire consideration).
101 See chapter 9, post.
102 For a full discussion, see *Coulls v. Bagots Executor and Trust* [1967] ALR 394, and chapter 9, post.

is of the court's own making: errors which, as we have seen, are being repeated unto the very present. Moreover, the doctrine of consideration, like most legal doctrines, should not be seen as absolute but as requiring an exception. Many of the difficulties arising from the doctrine of consideration are almost exclusively as a result of both the late development of the complementary doctrine of promissory estoppel and a failure to use that doctrine in an honest and straightforward manner. From the earliest of cases like *Pinnel* to the most recent such as *Williams* the courts have butchered the doctrine of consideration to bring justice to the case at bar, instead of admitting that, in certain situations, some promises simply do not require consideration. Even the prophets of doom for consideration have been forced to resort to a strict and unrealistic interpretation of the doctrine when the needs of justice demanded it: see Denning in *D and C Builders*. This has been recognised in the US for some time. We shall turn to a critical analysis of this next.

8.00

Enforcement without consideration

8.01 INTRODUCTION

We have already discussed in some detail that as a general rule at common law no contract is enforceable without the presence of consideration, unless the contract is made under seal.[1] But a more detailed analysis of the aforementioned discussion on consideration showed that this simplified statement is not all-embracing. The definition of consideration is quite vague. Consideration is often found in situations which might cause the ordinary person some confusion[2] and is not found in situations which an ordinary person would think incredible.[3] The courts have refrained from giving a strict definition of the concept for very good reasons. The flexibility afforded by vagueness can be immensely helpful. In the US, attempts to formulate a rule for consideration in the Restatements have necessitated the formulation of exceptions to such rules.[4]

Indeed, while consideration is a creature of the common law, its acceptance has not been without question.[5] In this work it is proposed to deal with the issue of enforcement of contracts without consideration in three distinct areas. Firstly, there will arise situations where the conduct of the past will impose an obligation

1   See chapter 7.
2   *Thomas v. Thomas* (1842) 2 QB 851 (the payment of £1 per annum for a house held to be a valid consideration); *Sturlyn v. Albany* (1587) Cro Eliz 67 ('when a thing is to be done by the plaintiff be it ever so small, this is a sufficient consideration to ground an action'); *Sibree v. Tripp* (1846) 15 M&W 23 (a change of the method of payment from cash to a negotiable instrument was held to be valid consideration: 'if for money you give a negotiable security you pay it in a different way', *per* Alderson B, now overturned in *D & C Builders v. Rees* [1965] 3 All ER 837).
3   Past consideration is normally the most difficult for the layman to understand: *Roscorla v. Thomas* (1842) 3 QB 234 (a warranty to fitness, given after contract completed, was held to be without consideration and not enforceable); *In re McArdle* [1951] 1 All ER 905 (a sister-in-law made improvements to the home of her in-laws. Afterwards, these in-laws signed document promising to pay her a sum of money for these improvements. When they failed to honour the agreement, the sister-in-law sued. *Held* the consideration was past).
4   Restatements, Second, Contracts, s. 71 et seq.
5   *Hawkes v. Saunders* (1782) 1 Cowp 289.

on the parties which renders an agreement enforceable despite the lack of present consideration. In some senses this is a method of using past consideration in a present contract, and it normally requires some moral obligation to so enforce the contract. Although the presence of such moral obligation will not guarantee success, its absence is virtually always fatal. It should also be noted that, while the phrase moral obligation may no longer be fashionable within this jurisdiction, the practical reality is that it is often used by a court, whatever the terminology. Secondly, there is variation of an existing contract whereby the variation should be supported by fresh consideration but the variation agreement is deemed enforceable despite the absence of such consideration. Here again the rulings have more to do with justice than application of rules. Finally, there is the purest concept of enforceability without consideration, sometimes known as 'promissory estoppel', which involves the imposition of a legally binding contract merely on the basis of a promise; to that extent it is in direct conflict with common law theory and represents a battleground between two opposed factions in the legal world.

8.02 PAST CONDUCT

Pre-existing debts We have already seen that past consideration is no consideration at all, but at this point we will have to revisit this idea and raise some troubling questions. Let us pose a hypothetical situation. Suppose X owes Y £1,000 which is due to be repaid on 1 January. The due date passes without the payment being made. Somewhat irate, Y visits X and demands payment. X promises to pay the debt on 1 February and Y leaves, troubled but calmer than when he arrived. This date (1 February) comes and goes with no sign of payment. Y immediately visits his lawyer and seeks advice. Clearly Y has no major difficulty, since he can sue X on foot of the original promise to pay the sum outstanding on 1 January. But what of the promise to pay the amount by 1 February. Is this an enforceable promise? It is unsupported by any fresh consideration, so one would have expected the answer to be that this promise is not enforceable. However, Corbin believes that the earlier common law rule on this issue still applies, namely, that this second promise is enforceable—at least if the second promise is co-extensive with the pre-existing debt and perhaps even if the second promise made by X is to pay a smaller amount than originally due.[6] Moreover, under the UCC, such a promise is enforceable despite the absence of consideration if it is contained within an instrument.[7] It might be

---

6   1A Corbin, op. cit., ss. 211, 212; while this was so at early common law, it is no longer sustainable in modern jurisprudence, see *Pinnel's* case infra; if Corbin's proposition is restricted so as to apply only where the promise to pay is co-extensive with the debt, then it may be possible to distinguish *Pinnel*. Moreover, as stated in chapter 7, *Pinnel's* case represents unsatisfactory law in many ways.

7   S. 3-408.

argued that the question is in fact hypothetical and unlikely to be of practical relevance since Y can always sue on foot of the first promise, but of course this is not true. Suppose the first promise cannot be enforced under the Statute of Limitations, or for some failure of technical form. It would then be important to know which of the promises was enforceable, and there are a number of clear instances when this will arise. However, it is equally true to say that where the existing debt is not suffering from a legal defect, the proper course of action should be to sue to enforce the first promise and not the second promise, which is unsupported by consideration.[8]

Where the pre-existing debt has been discharged by operation of law,[9] such as bankruptcy, Statute of Limitations, etc., it is a general rule that a subsequent promise made by the debtor to pay the amount owing, or such other amount, is enforceable without any further consideration.[10] This has now been legislatively overturned in the UK with the Limitation Act 1980, which makes the acknowledgement of a statute-barred debt inactionable but does permit an acknowledgment, duly signed, to delay the operation of the limitation period despite the absence of consideration.[11] The rationale behind the common law approach is less than satisfactory and appears to be based more on the older rule that a promise to pay an antecedent debt has sufficient consideration from the antecedent debt itself. This, as was stated earlier, was over-ruled by the decision in *Pinnel's*[12] case. If, in the above example, Y's promise (not to sue to enforce the debt if X pays part of the debt) is unenforceable by virtue of lack of consideration, it is difficult to see how X's similar gratuitous promise to pay an entire debt that is not legally recoverable can be enforceable. Indeed, in some cases in the US, the application of the above principle has not been extended to actions seeking enforcement of a tort claim barred by the Statute of Limitations.[13] Moreover, abuse of such acknowledgments by financial institutions after bankruptcy proceedings has led to the express prohibition of such promises by virtue of the Bankruptcy Reform Act 1978 in the US.[14]

8   See *Pinnel's* Case (1602) 5 Co Rep 117; *O' Neill v. Murphy* [1936] NI 16; *Foakes v. Beer* (1884) 9 App Cas 605; this is, however, inconsistent with the rule concerning composition of creditors, see ibid and chapter 7.
9   The rules discussed below concern debts discharged by operation of law, and thereby exclude debts entered into by infants, which are subsequently ratified when the infant reaches the age of majority, for a fuller discussion of this see chapter 5.
10 *Hyeling v. Hastings* (1699) 1 Ld Raym 389; *Flight v. Reed* (1863) 1 H & C 703; *Evans v. Heathcote* [1918] 1 KB 418.
11 S. 30; this was probably true at common law in any event, see Restatement, Second, Contracts, s. 82.
12 (1602) 5 Co Rep 117; of course, *Pinnel's* case applies only to a promise to forebear from suing in return for a promise of part payment, not a promise of full discharge of the debt at a later date. This is what supports Corbin's earlier assertion that the old common law rule for a promise of full discharge at a later date is enforceable, but see 1 Williston, s. 143 for a contrary view.
13 Restatement, Second, Contracts, s. 82, Comment b.
14 11 USCA s 524(c).

The courts should reject this rule (that a subsequent promise to pay a debt which is statute-barred requires no consideration to be enforceable) as an error based on the confusion of moral obligation and past consideration. Of more concern is a failure on the part of the courts to view this rule in conjunction with *Pinnel's* case and the *Williams v. Roffey*[15] case referred to earlier. Williston is correct in his view that an antecedent debt cannot be sufficient consideration to render a promise to pay that debt enforceable,[16] and this is so whether the debt suffers from a legal defect in terms of its enforceability or not.

Past benefits received   We have already seen that an agreement may envisage the existence of consideration yet the quantum is not determined until after the completion of the events in question.[17] The crucial element in this principle is that the acts so undertaken are undertaken at the request of the party who makes the subsequent promise of a quantum of payment. There will, however, arise situations where the acts undertaken are not undertaken at the request of the party in question. Ordinarily, the provision of unrequested services followed by a promise to pay for those unrequested services is unenforceable,[18] but some support has emerged for the concept of restitution;[19] thus, in the New York case of *Yarwood v. Trusts & Guaruntee Co.*[20] a wealthy man who purported to be a vagrant was offered shelter from the cold by the plaintiff. Subsequent to this the wealthy man promised the sum of $5,000 as payment for this charitable act. It was held that this was a case of promissory restitution and the promise was enforceable.

Moreover, the Restatement, Second, now holds such promises to be enforceable, at least to the extent necessary to prevent injustice.[21] However, there are limitations to the doctrine. First, there must be an express intention to be so bound. Second, the right to enforcement is refused if the promise confers a benefit as a gift or if for some other reason the promisor has not been unjustly enriched. To an extent, this may be said to be a revival of the moral obligation argument so roundly rejected previously. Certainly Corbin postulates that moral obligation must always form part of the common lawyers arsenal in order to escape the 'more hardened and definitely worded rules of law.'[22] The Restatement, Second, does try to make a distinction between moral obligations

---

15   [1991] 1 QB 1.
16   Op. cit., s. 143.
17   *Lampleigh v. Braithwait* (1615) Hob 105.
18   *Argy Trading & Development Co. v. Lapid Development* [1977] 1 WLR 444 (failure to keep a gratuitous promise to insure premises. *Held*, there was no breach of contract as no contract had occurred).
19   Henderson, 'Promises Grounded in the Past: The idea of unjust enrichment and the law of contract', 57 *Va Law Rev* 1115; 1A Corbin, op. cit., s. 230.
20   94 AD 47, 87 NYS 947 (1904).
21   Restatement, Second, Contract, s. 86.
22   1A Corbin, op. cit., s. 230.

involving sentiment or gratitude and moral obligations of true unjust enrichment, concentrating on benefits received in emergencies, business settings or
rectification of mistakes. Moreover, the *Yarwood* case mentioned earlier would
clearly fall outside the Restatement, Second.

In this jurisdiction, such problems are probably best dealt with using the
modern concept of unjust enrichment as a remedy rather than looking for
coherence with notional contract rules. However, a full discussion of this
concept is outside the ambit of this work and is best pursued in more specialised
works such as Burrows, *Restitution* and Goff and Jones, *Law of Restitution*
among others.

8.03 VARIATION OF CONTRACT

Traditionally, a variation or modification of the terms of an existing contract
was never enforceable unless supported by fresh consideration,[23] the one
exception to this being where the original contract permitted unilateral alteration
of the contract subsequent to its formation. However, this general rule no longer
applies. In the previously discussed case of *Williams v. Roffey*[24] it was found
that the variation of the terms of an existing contract freely entered into by both
parties would be enforceable without the presence of further consideration. This
ruling was used in the case of first instance, *Anangel Atlas Compania Naviera
SA v. Ishikawajima- Harima Heavy Industries Co. Ltd (No. 2)*,[25] by Hirst J. The
facts of the case are relatively straightforward. The plaintiffs were to purchase
a ship built by the defendants. Before completion the shipping market collapsed
and the plaintiffs discovered that the defendants were offering better prices and
terms to new purchasers. Both plaintiffs and defendants agreed that the original
contract should be concluded on the basis of 'most favoured customer'. Subsequently the plaintiffs discovered that another customer had obtained a better
deal and they sued to enforce the variation agreement. The defence rebutted that
the agreement was unsupported by consideration and therefore unenforceable.
Hirst J held otherwise and followed his view of *Williams* that there was a
practical or subjective benefit which rendered the variation enforceable. The
difficulty with this line of reasoning, of course, is that it places a thin line
between practical or subjective benefit and economic duress. The variation both
in *Williams* and *Anangel* resulted from a change in market conditions that
effectively meant the defendants would suffer if the plaintiffs elected not to
honour his original agreement, thus in reality leaving the defendants little room
for manoeuvre.

The result in both cases may be justifiable, but the legal theory used is

---

23   *Stilk v. Myrick* (1809) 2 Camp 317; [1990] 2 Lloyd's Rep 526.
24   [1990] 1 All ER 512.
25   [1990] 2 Lloyd's Rep 526, *The Atlantic Baron* [1975] QB 705.

somewhat dubious.[26] It requires the court to 'find' benefit to the defendant[27] and distinguish it from duress against the defendant.[28] The distinction between the two is not always as clear as one would hope.[29] It would be far better if the court merely had to adjudicate on the presence or absence of duress. In America, the UCC permits variation or modification of a contract to be enforceable in the absence of consideration;[30] this seems to be intellectually more honest and carries less scope for confusion than the unsatisfactory concept in *Williams*. Effectively, the UCC recognises that once the parties have entered into a legally binding contract they have evidenced sufficient acts for a court to impose legal obligations, not merely on the contract itself but also on any modification or variation arising from within it, including presumably its termination. This variation or modification is subject only to the rules of duress and undue influence, and there is no requirement to search for an artificial benefit to either party.[31]

One further point must be raised at this stage, which we referred to briefly in the chapter on consideration, namely, composition agreements with creditors. We have already seen in *Pinnel's* case that an offer to pay part only of a debt in full satisfaction and a promise by the creditor not to sue to enforce the balance, is unenforceable unless new consideration has been supplied. Yet, in the commercial world, part payment of a debt today is generally preferred to pursuing full payment through the legal system, which tends to be expensive, time-consuming and not always successful. Suppose X owes Y £1,000. X offers to pay Y £500 if Y will promise to forego the balance. Y so promises. The question that springs to mind is: why should Y even contemplate such an agreement? Firstly, Y will receive his money today and not a year from now, as is often the case if full court procedures are followed. Secondly, Y would

---

26 It does find some early support in *Watkins v. Carrig*, 21 A 2d 591 (1941) (the defendant, when excavating, struck rock which had not been expected. The contract was varied to cater for the turn of events, this variation had no consideration but the court held it to be enforceable).

27 It is difficult to see why there was no benefit in *Stilk v. Myrick* but was in *Williams*. *Williams* does not expressly overrule *Stilk* (see *Williams* [1991] 1 QB 1, 20, *per* Purchas LJ, though Glidewell LJ talks of refining and limiting it (at p. 16).

28 *The Atlantic Baron* [1975] QB 705; *Cotter v. Minister for Agriculture*, unreported, High Court, 15 November 1991 (Murphy J held, in a case similar to *Watkins*, that liability arose in either contract or quasi contract).

29 Indeed, the distinction between duress and a dominant bargaining position is not always easily discerned: *Pao On v. Lau Yiu Long* [1980] AC 614.

30 S. 2-209(1); *Skinner v. Tober Foreign Motors*, 187 NE 2d 669 (1963) (oral promise to reduce contract payments from $200 a month to $100 a month, held to be a valid modification of contract and enforceable without consideration); McKinney's NY GOL s. 5-1103 (New York statute requires writing before the modification is acceptable); *Morans v. Armstrong* (1840) Arm Mac Og 25.

31 It should be noted that if the variation or modification goes so far as to effectively rescind the first contract then this is enforceable as having valid consideration (notably the discharge of the first contract).

have to pay his legal team for the costs of pursuing the action; these costs, while notionally collectible from the debtor, might add another financial burden to the debtor that he is unable to carry. Finally, X may decide to spend the balance of his assets leaving the creditor with nothing at the end of a year's legal process.[32] Yet the law permits the creditor to have the best of both worlds, for he can collect the £500 now and promise whatever he likes and still pursue the balance from the debtor. The rule was a direct result of the doctrine of consideration, but in practice few business people would act in such fashion. Moreover, it becomes troublesome in situations where there is one debtor but many creditors, so that an agreement between the parties as to part payment of the entire amount outstanding should be enforceable both as a recognition of existing business and commercial practice and to encourage the extra-judicial settlement of disputes and thereby free valuable court time. Thus, it is well established that an arrangement between a debtor and a number of creditors where the amounts owing are paid off as a percentage, say 50p in the £, is a valid and enforceable agreement, and the creditors cannot subsequently resile from their promise not to sue to enforce the balance.[33] This sort of arrangement is commonly known as a 'composition with creditors'; many theories have been advanced to reconcile this ruling with that of *Pinnel*, but the reality is that no such reconciliation is possible.

In light of recent case law, the difficulties have now nearly evaporated. The ruling on composition with creditors reflects commercial practice, whereas the doctrine of *Pinnel* reflects the logic of consideration; but that logic is clearly changing as a result of *Williams*. If we view the existence of a debt as a contract, an offer of part payment would constitute a variation on the terms of that contract. This could be a subjective benefit to the defendant which would now appear to be enforceable despite the absence of fresh consideration. Thus, *Pinnel's* case is now no longer merely inconsistent with the composition with creditors theory but also with the ruling in *Williams*. *Pinnel* can no longer be held out as unquestioned good law but must instead be of dubious merit.[34]

Irish courts of course are not bound by English case law, and it is difficult to see why they should not avoid what clearly appears to be a potential minefield of analysis being offered by their English brethren and opt directly to adopt the UCC approach. Such a move would be supportable in theory. Once the parties have entered into a contract and have shown sufficient seriousness that they mean to be bound by its terms (such seriousness taking the form of consideration), any subsequent alteration, once freely made and not pursuant to duress or undue influence, should be enforceable to the extent that the original contract

---

32   Note the existence of the Mareva injunction may be available to alleviate this problem; see Keane, *Equity and Trusts in the Republic of Ireland*, 1988.

33   *Morans v. Armstrong* (1840) Arm Mac Og 25.

34   But note that *The Atlantic Baron* [1979] QB 705 is still considerable support for the view that *Williams* is incorrectly decided.

was enforceable. This is still consistent with the earlier approval of Williston's point of view that a promise to pay an antecedent debt requires fresh consideration to be supportable. The promise to pay in accordance with an earlier contract is not a variation and accordingly cannot come within the terms of the above rule. The above rule can only apply where the variation has been accepted prior to the events of the obligation under the contract falling due for performance. If the obligation has matured, and not been performed, then a subsequent promise creates a new contract which would require consideration. Thus suppose X owes Y £1,000 payable on 1 January 1993. In December 1992 X proposes that he pay Y £500 on 1 January 1993 and the balance a year later. This proposal, if accepted by Y, should, under the rule outlined earlier, be enforceable despite the absence of consideration, since the events of the obligation (payment of the outstanding amount) have not yet matured. But suppose none of this happens and X fails to pay by the due date of 1 January 1993. On 3 January 1993 X now promises to pay Y the £1,000 on 1 March 1993. This proposal, if accepted by Y, is not enforceable as it is a new contract and unsupported by consideration. It is not a variation of the existing contract since the events of obligation have matured. Of course, Y could still sue in that case on foot of the earlier contract to pay by 1 January 1993.

8.04 PROMISSORY ESTOPPEL

Introduction This concept gained popularity primarily as a result of the ruling of Denning in *Central London Properties v. High Trees*,[35] but its ancestry can be traced back to much earlier times when it started life as a creature of equity and principally a remedy. In *Hughes v. Metropolitan Railway*[36] Hughes, as lessor of a railway building, served notice on the company to repair the building within six months. The company responded by offering their interest in the building to Hughes for a price. The parties conducted negotiations on the possible purchase of the reversion by Hughes, during which time there was an implied promise by Hughes not to enforce the request for repairs. The negotiations broke down, and Hughes now sought the transfer of the property to himself, because the company had failed their contractual obligation of repair within the six-month period. This was because Hughes had impliedly promised that he would not enforce this provision; but he now claimed that the promise was unenforceable for lack of consideration. It was clear that the court would

---

35 [1947] KB 130; *Kenny v. Kelly* [1988] IR 457 (an assurance given by College authorities, which was intended to be acted upon, held to be enforceable, approves Denning J in *High Trees*).

36 (1877) 2 App Cas 439; at common law estoppel had a more limited application as an exclusionary rule of evidence: *Jordan v. Money* (1845) 5 HL Cas 185 (a statement of fact can give rise to estoppel at common law, not statements of intention); *Munster & Leinster Bank v. Croker* [1940] IR 185; *McNeill v. Miller* [1907] 2 IR 328.

not permit Hughes to use the legal rules to such benefit. The solution was to hold that he was estopped from denying his promise, despite the absence of consideration.

Hughes occured some seventy years before *High Trees*, yet it is the latter which is more notorious and which has come to represent the signature tune of this doctrine. In *High Trees* the owner of a block of flats had leased the entire block to a property company, which in turn would lease individual flats within the block to individual tenants, making a profit from the aggregate of the individual rents less the sum owing as rent to the owner. The owner received an income without having to lease every individual unit in the block. The agreement had been entered into prior to the Second World War when the demand for properties in Central London was relatively fixed. Unfortunately, during that war, which erupted during the currency of the lease arrangement, tenants had little desire to rent accommodation in downtown London which for the most part was in direct line of the bomb sights of Axis warplanes. It was clear that the property company would not be able to fill the block or charge such high rents to those brave or foolhardy enough to persist in renting flats in London. The owner of the block, realising that it did not matter which property company had the building, decided to reduce the rent payable by the property company for the duration of the war. This reduced rent was paid thereafter. The owner company went into liquidation at the end of the war and the liquidator brought an action for the arrears of rent, that is, the difference between the rent originally agreed and the rent paid pursuant to the variation as a result of the war. The argument from the liquidator was that the owner's promise to extract only half of the rent due was unenforceable since it lacked consideration. Denning MR ruled that the liquidator was estopped from denying the earlier promise not to enforce the full rent. Certainly this is in accordance with the decision in *Hughes*, although the decision was regarded as somewhat historic. In essence it involved little more than a variation of the terms of a contract and should therefore have been subject to the same rationale as the 1877 case. The innovative element in *High Trees* was the application of this rule to variations with respect to price which it was felt were not covered by *Hughes*. But this, of course, was incorrect, if one looks deeply at the instances where the rule was applied after 1877 and before 1945. It is clear that, since *Birmingham and District Land Co. v. LNWR*,[37] no distinction was to be made in the application of this doctrine on the basis of the nature of the contractual term so varied, and accordingly *High Trees* did not represent any dramatic change in the true rationale of promissory estoppel as understood since 1888. But the power of perception far outweighs reality, and the perception that *High Trees* represented a dramatic new departure spurred legal jurisprudence into action.[38] What had

---

37   (1888) 40 Ch D 268.
38   In the United States, such promissory estoppel has become part of the Restatement, Contracts, s. 90: taken from Williston's proposals in 1932 for the adoption of this concept.

been a quiet backwater weapon in the legal arsenal now began to be used more frequently. Courts began expanding or narrowing its ambit. There is no doubt that much of this occurred due to the circumstances after the Second World War, where numerous contracts had been changed in light of the exigencies at the time. To render most such variations unenforceable would have placed incredible hardship on many people, and this was something the courts were unwilling to let happen. But, as so often happens, once unleashed, the power of a weapon is often difficult to control both in ferocity and coverage.

Before examining in detail the ebb and flow of the doctrine of promissory estoppel, it would be useful to take some time to place the role of *High Trees* in context. We said earlier that the law as it stands at present is that in general a variation of an existing contract is unenforceable unless supported by fresh consideration and that the result of *Williams v. Roffey*[39] is to enable the court to find such consideration from the concept of subjective benefit. For a moment, let us ignore the modern twist of *Williams* and return to the old rule and its relationship to *Hughes* and *High Trees*. Both those cases involve what essentially were variations in the terms of an existing contract, and yet the result is diametrically opposed to that stated for such a situation. How is it that both rules still survive? The answer is quite simple. Promissory estoppel as understood in both of the mentioned cases is an extension of the variation rule. Let us use an example. Suppose X has promised to buy a ship for £10,000 from shipbuilder Y. While being constructed, X runs into difficulty and makes a re-arrangement with Y to pay only £8,000. Ignoring the decision of *Williams* for the moment, this agreement, since it lacks consideration, is unenforceable according to the variation rule and also under the *Hughes/High Trees* doctrine. The principle in these cases comes into effect only when the party has relied upon the agreement and has in some manner altered his position. This distinction is important. The agreement is not enforceable, but reliance upon that agreement which causes damage may result in granting of a remedy. To that extent the *Hughes/High Trees* doctrine *simpliciter* concerns merely the existence of an equitable remedy pursuant to reliance on the unenforceable contract. As an equitable remedy it is discretionary and cannot be claimed as a matter of right. Moreover, it is a remedy, no more, no less. It cannot be a cause of action in its own right. This is as far as the concept goes in its purest form. But what has happened is that this simplistic doctrine has been used by opposing forces in a legal war which still rages over the role of consideration in our legal system and which, we shall see later, meets up with the decision in *Williams* in one of the laws most complex of arguments.

Before looking at the growth of the *High Trees* doctrine it is interesting to note that if the courts were to adopt provisions similar to the UCC (which would make variations in a contract enforceable without further consideration) the

39   Op. cit.

need for the doctrine would almost disappear. Despite this, new concepts have arisen that may not be so easy to put away.

Promise   There must be a promise made which is intended to affect the legal relationship between the parties.[40] Such promise does not have to be express but can be implied from the circumstances.[41] However, it must be clear and unambiguous;[42] it must not be equivocal.[43] Thus, a promise to cancel a contract for non payment does not constitute a promise within the meaning of the doctrine.

Reliance   We have already seen that reliance on the promise is essential before it will be treated as enforceable by the courts. In other words, the litigant must show to the satisfaction of the court that he has relied upon the promise so made and, generally speaking it is this which will cause the biggest stumbling block in the use of the doctrine of promissory estoppel. As Denning LJ pointed out in *Alan v. El Nasr Export and Import*,[44] what must be shown is that the claimant conducted his affairs on the basis of the promise and that it would subsequently be inequitable not to enforce the promise. This has often been stated as a requirement that the reliance be at the claimant's detriment, that is, he must have unfavourably altered his position.[45] But this is clearly erroneous. Often the claimant will alter position with a resultant benefit.[46] Indeed, both *Hughes* and *High Trees* gave a resultant benefit to the claimant. In the former, the railway company was relieved of the need to repair the premises within the original six months; and, in the latter, the property company avoided forfeiting its lease for non-payment and could therefore continue in business. This has led some to postulate that reliance *simpliciter* is sufficient even if the reliance results in a benefit to the claimant, and this is to an extent in accord with attempts to limit the benefit/burden conundrum. This goes too far in the other direction, inasmuch as it merely requires the claimant to have relied upon the promise, and fails to

---

40   *Collin v. Duke of Westminster* [1985] QB 581; in the US, statements of future intent have been held not to be sufficient (*Burst v. Adolph Coors*, 650 F 2d 930) and neither have estimates (*Robert Gordon Inc v. Ingersoll Rand*, 117 F 2d 654).

41   *The Laconia* [1977] AC 850; mere inaction generally will not be sufficient: *Amherst v. James Walker Goldsmith and Silversmith* [1983] Ch 305; *Colin v. Duke of Westminster* [1985] QB 581.

42   *Keegan & Roberts v. Comhairle Chontae Atha Cliath*, unreported, High Court, 12 March 1981.

43   Merely failing to enforce the strict terms of the contract will not bring the doctrine into play; *The Scaptrade* [1983] QB 529, [1983] 2 AC 694.

44   [1972] 2 QB 189.

45   *Morrow v. Carty* [1957] NI 174; *McCambridge v. Winters*, unreported, High Court, 28 August 1984; *Industrial Yarns v. Greene* [1948] ICRM 15.

46   *Brikom Investments v. Carr* [1979] QB 467; *The Post Chaser* [1982] 1 All ER 19; *P v. P* [1957] NZLR 854; note however that the courts are keen to find detriment, see *In re JR* [1993] ILRM 657, *Coughlan* (1993) 15 DULJ 188.

have due regard to the latter part of the earlier formulation by Denning. After reliance on the promise, it must be shown that it would be inequitable not to enforce the promise or, put in a less oblique fashion, it must be shown that enforcement of the original promise would be unjust:[47] a more accurate representation of the reliance concept. Has the claimant relied upon the promise to the extent that to enforce the original contract is no longer justifiable? In making this determination, it is crucial to ascertain a number of items. Firstly, was the claimant justified in relying upon the promise? Secondly, was the promise outstanding for a sufficiently long enough period of time that its non-enforcement will result in injustice? Thirdly, did the promise induce the reliance? And finally, will the enforcement of the original contract result in injustice in any event? We shall deal with each of these in turn.

It is not sufficient for the claimant to plead reliance on a promise that is clearly a mistake: for example, where the promise to reduce the price of the item brings the price level far below what one would reasonably expect.[48] In other words, the claimant must act reasonably in relying on the promise and he is not entitled to rely on any unreasonable promise made.[49] Whether or not the promise is a mistake is irrelevant; what is important is the reasonable response of the claimant upon receipt. If an ordinary person would say that such a promise is unusual, then the claimant has no right to rely on same. If the promise appears on the surface to be reasonable, then it cannot be set aside merely because it was made by mistake. It would appear that the same rules of mistake apply as are discussed in a later chapter. This factor will have more impact subsequently when we discuss situations where promissory estoppel is used not merely to vary the terms of an existing contract but to form a new contract where none existed previously.

Moreover, it may well be that the promise has not been in existence for a sufficiently long period of time for any reliance by the claimant to be irreversible. If the promise is revoked before any reliance has occurred, then promissory estoppel will not apply; but where the reliance has occurred, and the promise is subsequently revoked, the doctrine will only operate where the reliance itself cannot be reversed, and presumably in this regard the claimant is under a duty similar to that of tort where a defendant must mitigate his loss. Thus, if the claimant enters into arrangements as a result of the promise, a failure on his part to resile from those arrangements on learning of the revocation of the promise may well deny the claimant the relief sought. Thus in *Societé*

---

47 *The Post Chaser* [1982] 1 All ER 19 (it is not inequitable to withdraw from a promise 2 days after making it); *Williams v. Stern* (1879) 5 QBD 409 (promise not to enforce security clause over goods for one week, withdrawn from two days later when it was discovered that another person was likely to seize the goods. Held not inequitable to withdraw in this manner).

48 *Robert Gordon Inc v. Ingersoll Rand*, 117 F 2d 654 (estimate so under-priced that any reasonable person would see it as incorrect).

49 This is the same rule that applies to offers, see chapter 3 generally.

Italo-Belge pour le Commerce et l'Industrie v. Palm and Vegetable Oils (Malaysia)[50] the promisor withdrew from his promise within two days. The court held that this was permissible. The short space of time during which the promise had been in existence meant that its revocation caused no injustice to the promisee.

The promise must have induced the reliance by the claimant, although there is no need for it to be the sole motivation behind the reliance.[51] In practice, provided the claimant alters his position after the promise, it will be presumed that he did so in reliance of the promise and the onus will be on the promisor to disprove such reliance—a difficult task.

Finally, even where the claimant has relied on the promise it may well be in certain situations that it remains unenforceable since either the claimant is not prejudiced by enforcement of the original contract or the actions of the promisor are not unjust. A classic example of this is the case of *Williams v. Stern*[52] where the claimant had purchased furniture on instalments and where, under a term of the contract, if payment were not made on the due date, it would be seized by the lender. During the currency of the agreement, the claimant asked the lender to give him an extra week to pay the latest instalment and refrain from exercising the right of seizure. The lender so promised, but three days later seized the furniture when he discovered that it was about to be seized by the claimant's landlord in satisfaction of arrears of rent. The promise was held unenforceable, for two reasons. Firstly, enforcement of the original contract would result in no injustice to the claimant since the property was being used to satisfy another debt; and, secondly, the revocation of the promise in light of the changed circumstances was not inequitable on the part of the lender. He had acted merely to preserve his own rights over those of another.

Pre-existing relationship   We have so far assumed that promissory estoppel is confined to variation of an existing contract; however, there is case law to the effect that this need not always be so. In *Durham Fancy Goods v. Michael Jackson (Fancy Goods)*[53] the doctrine was applied where there was no pre-existing contractual relationship but a relationship based on a statutory provision. It was postulated that all that was required was the existence of a pre-existing legal relationship. In *Maharaj v. Chand*[54] the doctrine was used where a man attempted to eject the woman he had been living with from the family home: there was no contractual relationship between the man and woman, yet estoppel was used by the court. Subsequent case law continues to

---

50   [1982] 1 All ER 19 (referred to elsewhere as the *Post Chaser* in the footnotes).
51   *Edgington v. Fitzmaurice* (1885) 29 Ch D 459.
52   (1879) 5 QBD 409.
53   [1968] 2 QB 839.
54   [1986] AC 898 (this case may be explicable on the basis of proprietary estoppel, see Snell, *Principles of Equity*, 28th ed. and *In re JR*, op. cit.

cast doubt on the proposition that there need be a pre-existing contractual relationship between the parties, but it has not been expressly over-ruled. Indeed, there would appear to be some authority which expands the proposition further by extending it to situations where there is no prior relationship of any description, or where the relationship is putative. In the *Henrik Sif*,[55] where the claimant was led to believe that he had made a contract with the promisor, whereas in fact he had made it with another person, the court held the doctrine applicable. However, both this case and the cases cited earlier to the effect that all that is required is a pre-existing legal relationship are far too tenuous to put forth as authorities.[56] As of now, in the absence of a firm statement from the courts, it requires a pre-existing contractual relationship to ground the relief of promissory estoppel.[57] Whether the presence or absence of any other pre-existing relationship is required is unclear. If the courts were to permit the application of promissory estoppel in the absence of any pre-existing legal relationship, it would move us closer to the position adopted in the United States (discussed in more detail below). The net effect would be to transform promissory estoppel from a defensive remedy to an independent cause of action. The US experience has shown that this is possible without destroying the doctrine of consideration.

Suspensory effect As a general rule, the application of the doctrine operates only to suspend rights accruing under a contract and not to extinguish them.[58] Thus, in the *High Trees* case it was never contended that the owners of the building could not claim the original rent from the date of notification of withdrawal of the promise to the defendants: only the arrears had been placed in suspense. Ordinarily, the variation can be revoked at any stage and the original rights arising under the contract re-invoked from that time on. It is, however, possible that in certain, admittedly rare, situations the rights are not merely suspended but extinguished. Thus in *Ogilvy v. Hope-Davies*[59] a promise not to enforce a completion date of 30 August on a contract for the sale of land made on 15 August could not be revoked so as to re-instate the original date. The case should be regarded with a certain amount of respect since, in this jurisdiction, the completion date for a conveyance is not of the essence in the contract: this can be shown from the fact that the party suspends the original closing date. Moreover, in the case at bar, the result was to delay the enforcement date but not to extinguish the enforcement itself. Promissory estoppel operates to suspend and not extinguish the rights under the original contract; however,

---

55 [1982] 1 Lloyds Rep 570.
56 See *Evenden v. Guildford City FC* [1975] QB 917 (the doctrine of promissory estoppel could apply to a putative contract).
57 *Folens v. Minister for Education* [1984] ILRM 265; for an opposite view see *Waltons Stores (Interstate) v. Maher* (1988) 76 ALR 513.
58 *Tool Metal Manufacturing Co. v. Tungsten Electric* [1955] 1 WLR 761.
59 [1976] 1 All ER 683.

the revocation of the variation must afford a reasonable opportunity to the other party where the context so admits.

However, suppose that the parties agree to terminate rather than vary the terms of their contract. Is such termination a variation and enforceable under the rules outlined earlier? An agreement to terminate a contract prior to its completion, inasmuch as that both parties still have not performed their obligations, will be enforceable, since the surrender by both of them of such rights under the putative contract constitutes sufficient consideration. But if one of the parties has completed his portion of the bargain, an agreement to terminate the remaining obligation will be unenforceable unless supported by further consideration.

Shield not sword   It is often stated that promissory estoppel can only be used by a defendant as a defence to a claim by a plaintiff. Thus in *Combe v. Combe*[60] Denning LJ took the opportunity to restate the principle enunciated earlier

> The principle stated in the *High Trees* case . . . does not create new causes of action where none existed before. It only prevents a party from insisting on his strict legal rights, when it would be unjust to allow him to enforce them.[61]

In that case a promise made by a husband with respect to the payment of maintenance to his wife was not honoured, but her suit for performance of the promise was dismissed since she could not plead it in the affirmative. Presumably it would have been possible for the husband to plead her agreement to the arrangement if he had been sued by the wife for increased maintenance, for then he would have been using the doctrine as a defence.

This limitation is somewhat questionable, particularly for those who would use promissory estoppel where no previous relationship existed. Moreover, there is little justification for so denying the plaintiff the opportunity to raise the issue. Failure to abide by the promise appears only enforceable where a party has been disadvantaged but not where a party has something to gain. It cannot be that the effect of the promise should go to the substance. The promise is either enforceable or it is not. If the other criteria are satisfied, why not allow promissory estoppel to be pleaded as a cause of action? This would bring us in line with the US position of detrimental reliance, and make the application of the doctrine more rational and utilitarian. Fears that it would cause the doctrine

---

60   [1951] 2 KB 215.
61   Ibid at p. 219; however see O'Dell, 'Estoppel and Ultra Vires Contracts' (1992) 14 *DULJ* 123 (he proposes that *In re PMPA (Longmile) Garage Ltd (No. 2)* (op. cit). is an example of estoppel as a cause of action; Mee, 'Taking Precedent Seriously.' (1993) 11 *ILT 255* (he proposes that *In re JR* (op. cit.) is another example of estoppel as a cause of action); but see Coughlan, 'Swords, Shields and Estoppel Licences' (1993) *DULJ* 188 for a different view); *Walton v. Maher*, op. cit.

of consideration to be effectively abrogated are over-stated, and, indeed, due to the latest rulings in the *Williams* case, somewhat redundant, since that case has done more to hole the doctrine of consideration below the water-line than any intelligent use of promissory estoppel could.

We turn therefore to deal with the use of detrimental reliance as a method of enforcing a contract.

8.05 DETRIMENTAL RELIANCE AS CONSIDERATION

There can be little doubt that the latest formulation of detrimental reliance in the Restatement, Second, offers the best way forward.[62] S. 90 states:

> (1) A promise which the promisor should reasonably expect to induce action or forbearance on the part of the promisee and which does induce such action or forbearance is binding if injustice can be avoided only by the enforcement of the promise. The remedy granted for breach may be limited as justice requires.

While this is conceptually close to the promissory estoppel formulation outlined above, it differs in a number of key aspects and removes the ambiguity that exists yet retains the inherent flexibility of the doctrine. Firstly, it removes any requirement for a pre-existing relationship, whether contractual or not. Thus all that is required is a promise.[63] Further, the promise must be sufficient to have invoked a reasonable reliance on it. If the promisee acts unreasonably he will not be able to avail of the doctrine. Moreover, the promisor must have anticipated reasonable reliance upon such a promise.[64] Secondly, it only operates to prevent an injustice from occurring. If no injustice has arisen, the doctrine cannot be used. Clearly this requires that the promisee has suffered some wrong that must be righted; this will normally mean that the promisee has acted to his detriment. If he has not so acted to his detriment, no injustice will have occurred.[65] Thirdly, unlike the original formulation,[66] the remedy is not that of

---

62 Williston introduced the idea of promissory estoppel into the first Restatement in 1932: simply put the argument was that reliance could make a donative promise enforceable, see Eisenberg, 'Donative Promises', 47 *Univ Chicago Law Rev*, 1.

63 See above, 8.04.

64 *Smith v. Boise Kenworth Sales*, 625 P 2d 417; 4 American Law Institute Proceedings 92 et seq., Clark, op. cit., p. 63.

65 A considerable degree of flexibility is left with the court to determine when an injustice has arisen. This is to be welcomed.

66 While not expressly stated, Williston himself believed that the full contractual obligation should be imposed; Williston IV American Law Institute Proceedings, Appendix, p 103, 'you have to take one leg [a contract is formed] or the other [it is not so formed].

automatically imposing a full contract with all its ramifications.[67] The remedy can be limited so as only to mitigate the injustice suffered. This might include imposition of a full contract,[68] but it could also be less severe. Finally, no restriction is placed upon the use of the doctrine as a cause of action in its own right.

Despite the existence of this provision, consideration, as we know, it has not vanished from US contract law.[69] The system still works and has not come crashing down around people's ears. But can such an approach be legitimately adopted by the courts in this jurisdiction? A simple legislative enactment would overcome any technical difficulties. In the absence of this legislative intervention, while acknowledging a contrary view exists,[70] the courts could indeed adopt this approach and are in fact not that far away from doing so. In *Smith v. Ireland*,[71]

Finlay P approved this *dicta* of Denning MR:

> Short of an actual promise, if he by words or conduct, so behaves as to lead another to believe that he will not insist on his legal rights knowing or intending that the other will act on that belief—and he does so act, that again will raise an equity in favour of the other, and it is for the court to say in what way the equity may be satisfied.[72]

Pushing the boundaries of these comments could, at one fell swoop, rationalise the whole area of enforcement of contracts in the absence of consideration. The courts in this jurisdiction should take the first opportunity to do so.

---

67 *Goodman v. Dicker*, 169 F 2d 684 (1948) (the plaintiff's claim was limited to loss of profits only); Fuller and Perdue, 'The Reliance Interest in Contract Damages', 46 *Yale LJ* 373.

68 Restatement, Second, Contracts, s. 90, Comment d; *Robert Gordon Inc v. Ingersoll Rand*, 117 F 2d 654 (the estimate was so low as to be palpably incorrect),

69 Though consideration in US law has a slightly narrower definition as a result of Holmes' urging in *The Common Law*, op. cit., p. 292; *Wisconsin & Mich Railway v. Powers*, 191 US 379 ('it is not enough that the promise induces the detriment or that the detriment induces the promise if the other half is wanting', at 386); see above, 8.04.

70 Clark, op. cit.

71 [1983] ILRM 300

72 *Crabb v. Arun District Council* [1976] 1 Ch 179; see also *The Hannah Blummenthal* [1983] 1 All ER 34, *Kenny v. Kelly* [1988] IR 457 for the use of injurious reliance and legitimate expectation as possible alternatives. However, they remain unsatisfactory.

9.00

Privity

9.01 INTRODUCTION

The doctrine of privity has been the subject of some considerable criticism. Simply put, it denies the right to a person who is not a party to a contract, and who therefore cannot be said to have supplied consideration, from enforcing the contract, despite the fact that the parties intended that person to be the beneficiary of the contract.[1] It receives perhaps its clearest expression in the case of *McCoubray v. Thompson*.[2] Here a landowner wished to give his property, in equal shares, to both the defendant and the plaintiff. The fact of the matter, however, was that the defendant desired all the property; the plaintiff would be satisfied with the monetary value of the share of the land he was to receive. For the sake of simplicity it was agreed between the owner of the property and the defendant that the land would be conveyed directly to him and in return he would promise to pay the plaintiff a certain sum of money. The property was duly conveyed, but the rest was silence from the defendant; no money was forthcoming to the plaintiff. In the meantime the owner had died, and the plaintiff now sought to have the agreement enforced. The court rejected the application, pointing out that the plaintiff had supplied no consideration with which he could enforce the bargain. If he had done so (even as a result of circumstances as in the case of *Barry v. Barry*)[3] he would have been allowed to recover. Clearly, the correct party to enforce the agreement was the owner (now dead). The deceased owner's estate similarly could not seek to enforce the contract because it would not be of interest to the estate itself and therefore it would be irresponsible and unlawful of the executors of the estate to waste assets in pursuit of another's benefit.[4]

The point of the matter is not that the plaintiff is not a party to the contract in its widest sense. It is difficult to see how, in the English case of *Tweddle v.*

---

1   Treitel, op. cit., p 523 et seq; Cheshire and Fifoot, op. cit., p. 437 et seq.; Calamari and Perillo op. cit., p. 691 et seq.; *Price v. Easton*, 110 Eng Rep 518 (KB 1833).
2   (1868) 2 IRCL 226.
3   (1891) 28 LR (Ir) 45 (the forbearance by a third party of a legal claim on the deceased's estate is sufficient consideration to enable him to enforce action).
4   See Wylie, *Irish Land Law*, 2nd ed., chapter 16 for general rules on the administration of deceased person's estates.

Atkinson,[5] for example, where the plaintiff sought to enforce an agreement between his father and his father-in-law (which involved a payment of money on the plaintiff marrying his father-in-law's daughter), that the plaintiff was not a party to the contract. Yet it was held that the plaintiff had not been a party to the contract and therefore the court did not allow him to recover. This reasoning is entirely fallacious. Most cases involve a situation where one of the parties to the contract is dead, and therefore unable to sue. This appears to negate the contract. Although the parties intended to benefit the plaintiff, the technical intervention of death has removed the whole basis upon which the common law of contract rests, namely, the enforcement of bargains freely entered into. The defendant obtains an unwarranted advantage from death: it is in the defendant's interest that his co-contractor should not survive. This must be of questionable policy value.

The other alternative is of course that the original party to the contract is not dead but has elected not to enforce the contract; however, this may well involve different policy considerations, as we shall see later.[6]

9.02 A DIFFERENT PERSPECTIVE

At early common law, this approach was not accepted and third-party beneficiaries were allowed recover. In *Dutton v. Poole*[7] the defendant promised his father that he would pay his sister £1,000 if the father would forebear from selling a particular property. The father refrained from the sale, but so too did the defendant from his promise to pay his sister. The plaintiff now sought to enforce the contract as third-party beneficiary. Clearly the act of forbearance from a particular act can constitute good consideration[8] so there was no question that the father could enforce the contract. But it was the sister who sought enforcement; to an extent this was logical: it was, after all, she who stood to gain. The court permitted recovery, and it seems clear that, in reaching that decision, much emphasis was placed on the family relationship between the parties. There exists a considerable body of case law prior to *Tweddle v.*

---

5   (1861) 1 B&S 393; *Dunlop v. Selfridge* [1915] AC 847 (a tyre manufacturer who had sold some of his tyres to a wholesaler could not enforce a clause preventing resale of these tyres below a certain price against third party retailer. The clause lacked both consideration and privity *vis-à-vis* the third party); *Murphy v. Bower* (1868) IR 2 CL (the plaintiff could not force the defendant (who had been employed by a contractor to certify plaintiff's work as satisfactory for payment) to issue certificates of satisfactory completion. The plaintiff was not a party to the contract between defendant and employer).

6   See for example *Snelling v. Snelling* (9.04 ibid) where the court decided the issue on the presence before it of all relevant parties. Normally, where the party is not deceased, his failure to enforce the contract is for some unconscionable reason.

7   83 Eng Rep 523 (KB 1677), affirmed 83 Eng Rep 156 (Ex Ch 1679).

8   *Hamer v. Sidway* (1891) 124 NY 583; See chapter 7 generally.

Atkinson that supports the decision in *Dutton v. Poole* as being sound in the common law, and it cannot be seriously refuted that *Tweddle* represents a modern departure from non-privity of contracts, at least with respect to family beneficiaries.[9] It is fair to say that, with respect to non-family contracts, it has been traditionally harder to find in favour of the third party; thus, in *Crow v. Rogers*[10] H owed C £70. H contracted with R to convey a house to R in return for which R would discharge the debt of £70 to C. C now sought to enforce the contract, but the application was dismissed.

The doctrine, while being long regarded as traditional common law orthodoxy as a consequence of consideration, nevertheless finds expression in Roman law. Oddly enough, Roman law did not have a similar concept of consideration, yet the exclusion of third parties to benefit or suffer from the terms of a contract to which they were not a party was well settled, and this has been carried over into many civil law jurisdictions today.[11] Given this reality, the concept of privity, which is so intimately linked with consideration, is more likely to be justified as a stand-alone policy decision by the courts. Thus, it would not be affected by the abolition of the doctrine of consideration.[12]

9.03 ALTERNATIVE APPROACHES

The injustice of such a rule has not been overlooked. Certainly there are cases where it is more inconvenient than unjust, but likewise there are cases where it is unjust and not merely inconvenient. In England several doctrines have emerged to mitigate the potential severity of the doctrine. Firstly, there is the principle of the 'undisclosed principal'. Secondly, the doctrine is a common law doctrine, and as such the courts of equity have given relief when appropriate. Thirdly, it has not received much application in the sphere of contracts dealing with land, presumably due to the equitable link. Finally, in *UDT v. Kirkwood*[13] Lord Denning MR pointed out that, in commercial activities where the parties

9   *Bourne v. Mason (1669) 1 Vent 6; Simpson, History*, pp. 475-485; *Coull's v. Bagot's Executor and Trustee* [1967] ALR 385; Palmer, 33 *Am Jl of Legal History* 3; the counter argument runs that cases like *Dutton* occurred at a time when the concept of consideration had not been finalised and included natural love and affection. In light of the *Eastwood v. Kenyon* decision, *Dutton*, and similar cases are now obsolete.

10   (1724) 1 Str 592.

11   See in particular France, referred to later; Buckland and McNair, *Roman Law and Common Law*, 2nd ed., pp. 214-217.

12   *Kepong Prospecting v. Schmidt* [1968] AC 810 (an enlarged definition of consideration in Malaysia could not affect the doctrine of privity, *per* Privy Council); but see Furmston, 23 MLR 383-384 and *Jacobs* [1986] JBL 466,467 for a contrary view; note that the decision of *Tweddle* is based on consideration, whereas that of *Bourne* is based on privity *simpliciter*. Note also, that US law still relies on the doctrine of consideration, but does not operate privity as an effective doctrine, see 9.03 ibid.

13   [1966] 2 QB 431, 454-455; This ruling may be useful in explaining the enforceability of bankers' commercial credits. Commercial credits facilitate international trade where

have all based their relationship on a practice that such third-party beneficiaries will be entitled to recover and enforce the contract, the courts will give effect to that intention. Before discussing these items in detail, it may be useful to look to alternative jurisdictions.

The position in France is not radically different. There, the Roman law rule of refusing to permit third-party beneficiaries to a contract to enforce their benefit was effectively adopted—but with two provisions to mitigate the obvious harshness of such doctrine. It seems clear, however, that the exceptions have become so abused in their application in that jurisdiction that the more accurate view of law would be that, with exceptions, third parties have the right to enforce benefits under a contract.[14]

Certainly, early jurisprudence in the United States seemed to follow this approach. In *Lawrence v. Fox*[15] the defendant received a loan from H in return for which he promised to repay a debt owed by H to the plaintiff. The defendant refused to honour this promise, and H was either unable or unwilling to enforce the contract himself. The plaintiff was therefore a third-party beneficiary but without the fortune of being in some sort of family relationship with the other parties. The decision occured before that of *Tweddle* and, therefore, relying on traditional common law and, under the influence of equity, the court gave verdict for the plaintiff, enforcing the contract because the justice of the case demanded it. The decision received general acceptance, although the need to limit its application became immediately obvious. The Restatement concerned itself with a classification of beneficiaries into three: creditor,[16] donee[17] and

---

a purchaser of goods arranges with his bank to open a line of credit in favour of the seller, in return for a promise to the bank to re-imburse the amount of credit given. The opened credit line is irrevocable. As a result, the seller forwards the goods secure in the fact that he will receive payment. The problem is that, if it should break down, and the bank revoke the credit, there is no privity between the bank and the seller. As a matter of practice, no bank has ever denied the enforceability of such arrangements and it would be unlikely that a court would do so, see generally Gutteridge and Megraw, *The Law of Bankers Commercial Credits*, 7th ed.; *Hamzeh Malas v. British Imex Industries* [1958] 2 QB 127; *Urquhart Lindsay v. Eastern Bank* [1922] 1 KB 318.

14   Lawson, *A Common Lawyer looks at the Civil Law* (1955).

15   20 NY 268 (1859), the case was felt by some of the judges to revolve around trust and agency concepts, but this was rejected in the lead judgment; see also Restatement, Second, Contracts, s. 302, Comment f; the case was not universally accepted, see *Green v. Green*, 298 Mass 19, 9 NE 2d 413 (1937) (Mass Commonwealth Courts refused to enforce third party obligations) overturned in *Choate Hall & Stewart v. SCA Serv*, 378 Mass 535, 392 NE 2d 1045 (1979).

16   Restatement, Contracts, s. 133(b): if the purpose of the promisee is to discharge an actual, supposed or asserted duty of the promisee to the beneficiary (such as where the promisee owes the beneficiary £100 and enters into a contract with the promisor where the money is paid by the promisor directly to the beneficiary), even where the promisee's obligation is not effective due to time limitation or formalities, such a beneficiary can enforce the contract.

17   Réstatement, Contracts, s. 133(a): if the purpose of the promisee is to confer a gift onto

incidental.[18] This has been refined in the Restatement, Second, to simply incidental and intended beneficiaries to a contract.[19] Any beneficiary that acquires rights under a contract is an intended beneficiary if it can be shown that recognition of such right to enforce performance is appropriate to effect the intention of the parties[20] and that either the performance will satisfy a monetary obligation of the promisee[21] or circumstances indicate that the promisee intends the beneficiary to benefit.[22] In reality this is similar to the original classification of creditor and donee beneficiaries,[23] though there are some important differences.[24] In both situations incidental beneficiaries may not enforce the contract, whereas intended beneficiaries effectively may.[1] This is rational; otherwise it might be possible that a prospective tenant of a building would be eligible to sue on foot of the contract between owner and builder for non-speedy erection of the building.[26]

the beneficiary; such a beneficiary can enforce the contract. *People ex rel Resnik v. Curtis and Davis* 78 Ill App 2d 381.

18 Restatement, Contracts, s. 133(c): a beneficiary who does not fall within the definitional provisions of footnotes 4 or 5 cannot enforce the contract.

19 Restatement, Contracts, Second, s. 302; it is true to say that the 'intent to benefit' approach was adopted in most States, in preference to the first Restatement formulation either by case law (*HR Moch Co v. Rensselaer Water Co.*, 247 NY 160; *Norfolk Western v. US*, 641 F 2d 1201 (1980); *Holbrook v. Pitt*, 643 F 2d 1261 (1981)) or by Statute (2 Williston s 326). In *Lucas v. Hamm* (15 Cal Rptr 821) a lawyer promised to draft a will for the testator. The will was to be made in favour of the plaintiffs, but was improperly drafted thereby excluding the plaintiffs from taking under it. The court held that it was sufficient if the promisor understood that the promisee intended the beneficiary to benefit. It is clear that there is an overlap with the area of the law of torts. The advantage of being able to sue in contract is that liability is strict, it does not depend on proof of negligence. Contrast this with a similar case in this jurisdiction, *Wall v. Hegarty* [1980] ILRM 124 where a beneficiary under a will could recoup his loss in tort, see also *Ross v. Caunters* [1980] Ch 279.

20 Restatement, Contracts, Second, s. 302; the Restatement, Second does not assist with the definitional problems of the concept of an intention to benefit, see Calamari and Perillo op. cit., pp. 693-700.

21 Restatement, Contracts, Second, s. 302, note that the obligation to pay must be actual and not supposed, as was the case in the first Restatement, *Rae v. Air-Speed*, 386 Mass 187, 435 NE 2d 628 (1982).

22 Restatement, Second, s. 302; confers a special status to gifts given outside the family relationship which had been essential in the first Restatement, *Seaver v. Ransom*, 224 NY 233, 120 NE 639 (1918).

23 See Calamari and Perillo, op. cit., pp. 700-701.

24 See footnotes 9 and 10 ibid; note that the concept of 'reliance' may also be available, if such reliance would be reasonable to enable a beneficiary to enforce recovery, see Restatement, Second, s. 302 ill. 11, 12.

25 Though incidental beneficiaries and intended beneficiaries under Restatement, Second, differ from those under the first Restatement, see *Rae v. Air-Speed*, 386 Mass 187, 435 NE 2d 628 (1982).

26 See Farnsworth, op. cit., p. 741 et seq.

Certainly, law reform in England has suggested the abolition of the privity doctrine,[27] but to date no action has been taken.

9.04 JUDICIAL INTERVENTION

The courts themselves have not been oblivious to the disadvantages of this doctrine and have attempted to move some way in this issue. Historically, the devices used by the courts to limit its implementation have posed considerable difficulties. The use of the trust is found in the case of *Drimmie v. Davies*,[28] whereby an agreement between father and son for the son to take over a dental practice on the father's death, subject to annuities to be paid to the other members of the family, was held to be enforceable by the father's wife and other children, despite their not being a party to the contract. The decision was on the basis that the promise constituted a trust, which was an equitable creation and thereby subject to the rules of equity, which would accordingly permit the plaintiffs to recover.[29] This method is clearly a fiction; no such trust was contemplated between the parties. In modern jurisprudence, the use of the trust as a method of avoiding privity has fallen into disrepute,[30] but it is important to remember that the trust concept may still be useful in certain situations.[31]

Another possibility has been the undisclosed principal theory, that is, that the

---

27   *Law Revision Committee*, 6th Interim Report, para 50(a) (1937); note some Common Law countries have removed the doctrine by Statute, see Date-Bah, 'Enforcement of third party contractual rights in Ghana.' 8 *U Ghana LJ*.

28   (1899) 1 IR 176; *Tomlinson v. Gill* (1756) Amb 330 (It was held that a promise made by the defendant to a widow that, if he were permitted to administer her deceased's husband estate, he would make up any deficiency in the estate to the creditors, was sufficient to permit the plaintiff (a creditor) to sue to enforce the promise. The promise to the widow was a trust for the benefit of the creditors); *Kenny v. Employers Liability Insurance Corporation* [1901] 1 IR 301.

29   But cf. *Clitheroe v. Simpson* (1879) 4 LR (Ir) 59 (S, father of D, and C agreed, by deed, to convey land to D in return for D paying C £100. D failed to pay, C sued to recover but failed. This case more accurately states the true position: no trust is created.).

30   *Vandepitte v. Preferred Accident Insurance* [1933] AC 70 (the Privy Council held against the plaintiff because of a lack of intention that he should benefit); *Cadbury Ireland v. Kerry Co-Op* [1982] ILRM 77; *In re Schebsman* [1944] Ch 83 (*per* DuParcq LJ 'It is true to say that, by the use possibly of unguarded language, a person may create a trust . . . without knowing it, but unless an intention to create a trust is clearly to be collected from the language used and the circumstances of the case, I think that the court ought not to be so astute to discover indications of such an intention . . . both parties intended to keep alive their common law right to vary consensually the terms of the obligation . . .' at p. 104. Note that this is a strong argument against the use of the trust, since, once created, the terms of such trust become unalterable).

31   *Green v. Russell* [1959] 2 All ER 525 (the mere existence of a promise between X and Y to benefit Z does not create a trust, but other surrounding circumstances may lead to this conclusion); *In re Webb* [1941] 1 All ER 321.

party to the contract acted as an undisclosed principal for the beneficiary.[32] Effectively, this means that the third party is deemed to be a party, albeit an unmentioned party, to the contract. Thus, the doctrine of privity is effectively side-stepped. It has culminated in the so-called *Eurymedon* case.[33] There, a contract to ship goods from England to New Zealand had been entered into by the parties,which contained a clause limiting the liability of the carrier in the event of the cargo being damaged. The cargo was subsequently damaged by the negligent actions of stevedores, and the defendant now sought to rely upon the benefit of the limitation clause of the agreement. The Privy Council held that they could rely on the limitation clause if it could be shown:

(i) that the contract clearly intended to protect the stevedores, and

(ii) the carrier was clearly acting as an agent for the purposes of securing a benefit for the principal, and

(iii) the agent had the authority to act for the principal, and

(iv) there was consideration.[34]

This too is a conceptual fiction, unless the concept outlined in that case is restricted to bailments of goods or to cases where a real agency relationship can be found, thus excluding many cases of difficulty where privity intervenes.

It should also be noted that the doctrine is avoided in the area of land law,[35] insurance contracts[36] and certain statutory provisions.[37] The usefulness of these particular methods of avoidance of the doctrine so outlined may be removed if a more dynamic approach is taken by the courts; there has been considerable evidence that they are in fact beginning the long slow move away from the narrow view of privity.

Rather than relying on the earlier mentioned artificial concepts, there has been a growing impatience with retaining a discredited doctrine. In *Beswick v. Beswick*[38] a nephew promised his uncle that in return for the uncle's business being transferred to him upon the uncle's death, he would, *inter alia*, promise to pay £5 per week to the uncle's widow. He failed to do so, and the widow sued both as administrator of the uncle's will and in her own name. Denning MR held that the widow could sue in her own right because privity was merely a common law rule of procedure. Other judges in the House of Lords have also

---

32 The problem is that before the relationship of agency can arise, it must be intended to be created (*Sheppard v. Murphy* (1867) 1 Ir R Eq 490). Normally in third party beneficiaries this is not so.

33 [1975] AC 154.

34 [1975] AC 154, 162.

35 See Wylie, *Irish Land Law*, 2nd ed., chapter 19 for covenants running with the land.

36 Road Traffic Act 1961, s. 76; Married Women's Status Act 1957, s. 7.

37 Married Womans Status Act 1957, s. 8; Sale of Goods and Supply of Services Act 1980, s. 32.

38 [1968] AC 58.

severely criticised the doctrine, so that in *Woodar Investment Development v. Wimpey*[39] Scarman LJ hoped that the House of Lords would reconsider *Tweddle* and the other cases that 'stand unjust guard over this rule'. Yet the ruling of the case itself by the majority casts doubt on the opening so created by Denning in *Beswick* and the subsequent case of *Jackson v. Horizon Holidays.*[40] In *Jackson,* a contract for a holiday entered into by a husband and a tour operator was held to be enforceable by the husband's family, his wife and children, and that they could recover in their own right. The decision seems justifiable, and the subsequent House of Lords' comment that it was incorrect as regards the principle enunciated by Denning is unwelcome. In *Snelling v. Snelling*[41] three brothers were directors of a company; they had entered into an agreement between themselves that, as long as certain debts were owed by the company to finance houses, none of the brothers would call in loans they had made to the company, and, in the event of any of them resigning his directorship, that brother's loan would be forfeit. The plaintiff resigned from the position of director and sued the company for repayment of the loan. The company, not being a party to the agreement, could not resist such application, but the remaining two brothers applied to be joined as co-defendants, which was allowed. Correspondingly, as all the parties were now involved in the action, the court dismissed the suit.

Snelling seems an eminently sensible decision; but taken in conjunction with the above cases, where does it leave us? It would seem that at equity, a beneficiary could force one of the parties to the contract to sue the other party for non-compliance with the agreement. Thus, if X makes a contract with Y whereby Z is intended to benefit, Z cannot sue Y directly to enforce this agreement since he is not a party to the agreement, but at equity he may sue X to force X to sue Y to have the bargain implemented. However, as we have seen earlier, the difficulty is that equity operates through the trust, and there has been considerable judicial reluctance to travel this path in recent times.[42] But, as a result of *Snelling*, it might be that all Z would have to do would be to join X and Y to the action and thus, having all the parties present, the court would be able to exercise its inherent equitable jurisdiction to see that justice is done in the case.

There is more than enough evidence to prove that the doctrine enunciated in *Tweddle* is a perversion of the original common law position. The practical experience of the operation of this unjust rule, and its critical assessment by some courts, warrants a revision of this area by the Irish courts. Moreover, a move closer to the American position of allowing intended beneficiaries of contracts to recover, despite their not being parties to the contract, would bring this jurisdiction into line with other civil law countries of the European Union

39   [1980] 1 All ER 571.   41   [1972] 1 All ER 79.
40   [1975] 3 All ER 92.   42   See footnote 3, ibid.

such as France, where the enforcement of third-party rights in contracts is the norm.[43] Irish courts have the power to do this without infringing any delineation of roles or strictures of constraint. Guidance could be taken from the joint judgment of Mason CJ and Wilson J in the Australian case of *Trident General Insurance v. McNiece Bros*,[44] where, in not applying a strict rule of privity, they said:

> it is the responsibility of this Court to reconsider in appropriate cases common law rules which operate unsatisfactorily and unjustly.[45]

It is not being suggested that any person with an interest in a contract should be allowed to enforce the agreement—merely those parties so intended to benefit from it. If the parties intended someone to benefit from the contract, and that contract is a valid and enforceable contract, it seems difficult to justify a refusal to permit the beneficiary so intended from enforcing the contract in his own right. It does not destroy the common law doctrine of consideration. We have already seen that the rule that consideration must move from the promisee is a distinct doctrine from that of privity. The abolition of privity will not affect the doctrine of consideration.[46] If X and Y enter into a contract intended to benefit Z but without consideration, Z should not be allowed to recover since the contract is unenforceable.

One should bear in mind that certain statutory provisions grant such a right in any event, albeit it in limited and special circumstances.[47]

9.05 CONTRACTS IMPOSING LIABILITIES

We have so far concerned ourselves with contracts bestowing benefits upon third parties, but the traditional argument against allowing their enforcement has been that it is not possible to impose a liability on persons who are not parties to a contract—a just statement of law—and as a corollary, it would be illogical to permit the enforcement of benefits.[48] This is inconsistent. Firstly, there is no good reason why one should treat a benefit the same as a liability. The two are

---

43   See 9.03, footnote 2, ibid; Nicholas, op. cit., 169-99.
44   (1988) 165 CLR 107.
45   (1988) 165 CLR 107, 123.
46   See *Kepong*, and related case discussion, 9.02 footnote 6, ibid; it follows if we accept that privity would survive the abolition of consideration, then the corollary also must hold true: consideration would survive the abolition of privity.
47   For example, Married Women's Status Act 1957, s. 7 (Insurance Policies), s. 8 (Contracts bestowing benefits upon spouse or children); see also *Oblique Financial Services v. Promise Production* [1994] ILRM 74 (an obligation of confidentiality under a contract, held not to be confined to the parties to that contract).
48   See Cheshire and Fifoot, op. cit., p. 448 et seq.

hardly the same, and it would make sense to apply different rules to both. Secondly, such dichotomy involves distinguishing what is a benefit and what is a liability. One man's benefit is another's liability. It cannot be the court's function to determine which it is for the third party. How, then, can we know whether it is benefit or a liability? In reality the puzzle is easily resolved. If the third party sues to have the contract enforced because he is an intended beneficiary of the contract, then it is a benefit, even if an objective person might say it is more in the lines of a liability. In other words, by suing to have the contract enforced, the third party, one would assume, views the import of the contract to be of benefit to him. He has volunteered to seek to have the contract enforced upon him. It is not being imposed but is rather the result of his own free will. On the other hand, if he determines it is a liability, he will not sue on the contract, and any action would be taken by the parties to the contract to have a contract imposed upon a person without their consent. This would be out of line with justice and jurisprudence. In summary, the modification of privity proposed above would not have any impact for the traditional view that liability cannot be imposed upon strangers, and it would remain similar to that operated with respect to disclaimers under a will.[49] We shall briefly explore the jurisprudence on this.

As a basic rule, a third party to a contract will not be saddled with any liability arising out of such contract, however, this rule is the subject of considerable modification in land law, particularly as a result of the decision in *Tulk v. Moxhay*[50] and the different considerations that apply in land law in general. Moreover, in two ordinary contractual situations special rules apply—contracts which impose restrictions as to use or price. In *Lord Strathcona SS v. Dominion Coal Co.*[51] the Privy Council dismissed an appeal by the defendants against an order of the Nova Scotia courts granting an injunction preventing the defendants from using a ship that they had purchased in a manner inconsistent with a charter that had been entered into by the original owner of the ship and the plaintiff. The reasoning was based on the fact that the defendants had notice of the agreement and followed the approach in *Tulk v. Moxhay*. The decision can be criticised, not perhaps as to the result but as to rationale. *Tulk v. Moxhay*, and the principle therein evolved, no longer relies on notice, and the fact that the application of this doctrine requires a proprietary interest (which might not always be found) is somewhat worrying. These criticisms were found in the judgment of Diplock J in *Port Line Ltd v. Ben Line Steamers*,[52] where he held the Strathcona case as being wrongly decided. He also pointed out that even if it were good law, it would not apply where the defendants had no notice of the preceding obligation. Moreover, it was not available where the remedy so

---

49   See Friel and Donegan, 'Disclaimers
     on Intestacy,' *Irish Tax Review*,
     March 1992.
50   (1848) 2 Ph 774.

51   [1926] AC 108; *DeMattos v. Gibson*,
     4 DeG&J 276 (1858).
52   [1958] 1 All ER 787.

sought was one of common law damages. If the principle were to operate, it would warrant only the equitable remedies of injunction and so forth. However, subsequently in *Swiss Bank Corp v. Lloyd's Bank*[53] the *Strathcona* case was approved, principally on the basis that such equitable jurisdiction was the counterpart to the tortious action of interference with contractual obligations. The better view of this situation may be found as follows:

> It is obvious that if X has let or pledged his chattel to Y and has transferred its possession to Y and if he then sells its to Z, Z can only take it subject to Y's legal rights, and since they are legal rights whether Z has notice of it or not.[54]

In summary it would appear that a liability imposed upon a stranger to the contract that concerns a restriction of use is enforceable, at least to the extent that the third party had notice of such restriction, although it is arguable also where no such notice is present. Diplock J's restriction on remedies to equitable remedies only would be inconsistent with the above quotation and should be regarded as inapplicable.

Finally, a contract may impose a restriction as to price, but such clauses are not effective at common law;[55] also, in light of the competition policy regulation of contracts, they may be unenforceable even as against the parties themselves.[56]

In conclusion, the imposition of liabilities on third parties is perhaps better dealt with in the subsequent chapter on Assignment of Contractual Rights.[57]

53   [1979] 2 All ER 853.
54   Holdsworth, 49 LQR 576, 579.
55   *Taddy v. Sterious* [1904] 1 Ch 354.
56   Competition Act 1990; chapter 20, ibid.
57   Chapter 29, ibid.

10.00

Formalities in contract

10.01 INTRODUCTION

As a general rule, the courts at common law will enforce a contract even if there is no documentary evidence as to its existence or its terms.[1] In other words, there is no requirement that a contract be written, or take any particular form. We have seen that a contract under seal, by definition a written contract, is enforceable *per se*.[2] However, the mere fact that a contract is written is not sufficient to make it enforceable without the presence of consideration.[3]

Similarly, a verbal contract is not of itself unenforceable, but it may in practice be more difficult to prove should the contract or its terms be in dispute.[4] Often, contracts are a mix of written and oral, and we shall see later how this can be used to help construct the true terms of a contract.[5]

The law will normally lay down a general rule and then proceed to outline situations where it will not follow that rule. Such is the case here, and we shall now proceed to outline the kind of contract where some formality is required before the contract is enforceable and what exactly that formality is. One has to remember however, that mere compliance with these formalities is not of itself sufficient to found an enforceable contract, and that consideration will still be required. In this way contracts requiring formalities differ from contracts under seal.

---

1   Initially, oral contracts were not enforceable at common law but this changed with the advent of the writ of assumpsit, 2 Corbin, op. cit., 275.
2   See chapter 7.
3   In the US many states have abolished the seal and replaced it with the concept of the writing. Two states have enacted legislation equating a written instrument to a document under seal which requires no consideration to be enforceable (Mississippi Code Annotated, ss. 75-9-1, 75-9-3, 75-9-5 and New Mexico Stat s 38-7-2)—others have merely abolished the seal (New York Gen Constr Law, s. 44-a and Arkansas, Illinois, Indiana, Minnesota, Nebraska, Ohio Utah and Wyoming). Several states have enacted a rebuttable presumption of consideration in written contracts (California Civil Code Ann, ss. 1614, 1615 and 1629 and Arizona, Idaho, Iowa, Kansas, Kentucky, Missouri, Montana, Nevada, North Dakota, Oklahoma, Tennessee and Texas).
4   6, Holdsworth, *A History of English Law*, 379-397: following the enforcement of oral promises, perjury appears to have become commonplace.
5   See chapter 11.

10.02 STATUTE OF FRAUDS (IRELAND) 1695

The enforcement of oral contracts led to a corresponding increase in the number of perjury actions and indeed subornation of perjury actions that caused concern for the legislature on two grounds. On the one hand, such actions were tending to block the processing of actions through the courts because cases were effectively tried and then retried on perjury. Moreover, considerable doubts arose concerning the risk of fraud on the courts, whereby the better liar would prevail over the poorer truth-teller. Nor should it be forgotten that recollection of events past is often unreliable, even where the parties are honest in their assertions.[6] Accordingly, in 1677, the Act for the Prevention of Fraud and Perjuries was enacted to require written evidence in certain contracts if they were to be enforceable.[7] This was enacted in this jurisdiction by virtue of the Statue of Frauds (Ireland) Act 1695. The need to have written evidence to enforce contracts has received different treatment in the United States and the United Kingdom. In the United Kingdom the Statute of Frauds has been repealed, except with regard to contracts for the sale of land and suretyship.[8] Much of the reason for this repeal has to do with the narrow interpretation given by the courts to the application of the Statute, though it has been argued that the Statute is not coherent any event, having been written over three hundred years ago.[9] On the other hand, in the US repeal is extremely unlikely, with the emphasis on its extension to other areas in many States[10] and the adoption of an expurgated version in the Uniform Commercial Code,[11] perhaps pointing the way forward for a modern version of events.[12]

---

6   Treitel, op. cit., p. 161 views the formality requirement differently. First, he believes it promotes certainty and simplification of the contractual agreement. Secondly, it has a protective effect in making people think before entering into contracts thereby protecting the weaker party; for the use of formalities as consideration, see Holmes, *The Common Law*, p. 273.

7   It should be remembered that the Statute was not, primarly, enacted to regulate formalities in contracts, but rather to the protection of property rights following the Civil War and the Cromwell era.

8   Law Reform (Enforcement of Contracts) Act 1954; see also the amendment made by the Law of Property (Miscellaneous Provisions) Act 1989, s. 2 which amends the rules with respect to contracts for the sale of land by requiring that they not merely be evidenced in writing, but made in writing: a rule that has been criticised as unduly harsh by Clark, op. cit., p. 97.

9   6 Holdsworth, *History of English Law*, p. 396; Williams, *The Statute of Frauds*, section IV, p 283; two English Law Reform Commission Reports also recommended abolition in 1937 and 1952, see *Law Reform Committee First Report*, Cmnd 8809.

10   Restatement, Second, Contracts, Statutory Note to chapter 5: in particular, writing is required for contracts to leave property by a will, pay the commission of a broker or ratification of a debt incurred during infancy.

11   S. 2-201; for an overstated criticism of the UCC provision, see Cunningham, 'A proposal to repeal section 2-201: the Statute of Frauds Section of Article 2', 85 *Com LJ* 361.

12   This is certainly the view of Calamari and Perillo, op. cit., p. 776; see Bently and Coughlan, 'Proprietary Estoppel and Part Performance' (1988) 23 Ir Jur 38.

The choice would therefore appear to be up or out: either bring the Statute up to speed to cover modern events, or repeal it. The English have adopted the virtual repeal of the Statute; the Americans are in the long process of reforming the Statute to make it relevant to modern needs, but they seem somewhat stuck in the issue. In this jurisdiction, we have made no effort to do either; the Statute not only remains in force *in toto*, but also is not the subject of reform initiatives as one might have hoped. As against that background, the existence of the Statute for such a long period of time has served to leave a trail of case law that has done much to ameliorate the rigours of the provisions, particularly through equity.[13] We turn our attention to discover the formal requirements for enforcement of certain contracts.

The Act requires that such contracts be evidenced in writing and signed by the party against which the contract is alleged to exist, or his lawfully authorised agent. It is to be assumed that the agent's authority should also be evidenced in writing.[14] The written document is referred to as a memorandum, and there is no requirement that it contain all the details of the contract nor need it take any particular form.[15] A memorandum can in fact take many forms, including cheques,[16] receipts,[17] and even a letter of repudiation which was made in sufficient detail that all the terms of the contract were in fact set out.[18] Moreover, more than one document may be used to constitute a complete memorandum.[19] This process is known as joinder of documents,[20] but great care must be exercised in its application. The documents must refer to each other, either expressly or impliedly; thus in *Kelly v. Ross & Ross*[21] the court refused to join a total of nine documents because the documents which were signed did not refer to the remaining documents and there was insufficient material on the signed items to constitute a valid memorandum of its own. Logically enough, in order to come within the scope of a valid memorandum, the document which

---

13 Chapter 26, post.
14 But see *Callaghan v. Pepper* (1840) 2 Ir Eq R 399 for a contrary view; *Heath v. Chilton* (1844) 12 M&W 632 (held that there was implied authority where a husband stood by and let his wife sign on his behalf); signature of an agent, in general, should clearly be identified as such; otherwise, the agent runs the risk of being held personally liable: *Lavan v. Walsh* [1964] IR 87 and in particular Budd J at p 96.
15 There is no requirement that the parties intended to create a memorandum, *Murphy v. Harrington* [1927] IR 339 but the intention must be to create an authentic document, *McQuaid v. Lynam* [1965] IR 564.
16 *Doherty v. Gallagher*, unreported, High Court 1975 note that in this case details of the sale were found on the foot of the cheque. The principle may not be applied in the absence of such details.
17 *McQuaid v. Lynam* [1965] IR 564.
18 *Tradax (Ireland) v. Irish Grain Board* [1984] IR 1.
19 *McQuaid v. Lynam* [1965] IR 564.
20 Fridman, 'Joinder of Documents to form a memorandum.' (1958) 22 Conv 275; *Barratt v. Costelloe* (1973) 107 ILTR 239.
21 Unreported, High Court, 29 April 1980.

carries the signature must have been signed after all the documents with which joinder is sought have been created. Otherwise, it would be an attempt to claim signature to that which was not in existence at the time of its creation. Thus in *McQuaid v. Lynam and Lynam*,[22] Kenny J stated that

> The many cases on the issue whether a number of documents read together can constitute such a memorandum or note in writing show a progressively liberal approach by the Courts to this question. I think that the modern cases establish that a number of documents may together constitute a note or memorandum in writing if they have come into existence in connection with the same transaction or if they contain internal references which connect them with each other. But as the memorandum or note considered as a whole must be signed, it would seem to follow that the document which is signed must be the last of the documents in point of time, for it would be absurd to hold that a person who signed the document could be regarded as having signed another document which was not in existence when he signed the first.[23]

The memorandum must contain the essential content of the contract before it will suffice.[24] The minimum requirement is that the memorandum should be capable of identifying the parties to the contract,[25] enabling the price to be ascertained;[26] and it should refer to the subject matter of the contract.[27] It may well be that the parties consider other items to be essential to the contract, in which case the memorandum will not be sufficient unless it contains these terms.[28] Whether a term is essential to the contract will depend on the court's interpretation in light of all the surrounding circumstances.

The memorandum must be signed by the person against whom the contract is charged. The crucial element is that the signature or mark is intended to be a proof of authenticity and not one of information only.[29] This dividing line is a difficult concept but is the primary reason for differing decisions. In *Casey v. Intercontinental Bank*[30] a letter typed by a solicitor's secretary on headed paper,

22 [1965] IR 564.
23 [1965] IR 564, 569.
24 It must also accurately reflect the agreement, *Crane v. Naughten* [1912] 2 IR 318.
25 *Law v. Roberts* [1964] IR 292; *Murphy v. Harrington* [1927] IR 339.
26 Either by express statement, *Law v. Roberts* [1964] IR 292 or some specific method of obtaining the price, *Smith v. Jones* [1952] 2 All ER 907.
27 *Waldron v. Jacob* (1870) IR 5 Eq 131 (extrinsic evidence was admitted to illustrate what the phrase 'this place' meant) *Viscount Massereene v. Finlay* (1850) 13 Ir LR 496.
28 The test to be adopted is subjective, *Barrett v. Costelloe* (1973) 107 ILTSJ 239; *Hoon v. Nolan* (1967) 101 ILTR 99; *Stinson v. Owens* (1973) 24 NILQ 218; each case turns on its own facts, precedent may be of little value.
29 *McQuaid v. Lynam* [1965] IR 564.
30 [1979] IR 340; see also *Huckelsby v. Hook* (1900) 82 LT 117; *Dyas v. Stafford* (1882) 9 LR Ir 520.

but which was not personally signed by the solicitor concerned, was held to be signed within the meaning of the Statute. By contrast in *Kelly*, initials placed by a solicitor for reference purposes on the side of a document were held not to be sufficient to constitute a signature, they being for information only. Moreover, a rubber stamp has been held to be a signature for the Statute.[31]

10.03 CONTRACTS COVERED BY THE STATUTE

The operative section of the Act, s. 2, was passed to require that certain documentary evidence of the contract exist before such contract is to be enforceable. It covered the following contracts:

(a) contracts to pay the debt of another;

(b) contracts where the consideration was to be marriage;

(c) contracts for the sale of land or an interest therein;

(d) contracts that will not be performed within one year;

Let us now turn to each of the specified contracts in turn.

(a) Contracts to pay the debts of another   The Statute covers contracts of guarantee only, and not contracts of indemnity. A contract of guarantee occurs where one of the parties to the contract agrees to pay the sum due under the contract if another party to the contract should default in his primary obligation to pay that sum.[32] Such contracts must conform to the Statute.

On the other hand, contracts of indemnity occur where a party to the contract may be sued for the entire sum in his own right and independent of any other party's obligations. In essence, whereas contracts of guarantee involve secondary liability, contracts of indemnity involve co-equal primary liability. Contracts of indemnity are not required to conform to the statute.

Another way of phrasing this solution is to look at it in terms of the promise to pay the debt of another being original or collateral.[33] This is sometimes restated as the 'main purpose' rule which states that 'where the party promising has for his object a benefit which he did not enjoy before his promise, which benefit accrues immediately to himself, his promise is original, whether made before or after or at the time of the promise of the third party, notwithstanding that the effect is to promise to pay or discharge the debt of another.'[34] Such

---

31 *Bennett v. Brumfitt* (1867) LT 3 CP 28.

32 *Bull v. Collier* (1842) 4 Ir LR 107; *Fennel v. Mulcahy* (1845) 8 Ir LR 434; *Dunville v. Quinn* (1908) 42 ILTR 49.

33 *Mountstephen v. Lakeman* (1871) LR 7 QB 196; but for a caution on the usefulness of such terms, see 3 Williston, s. 463.

34 *Nelson v. Boynton*, 44 Mass 396 (1841).

original contracts are enforceable despite the absence of writing.[35] All other collateral contracts require the existence of writing before being enforced.

(b) Contracts for which the consideration is marriage   This part of the Statute concerns contracts donating a gift to the intended couple. Before such gifts may be enforced they must satisfy the Statute. Marriage contracts themselves are no longer enforceable today, and there is considerable merit in repealing this part of the Statute.

(c) Contracts for the sale of land or an interest therein   This is by far the greatest application of the Statute that concerns lawyers. The topic deserves much more detailed examination than the scope of this text would allow; suffice it to say that all such contracts must be evidenced in writing and the only difficulty is the phrase 'or interest in land' (this is better dealt with in the more specialised works on land law).[36] However, a plaintiff may find that it is in his interest to have the contract classified as a sale of goods rather than a sale of an interest in land.[37] By so doing, a plaintiff may absolve from himself the burden of providing a written memorandum and instead seek to use the sale of goods provisions referred to in 10.03 post. Thus, in *Scully v. Carboy*[38] the court held that an agreement to let the meadowing of a field was in fact the sale of a good and not an interest in land. Accordingly, the plaintiffs acts of part payment and the defendant's acceptance of them obviated the need for a memorandum. Part-payment of the sale of an interest in land does not obviate the need for a memorandum.

(d) Contracts that will not be performed within one year   This only covers those contracts which are not intended, at the time the contract was entered into to, to be performed within one year.[39] Thus, if the parties intended the transaction to be completed within one year, but in fact it takes much longer, the Statute cannot be pleaded to render the contract unenforceable.[40] The purpose of this provision is to minimise cases arising where the reliability of oral evidence has gone stale in the mists of time. In *Naughten v. Limestone Land Co.*[41] an oral agreement,

---

35 *Barnett v. Hyndam* (1840) 3 Ir LR 109.
36 In particular see Wylie, *Irish Conveyancing Law*, op. cit.
37 *Guardian Builders v. Sleecon and Berville* unreported, High Court, 18 August 1988 (the purchase of shares in a company which owned property, did not come within the statute as requiring the existence of writing. This was despite the real intention of the purchaser being to purchase the land: purchasing the company was designed to reduce stamp duty and gain tax advantages when compared with a straight purchase of the land).
38 [1950] IR 140.
39 *Tierney v. Marshall* (1857) 7 ICLR 308 (not possible to perform the contract within one year, therefore required writing).
40 *Hynes v. Hynes* unreported, High Court, 21 December 1984; *Murphy v. O'Sullivan* (1866) 11 Ir Jur (New Series) 111.
41 [1952] Ir Jur Rep 19.

whereby the plaintiff went to England to study so that on his return he would be employed by the defendant for a period of four years, was held invalid, as no memorandum of such an agreement existed. The plaintiff, however, was seeking payment of wages for the period when he was studying in England, arguing that this element of the contract was both intended to and actually did so take place within one year and therefore did not require to be evidenced in writing. Dixon J refused to hold that the contract was severable into what was intended to be performed within one year and what was to be performed more than a year in advance. This is patently correct: it cannot be that a contract which is intended to last more than one year should be initially valid in the absence of writing, yet one year later would be no longer valid for the absence of writing. Thus, in *Farrington v. Donohue*[42] an oral agreement, made by the defendant to maintain a child until such time as it could maintain itself, was held to require a memorandum, notwithstanding the plaintiff's argument that the child could have died within one year of the creation of the contract. Thus the contingency nature of any oral agreement would not seem to remove the need for written evidence of the contract.[43]

One interesting point to remember about *Naughten's* case is that it might be open to a subsequent court to find that, on similar facts, there existed not one but two contracts; entering into one would constitute the consideration for the other. Thus, in that case the court might have found that the plaintiff and defendant had agreed that the plaintiff would go to England for training and as a result of that he would on his return enter into a second contract of employment for four years. The first contract would not come within the Statute and therefore not require writing; the second contract would. Such an interpretation would be useful in some situations in an effort to ameliorate the harshness of the earlier rule.

10.04 SALE OF GOODS ACT 1893, S. 4

This section requires that contracts for the sale of goods in excess of ten pounds should be in writing. This provision was repealed in England and in the United States the Uniform Commercial Code raised the figure to $500.[44] Either process would appear preferable to the stubborn remains of this provision in Irish law.

Clearly, this rather ancient rule would be a considerable hindrance to modern business unless there were certain exceptions—and there are. Such contracts will be enforced despite the absence of written evidence if it can be shown that

(i) the buyer accepts and receives part of the goods sold,[45] or

42 (1866) IR 1 CL 675.
43 See *Dublin Corp v. Blackrock Com-
    missioners* (1882) 16 ILTR 111 (the
    contract was terminable at will, there-

fore, no writing required).
44 S. 2-201.
45 *Tradax (Ireland) v. Irish Grain Board*
    [1984] IR 1 (the acceptance of 1,800

(ii) the buyer has given something in earnest to bind the bargain,[46] or

(iii) the buyer has made full or part payment.[47]

(i) Acceptance and receipt Acceptance and receipt means that the buyer has 'done any act in relation to the goods which recognises a pre-existing contract of sale whether there be an acceptance in performance of the contract or not'. Thus, it is clear that it is the buyer's intent and actions that are crucial and not those of the seller.

It would seem that acceptance of part of the goods is sufficient. Thus, in *Tradax (Ireland) v. Irish Grain Board* the purchaser accepted a mere 1,800 tonnes of a grain order which was for 12,000 tonnes. Yet this constituted sufficient acceptance to obviate the need for a memorandum. Moreover, acceptance must be by the party it is sought to enforce the contract against and not by a third party who has no authority to act on behalf of the defendant. In *Hopton v. McCarthy* the plaintiff and defendant were involved in discussions for the purchase of some materials. The defendant ordered the materials but cancelled the order when he discovered that the price of the items were in fact far greater than he had been led to believe during the negotiations. The seller proceeded to send the goods to the defendant by rail, and upon arrival they were stored by the rail carrier for collection by the defendant. This did not bind the defendant because neither he, nor anyone authorised by him, had accepted the items in question.

Likewise, where the goods are left at the buyer's premises without his consent, this is not sufficient acceptance, nor where he takes possession of the goods as custodian to preserve them from deterioration or destruction, though such actions may be open to evidentiary challenge by the seller.

(ii) Something given in earnest to bind the contract It is clear that the payment of a deposit, or other sum of money of course constitutes something given in earnest that binds the contract; but it is equally clear that such action constitutes payment in part or in full (discussed below). If this is to have any meaning, it must refer to something other than payment of all or part of the price. Forde ignores the issue entirely,[48] and Clark offers the giving of a business card as being an act that is sufficiently earnest to bind the parties to the contract.[49] In the US, the UCC abolished this exception to the need for writing, and it seems preferable that the legislature should adopt this course of action here.

---

tonnes of an order of 12,000 tonnes, was sufficient not to require writing); *Hopton v. McCarthy* (1882) 10 LR (Ir) 266 (delivery to carrier not sufficient).

46 2 Corbin, s. 494; 3 Williston, s. 564; *Kirwan v. Price* [1985] Ir Jur Rep 56 (an offer of payment does not amount to something given in earnest).

47 *Scully v. Carboy* [1950] IR 140.

48 Forde, *Commercial Law in Ireland*, op. cit., p. 17: he assumes that it is the same as part payment. This is discussed below.

49 Clark, *Contract Law in Ireland*, op. cit., p. 220.

(iii) Full or part payment   It is not sufficient that the payment is merely tendered; it must be accepted by the other party. Thus, in *Kirwan v. Price*[50] an offer of payment made by the purchaser on completion of the agreement for the sale of a horse was refused by the seller. It was held that the seller's acceptance of same was vital if the need for a written memorandum was to be avoided. Likewise a cheque sent in the post which is returned uncashed cannot constitute full or part payment, but a cheque which has been cashed obviously can.

There is no authority in this jurisdiction as to the effect of part payment which has been accepted, particularly where the goods can be severed to the extent that the part payment can be said to cover a specified quantum of the goods involved. It would seem that the concept of giving something in earnest would be satisfied by the giving of part payment and that such part payment would cover all the goods it was contracted for.[51] However, if the 'in earnest' provision is to be removed as suggested earlier, it would leave open the possibility that part payment might be treated, as in the US, as covering only that portion of the goods contracted for which would be paid in full by the part payment unless the goods were unseverable.[52] Thus, a contract for 200 television sets at £100 each and where the seller has accepted £1,000 as part payment would operate to bind the parties only to the extent of ten televisions, in the absence of a written memorandum. A contract to purchase a horse for £10,000 where the seller has accepted part payment of £1,000 would operate to bind the parties to the sale of the horse (it not being possible to say that the money refers to the horse's head or legs and can be severed), despite the absence of a written memorandum. This approach is incorrect; part payment should operate to the same extent as full payment, even if the legislature were to abolish the 'in earnest' category under the statute.

10.05 HIRE PURCHASE ACTS 1946-1980

Under s. 3 of the 1946 Act, a contract for the hire purchase of a good must be in writing signed by all the parties to the agreement if it is to be enforceable. This requirement is absolute, as decided in the case of *Mercantile Credit Company of Ireland v. Cahill*.[53] The Act goes on, however, to stipulate the contents of such memorandum of agreement;[54] however, the absence of these is not automatically fatal but lies within the court's discretionary power.[55] The

---

50   [1958] Ir Jur 56.
51   Restatement, Contracts, s. 205; *Scott v. Mundy and Scott*, 23 ALR 460 (1922) part payment and 'in earnest' are the same; but see 2, Corbin, s. 494, 3 Williston, s. 564 which contests this view since something in earnest does not go to the price.
52   UCC 2-201(3)(c).

53   98 ILTR 79.
54   S. 3(2) cash price of goods, hire purchase price, amount of instalments, time when payable, description of goods and a statement of the hirer's rights regarding termination and recovery.
55   *UDT v. Nestor* [1962] IR 140.

court may hold the agreement enforceable notwithstanding the omission of certain items if it believes that no one has been prejudiced by this omission and that it is just and equitable to do so, though the court may impose such restrictions as it sees fit.[56]

10.06 FAMILY HOME PROTECTION ACT 1976

According to this Act a contract for the conveyance of any interest in the family home[57] by one spouse will be valid only if the other spouse's consent in writing is obtained prior to the contract being concluded.[58] However, in *Nestor v. Murphy*,[59] both partners to the marriage signed the contract for sale and sought to put it aside on the basis that the prior consent of each spouse had not been obtained and that this rendered the agreement invalid. Henchy J rejected the assumption that the Act applied where both spouses joined in the contract for sale. The purpose of the Act was to prevent the sale of the family home by one spouse without the knowledge of the other spouse. Where both spouses had knowledge of the transaction, it would not require compliance with the Act. Presumably such knowledge would have to be in writing, as was the situation in the case at bar.

A failure to comply with the provisions of this Act renders the transaction void *ab initio*, thus strengthening the protection granted the spouse. There are exceptions to the provisions, contained in s. 3(3). Simply put, the exceptions exclude situations where the sale occurs by one other than the spouse (for example, a mortgage holder enforcing his security), a sale to a *bona fide* purchaser for value and without notice (for example, where reasonable enquiries could not have been reasonably expected to discover the existence of a spouse) and finally where certain provisions of the Act specify that it shall not apply (for example, where the agreement for sale was made before the marriage of the spouses).[60]

10.07 BODIES CORPORATE

As a general rule a body corporate cannot enter into a binding contract unless it does so under seal, though this rule has never been absolute. Moreover, s. 38 of the Companies Act 196 states as follows:

(1) Contracts on behalf of a company may be made as follows:

56 *Henry Ford and Son Finance v. Forde* unreported, High Court, 13 June 1986.

57 S. 2 (dwelling in which the protected spouse ordinarily resides or used to reside before so leaving).

58 S. 3(2) and 3(3).

59 [1979] IR 326.

60 See Generally, Shatter, *Family Law in Ireland*, p. 317 et seq.

(a) a contract which if made between private persons would be by law required to be in writing and to be under seal, may be made on behalf of the company in writing under the common seal of the company;

(b) a contract which if made between private persons would be by law required to be in writing, signed by the parties to be charged therewith, may be made on behalf of the company in writing signed by any person under its authority, express or implied.

(c) a contract which if made between private persons would by law be valid although made by parol only, and not reduced into writing may be made by parol on behalf of the company by any person acting under its authority, express or implied.

It is clear, therefore, that the Act attempts to treat dealing by companies registered under the Act as equivalent to dealings by private individuals. This section should, however, be read in connection with the concept by which individuals have the power to bind a company and depending on the extent an individual dealing with a company may regard certain of the company's officers as having the power to bind the company at least to the extent that it will protect third-party interests. For a fuller discussion of this topic one should look at specialised company law works such as Keane, *Company Law in the Republic of Ireland* and Ussher, *Company Law*.

10.08 CONCLUDING ISSUES

Contracts which require to be evidenced in writing will be unenforceable at common law for lack of such documentary evidence. There has, however, developed a substantial body of law whereby in certain circumstances such contracts may be enforceable, despite the lack of written evidence, notably through the concepts of equity. It is also true to say that the scope of such litigation has continued to burgeon and revolves around rather subtle and technical niceties that have served to prolong litigation. These principles are looked at later, as part of the chapter on Remedies, where it is felt they are more appropriately dealt with.[61] Yet it is important to realise at this stage that much energy is expended in avoiding these provisions, which have led some to posit that all writing requirements should be abolished. There is indeed merit in such a proposal, though less controversially a modern reform of the Statute might be acceptable. In any event, a change requires legislative activity and is not open to the courts themselves.

61   See chapter 26.

11.00

Express terms

11.01 INTRODUCTION

The 'express terms' of a contract are those terms found from either the written agreement (if any) or the oral communications which passed between the parties, or both.[1] In the absence of any written agreement, the terms of the contract are to be found exclusively in the oral communications between the parties. The common law does not require any formality in the creation of contracts save in a few statutory provisions,[2] and an oral contract is as effective as a written one. Most contracts are in fact a mix of both written and oral terms. Neither takes precedence over the other.[3] However, it is obvious that proving oral terms of a contract may pose some difficulty if the other party now disputes that such words were said, but, on the whole, basing an action on an oral agreement is not fatal in this jurisdiction. It is the role of the courts in the adversarial system to decide who is telling the truth and who is not. This will also be true where there is a conflict in evidence between written and oral terms of the contract, of which more will be said later.[4]

However, there are a number of points that we should make before analysing the express terms of the contract in detail. Firstly, we are concerned here only with terms that have become part of the contract. Many negotiations concern themselves with statements that are designed to induce the parties to enter into the contract but which will not subsequently form part of the contract; for example, a claim that 'this is the finest car I have ever driven' made by the seller.

---

1   Joinder of documents (that is, using two or more documents as a single document) is possible by express reference: *Adamastos Shipping v. Anglo Saxon Petroleum* [1959] AC 133 (the joinder occurred in the written contract by express reference to another Act which was to take effect as part of the terms of the contract, despite the fact that the Act and the express terms of the contract conflicted), there is no reason why an oral joinder of a written document cannot occur; *LAC Minerals v. Chevron Corp.*, unreported, High Court, 6 August 1993; See chapter 10; *Governors of National Maternity Hospital v. McGouran*, unreported, High Court, 3 November 1993 (the court had to discover the intention of the parties to see whether they created a lease or a licence).
2   See chapter 10.
3   However, contracts made orally are to be determined as a question of fact from a jury, *Smith v. Hughes* (1871) LR 6 QB 597 whereas the interpretation of a contract is the task of the judge as a matter of law, *Bentson v. Taylor & Sons (No. 2)* [1893] 2 QB 274. This distinction is of less significance since the abolition of juries in most civil cases.
4   Sometimes referred to as the parol evidence rule, see 11.03 ibid.

They are known as 'representations' and, if they are false, or untrue, as 'misrepresentations'. They are not part of the contract, and breach of such a representation or misrepresentation will not automatically constitute an actionable claim, though it may in certain cases. For a fuller discussion see chapter 17 on Misrepresentation. Secondly, as well as identifying the express terms of the contract, it falls to the courts to interpret such terms; that interpretation may be far removed from that which the parties intended at the time of the agreement,[5] so, even if a term is found to be part of the contract, the effect of such a finding may bring a surprise to either or both litigants.[6] Finally, not all terms of the contract will be treated equally; therefore each term must be classified according to the consequences a breach of that term will have. This is discussed fully below.[7]

One final word of caution: the term 'written agreement' does not necessarily imply a signed agreement. There is no requirement for any formality to exist with the writing: a hastily scribbled note on the back of a cigarette packet, unsigned, is valid, though, of course, its probative value in such a situation may be closer to that of an oral communication.

11.02 A TERM OF THE CONTRACT

How is it determined that a particular element of the negotiations will constitute a term which forms part of the contract? It is true to say that the need to determine whether a statement forms part of the contract or not has been marginalised, primarily as a result in the increase in remedies available for misrepresentations (statements that do not form part of the contract but which induced the party into making the contract). However, it is still necessary to distinguish whether the term is part of the contract or not, for, if it is, breach of that term is actionable at common law as of right, whereas an action for misrepresentation is at the court's discretion.

A number of factors will influence whether or not a statement is a term of the contract. Firstly, when was the statement made? We have already seen that a statement or promise made after completion of the contract cannot be enforceable unless it contains fresh consideration,[8] but what of statements made prior to the conclusion of the contract? In *Schawel v. Reade*[9] the seller represented to the plaintiff, some four weeks prior to the completion of the contract, that the horse was perfectly sound for stud purposes, yet this was held by the court to

---

5   *Thake v. Maurice* [1986] 1 All ER 497 (a statement by a medical doctor that a vasectomy would make the plaintiff sterile could not be intended literally, since certainty in medical treatment is unattainable).

6   It is also their role to interpret the meaning of such agreements: *Baha-*

mas International Trust v. Threadgold [1974] 3 All ER 881 (a concession by one party as to the meaning of a particular contract term is not binding on court).

7   See chapter 13.

8   *Roscorla v. Thomas* (1842) 3 QB 234.

9   [1913] 2 IR 81.

form part of the contract. In *Routledge v. McKay*,[10] however, a similar delay of over four weeks resulted in the court's holding that a statement as to the age of a motorbike was not part of the contract. The difference in approach is only explicable on the basis that in *Shawel* the defendant appeared somewhat less than honest, whereas the defendant's error in *Routledge* was an honest mistake (arising from the registration book in his possession). However, other explanations are of course possible, as we shall see. Secondly, if the oral agreement is reduced to writing, did the parties intend that the written document should contain all the terms of the contract to the exclusion of any oral terms? In *Birch v. Paramount Estates*[11] a statement by the defendant that the house to be built would be as good as the show house was not contained within the subsequent written document, yet the court held that the written document did not exclude the oral statement of the defendant. And this leads us on to a third possibility, namely, the difference in skill or knowledge between the two parties to the contract. This is a politically correct method of justifying what, in essence, is an equitable ruling given the justice of any particular case.[12] It has been argued that the decision in *Schawel* is based on the skill of the seller, who was in a position to know of the true health of the horse, whereas *Routledge* is explicable on the basis that the seller relied only on the details of the vehicle's registration, which he would have no reason to doubt. This would also explain the difference between *Oscar Chess v. Williams*[13] and *Dick Bentley Productions v. Harold Smith Motors*.[14] In the former, the action of the plaintiffs (a car dealer) failed against the defendant (an ordinary person) where the age of the vehicle was stated inaccurately by the defendant, in reliance of the registration details, which had, unknown to the defendant, been altered. In the latter case the plaintiff (an ordinary person) succeeded against the defendant (a car dealer) for a statement made by the defendant with respect to the mileage of the vehicle in question, the statement being held to be a term of the contract. Denning LJ was present for both decisions and explained them on the basis of negligence, yet it is difficult to see that this is so in the area of contract.[15] Moreover, such a

---

10 [1954] 1 All ER 855.
11 Cited in *Oscar Chess v. Williams* [1957] 1 All ER at 329 [1956) 16 *Estates Gazette* 396)].
12 *Bannerman v. White* (1861) 10 CBNS 844 (an inquiry by the purchaser as to the use of sulphur in a product made by the seller, accompanied with a statement that if it had been, the purchaser would go no further, was held to constitute part of a complete transaction. The promise that sulphur had not been used could not be severed from the contract).

13 [1957] 1 All ER 325.
14 [1965] 2 All ER 65.
15 But for a reiteration, see *Hummingbird Motors v. Hobbs* [1986] RTR 276 (an odometer reading of 34,000 miles was not accurate—the vehicle had in fact covered 80,000 miles. This was not known to seller at time. *Held* that it was not reasonable for the purchaser to believe that the odometer constituted a promise from the seller. The seller was a private citizen; the buyer a car dealer).

distinction is now no longer justifiable on the basis of the principle of *Hedley Byrne v. Heller*,[16] which concerns liability for negligent mis-statement and which would seem to cover such situations.

One further possibility used by the courts has been the concept of the collateral contract, that is to say, the statement complained of does not form part of the contract itself but constitutes a separate contract, or a collateral one, which comes into effect by consideration of entering into the main contract.[17] Thus, for example, in *Bentley's* case it could be construed that the defendant contracted with the plaintiff that, if he purchased the vehicle, the defendant vouched that the vehicle had done only so many miles. Thus, the statement as to mileage is actionable as a contract of its own made in consideration of entering into another contract.

The law is somewhat unsatisfactory in this area. Further, it is illogical and inconsistent. Denning's approach as to the skill or negligence of the litigants is highly undesirable.[18] The collateral contract theory, while effective, has several drawbacks, not least of which would be a profusion of contracts arising out of what is in reality a single contract. For example, there might be hundreds of collateral contracts involved in the sale of any item, but the existence of these collateral contracts is only necessary because the court has, in the first instance, failed to hold certain statements as terms of the main contract.[19] Why invent collateral contracts when the court could just give true effect to a larger contract? Collateral contracts should be confined to those cases like that of *City and Westminster Properties v. Mudd*,[20] where the defendant signed a lease restricting the user of the premises involved to showrooms only, whereas he had in fact been sleeping in a part of the property. He signed the written lease on the basis of an oral promise that the written condition would not be enforced. The plaintiff now resiled from the oral promise that the written condition would not be enforced. The court found that he was in breach of his written obligations under the lease but was saved by the collateral oral contract that the particular covenant would not be enforced. The oral contract had been instrumental in getting the defendant to enter into the main contract.

Whether a statement forms part of the terms of a contract is a question of fact based on the totality of the evidence, including any written evidence, and varying from case to case.[21] Cynics would no doubt add, with some justification,

16   [1963] 2 All ER 575.
17   *Shanklin Pier v. Detel Products* [1951] 2 All ER 471 [1958] 2 All ER 733.
18   See *Harling v. Eddy* [1951] 2 All ER 212 for further support of the argument that the skill of the parties is a contributory factor.
19   In *Evans v. Andrea Merzario* [1976] 2 All ER 930 Denning felt compelled to use the collateral contract. By con-

trast, from the same facts, his fellow judges established a single contract, partly written and partly oral.
20   [1958] 2 All ER 733.
21   *Bank of Ireland v. Smith* [1966] IR 161 (there is a tendency of courts to hold that the representation which induces the sale is a warranty, unless it can be proved that the representation is made innocently and in ignorance of the error, *per* Kenny J).

that the consequences of finding it to be a term of the contract play an immense part in the *ex post facto* reasoning of the courts.

11.03 CONFLICT BETWEEN WRITTEN AND ORAL TERMS OF A CONTRACT

Since it has been stated that a contract can consist of both written and oral terms, it is quite possible that such terms will be in conflict with one another. The traditional rule, known as the 'parol evidence rule', has been that, where there is written evidence of the terms of a contract, it is not possible to adduce oral evidence to contradict, add to or vary the written agreement.[22] In other words the contract is bordered by the four walls of the written document. The reason for such a rule is obvious: to allow otherwise would be to leave written communications open to perpetual challenge. However, this archaic rule has been virtually abolished by various judicial pronouncements since its practical impact was to work considerable injustice.

Firstly, the written agreement might not contain the full scope of the contract, and therefore oral evidence would have to be admitted to elaborate on the contract. Thus, in *Walker Property Investments v. Walker*[23] the parties omitted from the written agreement an earlier oral agreement whereby the plaintiff was to have the use of some storage rooms if he agreed to lease the flat in question; the court admitted the oral evidence and found in favour of the plaintiff.

Secondly, a written term may need to be understood or interpreted in the light of oral terms and agreements or indeed that of custom and practice. For example, in *SS Ardennes v. Ardennes*,[24] a bill of lading permitting the ship operator to travel by any route, directly or indirectly, was held to be contradicted by an oral promise from the defendants that the ship would in fact travel directly to London. And in *Moroney v. Revenue Commissioners*[25] oral evidence was admissible to show that the transaction which appeared from the written agreement to be a sale was in fact a gift from father to children. And, as Parke B stated in *Hutton v. Warren*,[26]

---

22 *Jacobs v. Batavia & General Plantations Trust* [1924] 1 Ch 287; *Hawrish v. Bank of Montreal* (1969) 2 DLR (3d) 600.

23 (1947) 177 LT 204; *Howden v. Ulster Bank* [1924] IR 117 (parol evidence admitted, since the contract was made up of both written and oral terms); *Clayton Love v. B+I* (1970) 104 ILTR 157 (a telephone conversation was held admissible to enlarge written contract).

24 [1950] 2 All ER 517.

25 [1972] IR 372; *Ulster Bank v. Synnott* (1871) 5 IR Eq 595 (oral evidence was admitted to give meaning to a written phrase); *Chambers v. Kelly* (1873) 7 IRCL 231 (the meaning of a phrase, 'all other trees', could be limited by oral evidence showing that only larch trees were meant).

26 (1836) 1 M&W 466.

It has long been settled, that, in commercial transactions, extrinsic evidence of custom and usage is admissible to annex incidents to written contracts, in matters with respect to which they are silent. The same rule has also been applied to contracts in other transactions of life, in which known usages have been established and prevailed.[27]

Thirdly, oral evidence could be adduced to show that no contract had in fact come into existence—for example, where the implementation of such a contract was to be suspended for some reason or was not in reality to occur in the manner so described. Thus, in *Pym v. Campbell*[28] oral evidence was admitted to show that a written agreement was not to have effect until an engineer had given his approval to the subject matter of the contract. And as we have seen in *City and Westminster Properties v. Mudd*[29] it was held that a collateral oral contract not to enforce the written terms of a lease was valid.

Finally, where the written evidence contains a mistake, a remedy through equity may be available under the principle of rectification; that is, the document may be rectified so as more truly to represent the agreement of the parties in question.[30]

The cumulative affect of these judgments is to remove, in a practical sense, the parol evidence rule. A better rule would be that written evidence of the terms of a contract is presumptive evidence only, and the presumption can be rebutted by oral or other evidence.

11.04 INTERPRETATION OF THE EXPRESS TERMS OF THE CONTRACT

Assuming that a statement has become a term of the contract as outlined above, then it falls to the courts to give meaning to such terms. This has led some to differentiate between interpretation and construction of the terms of the contract. Interpretation relates to the meaning of the words used, whereas construction concerns the legal effect of such words; and it is not always necessary that the two should coincide.[31] While this is a useful dichotomy, it has neither sufficient general usage by the courts nor analytical merit to warrant further investigation. The real crux of the issue of interpretation or construction

---

27   Ibid, 475; *Wilson Strain v. Pinkerton* (1897) 3 ILTR 86 (the court admitted evidence of a custom that it was the practice that the employer took over the debts of a bread delivery man); *Page v. Myer* (1861) 6 Ir Jur Rep (NS) 27 (evidence of custom was admitted where the contract was silent on the relevant issue).
28   (1856) 6 E&B 370; see chapter 6 ibid.
29   Op. cit.
30   See chapter 26 ibid.
31   Restatement, Second, Contracts, s. 200; 3 Corbin s. 534; *Fashion Fabrics of Iowa v. Retail Investors*, 266 NW 2d 22.

revolves principally around two distinct schools of thought: objective[32] and subjective.[33] In the former, a meaning should be ascribed to the terms of a contract totally independent of the intention of the parties involved, while the latter would see that words are coloured by the people who say them and argue that the courts should seek the intention of the parties in question.[34] In the United States, Corbin and the Restatement, Second adopt the subjective intention of the parties,[35] while it has been Williston who has espoused the objective approach. In this jurisdiction the first step is to give the words of a contract their ordinary meaning as understood by a reasonable third party; that is, the objective test should apply.[36] This may result in a finding that was far from the intention of the parties, but it has the advantage that it avoids an artificial attempt to divine the mental intention of the parties at some distant point in history.

It is, of course, not true to say that the objective test is operated entirely in the abstract, for it is permissible to admit extrinsic evidence where the terminology is ambiguous[37] or technical[38] or requires to be read in light of a particular custom or practice.[39]

11.05 RELATIVE WEIGHTING TO CONTRACTUAL TERMS

Not all contractual terms can be considered of equal importance. This is not to say that there is no legal sanction for the breach of certain terms of the contract; quite the contrary. A breach of a term of the contract entitles the injured party to some remedy, but the nature of the remedy is defined by the importance of the term breached. The ordinary remedy for any breach of contract is in the

32 See 4 Williston, s. 605.
33 3 Corbin s. 542.
34 *Towne v. Eisner*, 245 US 418 (1918) ('A word is not a crystal, transparent and unchanged; it is the skin of a living thought and may vary greatly in colour and content according to the circumstances.' per Holmes J, at 425); even to the extent where a party can claim that 'buy' means 'sell'!, see Corbin, 'The Interpretation of Words and the Parol Evidence Rule.' 50 *Cornell LQ* 161.
35 See in particular Restatement, Second, Contracts, s. 201(1) (where the parties have attached the same meaning to a promise or agreement or a term thereof, it is interpreted in accordance with that meaning).
36 *Eyre v. Measday* [1986] 1 All ER 488; in *In re Wogans (Drogheda) (No. 3)* [1992] 3 IR the subsequent conduct of the parties to the contract was not admissible as to the interpretation of the contractual terms. It has been argued that this tends to support the objective test of interpretation.
37 *Raffles v. Wichelhaus* (1864) 2 H&C 906, 159 ER 375 (once it was shown that there were two ships of the same name (Peerless), then the defendant could adduce evidence to show which ship was intended); McBaine, 'The rule against disturbing plain meanings of writings.' 31 *Cal Law Review* 145.
38 *Schuler (L) AG v. Wickman Machine Tool Sales* [1974] AC 235 (the use of technical distinctions in this area is no longer highly relevant).
39 See ibid.

nature of a monetary compensation payment termed in law as 'damages'. Damages are designed in contract so as to place the injured party in the same position as if the contract had been fully carried out according to its original terms. However, certain terms will be considered to be so important that a breach of same might enable the injured party not merely to claim damages but to treat the contract as repudiated. Traditionally, lawyers felt that all contractual terms could be classified as conditions or warranties. Breach of a condition enabled the injured party to treat the contract as repudiated, whereas breach of a warranty entitled the injured party to damages, but not to treat the contract as repudiated. Modern jurisprudence now holds that these terms are not exhaustive, and the categorisation is a matter of case by case analysis. Since, however, such classifications apply equally to express and implied terms, we shall discuss the concept of the implied term in contract before analysing the relative weighting of such terms in detail.[40]

11.06 BATTLE OF STANDARD FORM CONTRACTS

Increasingly, contracts are formed on the basis of an exchange of negotiations between two or more firms, each of which is adamant that the contract is concluded on their terms and conditions. In many instances these terms and conditions are to be found printed on the reverse side of the relevant communications. The question then arises as to what terms constitute the express terms of the contract.[41] This is often referred to as the 'battle of the forms'. In some ways it is a question of offer and acceptance, for, whatever communication constitutes the offer, there is still the question of whether it has been validly accepted without variation. Since an acceptance operates on the basis of its own terms and conditions, and therefore does not 'mirror' the offer, it is more likely that no contract will have come into existence.[42]

An example will help to evaluate this. Let us suppose that X Ltd has written a letter to Y Ltd asking if they will sell a product at £5 per tonne, the letter being written on paper that clearly states that any contract is to be formed on the basis of X's usual terms and conditions printed overleaf (Letter 1). Y Ltd writes back saying the goods will be sold at £5 per tonne on Y's usual terms and conditions, again printed overleaf (Letter 2). X Ltd replies by enclosing details of where the product should be delivered to, again referring to their usual terms and conditions (Letter 3).

The first difficulty is to determine if Letter 1 or Letter 2 is the offer. If Letter 1 is the offer, then the only possible acceptance can be Letter 2. Let us assume that Letter 1 is the offer. Can Letter 2 validly accept it? It is not a mirror image

---

40   See chapter 13.
41   *Butler Machine Tool v. Ex-Cell-Corp* [1979] 1 WLR 401.
42   See chapter on Acceptance for a detailed discussion of this issue.

of the offer unless, in the highly unlikely event that Y Ltd is using the same printed terms and conditions. Failing this, there are really two possibilities: firstly, the court can construe the contractual terms as a synthesis of the two forms; secondly, it can declare a winner to the battle and opt for one of the party's terms and conditions only. The synthesis approach appears to have no judicial support in any common law country, for it would involve writing contracts for the litigants.[43] The declaration of a victor in the battle has a number of drawbacks.[44] It involves a decision as to which document constitutes the offer and which the acceptance. In the above example, this will mean that the contract will be performed on X Ltd's terms if Letter 1 is the offer and Y Ltd's terms if Letter 2 is the offer. In the absence of any UCC equivalent, which would relax the mirror image acceptance rule,[45] if the response to the offer is too overt as to the terms and conditions that the contract is accepted on, this will be more likely to render the contract non-existent.[46] Moreover, the use of standard form contracts where the parties are not equally met raises some difficulties for consumers when dealing with monopoly suppliers, though the courts have been alive to this.[47]

It would be preferable to adopt the UCC approach, but in its absence it might be necessary to use to the synthesis approach. This is preferable to denying the existence of the contract.

---

43 Though see Anson, op. cit., p 33.
44 It is however the accepted method used by English Courts, see *Butler Machine Tool v. Ex-Cel-O Corp*, ibid.
45 UCC s. 2-207, see chapter on Acceptance, ibid.
46 See *British Road Services v. Crutchley & Co.* [1968] 1 All ER 811; *Mack and Edwards v. McPhail Bros.* (1968) 112 Sol Jo 211 (Australia); *British Steel Corp. v. Cleveland* [1984] 1 All ER 504.
47 See *McCord v. ESB* [1980] ILRM 153 (so called 'contracts of adhesion', such as the supply of electricity, which are made on a take it or leave it basis, will be scrutinised quite intensely); *Farrelly v. ESB* (the disconnection of electricity, without giving the customer a reasonable opportunity to prove that the bill had been paid, led to award of damages).

12.00

Implied terms

12.01 INTRODUCTION

There are, of course, some terms of the contract which will not be either expressly written or stated but which, for one reason or another, will form part of the contract in any event.[1] Such terms are known as 'implied terms', but, beyond that loose connection by way of nomenclature, these implied terms have little in common between themselves.[2] In some situations implied terms are imposed by external sources;[3] in others they are implied as the unspoken intention of, variously, the parties, third parties or practice and tradition.[4] Finally, the courts may impose such implied terms in order to give efficacy to the contract, though such action is relatively controversial.[5] Whether the term is express or implied will not affect the consequence that flows from it, or the way it is interpreted.[6]

1   *Roxborough v. Crosby* [1918] VLR 118 ('where parties have entered into a written contract, and particularly a carefully drawn formal written contract, expressions admitting ground for an implication may be met by a counter presumption that the parties must be taken to have provided for everything which they thought necessary', *per* Cussen J at 130).
2   The classification of implied terms is of dubious merit, but it cannot be avoided in an analytical text, see *Liverpool City Council v. Irwin* [1977] AC 239 (per Wilberforce LJ 'shades of a continuous spectrum'), *Shell v. Tostock Garage* [1976] 1 WLR 1187.
3   See for example statutory implied terms under the Sale of Goods and Supply of Services Act 1980, chapter 15 ibid.
4   *The Moorcock* (1889) 14 PD 64; *Helicopter Sales Australia v. Rotor-Work Property* (1974) 132 CLR (terms are not 'implied into contracts merely so as to give effect to some policy thought likely to promote the attainment of desirable social ends. Terms are implied so as to better give effect to the bargain arrived at between the parties, the carrying out of their presumed intention', *per* Stephen J at 13); *Ward v. Spirack* (1945) Ir Jur Rep 59; but cf. *Hamlyn v. Wood* [1891] 2 QB 488 ('a court has no right to imply in a written contract any such stipulation, unless on contracting the terms of the contract in reasonable and business manner, an implication necessarily arises that the parties must have intended that the suggested stipulation should exist', *per* Esher MR at 491).
5   But cf. *O'Toole v. Palmer* (1945) Ir Jur Rep 59; *Aga Khan v. Firestone and Firestone* [1992] ILRM 31, discussed later.
6   But no term will be implied if it conflicts with an express term of the contract (*Les Affreteurs Reunis v. Leopold Walford (London)* [1959] AC 801) or the tenor of the contract (*Gonnell Power Farming v. Nies* (1935) 35 SR (NSW) 'If the express term appears to be intended to cover the field that would otherwise be occupied by the implied term, the implied term is excluded', at 477).

We turn our attention now to discuss in detail the situations when terms will be implied into a contract.

12.02 CUSTOM AND PRACTICE

Business or other contractual transactions do not occur in a vacuum. There is a world outside through which people have come to expect certain things as being a given factor in their dealings. These are classified as 'custom and practice', and they will, of course, vary from transaction to transaction. Normally they will be so well accepted that very often they will not form part of the express terms of the contract simply because no one would have thought it necessary to state them expressly. Thus, in *O'Connail v. Gaelic Echo*[7] a custom that involved the payment of holiday pay to journalists was upheld, despite its express absence from the contract. Moreover, in *Hutton v. Warren*[8] evidence of local custom was admitted to show what an agricultural tenant was entitled to on quitting the land and, as Parke B stated,

> The common law, indeed, does so little to prescribe the relative duties of landlord and tenant, since it leaves the latter at liberty to pursue any course of management he pleases, provided he is not guilty of waste, that it is by no means surprising that the courts should have been favourably inclined to the introduction of those regulations in the mode of cultivation which custom and usage have established in each district to be the most beneficial to all parties.[9]

It is clear from this that custom and practice can vary not only from transaction type to transaction type but also from area to area, so that what might be acceptable in one area would not form part of the local custom in another. This results in the danger of a certain amount of regionalisation of the law and should be treated with some caution.

Indeed, the whole import of custom and practice has limits in implying a term into a contract. Firstly, the onus of proof on the party claiming the benefit of the custom is quite high to prove not merely its existence[10] but its notoriety.[11] In other words, the law will not impose obscure customs on the parties but only those that it is sufficiently satisfied are well enough known to the general public as to warrant such implication.[12] Secondly, even if such a custom and practice

---

7   (1958) 92 ILTR 156.
8   (1836) 1 M&W 466.
9   Ibid, 476.
10 This can be quite a difficult onus to discharge, *Taylor v. Hall* (1869) IR 5 CL 477; *O'Reilly v. Irish Press* (1937) ILTR 194.

11 *O'Reilly v. Irish Press* (1937) ILTR 194; *Majeau Carrying Co. v. Coastal Rutile* (1973) 129 CLR 4.
12 *Halsbury's Laws of England*, Vol. 11, para. 361, p. 797; even so the custom must be reasonable, *Produce Brokers v. Olympia Oil and Cake Co.* [1917]

can be established, this will not automatically mean that the custom will in fact be implied into the contract. It must be shown that the custom does not contradict an express term of the contract. If an express term of the contract is inconsistent with the custom or practice, it must be assumed that the parties have chosen to depart from such custom or practice. Thus, in *Les Affretuers Reunis Societié Anonyme v. Walford*[13] the defendants attempted to resist a claim by the plaintiff seeking payment of commission on the signing of the charterparty as expressly stated in the contract. The defendants sought to use a custom whereby payment of commission arose only after hire had been earned, it not having been earned in this case since the French government had requisitioned the boat. Rejecting the argument of the defence, Lord Birkenhead on appeal took the opportunity to point out that the parties had entered into the agreement in full knowledge of the custom and, accordingly, in full knowledge that the express terms of the contract were in direct conflict with that custom. The only logical conclusion is that the parties intended to displace the custom and practice. Finally, it may also have to be shown that the custom acts in a positive sense in fulfilling the contract. This means that a term of custom and practice will not be implied into a contract unless it is required to give a completeness or efficacy to the contract which does not exist in its absence.[14]

Before too critical a view is taken of the role of custom in implying terms into a contract, it should be remembered that, in many instances, the existence of a custom or practice is so widespread and notorious that, ultimately, it is not merely the courts that give recognition to such custom and practice, but subsequently the legislature will adopt statutory provisions of general application. There are many instances from the commercial world where business people's custom and practice has resulted in major pieces of legislative activity which merely served to formalise the existing position.[15]

12.03 TERMS IMPLIED BY THE COURT

There has been a long history of courts implying terms into a contract and justifying such inclusion on different grounds. In some cases the courts will say

1 KB 320; a question arises with respect to the knowledge of persons new to the business: *Strathlorne Steamship Co. v. Hugh Baird and Sons* [1916] SC HL 134 (does not have to be the knowledge of the person themselves, presupposes knowledge of the business environment. The test is objective, not subjective).

13   [1919] AC 801.
14   *London Export Co v. Jubilee Coffee Roasting Co.* [1958] 2 All ER 411 ('an alleged custom can be incorporated into a contract only if there is nothing in the express or necessarily implied terms of the contract to prevent such inclusion and, further that a custom will only be imported into a contract where it can be so imported consistently with the tenor of the document as a whole', *per* Jenkins LJ at 420).
15   Bills of Exchange Act 1898; Sale of Goods Act 1893.

they do this to give effect to the unexpressed intention of the parties; in other cases it will be to give so-called 'business efficacy' to the contract. Both of these principles, while probably having little to differentiate them, have gained widespread acceptance from the courts. In *The Moorcock*,[16] the plaintiff's ship was being unloaded at the jetty of the defendant when the tide ebbed and the plaintiff's ship hit a ridge of hard rock under the river mud, damaging the vessel. The plaintiff's action was met with the defence that the contract contained no guarantee of safety with respect to the anchorage of the ship. The court, in rejecting the defendant's argument, went on to state

> . . . if one were to take all the cases and there are many, of implied warranties or covenants in law, it will be found that in all of them the law is raising an implication from the presumed intention of the parties, with the object of giving to the transaction such efficacy as both parties must have intended that at all events it should have. In business transactions such as this, what the law desires to effect by the implication is to give such business efficacy to the transaction as must have been intended at all events by both parties who are businessmen. . . . The question is what inference is to be drawn where the parties are dealing with each other on the same assumption that the negotiations are to have some fruit, and where they say nothing about the burden of this unseen peril, leaving the law to raise such inferences as are reasonable from the very nature of the transaction.[17]

As can be seen from the clear wording of this passage, the court is concerned with implying terms into a contract that the parties would have intended but through oversight omitted, and even then such terms will be implied only when it is necessary to give effect to the agreement. In more modern jurisprudence the first part of this principle is often referred to as the 'officious bystander' test. In other words, if at the time the parties were entering into the contract an interfering bystander were to interject in the negotiations and ask, 'What about such and such?' both of the parties would turn on that bystander and with a shared contempt for him roundly declare, 'But, of course, that is taken as read!'[18] This is what happened in *Kavanagh v. Gilbert*,[19] where a piece of land was sold at auction but the sale was not binding because the auctioneer failed to create

16   (1889) 14 PD 64; *Butler v. McAlpine* [1904] 2 IR 445.
17   Ibid, 68 per Bowen LJ.
18   *Shirlaw v. Southern Foundries* [1939] 2 KB 206 (if, while the parties were making their bargain, an officious bystander were to suggest some express provision for their agreement, they would testily suppress him with a common 'oh of course'!) contrast with *Spring v. NASDS* [1956] 2 All ER 221 (the officious bystander, in response to the question as to whether or not the Bridlington agreement should form part of the contract, would say 'what's that?').
19   (1875) IR 9 CL 136.

the necessary memorandum of agreement. The court held that a bystander who might have asked both parties whether or not such a memorandum should have been completed would in all likelihood have been berated for stating the obvious.

Unfortunately, it has been promulgated that the second part of the principle, that of business efficacy, is a separate and distinct principle capable of independent application from the officious bystander test. The bystander test implies an unexpressed intention of the parties, whereas the efficacy principle implies a term not because the parties intended it (indeed, it might even be that the parties did not intend it), but because it is necessary to give effect to the contract. This has been further confused by the likes of Denning MR who have advocated the concept of implying such terms as are reasonably necessary for the efficacy of the contract.[20] On such rationale the term is implied not by presumed intention or necessity but on the grounds of reasonableness. The danger in such an approach is obvious. It has been roundly condemned by Wilberforce LJ in *Liverpool City Council v. Irwin.*[21] In that case the defendants were tenants in a tower block who lived on the ninth floor. The elevator to that floor was inoperative and the defendants withheld the payment of their rent claiming the existence of an implied term of access to their apartments. The plaintiffs rejected such an implied term. The court held that there was an implied term that access should be given to the defendants, but this term offered only a reasonable right to access and not an absolute right, and the defendants had failed to show that the plaintiffs had not discharged this obligation to maintain a reasonable level of access. If we examine this case in greater detail, many of the finer points become clearer, as do the errors in certain theories. Firstly, the case clearly shows that the test of *The Moorcock* is an indivisible test, that is, it requires the existence of an unexpressed intention of the parties together with the fact that the term be required in order to give business efficacy to the contract. In the case at bar, it is clear that if a bystander had said to the tenants and the landlord, 'What about the provision of access to the ninth floor of the building?', both parties would have berated the bystander for stating the obvious. But this in itself is not sufficient to imply a term into the contract; something more is required. The term must be needed to give efficacy to the contract,[22] and clearly the question of access to the apartment is a term that would be so required. But the final element in *The Moorcock* formulation concerns itself with 'leaving it

---

20 *Greaves & Co. v. Baynham Meikle* [1975] 3 All ER 99 (a term is implied which is reasonable in all the circumstances, not necessarily the unexpressed intention of the parties).

21 [1976] 2 All ER 39

22 *Liverpool City Council v. Irwin*, ibid, ('such obligation should be read into the contract as the nature of the contract implicitly requires, no more no less: a test in other words of necessity', *per* Wilberforce LJ, at 254); *O'Toole v. Palmer* (1945) Ir Jur Rep 59 ('I do not think there is any necessity to imply a term for the purpose of giving the contract a business efficacy', *per* Gavan Duffy J).

to the law to raise such inferences as are reasonable from the very nature of the transaction'. Thus the implied term, though required for business efficacy is only required to the extent that it would be reasonable. There is therefore only one test, that of *The Moorcock* which consists of two limbs—unexpressed intention and necessity to ensure efficacy, of the contract to the extent that such term is reasonable. Secondly, the decision in *Liverpool City Council v. Irwin* is a clear rebuff of the 'reasonable' concept.[23] The *Moorcock* principle is not a case of alternative rules. In *Liverpool City Council v. Irwin*, it would have been very reasonable to imply a term into the contract absolutely obliging the landlords to provide access to the ninth floor, but this would be beyond what would be required to give efficacy to the contract. All that was required or necessary for efficacy was to give reasonable access to the ninth floor. In the words of McCarthy J in this jurisdiction,

> It is not the function of the court to rewrite a contract for parties met upon commercially equal terms; if such parties want to enter into unreasonable, unfair or even disastrous contract that is their business, not the business of the courts.[24]

However, it goes too far to limit the doctrine to that of commercial contracts, and it is perhaps better stated with the gloss of the *dicta* of O'Higgins CJ in the same case:

> The courts have no role in acting as contract makers, or as counsellors, to advise or direct which agreement ought to have been made by two people, whether businessmen or not, who chose to enter into contractual relations with each other.[25]

The net result is that courts will imply terms into a contract that are the unexpressed intention of the parties and are necessary to give efficacy to the contract. The unexpressed intention is determined by the officious bystander test, and the efficacy goal is limited by the fact that such terms must be reasonable.

---

23   Advanced by Denning MR in *Trollope and Colls v. NW Metropolitan Hospital Board* [1973] 1 WLR 600.
24   *Tradax (Ireland) v. Irish Grain Board* [1984] IR 1.
25   Ibid. at 7; but see *Trustee Savings Bank v. Maughan* [1992] 1 IR 488 where Costello J held in the High Court that a term, clearly stating that a loan account with the bank was to be operated in the 'usual' manner, did not give the bank the right to impose compound interest on the overdue amount, despite this being the usual policy of the bank. The case is indicative of an emerging tendency to protect the weaker party to a contract, and use the inherent powers of the court to ensure that fairness is achieved in contractual relationships. Whether this will be seen in future applications of implied terms remains to be seen.

But the question still remains as to whether the courts may impose terms on a contract which were not intended by the parties to that contract. The answer is a limited yes.[26] In certain specialised situations, the courts will, as a matter of policy, impose terms on a contract which were not the intention of the parties concerned. In doing so, it acts on the basis of a legitimate public policy that is desirable to uphold; for example, in contracts for the lease of furnished premises, there is an implied term that the premises is in fact fit for human habitation;[27] likewise, a contract of landlord and tenant will have an implied term that the tenant can have peaceable possession of the premises.[28] Such terms are implied, not to aid the working or otherwise of the contract, but solely on the basis of judicial policy.[29] Implied terms of this nature are, therefore, quite common in contracts for landlord and tenant[30] and in employment contracts,[31] to the limited extent that they are still governed by the ordinary law of contract. Indeed, it is probably true to say that, where judicial interference has been pronounced in this manner, the legislature has tended to intervene in modern times to give statutory certainty to the policy issues involved.

26 *Tournier v. National and Provincial Union Bank of England* [1924] 1 KB 461; *Potter v. Carlisle and Cliftonville Golf Club* [1939] NI 114 (a term was implied that a golfer undertook usual risks in a golf course and so could not recover damages where he was injured by flying golf ball).

27 *Siney v. Dublin Corporation* [1980] IR 400 (but note that it is not implied if the premises is unfurnished); *Burke v. Dublin Corporation* [1991] IR 341; *Coleman and Coleman v. Dundalk Urban District Council*, unreported, Supreme Court, 17 July 1985.

28 As in *Byrne v. Martina Investments* [1984] 3 JISLL 116 (failure of landlord to keep property in good repair. *Held* that tenants had a good cause of action, despite absence of express covenant placing obligation on landlord to keep the property in good repair).

29 Judicial policy can be classified, tentatively, as follows: (1) protection of a contracting party as outlined in landlord and tenant and employee/employer cases outlined earlier, ibid.; (2) incomplete contracts, see *Hillas v. Arcos* (1932) 38 Comm Cas 29, *Ornamental Steamship Co. v. Tyler* [1893] 2 QB 578; (3) imposition of equitable rights, see *Hospital Products v. US Surgical Corporation* (1984) 156 CLR 411 (exclusive dealing agreement between plaintiff and defendant. Defendant had own manufacturing process and made copies of the plaintiff's product, which were the subject of the agreement. Action by the plaintiff succeeded on the basis, not of fiduciary breach, but breach of implied terms — along the lines of UCC s. 2-306(2)).

30 See ibid.; *Wettern Electric v. Welsh Development Agency* [1983] QB 796; *Brown v. Norton* [1954] IR 34; *Morris v. Redmond and Wright* (1935) 70 ILTR 8 (terms that a house was to be built in efficient manner and be capable of habitation implied into the contract), but see *Curling v. Walsh*, unreported, High Court, 23 October 1987 (the vendor of an existing house does not warrant, as an implied term, the premises are fit for habitation or free from structural defects).

31 *Royal Trust Co. of Canada v. Kelly*, unreported, High Court, 27 February 1989 (implied term in contracts of employment for a non fixed duration that termination can be on reasonable notice); *Orr v. University of Tasmania* [1956] Tas SR 155 (there is an implied term in a lecturer's contract of employment not to seduce students); *AF Associates v. Ralston* [1973] NI 229 (implied term that an employee could not directly compete with employer); *Imperial Group Pension Trust v. Imperial Tobacco* [1991] 2 All ER 597 (implied term that an employer was to act in good faith over pension fund); *Fluid Power*

12.04 TERMS IMPLIED BY THE CONSTITUTION

It has been suggested that certain terms will be implied into contracts by virtue of the existence in this jurisdiction of Bunreacht na hÉireann, 1937. The argument runs that if the common law can imply terms into a contract, then Constitutional provisions which take precedence over the common law must also be capable of implying terms into a contract.[32] This appears fallacious. Firstly, almost all of the cases can be resolved without implying any term into the contract.[33] Instead, it seems clear that the Constitution can limit the application of contractual terms and that this is the basis of the decisions so cited. In other words a contractual term cannot be used to oust the superior nature of constitutional rights, but this does not necessarily mean that there is an implied term in the contract. It is the exercise of rights under the contract which are subject to constitutional scrutiny.[34] Secondly, terms implied into a contract by operation of law can be excluded by the express agreement of the parties. Could it therefore be that constitutional rights can be excluded by contractual agreement? It follows if one accepts the earlier argument that they can be so excluded—but it would be difficult to envisage such a situation. Moreover, the waiver of constitutional rights is surely a matter of constitutional law and not something to be left to the vagaries of contractual analysis.[35] Finally, it seems excessive to resort to constitutional provisions to remedy a defect in a contract. To an extent it demeans the constitution and falls into the trap (so often the last straw for the desperate lawyer to grasp at, the final hope of a poor case)—a constitutional right. The Constitution protects the exercise of rights guaranteed by it in any given relationship, it does not mould the relationship itself.

12.05 TERMS IMPLIED BY STATUTE

Certain terms will be implied into a contract by virtue of statutory provisions. We have seen earlier that this often occurs in recognition of the fact that the courts have for some time implied terms into a contract exclusively on the basis

---

Technology v. Sperry (Ireland) unreported, High Court, 22 February 1985 (there is an implied term concerning the exercise of rights under the express terms of a contract, in this case the termination of contract. Express terms had to be exercised in a reasonable manner).

32   *Meskell v. CIE* [1973] IR 121.
33   *Meskell v. CIE*, ibid. (right to dismiss subject to implied term that it will be exercised only in accordance with the rights of the employees); *Glover v. BLN* [1973] IR 288 (implied term that fair procedures will operate in the exercise of contractual rights) for other examples of fair procedures see *AIB v. Lipton* ibid., *Gunn* [1990] 2 IR 168; *NEETU v. McConnell* [1983] ILRM 422.
34   *Allied Irish Bank v. Lipton* (1984) 3 JISLL 107 (disciplinary hearing had to be impartial).
35   See Casey, *Constitutional Law in Ireland*; Forde, *Constitutional Law in Ireland* and Kelly, *The Irish Constitution*.

of public policy or custom and practice. However, it also occurs where the legislature wishes to mould the activities of society in a different direction.

One of the most important statutes would affect contracts for the sale of goods as contained in the Sale of Goods and Supply of Services Act 1980. We look at this in more detail in chapter 15. A number of other statutory provisions also impact on contracts, but they are too disparate and unconnected in terms of analysis for any benefit to be achieved from a review of them.

13.00

Conditions and warranties

13.01 INTRODUCTION

It has already been said that not all the terms of a contract, whether express or implied, carry equal weight. Breach of some terms will entitle the aggrieved party to damages only, whereas breach of another term may well entitle him to treat the contract as if it were at an end. The traditional classification has been that of conditions and warranties. A condition is a term of the contract breach of which entitles the party to treat the contract as rescinded.[1] A warranty is a term of the contract for which a breach thereof raises a claim in damages but does not permit recission of the contract itself.[2] It is true to say that this view of the classification of the terms of a contract has not been historically absolute but represents a modern formula based heavily on the legislative provisions for the sale of goods. The present use of the terminology, although adopted by extension from the provisions for the sale of goods, is far superior to that which reigned beforehand.[3] The one difficulty is that the word 'condition' is used not only in this sense but also to refer to both a condition precedent and a condition subsequent. A condition precedent (where something must be fulfilled before the contract comes into effect)[4] and a condition subsequent (where if the contract

---

1   *White Sewing Machine v. Fitzgerald* (1894) 29 ILTR 37; Sale of Goods Act 1893, s. 11(1)(b), Restatement, Second, Contracts, s. 224.
2   See Sale of Goods Act, ibid; S. 62(1) which defines a warranty as that which is collateral to the main purpose of the contract.
3   *Kingston v. Preston* (1773) 2 Doug 689. This case involved the order of performance of the contract and the related problem discussed in footnote 45 ibid (whether a failure to perform obligations by one of the parties to the contract could be held to be a condition precedent which would obviate the obligation of the other party to perform his or her obligations). The transfer of a business did not have to be performed, since the obligation of the purchaser to provide security for the transfer was a condition precedent; in *In re Application of Butler* [1970] IR 45 a failure to disclose a prior accident to the insurance company, released the insurance company of the obligation of performing the contract of insurance. The requirment of notification was held to be a condition precedent.
4   *Pym v. Campbell* (1856) 6 E&B 370 (contract was not to come into effect until subject matter was examined by an engineer—condition precedent); Restatement, Second, Contracts, s. 225(2); the condition must not lack certainty: *Lee Parker v. Izzet* [1972] 2 All ER 800 (a term 'subject to obtaining a satisfactory mortgage' was held void for uncertainty); It might be that both parties have conditions to fulfil concurrently, in that there are conditions precedent for both parties (see Restatement, Contracts, s. 251 and

is to remain enforceable something must be done after the contract has been created)[5] are technically different from the meaning ascribed to the term 'condition' in the sense of a term of the contract. Conditions precedent and conditions subsequent connote some external event which impacts on the operation of the contract, whereas in the sense used here 'condition' refers to the importance placed upon the internal terms of a contract in a situation where such term has been breached.

We turn now to analyse the dichotomy between conditions and warranties as terms of a contract.

13.02 THE DICHOTOMY EXPLORED

The classification of the terms of a contract into conditions and warranties, while useful, is not, as had been once thought, exhaustive. This is clear from the *Hong Kong Firs* case.[6] In this case, the defendants had chartered a ship from the plaintiffs for two years as and from February 1957. However, the ship was under-manned by inexperienced staff in the engine room, as a result of which delays of nearly twenty weeks had occurred. Accordingly, by June the defendants had repudiated the contract. The ship was seaworthy by September. The plaintiffs now sued for damages arising from the repudiation of the contract. The term of the contract breached was that of seaworthiness of the vessel. One might have been forgiven for believing that seaworthiness would be a condition of a contract of charterparty and that breach of such a condition would permit repudiation of the contract and that therefore the plaintiff's case was unsustainable. However, the Court of Appeal did make some valuable observations. It held that a simple dichotomy between a condition and a waranty would not be appropriate where the term in question was of a complex nature and that the concept of sea-worthiness was such a complex term. As Upton LJ said,

the role of the constructive condition). This requires that one of the parties must tender performance, thus rendering the other party liable on his condition precedent, see Calamari and Perillo, op. cit., p. 441.

5   *Head v. Tattersall* (1871) LR 7 Exch 7; Restatement, Contracts, s. 250(b); conditions subsequent are comparatively rare: *Kindler v. Anderson*, 433P 2d 268; *Berman v. Palatine Insurance Co.* 379 F 2d 371 (there was a failure to claim under an insurance policy for a valid claim. The court held the requirement of making a claim is a condition subsequent to the contract of insurance); Holmes, *The Common Law*, op. cit., pp. 316-318 (conditions operate so as to shift the onus of proof from one party to another); the court's use of language is somewhat ambivalent, see *Bentworth Finance v. Lubert* [1967] 2 All ER 810 (a condition requiring that the logbook be delivered to the purchaser was held to be a condition precedent. But it cannot have been that no contract existed where the plaintiff gave a car to the defendant on hire purchase without the log book. This is more accurately described as a condition precedent).

6   [1962] 1 All ER 474.

If a nail is missing from one of the timbers of a wooden vessel, or if proper medical supplies or two anchors are not on board at the time of the sailing, the owners are in breach of the seaworthiness stipulation. It is contrary to common sense to suppose that in such circumstances, the parties contemplated that the charterer should at once be entitled to treat the contract as at an end for such trifling breaches.[7]

This simple argument exposes many of the weaknesses of the traditional dichotomy of condition and waranty. Firstly, it illustrates the complete fallacy of divorcing the term of the contract from the effect of the breach of that term. Let us suppose that a nail is missing as Upton LJ has postulated, and that the nail is missing without any negligence. Suppose, too, that the ship sails and completes its voyage. The contract cannot be repudiated on the basis that the ship was not seaworthy. The corollary must also be true: if a nail is missing, and the ship flounders, then the ship has proved itself to be unseaworthy and the injured party can repudiate the contract. The same term has had a different consequence depending on the nature of the breach of that term. Secondly, it further illustrates that attempting to classify the terms of the contract prior to their breach is unsatisfactory; the only way certainty as to the classification can be achieved is *ex post facto*, but at that stage the need to classify the term pales into a certain amount of insignificance in light of the need to obtain a suitable remedy. In the *Hong Kong Firs* case the defendants erred in selecting repudiation as a remedy for the unseaworthiness of the vessel, since an award of damages could have compensated them without terminating the contract. Remember, the fault complained about was one of delay which could have been remedied given time, that time to be paid for by the plaintiffs. At no stage was the defendant exposed to such damage as could not be compensated by an award of money. It presumably would have been different if the unseaworthiness had not merely caused delay but had rendered the vessel likely to capsize and thereby left it unusable as distinct from just being tardy. When it is said that the injury was not capable of compensation by an award of damages we mean this in the loosest sense possible. It might be clearer to say that the injury complained of is more appropriately remedied by damages rather than repudiation. Finally, the example illustrates a certain naivety in postulating that all the terms of a contract can be artificially divided into two categories and two categories only. The terms of most contracts are complex and difficult, and to believe that they are capable

---

7   Ibid, at 483; but see *In re Moore v. Landauer* [1921] 2 KB 519 (contract for 3,000 cases of tinned fruit with each case to be packed with 30 tins. In fact the fruit was delivered with some cases of more and some of less than thirty tins but the overall number was correct. *Held* that this was a breach of a condition. The decision is justifiable in that it concerned a breach of condition under s. 13 Sale of Goods Act, moreover the argument might be that the quantity in the each crate rendered the crate of fruit less valuable whereas the simple missing of a nail in a ship would not render the voyage less effective).

of easy resolution into neat labels underestimates the ability of people to organise their affairs in a highly complex fashion.

It is clear therefore that a term of a contract may be either a condition or a warranty depending on the nature of the breach of that term and its impact on the injured party. It thus becomes quite difficult to tell in advance whether a particular term is a condition or a warranty, and the injured party's lawyers have the unenviable task of pre-guessing the judgment of a court as to the consequence of the breach. The net effect is, of course, to discourage the use of repudiation in contract breaches, thus moving people away from the concept of self-help and towards a resort to either litigation or negotiated damages. It is clear that this is the policy choice made by the courts, for, if the *Hong Kong Firs* case is to be reconcilable within the orthodox classification, then it must be that the seaworthiness clause was a warranty, yet it cannot be that it is always the case that such a clause would be held to be a warranty. There must be some situations where the breach of it would be a condition. But those situations must be quite exceptional, and the party who chooses to exercise a supposed right of repudiation does so at considerable peril.

The failure to fix the terms of a contract into immutable categories, while allowing for individual justice, makes the process of advice giving relatively inaccurate. To that extent there are some who argue, and it must be said quite convincingly, that the search for warranty and condition classification is a moot point.[8] Further, they go on to point out that the problem should be looked at from the viewpoint of discharge by breach, rather than by devising an elusive notional classification. There is much to commend this sort of an approach.

There will however be situations where the parties would prefer, prior to the contract coming into effect, to know what terms will be regarded as sufficiently important to enable repudiation to be exercised; to this matter we now turn.

13.03 TILTING THE BALANCE

There is nothing to prevent the parties from altering the common law position by prior agreement. Thus, if the parties decide to stipulate that a term of the contract is a condition, breach of which will entitle repudiation, then this will be enforceable. Such an agreement must, of course, be express, and there should be no doubt as to the nature of the commitment being made.[9] Moreover, where such prior agreement is made, the right to repudiate the contract is independent

---

8   *The Hansa Nord* [1975] 3 All ER 379 (the court considered the effect of the breach in classifying a clause as a condition or warranty) approved in *Reardon Line v. Smith* [1976] 3 All ER 570; *Bunge Corporation v. Tradax* [1981] 2 All ER 513; but cf. *Mihalos Angelos* [1970] 3 All ER 124 (the usefulness of dichotomy of condition and warranty still remains, despite *Hong Kong Firs*).

9   *Reardon Line v. Smith* [1976] 3 All ER 570; *Schuler AG v. Wickman Machine Tool Sales* [1973] 2 All ER 39.

of the consequence of the breach. There is no requirement to show loss or damage. This merely recognises the freedom-of-contract concept upon which the common law supposedly rests. It does, however, presuppose a degree of far-sightedness which could well escape most, if not all, of those engaged in the negotiation of a contract. Few people like to concern themselves with what could go wrong with a contract during the first flush of euphoria at a satisfactory agreement on things like price, time and so forth.

It has been suggested that the whole context of the contract may permit an implication that certain of its terms are conditions entitling repudiation, even where this is not expressly so stated.[10] However, this idea should be treated with considerable caution. If a court could imply into the terms of a contract that these terms granted the right of repudiation, how would it differ from the earlier view that the terms of a contract themselves can be classified into conditions and warranties? If the implication of a right to repudiate a contract for breach of certain terms is to have any effect, it must be limited to situations where there is a pre-existing practice, custom, statutory provision or precedent which directly governs the issue.[11] Beyond that any general power of implication merely serves to restate the automatic categorisation rejected earlier.[12]

13.04 CONCLUSION

The best way of ensuring that breach of a particular term enables repudiation of the contract to be effected would seem to be to stipulate expressly this at the time the contract is entered into. Where this is not done, reliance must be placed on external factors which clearly render the breach of such a term sufficient to enable repudiation. In the absence of any of these features, is it possible for a lawyer to advise a client with certainty as to whether the breach of a particular term warrants a justified repudiation of the contract? There is one remaining possibility, to be found from the adoption by Costello J in *Irish Telephone Rentals v. Irish Civil Service Building Society*[13] of *dicta* from Diplock LJ in the *Hong Kong Firs* case. In *Irish Telephone Rentals* the plaintiffs repudiated a contract concerning the installation of a telephone system, claiming it did not

---

10 *Schuler AG v. Wickman Machine Tool Sales* [1973] 2 All ER 39; *Mihalis Angelos* [1970] 3 All ER 125.

11 For example see *Behn v. Burness* (1863) 3 B&S 751 (a statement regarding when a ship would be ready to load, was held to be a condition).

12 Though it has been claimed that a term of a contract will be deemed to be a condition if it goes to the root of the contract itself, see *Bunge Corporation v. Tradax* [1981] 2 All ER 513 (a time requirement of 15 days notice was held to be a condition, despite the absence of any loss to the plaintiff, since time was an essential element in the particular mercantile contract: 'To such cases the "gravity of the breach" approach of Hong Kong Firs would be unsuitable', *per* Wilberforce LJ at 542.

13 [1991] ILRM 880.

work. In deciding the case, Costello J approved the following statement as applicable:

> The test whether an event has this effect or not [the discharge of one of the parties from the performance of his undertakings], has been stated in a number of metaphors all of which I think amount to the same thing: does the occurrence of the event deprive the party who has further undertakings still to perform of substantially the whole benefit which it was the intention of the parties as expressed in the contract that should obtain as consideration for performing those undertakings?[14]

This reduces the classification to one of *ex post facto* and therefore of limited usage: one can determine if it is a condition by testing the consequence of the breach—at which stage the classification of the terms of limited value. But what it does make clear is that the classification of terms into conditions and warranties is a futile exercise unless the classification is agreed on at the time the contract is entered into. Where this is not the case, and it cannot be implied, (from custom, practice, statutory provision or precedent) that the term is either a condition or warranty, then the question of classification is unimportant. Instead, the breach should be looked to see if it warrants a payment of damages only, or whether it entitles the contract to be discharged. A full discussion of these principles can be found in chapter 22.

14   Ibid.

14.00

Exclusion clauses

14.01 INTRODUCTION

In many contracts, the parties attempt to outline the remedies available when the contract is not correctly performed. Further, one of the parties may seek to exclude or limit the consequences of non-compliance with the terms of the contract. The party relying upon such a clause, variously described as 'exclusion', 'exemption', 'excepting' and 'exculpatory' clauses, attempts to restrict liability in damages either by requiring the other party to undergo certain steps before any claim will be entertained or by denying any remedy whatsoever to the injured party. In many ways such clauses receive unwarranted criticism because their role is seldom understood except in a negative sense, that is, the person relying on the clause is seeking to avoid a just liability. If we look at two types of exclusion clauses—sometimes referred to as procedural (where recovery is barred only after a failure to conform to certain specified requirements)[1] and substantive (where no liability is entertained)[2]—we shall see that such clauses can serve a very useful purpose.

In the case of *procedural exclusion clauses* (as where a company states in the contract that no claim will be entertained for goods damaged in delivery unless it has been notified within three days), the aim of the exclusion clause is clearly to avoid a prolonged exposure to potential liability. It would be unfair for the company to accept liability several weeks later, so the onus on the other party to notify is not unreasonable. Early notification makes identification of the problem and proving it easier. The procedural exclusion clause requires that both parties to the contract act in a responsible way and that defects are complained of within a reasonable time, thus enabling agreed and timely resolution of a problem.

---

1   A procedural clause may in fact limit liability to nothing, see *British Leyland Exports v. Britain Group Sales* [1981] IR 35 (a clause denying liability for consequential loss in supply of defective products was held to limit damages payable, it did not render the primary obligation unenforceable).

2   *Leonard v. Great Northern Railway* (1912) 46 ILTR 220 (the failure to comply with a requirment of notice meant the loss of rights to claim damages); *G.H. Renton v. Palmyra Trading Corporation of Panama* [1956] 3 All ER 957 (a clause permitting discharge of goods at the port of loading, or other convenient port in the event of industrial action, was held to define the obligation of the party under the contract).

Substantive exclusion clauses prevent the injured party from claiming any compensation for non-performance of the contract; it may be difficult to see the value of such clauses, yet their existence clearly reduces costs and avoids duplication of insurance coverage. Moreover, certain services might not be provided if such clauses were not permissible.[3]

It must also be said that, in looking at the application of such clauses, the courts will first examine the contract without benefit of the clause to determine what is supposed to be performed by the contract itself. Having identified the obligations pursuant to the contract, the exclusion clause is then read to see in what way if any the remedies for breach of these obligations are limited.[4]

Before examining this in detail, the courts will check to see that the exclusion clause actually forms part of the contract itself, a process often referred to as 'incorporation of the exclusion clause'. Given the potential for abuse with respect to such clauses, it is not surprising to discover that they are treated considerably more cautiously than other contractual terms.

14.02 INCORPORATION OF THE CLAUSE

Incorporation of the clause is achieved by giving actual notice of the term to other party. Requiring the other party to sign the exclusion clause incorporates the term into the contract,[5] but less than that may suffice: specifically bringing it to the attention of the other person will give him actual knowledge and make

3   If liability is imposed on the provider of a service, this may make the selling price prohibitive, particularly where the user may have already borne the costs of catering for the risk. A distinction may have to be drawn between consumer and non consumer contracts. It is difficult to justify exclusion clauses in consumer contracts, although procedural exclusion clauses may be justifiable provided that they are not drafted too strictly. The courts have shown this sort of approach but see *Hollins v. Davy* [1963] 1 QB 844 at 850 where the court made the point that a person who parks his vehicle at a car park where no exclusion clause operates (protecting the owner of the car park with respect to liability for damage to the vehicle), one of two situations will happen if the vehicle suffers damage: the owner of the car will have his loss doubly insured (by his own insurance policy and that of the owner of the car park), or, if the owner of the car carries no insurance, he gains a benefit that he was not himself willing to pay for, the cost of which is borne by the other patrons of the car park.

4   *Karsales (Harrow) v. Wallis* [1956] 2 All ER 866 but this has been contested elsewhere, see *State Government Insurance Office of Queensland v. Brisbane Stevedoring* (1969) 43 ALJR 456. The effect of Denning MR's view in *Karsales* is to regard exclusion clauses as a defence, not as defining the obligation *per se*.

5   *Duff v. Great Northern Railway* (1878) 4 LR (Ir) 178; *L'Estrange v. Graucob* [1934] 2 KB 394 ('the plaintiff having put her signature to the document and not having been induced to do so by any fraud or misrepresentation, cannot be heard to say that she is not bound by the terms of the document because she has not read them', *per* Scrutton LJ at 404); *Curtis v. Chemical Cleaning and Dyeing Co.* [1951] 1 KB 805 (an innocent misrepresentation as to the effect of a signature meant that the defendant could not rely on the exclusion clause); the doctrine of non est factum (it is not my deed) may also be raised, that is, the document is different from that which was signed, fraud is not essential

the term an enforceable part of the contract. If the other party is not aware of the term, the party seeking to rely upon it must do all in his power to take reasonable steps to bring it to the attention of the other party. Failure to do this will prevent anyone benefiting from the clause. *Parker v. SE Railway*[6] has been regarded as the leading case in this regard, particularly with respect to the so-called 'ticket' cases (see below). However, the guidelines arising from these 'ticket' cases are somewhat misleading and unhelpful. The requirement of actual knowledge is sufficiently flexible to avoid recourse to rote rules.

A reasonable attempt must have been made to bring the clause to the attention of the party who is to be subject to the exclusion of liability. This can be achieved in a number of ways. Firstly, the clause could be signposted and on public display—such as disclaimers of liability at car parks, laundrettes. In theory, any one who enters into a contract under such circumstances has been the subject of a reasonable effort to have the clause brought to his attention,[7] but the courts have been careful to ensure that the notice is prominently displayed and easily visible. The same is true where liability is sought to be excluded by a notice which appears on a ticket or other such receipt; this raises the second issue: such a clause will have no impact if the reasonable attempts at incorporation occur *after* the contract has been entered into. The theory is clear: an exclusion clause is valid only if it gives the party a reasonable opportunity to consider the advisability of entering into such a contract with that sort of a clause. An opportunity to refrain from entering into the contract must exist. Thus, in *Thornton v. Shoe Lane Parking*[8] the clause was not incorporated where the entry ticket to a car park had printed on it that the plaintiff had entered into a contract on the terms and conditions displayed, since the displayed terms and conditions could not be read until after the plaintiff had entered the car park. The incorporation of the displayed terms and conditions could not occur after the contract had been made. It follows, therefore, that any such exclusion notices should be placed clearly on public display at a location which affords a reasonable opportunity to resile from entering into the contract.[9]

(*Bank of Ireland v. McManamy* [1916] 2 IR 161). One cannot, however, sign a document carelessly, leaving it to another to fill up (*UDT v. Western* [1976] QB 813; see also *Saunders v. Anglia Building Society* [1971] AC 1004 applied in *Norwich and Peterborough Building Society v. Steed* [1993] 1 All ER 330).

6   (1877) 2 CPD 416; *Ryan v. Great Southern and Western Railway*, 32 ILTR 108; the tests can be outlined as follows: did the plaintiff know that the exclusion clause attached? If yes, then it will bind him, if not then it will not bind him, unless notice has been given and it was reasonable to expect the plaintiff to know from the notice that conditions of exclusion were attached.

7   *Brady v. Aer Rianta* and *O'Beirne v. Aer Rianta* both cited in Clark, op. cit., p. 136, footnote 23. According to Clark, both these cases involved upholding exclusion clauses that were prominently displayed on the entrance to an airport car park.

8   [1971] 1 All ER 686.

9   *Olley v. Marlborough Court Ltd* [1949] 1 All ER 127; *Burnett v. Westminster Bank* [1965] 3 All ER 81.

The difficulty arises with respect to the so-called 'ticket' cases. It has been held that a ticket or receipt which is given, and which contains notice of an exclusion may be validly incorporated into the contract. This is clear from *Parker v. SE Railway.*[10] Simply put, if the party is given a ticket or other such notice but is unaware that there is any writing on it, then he will not be bound by the exclusion clause. If the person is aware of the existence of writing but is unaware of what that writing is about, then it will depend on whether or not reasonable notice of the conditions were given. Of course, if the person knows that the writing contains conditions of the contract, he will be bound by them. These guidelines must be treated with a certain amount of suspicion both in their application and their theoretical base. In application, *Early v. Great Southern Railway*[11] is difficult to justify, for in that case the ticket referred to terms and conditions of the contract which could only be inspected at the head office of the railway company, yet the exclusion clause was held to be incorporated. Theoretically, tickets or receipts are given at a stage in the contract where there is no freedom to resile from the contract, where no opportunity exists to re-consider.

Let us take the case of X, a first-year law student who has been horrified at the injuries suffered by people where liability is excluded by exclusion clauses; he has developed a phobia about entering into any contract with such clauses. If X walks onto a bus, offers the correct fare and is handed a ticket, which he then reads, is it really the case that the contract can be resiled from. Certainly, it would be difficult to see the bus driver willingly handing back the fare as the passenger hands back the ticket. If X then decides to book a holiday trip to recover from the altercation with the bus driver, he will first visit a travel agent who makes a telephone reservation with the airline and then asks X for the correct fare. X pays the money and the travel agent asks him to wait until the tickets are printed. This is done and the tickets handed over. X leaves the travel agent, now reading the back of the ticket, which contains an exclusion clause, and immediately returns to the agent. He demands that the contract be set aside but is told that will constitute a cancellation and, accordingly, 20% of the fare is non-refundable. In despair X hails a taxi and jumps in and asks to be taken home. As he is recovering, he spots the sign that says liability for certain events is excluded. Demanding the taxi driver halt, he jumps out and runs away, leaving

---

10   Ibid.
11   [1940] IR 414; *Shea v. Great Southern Railway* [1944] Ir Jur Rep 26 (the plaintiff took a bike on board a bus, the ticket excluded liability for theft. The court held that it had been incorporated since the plaintiff had the choice of leaving the bus if he was unhappy with the terms of the ticket); In general Irish Courts have been unsympathetic to plaintiffs in this regard: *Knox v. Great Northern Railway* [1896] 2 IR 632, *Slattery v. CIE* (1972) 106 ILTR 71. Both cases were justified by the court as being the reduction of agreed contractual terms to written form, despite the fact that this reduction to writting occurred after the contract was completed. It is to be hoped that this view is not strictly enforced in consumer cases.

the taxi driver screaming for the fare. He then returns to the taxi, pays the fare and goes to the shopping centre to put his jacket into the dry cleaners. He pays a deposit and receives a collection docket, which (of course), despite its label, contains terms and conditions of the contract, including the ubiquitous exclusion clause.

The above set of hypothetical facts gives a small sample of the extent to which the exclusion clause has become part of our everyday life; yet it is difficult to see how such clauses are validly incorporated into the contract. In almost all of the above instances the clause could only have been discovered at a point where no opportunity existed for X to resile from the contract. Moreover, no real effort has been made by the person seeking its inclusion to bring it to the other person's attention. Exclusion clauses are treated differently because they are onerous and traditionally speaking unusual, although this is probably less true today. The courts require that attention be drawn to them, but, quite rightly, do not require the person who will be the subject of the clause to have actually read it, for this would clearly be an onus too far. The law should be really construed more logically. The notice of exclusion clauses must occur prior to the contract, not contemporaneous with it, and such notice must be clearly given so that a reasonable person would be expected to have been aware of it, even if the party concerned was not actually aware of the exclusion clause. If this rule were correctly applied, most of the ticket situations would be ineffective with respect to exclusion clauses, at least as far as such tickets are presently operated.[12] Yet compliance with this in its fullest sense is not onerous for someone wishing to avail of the clause. Signature is not required (indeed, there is some Canadian authority that signature to an exclusion clause should not be treated as conclusive where the clause is surrounded by other non-contentious clauses,[13] but this may be a step too far, for if one's signature does not bind, it is difficult to see what can). Signposting the exclusion clause, highlighting its presence on the written document, orally notifying its existence—all these are more than sufficient.[14]

12 For support, see *Chapleton v. Barry Urban District Council* [1940] 1 All ER 356 (it was not reasonable to expect an exclusion clause to be found on a ticket given for the hire of a deck chair); *McCutcheon v. MacBrayne* [1964] 1 All ER 430.

13 *Tilden Rent-a-Car v. Clendenning* (1978) 83 DLR (3d) 400 ('in modern commercial practice, many standard form contracts printed documents are signed without being read or understood. In many cases the parties seeking to rely on the terms of the contract know or ought to know that the signature of a party to the contract does not represent the true intention of the signer, and that the party signing is unaware of the stringent and onerous provisions which the standard form contains. Under such circumstances, I am of the opinion that the party seeking to rely on such terms should not be able to do so in the absence of first having taken reasonable measures to draw such terms to the attention of the other party and, in the absence of such reasonable measures it is not necessary for the party denying the knowledge of such terms to prove fraud, misrepresentation or *non est factum*,' at 408-409); but cf. *Regan v. IAC* [1990] 1 IR 278, *O'Connor v. First National Building Society* [1991] ILRM 208.

14 A course of past dealing would also suffice, *Spurling v. Bradshaw* [1956] 2 All ER 121;

In many cases the courts have adopted such an approach. However, it would be wrong to think that the courts are eager to enforce these clauses. Thus, in *Olley v. Marlborough Court*[15] the majority of the court were of the view that the contract was concluded before the plaintiff reached the hotel room and that the exclusion notice situated within the room itself was not incorporated. In *Burnett v. Westminster Bank*[16] the plaintiff had two bank accounts, each was held with a different branch of the defendant's bank. The plaintiff, by crossing out the printed name of the branch, used cheques printed for use on one of the branches to write a cheque drawn on the other branch. He then sought to stop the cheque with the branch on whom he had drawn the cheque, but the cheque was paid in the other branch by a computer scanner that could only read the pre-printed magnetic ink and not the plaintiff's hand-written alterations. The defendant pleaded the existence of words written on the face of the chequebook that they would only be applied to the account for which they were prepared for. The plaintiff was successful, since it was not reasonable to expect the cover of a chequebook to contain contractual terms of importance.

Moreover, in general it is true that the courts are moving in the direction of requiring some additional effort on the part of the person relying on any unusual clause to bring such a clause to the attention of the person to whom it is to be applied against. Thus, in *Interfoto Picture Library v. Stiletto Visual Programmes*[17] a clause which imposed an expensive penalty for delay in returning some photographs was held to be sufficiently unusual so as to require it to be 'fairly brought to the attention of the other party'. This would seem to be a judicial insight to the future in many respects. The courts often use the process of incorporation to limit the effect of exclusion clauses by holding the clause was not properly incorporated. This is particularly evident in consumer cases where the courts have exhibited a marked desire to protect the consumer *vis-à-vis* the retailer.[18] Despite this, there will arise situations where the incorporation of the exclusion term into the contract cannot be avoided—for example, where it has been clearly brought to the attention of the other party. The principal justification for the incorporation of exclusion terms, where the party against whom it is operating is aware of its existence (namely, that these terms are willingly accepted, since, if they were not, there was an opportunity not to enter into the contract), presupposes that there is a similar contract available elsewhere without the exclusion clause. Yet this is not so. If the ESB clearly tell me, before I enter into a contract for supply of electricity to my house, that certain liabilities are excluded, can it really be said that I have any freedom to

---

Miley v. McKechnie (1949) 84 ILTR (a previous course of dealing by the plaintiff implied a term into the contract, though note the effect of s. 40 Sale of Goods and Supply of Services Act 1980).

15   [1949] 1 All ER 127.
16   [1965] 3 All ER 81.
17   [1988] 1 All ER 348.
18   For evidence of a different Irish approach, see ibid.

go elsewhere or do without an electricity supply? Of course not; so the courts have had to devise other limitations on the use of exclusion clauses even where they have been validly incorporated into the contract. Chief among them is the interpretation of the exclusion clause, and it is to this which we now turn.

14.03 CONSTRUCTION OF THE EXCLUSION CLAUSE

In general, because courts regard exclusion clauses with a high degree of suspicion, they take a fairly restrictive view of their ambit, where they are part of the contract. Firstly, it should be borne in mind that the person who framed the clause had the opportunity to frame it in a manner most favourable to himself.[19] Time, advice and choice are on the side of the drafter. The same is not true of the person who is bound by the clause. Even if he has alternative options (which as we have seen is not always so), a decision must be made quickly, legal advice is not readily to hand, the circumstances are different. The courts, therefore, wisely adopt what is called the *contra proferentem* rule; that is, they will construe the clause, in the event of any ambiguity, against the person who drafted it.[20] It should be understood that there must be some ambiguity in the interpretation of the exclusion clause *before* the *contra proferentem* rule applies, but at times the courts have clearly found an ambiguity in the exclusion clause, simply in order to apply the rule. Thus, in *Andrews v. Singer*[21] a clause which excluded 'any warranty or condition implied by common law, statute or otherwise' was held not to apply to an express term of the contract for sale that the car sold should be new. The car supplied had 500 miles on it and could hardly be described as 'new'. The exclusion did not cover the case, and the plaintiff could recover. Even more startlingly, in *Hollier v. Rambler Motors (AMC)*[22] a term which excluded liability to owners of vehicles arising from damage caused by fire was held not to cover a situation where the fire was started negligently. The court effectively held that the term could be read to cover deliberate fire or negligent fire but not both. This 'ambiguity' was resolved against the drafter and the exclusion clause did not apply.[23] The *contra*

---

19 *McNally v. Lancashire and York Railway* (1880) 8 LR (Ir) 81 ('There can be no hardship imposed by requiring companies to be clear and explicit in the framing of conditions designed for their own security. The humble and ignorant dealers who enter into transactions are at a disadvantage and at least they should be held strictly to the terms of the contracts deliberately prepared by their skilled advisors', *per* O'Hagan J at 92).

20 *Sproule v. Triumph Cycle* [1927] NI 83; *Hollier v. Rambler Motors* [1972] 1 All ER 399.

21 [1934] 1 KB 17.

22 [1972] 1 All ER 399.

23 *White v. John Warwick* [1953] 2 All ER 1021 (an exclusion clause for the liability of an owner of bicycles for hire, that he would not be liable for personal injury, was held not to cover the exclusion of tortious negligence).

proferentem as practised to these extremes clearly has critics. The need for the
English courts to implement the *contra proferentem* rule *in extremis* is obviated
by specific legislation on the issue and renders subsequent case law from that
jurisdiction suspect.[24] But it remains live in this jurisdiction in the absence of
such legislation.[25]

Of course, a carefully drafted clause might be capable of withstanding the
above rule; therefore, the courts have other elements in their armoury. Thus, if
the proferens (the person seeking to rely on the benefit of the exclusion clause),
or his agent, is guilty of wilful acts of destruction, he cannot rely on the benefit
of an exclusion clause.[26] The exclusion of liability can, therefore, only be used
to non-wilful acts, and the clause must be clearly worded so as to expressly state
which liability is excluded. For example, the clause might just exclude 'liability', and this might be taken to exclude strict liability only under the contract
and not necessarily liability for negligence.[27] Normally, exclusion clauses seek
to exclude all liability, no matter how arising: correctly drafted, these clauses
will be upheld by the courts.[28]

Finally, the exclusion clause cannot be used other than for its main purpose.
Thus, in *Glynn v. Margotson*[29] a clause which permitted the captain of a vessel
to stay at any port in the Mediterranean was designed to ensure the safe passage
of the vessel and not to permit the captain to delay unnecessarily in the voyage.
Accordingly, damage the fresh produce on board. And in *Sze Hai Tong Bank
v. Rambler Cycle*[30] a clause which discharged the defendant from liability once
the goods had been released from the port, would not apply where the release
was made to a person other than to whom it was supposed to be made.

14.04 EXCLUSION OF THE CORE OBLIGATION OF THE CONTRACT

Can a carefully drafted exclusion clause exclude liability for performance of
the contract? Clark gives the example of a contract to fly a passenger from X
to Y which contains a term excluding liability in the event of the airline deciding

24 Unfair Contract Terms Act 1977; *Mitchell v. Finney Lock Seeds* [1983] 2 All ER 737
    (Denning MR says that the rule should not be needed in light of the Unfair Contract
    Terms Act 1977).
25 Whether such clauses should be given a hostile interpretation remains open to debate
    in this jurisdiction; *Ailsa Craig Fishing v. Malvern Fishing* [1983] 1 All ER 101 ('one
    must strive not to create ambiguities by strained construction . . . the relevant words
    must be given, if possible, their natural plain meaning', *per* Wilberforce LJ, at 104).
26 *Ronan v. Midland Railway* (1883) 14 LR (Ir) 157.
27 *White v. John Warwick* [1953] 2 All ER 1021.
28 *Token Glass Products v. Sexton*, unreported, High Court, 13 October 1983.
29 [1893] AC 351.
30 [1959] AC 576.

to cancel all flights from X to Y.[31] This is termed an 'illusory' contract, for non-performance is excused from the start. It should be borne in mind that such clauses are unlikely to be construed by the court as having the effect of a total exclusion for non-performance of the contract in the first place, so that in *O'Connor v. McCowen*,[32] where turnip seed supplied to the plaintiff subject to the defendants' caveat that they could not 'guarantee it', it was held that the defendants could not rely on this statement when it transpired that the seed produced plants that were worthless and certainly not turnips. The wording was construed so as to cover only quality of the turnip seed, not its very identity. On the other hand, in *George Mitchell (Chesterhall) v. Finney Lock Seeds*,[33] involving a contract which permitted the described goods to be substituted by different goods at the discretion of the supplier but which also contained a clause excluding liability for any loss arising from such substitution, the court held the exclusion clause was effective where the substituted seed produced a commercially worthless crop. The defendant had been given the power to vary the subject matter of the contract.

But if the defendant is not given the power to vary the subject matter of the contract, can non-performance, as distinct from partial or defective performance, be excluded from liability? In *Karsales (Harrow) v. Wallis*[34] a car was supplied which was incapable of self-propulsion, and despite a clause excluding liability, it was held that the defendants were not entitled to rely on it where the entire basis of the contract was breached. In other words, what had occurred was not a breach of the contract but a failure to supply that which was contracted for, and accordingly the clause could have no effect. So, if the defendant steps outside of the contract to that extent, he cannot rely upon any benefit that the contract might claim to bestow upon him. In the only case in point in this jurisdiction, *Clayton Love v. B+I*,[35] the Supreme Court adopted the concept as outlined by Denning MR, namely, that it is a rule of law that fundamental breach prevents the defendant from relying on the exclusion clause. However, later cases in England, in particular *Harbutts Plasticine v. Wayne Tank Corporation*,[36] gave rise to some concern. In that case the contract contained a clause which limited damage to £15,000 in the event of a breach of contract. In fact, the materials supplied were inappropriate (the plastic pipes which were to carry hot material from one part of the factory to another could not withstand the heat) and damage close to £1,000,000 was sustained. The court held that the defendants could not rely on the limiting clause because a fundamental breach had occurred by operation of law; in other words, the facts could only be construed as creating a fundamental breach. Yet both parties were equally met and had an

---

31   Clark, op. cit., p. 146; *MacRobertson Miller Airlines v. Commissioner of State Taxation* (1975) 133 GLR 125; *Fogarty v. Dickson* (1913) 47 ILTR 281.

32   (1943) 77 ILTR 64.
33   [1983] 2 All ER 737.
34   [1956] 2 All ER 866.
35   (1970) 104 ILTR 157.
36   [1970] 1 All ER 255.

opportunity to examine the contract, to negotiate the allocation of risk if the work went wrong. If the doctrine arises by operation of law, none of these are relevant concerns, yet clearly it should be possible to enter a contract where both parties may themselves use clauses which limit the fundamental obligation of the contract. This was dealt with in an earlier case, *Suisse Atlantique*,[38] where the court held that fundamental breach was a matter of construction, not a rule of law; and in *Photo Production v. Securicor Transport*[39] the court overruled *Harbutts*, re-affirming the doctrine as one of construction rather than of operation of law. This certainly seems preferable. By being a rule of construction it is open to the courts to determine what the parties agreed: an extensive core obligation with exclusions for liability arising from breach whereby a fundamental breach is not to be covered by the exclusion clause, or a narrow core obligation by use of exclusion clauses (and accordingly with much less likelihood of fundamental breach actually occurring). The parties are free to allocate the risks between themselves as appropriate. Moreover, this is more in line with the general approach taken in applying exclusion clauses to which we referred to at the beginning of this chapter: the contract is first read to see what obligations arise and only then are exclusion clauses applied to those obligations. This jurisdiction is likely to follow the later English case law, *Clayton Love v. B+I* is of dubious authority.[39]

14.05 THE EXCLUSION CLAUSE AND PRIVITY

In the earlier discussion we have assumed that the parties are in a direct contractual relationship with each other. But it is often the case that the exclusion clause arises in connection with a third party and the defendant is seeking to rely on an exclusion clause of which he himself is not the author. For example, in *Morris v. C.W. Martin Ltd*[40] the plaintiff gave a fur coat to a furrier for cleaning. The furrier could not undertake the work himself but informed the plaintiff that the defendants could do the work and that he would arrange same. Acting as a principal, the furrier entered into a contract with the defendant which contained an exclusion clause. The fur coat was stolen due to the defendant's negligence and the plaintiff sued the defendant. The furrier, because he had acted as a principal, would have been precluded from suing, since the exclusion

---

37   [1967] 1 AC 361.
38   [1980] 1 All ER 556; cited with approval in the High Court in *Western Meats* [1982] ILRM 101, *Fitzpatrick and Harty v. Ballsbridge International Bloodstock Sales*, unreported, High Court, 25 February 1983.
39   However, it remains that fundamental breach is a vital concept in this jurisdiction given the lack of an analogous UCT Act 1977. The Courts here should not adopt its downgrading as has occurred in Australia, see Greig and Davis, op. cit., p. 652 et seq.
40   [1965] 2 All ER 725.

clause of the contract would deny liability, and if the furrier had acted as agent of the plaintiff this would also have barred the plaintiff's claim. But by suing the defendant directly, it was sought to avoid the exclusion clause. The case did not fall to be decided on the direct point; instead, the court held that the defendants were bailees[41] and the clause was insufficient for them to rely upon. The case could have been resolved more directly in either of two ways. Firstly, the exclusion clause was not effective, since insufficient notice had been given of it to the plaintiff. Denning attempted to deal with this (though the rest of the court left the question unresolved) by inferring that the plaintiff had given the coat to the furrier on the assumption that the 'usual trade terms and conditions' would apply. However, the assumption of 'usual terms and conditions' is difficult to reconcile with the need make the parties to a contract aware of exclusion clauses, particularly in this case where the exclusion was unusual. Denning's view of an exclusion clause incorporated on the assumption of 'usual terms and conditions' should, therefore, be treated with caution. Secondly, and perhaps more importantly, it is difficult to see any contract between the plaintiff and the defendant. Accordingly, since there was no contract between the plaintiff and the defendant, there was no operative exclusion clause; the relationship was one of possession or bailment.

This was the approach taken in *Scruttons v. Midland Silicones*,[42] where the defendants were stevedores who were subcontracted by the shipping company to unload the plaintiff's goods. The goods were damaged by the negligence of the defendants, who sought to rely on the contractual term between the plaintiff and the shipping company which limited the amount of damage payable. While that clause could clearly benefit the shipping company, could it be extended to cover his agents? The answer in a jurisdiction which still eschews a strict view of privity was unavoidable: the defendants could not avail of a contractual term to which they were not a party. If the doctrine of privity were amended, in the way we have already suggested (see chapter 9), most of the problems would disappear, since the test would be to see if the parties to the contract intended a third party to benefit from the exclusion clause. Failing such a reform of privity, *Scruttons* represents sound law.

But sound law does not always justice make. The courts have been conscious of the difficulties a simplistic implementation of this rule creates and in *The Eurymedon*[43] the Privy Council went to unrealistic lengths to extend the exclusion clause to cover third parties. In that case the court refused to hold that the defendants had been made a party to the contract but instead based its

---

41 A 'bailee' is one who has possession of goods which they do not own, for example, if I loan my book to you, you are a 'bailee' since you now have possession of goods which you do not own. I would be the 'bailor' and the relationship between us is a 'bailment'. The bailment can be for reward, for example, the hire of a rental car.

42 [1962] 2 All ER 1; *Adler v. Dickson* [1954] 3 All ER 397.

43 [1974] 1 All ER 1015.

decision on a unilateral offer that, if the contract were performed, the plaintiff would release those involved from any liability. This is extremely doubtful reasoning and indeed somewhat tortuous. It has been rejected in many other common law jurisdictions, such as Australia.[44] Indeed, subsequent English case law tends to suggest that a third party (that is, someone who is not a party to the contract in the legal sense) may well come within the scope of protection offered by the exclusion clause without recourse to artificial concepts. These cases can be only justified on the basis of contractual expectation; that is, the parties to the contract were aware, under normal commercial practice in the particular industry, that a third party could have benefit of the exclusion clause. *Norwich City Council v. Harvey*,[45] where the exclusion clause benefited a subcontractor in the construction industry despite the express mention of subcontractors' liability, is rationally explicable on the basis that the industry operated a standard form contract whose function was not merely to set down a standard contract but which was designed to allocate the risks in any such contract prior to entering into it and, accordingly, permit the parties to obtain their own insurance against such risks or operate at their peril. Commercial practice thus supersedes legal reasoning in this regard.

In conclusion it is true to say that, due to the doctrine of privity, a defendant who is not a party to a contract may not avail of any exclusion clause contained therein. However, in certain cases, commercial reality may dictate the prior allocation of risks to be born in contracts and thereby permit a defendant to avail himself of the protection of the exclusion clause. Finally, it should be noted that the problem would disappear if the doctrine of privity were to be amended along the lines suggested in this text.

14.06 STATUTORY EXCLUSION

The legislature may, of course, intervene and specifically deny the efficacy of an exclusion clause in a contract; this has happened under the Road Traffic Acts, where a driver of a mechanically propelled vehicle cannot exclude liability to a passenger. In pursuing this course of action, the legislature is pre-allocating the risks involved in any transaction. In the United Kingdom, the Unfair Contract Terms Act 1977 provides a general solution to many of the problems discussed earlier. A general statute on exclusion clauses, as distinct from piecemeal legislation, may also be preferable in this jurisdiction. In the meantime, the use of English precedent should be limited, given that English law is now formulated against a background of a general statutory remedy; the value of such cases post-1977 must be slight. Notice should also be taken of the impact of the EC Directive on Unfair Contract Terms (Chapter 15).

---

44   *The New York Star* [1979] 1 Lloyds Rep 298.
45   [1989] 1 All ER 1180.

Implied terms in contracts for the sale of goods or supply of services

15.01 INTRODUCTION

Contracts for the sale of goods form the basis of many commercial transactions, yet the regulatory aspects of these contracts have received limited attention. The cornerstone of the protection available in such contracts is to be found in the 1893 Sale of Goods Act, which in this jurisdiction remained unaltered until the Sale of Goods and Supply of Services Act 1980. Even that Act merely extended the scope of the provisions, with the relevant amendments, to include contracts for the provision of services—something which had been omitted from the earlier legislation. A fuller discussion of the Sale of Goods provisions is worthy of a text in its own right;[1] what follows is merely an attempt to give the salient features of the legislation.

While this chapter will concentrate on the provisions of the 1980 Act, it should be noted that, as a result of our membership of the European Union, further legislative measures have been enacted which impact on the implied terms of a contract—for example, the directive on misleading advertising,[2] on contracts negotiated away from business premises[3] and the directive on liability for defective products.[4]

15.02 SCOPE OF THE ACT

The Sale of Goods and Supply of Services Act 1980 applies to two types of contracts: contracts for the sale of goods and contracts for the supply of services. The question arises as to what constitutes goods and services. A good is defined in s. 62 of the Act as

---

1   See Benjamin, *Sale of Goods*, Atiyah, *Sale of Goods*, 8th ed., see also Forde, *Commercial Law in Ireland*, pp. 1-100.
2   See European Communities (Misleading Advertising) Regulations (SI No. 134 of 1988).
3   See European Communities (Cancellation of Contracts Negotiated Away from Business Premises) Regulations (SI No. 224 of 1989).
4   Dir 85/374/EEC, now enacted in the Liability for Defective Products Act 1990.

includ[ing] all chattels personal other than things in action and money, emblements, industrial growing crops, and things attached to or forming part of the land which are agreed to be severed before the sale or under the contract of sale.

While there is a clear distinction between chattels personal and chattels real, there had been some difficulty with the distinction of chattels personal and a contract for the supply of services. Thus, a contract to paint a portrait was held not to be a contract for sale of a good whereas a contract to build a ship is such a contract.[5] This is now resolved by the inclusion of services under the 1980 Act, which effectively renders these cases moot, though it should be noted that the provision extending the statute to cover services does not cover such services arising under a contract of service. Thus, in the above example, the painting of the portrait is covered under the Act, provided that the painter was not an employee, that is, operating under a contract of service (in which case the issue is dealt with under employment law provisions).[6]

Moreover, the contract must be one of sale and therefore excludes gifts, an exchange or other such transaction. This does not mean that the contract must be paid for in money or money's worth—merely that the purchase price can be expressed in money and the agreement is so expressed. Thus, in *Flynn v. Mackin*[7] Walsh J made the point that, in the purchase of a new car, it is often the case that another car is traded in as part of the price. Where this happens after a price has been agreed for the new car, the transaction remains a contract for sale—but the consideration is to be satisfied partly by cash, partly by the car being traded in. Presumably, however, if the contract was to sell a new car for £5,000 plus the old vehicle this is not necessarily a contract for sale within the statute, since it is part sale and part exchange.

Finally, the sale must transfer the ownership to the purchaser and not some other party. Thus, contracts of hire purchase or lease, by which the ownership in the property normally passes to the finance company and the goods in question are held on bailment, do not come within the Act, although other statutory provisions apply.[8]

15.03 TERMS OF THE ACT

For convenience sake we will deal with contracts for the sale of goods as distinct from the supply of services. There are a number of reasons for this, chief among

5   *In re Blyth Shipbuilding Co. Ltd* [1926] Ch 494.
6   See Fennell and Lynch, *Labour Law in Ireland* (1993).
7   [1974] IR 101.
8   In particular the Hire Purchase Act 1946, s. 9, imports the sale of goods provisions in contracts of hire purchase. The 1980 Act extended this to leasing arrangements (s. 38), see *O'Callaghan v. Hamilton Leasing* [1984] ILRM 146.

which is the more extensive judicial pronouncements with respect to sale of goods contracts. Moreover, much of what is said with respect to sale of goods contracts applies equally to supply of service contracts, although obviously allowances have to be made for the very different nature of the two transactions.[9]

The primary aim of the legislation is to imply certain terms into all relevant contracts. These are now analysed in more detail. Remember that these terms, or similar terms, may be in existence in the contract in any event and the Act is designed to insert terms that would not be implied at common law if they did not form part of the express terms of the contract. We shall see later the impact of conflict between these implied terms and other agreed terms of the parties.

Where the Act specifies that the implied term is a condition, normally breach of such condition entitles the parties to repudiation of the contract, whereas a warranty enables a claim in damages only. This bears the caveat that the distinction between conditions and warranties is not as clear cut as was once thought; for further discussion see chapters 13 and 22.

Implied term as to title (s. 12)   This has now been amended by s. 10 of the 1980 Act and effects two implied terms into the contract. Firstly, it is a condition that the seller has good title to sell the goods either at the time the contract is made or by such time as the terms of the contract fall to be performed. Secondly, there is an implied warranty that the goods in question are free from encumbrances other than those disclosed. Both these implied terms can be limited where the seller intends to transfer only such title as he or a third party actually has. The title requirement is then limited to the extent that the seller's rights have been fully disclosed. Disclosure is to occur prior to the contract being made.

The term applies even where the seller is unaware of the fact that he has no title to pass.[10] Finally, it should be remembered that the term does not operate to transfer a title which the seller does not have. It merely means that the purchaser can repudiate the contract and sue for consequential loss in the event of the seller not being the true owner. If the seller has stolen the items in question, such a solution may be of somewhat unrealisable value.

Sale by description (s. 13)   Again this is now found in s. 10 of the Act; simply put, it requires that where goods are sold by description they should correspond to that description. The question that immediately springs to mind is what constitutes a description. Clearly a label can constitute sale by way of description just as much as a description of goods not yet in existence can. In *O'Connor*

---

9   Part IV, Sale of Goods and Supply of Services Act 1980, s. 39: for services it shall be implied that: (a) the supplier has the necessary skill to render the service; (b) the service is supplied with due skill, care and diligence; (c) that the materials used will be sound and reasonably fit for the purposes intended and (d) any goods supplied under the contract must be merchantable, pursuant to s. 14(3).

10   *O'Reilly v. Fireman* [1942] Ir Jur Rep 36.

v. Donnelly,[11] where the purchaser asked for a particular brand of a product, this was held to constitute a description, but in *Oscar Chess v. Williams*[12] statements as to the age and mileage of a motor vehicle were held not to be a sale by way of description, and in *Reardon Smith Line v. Ynguai Hansen Tangen*[13] describing the ship as being one built in a certain ship-yard in Osaka, Japan, was held not to be a sale by way of description because the statements merely served to identify the ship and not describe it. It appears from the case law that the term 'description' excludes quality or condition but must describe the items essential characteristic. Thus, to sell a tin which is labelled 'Prime Fillets of Salmon' is a sale of salmon by description; the contents of the tin must be salmon, not some other fish that once went out with a salmon.[14] However, the phrase 'prime fillets' is one relating to quality and condition, and if it transpires that the tin consists of salmon but in fact is far from prime fillets of the fish but the scrag end of salmon, no cause of action arises under this section. It might, of course, be actionable as a misrepresentation; this is discussed elsewhere.

No liability attaches where the description given is not relied upon by the purchaser. For example, a car is being sold privately and an advertisement has been placed in a local newspaper; the car does not correspond with the advertisement; the purchaser does not see the advertisment but hears of the sale through a friend. The purchaser cannot take an action claiming the car does not fit the description in the newspaper advertisment. Reliance by the purchaser upon the description is crucial.[15]

Merchantable quality (s. 14)   Since 1893 all contracts for the sale of goods have had a term of merchantable quality implied into them. It should be noted that such an implied term only arises where the goods have been sold in the course of business, thereby excluding a private sale. However, the provisions extend to include those goods which do not, strictly speaking, form part of the contract for sale; thus, in *Gedding v. Marsh*[16] the returnable bottle in which the

11   [1944] Ir Jur Rep 1.
12   [1957] 1 WLR 370.
13   [1976] 3 All ER 570.
14   *O'Connor v. Donnelly* [1944] Ir Jur Rep 1.
15   *Beale v. Taylor* [1967] 1 WLR 1193; *Joseph Travers v. Longel Ltd* (1947) 64 TLR 150; *Harlington v. Hull Fine Art* [1990] 1 All ER 737 (a painting was sold as an original but in fact it was a copy. One argument of the plaintiff was that the sale was by way of description and therefore infringed s. 13. The court held against plaintiff on a number of grounds, but the claim that the sale was by way of description, and thus covered by s. 13, was rejected. Before the sale could be by way of description, the description had to be so essential as to become part of the terms of the contract. Reliance was a relevant and important fact, but was not conclusive. It had to be within the contemplation of both parties that the description was part of the contract, see also chapter 16 for a further discussion of this case on a related issue).

16   [1920] 1 KB 668.

mineral water came was held not to form part of the contract for sale but nonetheless was covered by the provisions of the Act.

All contracts for the sale of goods have an implied term as to their merchantable quality save with respect to defects which have been specifically drawn to the attention of the purchaser or (if an examination is made by the purchaser prior to the contract being concluded) to any defects which an examination ought to have revealed. The concept of merchantable quality lacked statutory definition until the 1980 Act, but this now clarifies previous judicial precedent in this area. Merchantable quality now means that the goods are fit for the purposes for which they are intended and as durable as can be reasonably expected. The two-limbed approach to this concept needs to be examined further. With respect to 'fit for the purposes intended', we must first examine the purpose for which the good is in fact intended. A car, for example, is intended to get the owner from X to Y, but there are many other purposes for which it is intended. Thus status, comfort, convenience and so forth are all equally important. To illustrate this, suppose I buy a new car tomorrow and it is clearly capable of transporting me from X to Y but little else; can the item said to be fit for the purposes intended? In *Bernstein v. Pamson Motors*[17] the court distinguished between two different situations, a secondhand car and a new car. In the former

> two basic requirements [are] first that it should be capable of being driven and, second, that it should be capable of being driven in safety,

whereas for the latter

> it would only be in the most exceptional case . . . that [if] on delivery [it] was incapable of being driven in safety [it] could ever be classed as being of merchantable quality,

and of course, the purchaser of a new car can expect

> the appropriate degree of comfort, ease of handling and reliability, of pride in the vehicle's outward and interior appearance.

Price, presumably, is a relevant issue here. Yet it little explains the different approach to two cases of great similarity. In *Leaves v. Wadham Stringer*[18] a vehicle with a defective bonnet light, a faulty fan belt, a leaking boot, some rust and a loose door was held merchantable whereas, in *Rogers v. Parish*[19] a Range Rover, which had substantial body defects, a misfiring engine and a noisy transmission system, was held to be unmerchantable. The reasoning behind the difference in approach is unclear. One suggested rationale is that the vehicles came from different market segments, yet this is somewhat dubious since in

17   [1987] 2 All ER 220.   19   [1987] 2 All ER 232.
18   [1980] RTR 308.

Business Appliance Specialists v. Nationwide Credit Corp[20] a second hand Mercedes, an expensive car of high quality, suffered very unusual wear which it should not have done, given the mileage and age of the vehicle in question. Yet the car was held to be of merchantable quality. Atiyah places this case at the borders of such reasoning.[21] Moreover, in *Shine v. General Guarantee Corp*[22] a car which was usable despite the fact that it had been submerged in water for 24 hours and had been classed as a write-off for insurance purposes, was held not to be of merchantable quality. The fact that the dealer believed that the car had been over-priced by £1,000 was held relevant. The price paid for a new car should have little bearing on the question of merchantabilty. The same is, of course, not true for a secondhand car, for such a vehicle sold at under-value must raise the presumption that the purchaser takes some risk in choosing to purchase it.[23] But a new car is sold according to a list price and it cannot really matter what price this is. The price represents the prestige of the marque and the features of that model. It seems absurd that a car in the lower market spectrum is merchantable despite the fact that a door fails to close properly, whereas a car in an upper market segment would not be if it had the same defect. Surely the purchasers of both models expect the car to perform identical functions; in other words, the door should be capable of closing properly. The upper market saloon may have doors that close with an expensive thud rather than the tinny clang of the cheaper car, and it may be expected to last longer, but in reality it cannot be that a failure to operate correctly as would be expected should receive this different treatment. The case law illustrates that the concept of 'fit' within the legislation is far from clear and is really quite subjective.[24]

The next question is the meaning of the phrase, 'for the purposes intended'. This raises a number of issues. Firstly, purposes intended by whom, exactly? The purchaser, the seller, a reasonable man, the manufacturer? If goods had only one use, few difficulties would arise, but most items have many uses. Clark points out that some items have a single use only: thus, hot water bottles are to be used to hold hot water, cakes and coal are to be consumed, and underpants are to be worn next to the skin.[25] Apart from a limited imagination as to what can be done with underpants (Madonna and other so called fashion icons have shown that underpants may be worn outside of clothing, at the very least), it is

---

20   [1988] RTR 3.
21   Op. cit., p. 175.
22   [1988] 1 All ER 911.
23   See *Lutton v. Saville Tractors* [1986] NI 327 (there is no legal distinction between new and second hand cars in terms of merchantability, it is a question of fact to be determined in each particular case).
24   *Harlington v. Hull Fine Art* [1990] 1 All ER 737 (a painting purchased in the belief that it was an original masterpiece, but which was later discovered to be a cheap replica with a drop in value from £6,000 to £100, was held by the court not to be unmerchantable, since one could still enjoy its artistic merit!).
25   Op. cit., p. 168.

doubtful if any item can be confined to a single use. This is not to say that s. 14 will be breached for every use made of a good, but that it would be difficult, if not impossible, to ascribe some abstract, exclusive use to a good without recourse to all the surrounding facts. Clearly, a good which is used in the manner intended by the manufacturer (or in a manner contemplated by the reasonable man) will bring itself within the provisions of the statute. But there may be other uses, not intended by the manufacturer, which would also be covered by s. 14. In *Stokes & McKiernan v. Lixnaw Co- Op*,[26] the plaintiff used alcohol purchased from the defendant for testing the quality of milk. One supply of the alcohol, while fit for drinking, was of insufficient quality to use for such testing. The defendants were held liable under this section because, despite the fact that the manufacturer, or the reasonable man, would have assumed alcohol was for drinking, it was also legitimate to use it for testing. Yet, in *Brady v. Cluxton*[1] a fur coat, which caused irritation when worn directly next to exposed flesh, was held not to be of unmerchantable quality. These cases cannot be reconciled as they stand, since in both cases the use made of the items was a legitimate use, albeit not one normally associated with the items in question. The key difference would appear to be the knowledge of the seller as to the use of the goods. In *Lixnaw Co-op* the use of the alcohol was known by implication since it can hardly have been reasonable that the co-op went in for heavy drinking, whereas in *Brady* the use could not have been known by the seller. Thus, a seller is presumed to know that a good which he is selling can be reasonably expected to be used in a certain manner, but where a good is to be used in another manner which would not be normal, liability will only attach to the seller where he is aware, or should have been aware, of the different use to which the item is intended to be put.

It should be remembered that all that is required is that the seller is, or should have been, aware of the use the item is intended for, not that the seller should know that it is incapable of performing that function.[28] Thus in *Wallis v. Russell*,[29] where boiled crabs were given by the seller in place of the fresh crabs requested, it was held that the seller was liable under s. 14 of the Act when the boiled crabs were bad, because the seller knew that they were to be eaten for tea. It did not matter that the seller could not tell if the crabs were good or bad, or that he had taken all reasonable steps to determine their status. Liability was strict. It does show that the buyer can rely upon the seller's skill and knowledge and thereby transfer the risk from one to the other. If the buyer asks the seller for a table that can withstand the weight of a computer system and is given one by the seller who is unaware of the fact that it will not support such weight, then the responsibility for the damages lies with the seller because the buyer relied on his skill and knowledge. If, however, the buyer exercises independent action

26 (1937) 71 ILTR 70.
27 (1927) 61 ILTR 89.
28 *Egan v. McSweeney* (1955) 90 ILTR

40 (a copper detonator in a bag of coal rendered the coal unmerchantable).
29 [1902] 2 IR 585.

and selects a table without seeking the advice of the seller, then the seller's liability will depend on whether or not the table in question would reasonably be expected to support such weight.

The question then arises as to how far the buyer's own skill and knowledge can displace the reliance upon the seller's skill and knowledge. If the buyer is a computer expert and seeks advice from the seller as to the suitability of a particular computer system, can the seller claim, if the system fails to meet the requirements, that the buyer's expertise removes the obligation from the seller? This might be an interpretation of *Draper v. Rubenstein*,[30] where an experienced butcher who purchased some cattle at a mart for slaughtering and subsequently found them unfit for consumption failed to succeed in an action under this provision; however, this is an unusual case and should not be authority for such a proposition. Is it suggested that a mechanic cannot buy a car without losing the protection of this section or that an experienced person in any field falls outside the scope of the Act? The correct view of *Draper* is that where the merchantability of an item cannot be ascertained from examination alone (capable of being performed equally by the seller and the buyer) and both the seller and the buyer are of equal status in terms of experience, then the normal rule of *caveat emptor*[31] applies. In this regard, the case is probably best treated as *sui generis* on its particular facts.

In summary, liability attaches to a good which is not fit for the purposes intended. 'Fit' is a subjective concept that will vary from good to good and is influenced by the price paid and other relevant factors. The purposes intended are those that a reasonable person would assume as being the primary purposes, or, where the good is used for another reasonable purpose, then only if the seller is aware or should have been aware from the surrounding circumstances of its intended use,[32] or where the good is being used for a non-reasonable purpose only if the seller is actually aware of the said use and has accepted liability for such use. Where a buyer expressly relies on the seller's skill and knowledge as to the use of the item, liability rests with the seller.

Finally, the item is expected to be as durable as one would reasonably expect from all the surrounding circumstances. It is commonly believed that many household goods have a twelve-month guarantee, yet this is not strictly speaking true. If a washing machine fails twelve months and one day after purchase, this does not preclude an action under the Act. It might preclude enforcement of the manufacturer's guarantee, but that is something separate from the Statute. Of course, the further one moves away from twelve months, the harder it will be

---

30 (1925) 59 ILTR 119; compare also *Harlingdon v. Hull Fine Arts* [1990] 1 All ER 737 (purchasers reliance on the seller as to the nature of the painting, supra).
31 Let the buyer beware!
32 *Brown v. Craiks* [1970] 1 WLR 752 (denim supplied by the seller was used to make jeans. The denim was unsuitable for jeans, it was only suitable for dresses. *Held* that there was no breach of merchantability when the use was not known to the seller).

to prove the case; but it is not impossible to do so. Moreover, some items might be expected to have a much longer durability, such as a ship or plane.[33]

Sale by sample (s. 15) Where a sale takes place by way of a sample, that is, where a sample is used to represent the bulk, it is an implied condition that the bulk corresponds to the sample. This means that the sample must be representative of the bulk, although it cannot be that such a criterion should be taken too literally, since to do so would render such sales impossible. A negative way of phrasing it is to say that the sample should not consist only of the best of the bulk or consist of items that would lead one to believe that the quality of the bulk is different from that which it in fact is. Moreover, there would be little point in requiring that the sample correspond to the bulk if the buyer were unable to have a reasonable opportunity to inspect the sample for any defects that may be present; therefore, such an opportunity is implied in the contract. Finally, a defect in the bulk should be capable of discovery on a reasonable examination of the sample. If it is not, then liability will attach.

Motor vehicles The 1980 Act, s. 13, imposes a new implied term into contracts for the sale of motor vehicles. Such contracts now carry an implied condition that, on delivery, the vehicle is free from any defects which would render the vehicle unsafe or dangerous to its occupants, to road users, or to the public in general. This is quite an onerous condition and exposes the seller to considerable liability, as in the case of *Glorney v. O'Brien*,[34] where a car sold for £250 rendered the seller liable for damages in excess of £18,000 when the suspension collapsed on the vehicle, injuring the occupants. Effectively this provision renders private sales of motor vehicles relatively risky, since the seller operates as insurer for the purchaser with respect to the safety of the vehicle.

15.04 CONTRACTING OUT OF THE ACT

Can such terms as are implied by the provisions of the Act be excluded by agreement between the parties? The Act makes provision for such exclusion, albeit in limited circumstances.

The implied term as to title (s. 12), cannot be excluded in any circumstance, but there is provision for excluding sections 13, 14, and 15 in non-consumer contracts. A person deals as a 'consumer' when he enters into a contract (outside the course of his business) with another party who makes the contract in the course of business, and where the goods in question would reasonably be expected to be for private use or consumption.[35] The definition of a consumer

---

33 In general see *Wills v. Davids* (1956-57) 98 CLR 77, *Lambert v. Lewis* [1982] AC 225, *Mash and Murrell v. Emmanuel* [1961] 1 All ER 485.
34 Unreported, High Court, 14 November 1988.

is somewhat cumbersome, and leaves a considerable amount of latitude to the court as to a determination of the status of the party to the contract. Remember, whether a party is a consumer depends on the current transaction, not his normal status. Thus, a business person can enter into a consumer contract and a consumer can enter into a non-consumer contract. There is a divergent approach to the question of consumer contracts between the courts in this jurisdiction and those in the United Kingdom which operate similar provisions. In the UK, the tendency has been to find that a person deals as a consumer even when he or she is a business person,[36] whereas the courts here have taken the view that most business people do not deal as consumers.[37] Having said that, the courts here have seldom been faced with the borderline cases that have arisen in the UK; therefore, it may be wrong to assume that the divergence concerning consumers and non-consumer contracts is as large as it might seem from first glance. A person never deals as a consumer when a contract arises from an auction or a tender.[38]

Where a person deals as a consumer, the provisions of the Act may not be excluded from the contract, but where the person deals as a non consumer they can be excluded from the contract where it is fair and reasonable to do so.

The Act contains a schedule of some of the reasons—but not all—which will warrant the exclusion of the terms of the Act. They are:

- relative bargaining power of the parties and the possibility of an alternative method of meeting the customer's requirements;

- whether there was an inducement to enter the contract;

- whether the customer had actual or constructive knowledge of the exclusion term;

- if there was an obligation on the customer, was compliance practical;

- were the goods made to special order for the customer at his request.

It is now apparent that the availability of insurance to the seller which would not disproportionately affect the price of the item will also be a major factor.[39] However, a large number of issues remain to be resolved with respect to the availability of insurance: it is unclear whether the insurance should have been available to either or both parties or whether the issue of insurance has to be raised by the parties. Nonetheless, a legitimate factor in determining the

---

35   S. 3(1)
36   *R&B Customs Broker v. UDT* [1988] 1 All ER 847; *Davies v. Sumner* [1984] 1 WLR 1301.
37   *O'Callaghan Leasing v. Hamilton Leasing* [1984] ILRM 146 (the supply of a ´drinks vending machine to the

owner of a take-away food outlet was held not to be a consumer transaction).
38   S. 3(2)
39   *George Mitchell v. Finney Lock Seeds* [1983] 1 AC 803.

exclusion of the statutory provisions is the availability of insurance and, like most of the cases where loss distribution is possible, the courts have shown a certain willingness to place the loss with the insured party.[40]

Finally, the provisions with respect to motor vehicles under s. 13 of the 1980 Act as mentioned above may also be excluded where the sale occurs to a buyer who is a dealer in motor vehicles or where the vehicle is to be exported from the jurisdiction and a document excluding liability, which has been entered into on a fair and reasonable basis, has been jointly signed.

15.05 HIRE PURCHASE AND LEASING AGREEMENTS

These agreements are controlled by the Hire Purchase Act 1946, which gives virtually identical rights, of the type outlined in ss. 12-15, to a person who obtains goods by way of a hire purchase agreement as to one who engages in a contract for sale *simpliciter*. Moreover, the distinction between a lease, which has become a popular method of financing personal property such as cars, computers etc., and a hire purchase arrangement has been assimilated under the 1980 Act. It remains the case, however, that rights of enforcement of hire purchase agreements and leasing agreements are substantially different.

15.06 UNFAIR CONTRACT TERMS AND THE EUROPEAN UNION

By the end of 1994, Member States should have enacted provisions dealing with unfair contract terms in consumer contracts pursuant to Directive 93/13/EEC.[41] In future a contract term is considered unfair if two conditions are fulfilled:

(a) the term has not been individually negotiated and

(b) the term causes a significant imbalance in the parties rights and obligations to the detriment of the consumer.[42]

It follows that, as a general rule, where a contractual term is to be found in a standard printed contract document, the presumption must be that it is unfair.[43] The presumption is open to rebuttal.[44]

---

40 *Smith v. Bush* [1989] 2 All ER 514 (a negligent survey undertaken by the defendant did not reveal that a house was defective. *Held* it was unreasonable to permit the loss to lie with the plaintiff, given the defendant's access to liability insurance as a professional surveyor).
41 OJ L 95 (21 April 1993). Enacted in the UK by SI No. 3159 of 1994.
42 Article 3(1).

Whether or not such a term causes a significant imbalance in the rights of the parties is a question of fact to be determined by the surrounding circumstances leading to the conclusion of the contract. The subject matter of the contract or the price agreed upon can never be the cause of a significant imbalance in the rights of the parties.[45]

All the terms of the contract must be in plain intelligible language;[46] otherwise, any ambiguity must be resolved in favour of the consumer.[47] Where a term is considered to be unfair, it can be severed so as to leave the remainder of the contract intact and enforceable.[48] The Directive gives some examples of typical terms which should be considered unfair, such as exclusion of liability for death and personal injury to the consumer.[49]

Finally, the Directive mandates that each Member State must take steps to ensure that unfair contract terms in consumer contracts are not permitted to continue.[50]

The Directive came into force on 1 January 1995, but the legislature should have availed of the opportunity not merely to enact the minimalist requirements of the Directive but should propose detailed legislation in the whole sphere of unfair contract terms.[51]

Note: This Directive applies to all consumer contracts not merely those for the sale of goods and will play an important role in the application of exclusion clauses in the future.

---

43   Pre-printed terms cannot have been negotiated between the parties, but are reminiscent of the French 'contrats d'ahesion', which are offered on a take it or leave it basis.
44   Article 3(2)—it follows that the presumption can be rebutted where the supplier can show that it is the practice to alter pre-printed terms of a contract, and that this was made known to the customer. It seems unlikely that the mere fact that the supplier was willing to alter the terms is sufficient, unless the consumer had a reasonable opportunity to know of this facility.
45   Article 4(2), although the subject matter, and the price thereof, must be in conformity with the requirement that they should be clear and intelligible, see below.
46   Article 4(2).
47   Article 5.
48   Article 6(1).
49   Annex to Directive, as are other examples such as unilateral alteration to the contract by the supplier or a disproportionate penalty to the consumer where the consumer fails to honour one of his undertakings in the contract.
50   Article 7(1), for example by state intervention in challenging common contract terms that exist in particular consumer contracts: for a common law approach to this problem, see the judicial pronouncements on over-the-counter temporary insurance policies for travel, ibid.
51   SI No. 144 of 1995 (retroactively applied). Note, in Australia there has been some judicial pronouncements to the effect that, despite the absence of a doctrine of good faith in general contract law, the courts should be mindful of the need for 'good faith' in the negotiation of terms; see Carter and Harland, op. cit.

16.00

Mistake

16.01 INTRODUCTION

Mistake in contract represents a major battleground between objective and subjective theories concerning the basis of the contractual relationship.[1] If the objective theory holds exclusive sway (and it is certainly true that at common law it does predominate), then there should be no need for a doctrine of mistake, since the contract, and its subject matter, would have come into existence solely on the basis of an objective third-party viewpoint, and the fact that the parties to the contract would hold a different view is irrelevant. But, of course, the objective view of contractual assent does not have exclusive domain; it is influenced by subjective concerns, many of which, originating from the civil law countries, sit uneasily into the legal theory.[2] What has emerged is a far from satisfactory approach to this subject area, making it difficult to propose a rational analysis of mistake in contract law. Instead, a series of rules have been devised to mitigate the effect of mistake in a contract; these rules are heavily influenced by the role of equity in the legal system, both in terms of substantive rules and remedies.[3]

There are a number of classifications of mistake that can be made, but care should be taken with any such categorisation since the terms are neither universal nor consistent. Often the courts themselves use the phrases interchangeably,[4] and certainly from an academic viewpoint there is little consensus on the issue;[5] however, while the terminology may vary, the facts seldom do and there a number of specific instances of mistake. First, both parties to the contract may be mistaken as to some element of the contract at the time the

---

1   Patterson, 'Equitable Relief for Unilateral Mistake', 28 *Columbia Law Rev* 859; Sabbath, 'Effect of Mistake in Contract: A Study in Comparative Law,' 13 *ICLQ* 798.
2   See Sabbath, ibid.
3   Perhaps further confused by the so called 'fusion fallacy' postulated in *United Scientific Holdings v. Burnley Borough Council* [1977] 2 All ER 62, approved in *Hynes v. Independent Newspapers* [1980] IR 204, but with respect this fusion fallacy is questionable at best, completely erroneous at worst, see Meaghar, Gummow and Lehane, *Equity: Doctrines and Remedies*, pp. 67-69; Baker, 'The Future of Equity' (1977) 93 *LQR* 529, Keane, op. cit., p. 25, doubts that *Hynes* is authority for the fusion proposition.
4   See *Nolan v. Nolan* (1954) 92 ILTR 94; *O'Neill v. Ryan* [1991] ILRM 672.
5   See Clark, op. cit., p. 201.

contract came into effect.[6] Here a number of possibilities offer themselves. Both parties may subsequently become aware of the mistake and decide to resolve the issue themselves without recourse to the legal process. More likely is that the mistake made alters the contract, so that it is to the benefit of one of the parties, and that party now wishes to enforce the contract despite the original mistake. This is sometimes referred to as 'common' or 'mutual' mistake, but we shall, as far as practicable, avoid the use of such traditional and misleading nomenclature. Secondly, one of the parties only to the contract may be operating under a mistake as to an element of the contract. This can then be further classified as to (a) situations where the mistaken belief of one party is known by the other party, who does nothing to clarify the situation, and (b) situations where the mistaken belief by one party are not known by the other party and both parties believe that the other is entering into the contract on the same basis even though this is not true. For the purposes of further analysis only, these will be categorised as Mistake Common to both parties, Unilateral Mistake and Cross Purposes respectively.

Before discussing each category we shall study a number of issues common to all three.

16.02 THE MISTAKE

In any given contract, there are a large number of factors that make up the content matter of the transaction. Thus, a simple 'I will buy your car for £5,000' may conclude a contract, but the subject matter of that contract will consist of a myriad of facts, such as the colour of the car in question, the engine capacity, whether or not the seat covers are included and so forth. Any contract, therefore, can contain a mistake as to one or more of these facts, but not all such mistakes can be treated equally. Not only will some mistakes be so trivial as to be irrelevant; external factors may result in the reality that a seemingly trivial mistake becomes one of major consequence. Thus, if I purchase a car believing it to be 1150cc and it transpires it is in fact 1220cc, the mistake in terms of the operating nature of the vehicle is to all intents and purposes irrelevant, yet this small mistake may mean that my tax and insurance liabilities are severely increased. The law will not come to the aid of a person for every mistake that occurs; it must be a mistake of consequence in that it is material to the performance of the contract. A mistake as to a subsidiary issue of the contract is of no concern to the courts; this is a natural implication of the objective theory of contract. But a mistake that is sufficiently material to somehow call into

6   The crucial date of the mistake is the date of the contract: *Amalgamated Investment and Property Co. v. Walker and Sons* [1976] 3 All ER 509 (an agreement on the basis of facts which were true at the time of conclusion of agreement, but which, before completion of the transaction, had changed. *Held* there was no question of mistake).

question the whole essence of the contract may force the courts to give some relief. The difficulty is in drawing the line as to what constitutes a material mistake sufficient to void the contract *ab initio* and what, even though it constitutes a mistake, is one that the parties will have to live with. The concept of the material mistake alters depending on the type of mistake, that is, joint or unilateral, and whether the court is willing to exercise its equitable jurisdiction.

Finally the term 'mistake' is commonly used by the layperson with a meaning that has no application within the law of contract. A purchaser may have made a 'mistake' in buying an item because he has seen it for sale elsewhere at a cheaper price, or because it does not really suit the purchaser or it will not fit where it was intended to go or, indeed, because the purchaser can ill afford the item. The court will not look into the quality of the bargain; it will not examine whether you were right to enter into the bargain. It is concerned only to ensure that you got what you bargained for, no matter how big a 'mistake' it may prove to be in reality.

16.03 MISTAKE AS TO FACT

It is clear that the mistake must revolve around an issue of fact. *Ignorantia juris non excusat*[7] applies in this specific situation, as well as being of general application.[8] The mistake must relate to past or existing fact.[9] There is, however, some confusion concerning mistakes as to the law and the definition to be afforded the word 'law' in this principle. It would appear to mean law in the general sense as opposed to private law rights. Thus, it is not a mistake of fact to be unaware that a contract to commit a crime is illegal, whereas it may be a mistake of fact to believe that the legal title to property was held by the seller when it in fact was not. In a sense, the latter mistake appears to be a mistake of law, an error in understanding the legal title to the property, but in *Cooper v. Phibbs*[10] Westbury LJ held that a private right of ownership, in that case a salmon fishery, was a matter of fact.

7 Ignorance of the law is no excuse.
8 *O'Loghlen v. O'Callaghen* (1874) IR 8 CL 116; *Brisbane v. Dacres* (1813) 5 Tart 143; but cf. *Kiriri Cotton Co. v. Dewani [1960] 1 All ER 177; Dolan v. Nelligan* [1967] IR 247; *Rogers v. Louth County Council* [1981] ILRM 143. There appears to be some considerable confusion between a mistake giving rise to contractual problems, and the law of restitution, where money is paid on a mistaken belief as to the law, see *Lord Mayor of Dublin v. TCD* [1986] ILRM 283. Restitution applies to most transactions, of which contract transactions form a large subset, and is available for any transaction arising from a mistake (see *Barclays Bank v. Simms* [1980] 1 QB 677—the double crediting of a customer account by mistake). For contract purposes we are concerned as to what constitutes a mistake sufficient to vitiate the contract.
9 And not to predictions: *Metropolitan Life Insurance v. Kase*, 718 F 2d 306 (on rehearing at 720 F 2d 1081).
10 (1867) LR 2 HL 149.

The distinction between fact and law is one which pervades our legal system, not just in the doctrine of mistake but elsewhere, such as restitution and the different roles of judge and jury at a trial (the judge decides issues of law, the jury determines issues of fact). It remains, however, one of the least clearly defined concepts, and it is true to say that often the concept of fact and law are indissolubly mixed.[11] Nonetheless, where the distinction can be made, relief for mistake is granted for mistake of fact and not law.[12]

16.04 THE EFFECT OF THE MISTAKE

If a litigant is successful in a claim of mistake, the result is to render the contract void *ab initio*, that is to say, the position of the parties must be reversed so as to restore them to their status as if the contract had never occurred.[13] Whilst this makes eminent sense, it also explains why courts are reluctant to apply this doctrine with a liberal hand, because the consequences of such an action often far outweigh any injury done to the parties. In many ways it is difficult to see where the line between cause of action and appropriate remedy can be drawn. In a number of situations the principle relating to the cause of action has been moulded by the appropriateness of the remedy of rescission.[14] At common law, for example, recission was unavailable where the parties could not be restored to their pre-contractual position. The difficulties caused by this prior to the Judicature Act and the fusion of the administration of equity and the common law cannot be over-estimated. Today, it is of marginal significance, since rescission at equity is possible in such circumstance.[15] Beyond that, however,

---

11 *Norwich Union Fire Insurance v. Price* [1934] AC 455; *Sharp Brothers and Knight v. Chant* [1917] 1 KB 771.

12 Though note Grieg and Davies, op. cit., p. 896 make the point that, despite pronounce-ments from Chitty, Anson, Cheshire and Fifoot, et. al., that relief is not granted for mistake of fact, care should be taken not to overstate the case. Many of the decisions really revolve around what is fact and what is law. Note that in *Pine Valley v. Minster for the Environment* [1987] IR 23, 42, Henchy J stated that 'so much of the purchase price as was attributable to the planning permission was paid under a mistake of law, but in my opinion it would be recoverable no less than if it had been paid under a mistake of fact'. How this affects mistake of law under contract is discussed in O'Dell [1993] *Restitution Law Review* 140 and in particular *Dublin Corporation v. Trinity College Dublin* [1985] ILRM 84 (High Court) and 283 (Supreme Court). Further, in Canada the mistake of law and mistake of fact distinction has been abolished (*Air Canada v. British Columbia* (1989) 59 DLR (4th) 161).

13 *Cundy v. Lindsay* (1878) 3 App Cas 459.

14 Effectively, the cancellation of the contract.

15 Considerable emphasis is placed by some courts on the effect of a mistake common to both parties, at law or equity. At law, the contract would be void *ab initio*, whereas equity is more flexible in its approach, see *Solle v. Butcher* [1950] 1 KB 671. Thus, a mutual mistake at common law is 'frowned upon and rare' (*Bell v. Lever Bros*, ibid., *AJB v. Credit du Nord* [1988] 3 All ER 902) but this is a distinction too far. The confusion is

any further discussion is best pursued in a dedicated work on remedies or equity as to the exact limit and extent of the doctrine of recission. What we are concerned with here is whether the facts of the case disclose sufficient material to ground the plea of mistake.

On a final note, it follows that the correct remedy for mistake is one of restitution and that damages can never be the appropriate remedy. Where a plaintiff seeks such a remedy, he must pursue a claim based on another doctrine such as misrepresentation.[16] However, where the terms of the contract are contained within a document, it is open to the claimant to seek relief by way of rectification at equity.[17] Again, the concept of rectification is one best described elsewhere, but it must be remembered that rectification is available only where there is a mistake as to the written document when compared to the oral agreement and as such therefore does not really fall to be dealt with under the issue of mistake *per se*, but rather the enforcement of written documents over spoken agreements. As Calamari and Perillo point out, 'Contracts are not [rectified] for mistake; writings are.'[18]

16.05 MISTAKE COMMON TO BOTH PARTIES

We are concerned here with a mistake shared between the two parties to the contract. It is the same mistake held by both.[19] Thus, both the offeror and the offeree may believe themselves to be contracting for the sale of a rare Van Gogh, but in reality it may in fact be an oil painting by some obscure artist from the same era. Both parties share the mistake; both believe it to be something which it is not.[20] Should such a contract be enforceable when the mistake is discovered, or can the purchaser demand that it be set aside as not being what the parties intend to bargain for? There are two ways of looking at this. First, the parties contracted for a Van Gogh and the fact that it was a painting was a subsidiary feature. Alternatively, the parties contracted to sell a painting, an attribute of which was that it was painted by Van Gogh. Here the identity of the artist is subsidiary to the essence of the contract. On an objective basis of contractual

understandable given the mix of law, equity, rights and remedies. Steyn J comments in *AJB* ibid., that, if the contract makes provision for the contingency, there is no place for mistake. This is doubtful. If there has been a mistake, there could be no contract, unless you interpret part of the agreement as a separate agreement in the event of a mistake in the main agreement occurring!

16   See chapter 17, ibid.
17   See chapter 26, ibid.
18   Op. cit., p. 392.
19   *Harrison and Jones v. Bunten Lancaster* [1953] 1 All ER (both parties misunderstood the term 'Calcutta Kapok'); *Rose v. Pim* [1953] 2 All ER 739 (the meaning of 'feveroles' was misunderstood by both vendor and purchaser).
20   Restatement, Second, Contracts, s. 152.

agreement, it would depend on what an independent third party looking on would believe the contract to be about. Thus, in the second case, even though there is a mistake as to a part of the contract, it is insufficient to displace the entire contract, though in equity some relief may still be available.[21] In the former case, the mistake goes to the essence of the contract and therefore the case should be suitable for the operation of the doctrine of mistake.[22] We shall turn to look at these situations separately.

Mistake as to identity, existence or ownership of the subject matter A mistaken belief by both parties as to the identity of the item in question is normally sufficient to ground relief for mistake and have the contract voided. The problem involves distinguishing the identity of the subject matter of the contract from the quality of the subject matter. While in theory it is possible to have a contract set aside for a mistake as to the identity of the subject matter (provided the mistaken belief is held by both parties), the courts have shown an incredible ability to refuse to find that any such mistake as to identity occurred; instead, they have looked upon the mistake as one of quality (not identity), granting or denying relief depending upon the presence or absence of a warranty. Thus in *Diamond v. British Columbia Thoroughbred Breeder's Society*[23] a mistake between two horses at auction made by both the auctioneer and the bidders was held not to be mistake as to identity but quality.

It is true to say that few problems present themselves under this heading. Most problems would in fact, come under the cross purposes category, where both parties are mistaken but with respect to different matters, such as in the sale of a car where one party believes that he is selling a Ford Escort, the other believes himself to be buying a Ford Mondeo. This is not a common mistake as to identity: the resolution of such a problem is discussed below. Moreover, care should also be made to distinguish a mistake arising from misdescription. Not only is this covered by specific legislative provisions: it is also a clear case of cross purposes. Thus, *Megaw v. Molloy*[24] is a clear case of cross purposes where the parties entered into a contract on the basis of a sample which was unrepresentative of the bulk to be sold. The parties were at cross purposes, since the purchaser agreed to buy the bulk of the sample and the seller agreed to sell the contents of a given ship from which he mistakenly believed the sample came.

A mistake as to the existence of any item is far more common. It is crucial here to determine when exactly the contract came into existence, for, if it was

---

21   *Solle v. Butcher*, ibid.
22   *Kennedy v. Panama New Zealand and Australia Royal Mail* (1867) LR 2 QB 580 ('. . . The case is to determine whether the mistake or misapprehension is as to the substance of the whole consideration going as it were to the foot of the matter, or only to some point even though a material point, an error as to which does not effect the substance of the whole consideration', *per* Blackburn J, at 589.
23   (1965) 52 DLR (2d) 146.
24   (1878) 2 LR (Ir) 530.

completed prior to the item ceasing to exist, then in our law, as a general rule, the risk passed to the purchaser at the time the contract was concluded, and any subsequent loss to the item is that of the purchaser (the seller has the right to obtain a court order for payment of the agreed price).[25] That is why, in contracts for the sale of a house, the purchaser takes out insurance from the date of the agreement, even though it may be many weeks before he moves into the property in question. The corollary is also true: if the parties negotiate a contract when the subject matter of the agreement is no longer in existence, then this will render the contract non-existent by virtue of mistake. Very often the issue becomes confused by the fact that the courts have honoured a contract with respect to a subject matter which was not in existence at the time of the contract; but this is done on the basis that the seller has guaranteed that the subject matter is in fact in existence and it is on foot of this that the purchaser can sue. In the absence of any such guarantee, the contract can be set aside for mistake. The question arises as to when a seller would be unaware of the non-existence of the subject matter of the contract. In *Couturier v. Hastie*[26] the plaintiffs were the consignors of a quantity of corn which they had sold to the defendants. Prior to the sale, and unknown to either plaintiff or defendant, the ship carrying the corn had called into a port where the cargo was found to be unfit to proceed further and was, therefore, sold to a third party. The defendants refused to pay on the basis that the goods had ceased to exist prior to the completion of the sale. The court held, rightly, that the parties had not contracted for an 'adventure' or 'goods lost or not lost' but had contemplated the purchase of something existing. Nowadays, this case might be more appropriately dealt with by virtue of the implied provisions under the Sale of Goods and Supply of Services Act 1980, dealt with below. But the case remains relevant for its principle, namely that since both parties were under a mistake as to the existence of the subject matter, the contract could be set aside as void for mistake. In *Couturier* justice was done, but if we compare this to *McRae v. Commonwealth Disposals Comm*[27] the same cannot be said. In *McRae* the plaintiff tendered for the salvage rights to the wreck of vessel at a given location. This tender was accepted by the defendant, who then gave detailed information as to the shipwreck's location. The plaintiff expended considerable time, money and effort in attempting to locate the shipwreck but discovered that there in fact was never any such shipwreck. The defendant clearly desired that the court hold that the contract was one of mistake as to existence and should therefore be rendered void and

25 Restatement, Second, Contracts, s. 266; 13 Williston 1561-1562; *Strickland v. Turner* (1852) 7 Exch 208 (a policy of life insurance was mistakenly taken out on a person who was dead. *Held*, the contract was void).

26 (1852) 8 Exch 40 affirmed (1856) 5 HL Cas 673; *Galloway v. Galloway* (1914) 30 TLR 531 (a separation agreement mistakenly entered into by a couple who thought that they were married but were not, was held void for mistake).

27 (1951) 84 CLR 377.

set aside. The court refused to do so and the reasoning becomes clear from the following passage of the judgment:

> It is not a case in which the parties can be seen to have proceeded on the basis of common assumption of fact so as to justify the conclusion that the correctness of the assumption was intended by both parties to be a condition precedent to the creation of contractual obligations. The officers of the Commission made an assumption, but the plaintiffs did not make an assumption in the same sense. They knew nothing except what the Commission had told them.[28]

The court clearly placed considerable reliance upon the fact that the Commissioners were the effective source of the plaintiff's belief as to the existence of the subject matter and, accordingly, there was an implied warranty as to the existence of that subject matter. This would appear to better resolve the issue. If the goods are not in existence at the time the contract was made, and this was not known by either party to the contract, then the contract is void by virtue of mistake, save where the seller has expressly warranted the existence of the item or has done so in an implied manner where the buyer's belief as to the existence of the subject matter has been induced by the seller.[29] The seller, having so relied upon his ability to convince the buyer of the existence of goods, cannot now claim benefit from their non-existence. *McRae's* case also raises the possibility of an action in tort for negligence on the part of the seller in stating the existence of goods which are in fact non-existent. This would seem to have confused the Australian court in the case at hand, since there is some indication of refusing relief on the basis of mistake where that mistake results from the carelessness of the defendant himself. This imports tortious principles of negligence and recklessness into the strict liability basis of contract. It would be strange if *McRae's* case were to depend on whether the seller had been negligent in implying the existence of the shipwreck or not.

Finally, we turn to the concept of mistake as to ownership. For contracts dealing with the sale of goods, the Sale of Goods and Supply of Services Act 1980 implies into every such contract a clause which warrants that the seller has title to the item sold. This cannot be waived by the terms of the contract itself. However, there will be contracts which do not involve the sale of goods and for which, therefore, the common law rules apply. Unless the risk is expressly passed, the rule remains that the purchaser buys an item with no

---

28 Ibid., at 387.
29 However the case is justifiable if it is to be viewed as a speculative venture, where the existence of the item itself is in question: *March v. Pigot* (1771) 5 Butt 2802 (the parties were held to have taken the risk that the subject matter of the contract might already be dead at the time the contract was entered into. The contract was a wager on which the father of the parties to the contract would die first. One of them was already dead at the time but this was unknown to them. A case of conscious uncertainty? See ibid.).

warranty as to the title of the seller with respect to the subject matter of the contract. However, the reality is that most courts would be willing to imply a warranty as to title being held by the seller of the subject matter of the contract. Unless the contract was deemed to be an adventure or gamble, it is difficult to see a seller being victorious at court.

Mistake as to quality or other attribute As a general rule the courts will not hold a contract void by way of mistake with respect to the subject matter or other attribute of the contract unless the mistake goes to the essence of the contract in question. In *Bell v. Lever Bros*[30] the plaintiff dismissed an employee and paid a generous severance allowance. Unknown to both the plaintiff and the employee, the employee's contract of service could have been summarily terminated for his misconduct without any compensation having to be paid. On discovering this, the plaintiff sought to have the contract declared void and the money returned. The court rejected the claim, stating that the mistake was not sufficiently important to warrant the voiding of the contract. However, further *dicta* from Lord Atkins have often been interpreted as refusing to allow a mistake as to quality rendering the contract void. This is clearly incorrect. In *Sherwood v. Walker*[31] a contract to sell a cow believed by both buyer and seller to be sterile and, accordingly, worth little was set aside on the basis of mistake as to quality when it was discovered that the animal was in fact pregnant and thus worth much more. The court held that the nature of the contract was no longer of the same kind contemplated by the parties. This is the better approach, for there will be situations where the subject matter of the contract is of a different kind from that believed by the parties. *Bell v. Lever Bros* is explicable on the basis that although there was a mistake as to quality, the contract sought to compensate for the prior employment of the employee and the mistake did not render this different in kind. A few points of caution should be noted. First, the courts tend to find that no mistake has occurred; instead, they tend to imply a term of warranty and give a remedy for the breach of this implied warranty. The relief, however, is clearly at equity and is discretionary. Secondly, there is a concept of conscious uncertainty, familiar to American jurists but which operates in this jurisdiction on a subliminal level. If we look at the case of *Wood v. Boynton*,[32] this concept becomes clear. The plaintiff found an unusual stone which he showed to the defendant. Both believed the stone to be a worthless topaz, but the defendant liked it so much that he offered the plaintiff $1 for the item. Subsequently it was discovered that the stone was in fact an uncut diamond worth nearly $1,000. The plaintiff sought to have the contract set aside. The court refused to do so, holding that the parties had entered into the contract with

30 [1932] AC 161.
31 33 NW 919; *Western Potato Co-Op v. Durnam* [1985] ILRM (the contract was held void as both parties mistakenly believed the seed was usable when it was not).
32 25 NW 42.

conscious uncertainty. Conscious uncertainty means that the parties are aware of the fact that the subject matter of the contract is somewhat fluid, so to speak. Thus, Calamari and Perillo give the example of a paternity suit which the parties have settled: the settlement cannot be revisited simply because new technology now proves that the plaintiff is not the father; the basis of the settlement included that prospect.[33] Courts will not continually re-open agreements, unless the agreement specifically allows for the re-opening of the agreement.

16.06 UNILATERAL MISTAKE

In unilateral mistake we concern ourselves with a situation where only one party to the agreement is mistaken and the other party knows of the mistake or should have known of it. In general no relief is granted by unilateral mistake.[34] The case law can best be understood by a distinction between common law and equity. If one of the parties to the contract knows of the mistaken belief of the other party at the time that the contract is entered into but proceeds with the contract nevertheless, at law, the contract is void *ab initio*. This has to be so if the law is to be consistent since the parties are not *ad idem*. But where, at the time the contract is entered into, one of the parties was mistaken and the other party was not actually aware of the mistake but should have been aware of it, using the 'reasonable man' test, then the contract can be set aside in equity on such terms as the court sees fit and retaining the general equitable discretionary approach to the granting of a remedy. Where one of the parties is mistaken and the other party is neither aware nor should have been aware of the mistake, then the contract cannot be set aside, for this is the same as trying to set aside a contract because the purchaser subsequently discovers he cannot afford the item; this could not have been known to the seller, therefore the contract stands.

The rule is well typified by the case of *Hartog v. Colin and Shields*,[35] whereby an agreement sold hare skins on the basis of weight, whereas the trade practice was to sell them by the piece. It was held that the defendant should have known that an error had occurred and the contract was void for mistake. It is clear the decision would have been different if the mistake would not have been known to a reasonable man, given the surrounding circumstances. But it goes too far to say that there is an absolutist view on this; relief for the mistake is not available in all situations where one of the parties should have known of the unilateral mistake.

Firstly, the mistake must be palpable, that is, is readily discernable by a reasonable person. Thus, a quote for the erection of a building of, say, £100,000

33   Op. cit., p. 382.
34   Foulke, 'Mistake in the Formation and Performance of a Contract', 11 *Columbia Law Review* 197; Restatement, Contracts, s. 12; but cf., 3 Corbin 608, 675.
35   [1939] 3 All ER 566.

made by virtue of computational error and which should be £1,000,000, is palpably mistaken and ordinarily would justify setting the contract aside. On the other hand, if the quote had been £900,000 due to computational error, this is not so palpable as to suggest the voiding of the contract.[36] This does, of course, leave us with the messy task of gauging what is palpable and what is not. Moreover, there has been a tendency, in the United States at least, to grant relief for mistakes which are not palpable but are vital.[37] This would further confuse the issue and should be avoided in this jurisdiction. The mistake is either palpable (permitting relief) or it is not. To add a further layer of categorisation merely serves to muddle.

Secondly, should any difference be discerned between mistakes of which the party is aware and mistakes of which he ought to be aware? There should be a difference. Where the mistake is known to the parties, the relief should be one at law and thus available as of right, for to do otherwise would be to allow one to profit from one's own wrongdoing. However, where the party was not actually aware of the mistake but should have been, it goes too far to give relief at law, but the court's broader equitable jurisdiction should be allowed to operate. Thus, even though the facts of the case are proven, relief should be granted only where the court thinks it right to do so. In coming to this decision, the court should examine two concepts: the effect of enforcement of the contract against the mistaken person, and the consequences imposed on the other party. If to enforce the contract would be oppressive or lead to an 'unconscionable exchange of values', then it should not be so enforced. On the other hand, the consequence of failing to enforce the contract on the other party should lead to no 'substantial hardship'.[38] In short, in assessing the balance of convenience between the seller and the buyer, the presumption lies in favour of refusing to enforce the contract, but this presumption can be rebutted. In *Taylor v. Johnson*[39] a contract for the sale of land stated that the purchase price was to be $15,000. The seller mistakenly believed the figure to be $15,000 per acre, giving a total sale price of $150,000 for the ten acres. The purchaser was aware of the mistake and proceeded to prevent the seller from discovering the error. In fact, the land sold was worth $60,000 at the time and after rezoning, of which the seller was unaware, would have been worth $195,000. The court held that at common law the contract was valid. The only valid basis for such a decision

36 *Webster v. Cecil* (1861) 30 Beav 62 (defendant had earlier refused to sell to the plaintiff a parcel of land for £2,000. The defendant wrote to the plaintiff offering the land for sale at £1,250—this was a mistake, the plaintiff meant £2,250. A decree of specific performance was refused).

37 *Boise Junior College District v. Mattegs Construction Co.*, 450 P 2d 604 (the mistake was considered a vital mistake when it negated the profit on a transaction); *Collen Bros v. Dublin County Council* [1908] 1 IR 503 (there was a clerical oversight in the computation of a tender. The court allowed rectification).

38 Restatement, Second, Contracts, s. 153(a), Comment (d); 13 Williston 1577-1578.

39 (1983) 151 CLR 422.

was that, at the time the contract was entered into, the buyer was unaware of the vendor's mistake and, accordingly, the contract could not be set aside; this was the finding of fact at the trial court which Dawson J on appeal, dissenting from the majority verdict, refused to overturn. The buyer's actions after discovering the mistake were sufficient at equity to permit rescission. Even if the buyer had not subsequently set out to deceive the vendor, the contract could still have been set aside at equity if it could be shown that he ought to have known of the vendor's error. The verdict would, therefore, be justifiable on the basis of the 'unconscionable bargain' outlined earlier; since the property was worth $60,000, a sale price of $15,000 should have been recognised as an error by the purchaser and it would be oppressive to enforce such a sale price since the land was now worth much more. Of course, because the relief is given at equity, the court could order relief as it saw fit, for example, rectifying the deed to read $15,000 per acre.

Mistake as to the identity of a contracting party   Many cases of unilateral mistake concern questions of the identity of one of the contracting parties; these cases should be treated as a subset of unilateral mistake and the principles contained therein should not necessarily have a wider implication. With mistake as to identity, one party is usually attempting to defraud the other mistaken party. If the case then involved a straightforward action against the fraudulent party by the original owner of the item, the issue would be resolved more easily. Instead, the normal fact pattern involves the transfer of the items by the fraudulent person to a *bona fide* purchaser for value without notice of the fraud.[40] Thus, the courts are involved in resolving the dispute between two innocent parties, the original owner and the new owner, both of whom have been conned by the fraudulent person. The substantive law has, therefore, been heavily influenced by the remedy available and the consequence of that remedy. Thus, in reality, in the case of identity, where one person deliberately misleads another as to his identity, the contract should be one of unilateral mistake and void *ab initio*. However, if that were so the *bona fide* purchaser for value without notice would gain no title whatsoever to the item; it is this conflict of principles that has led the courts to apply different rules with respect to mistake as to the identity of the person with whom the contract is made. Thus, in *Phillips v. Brooks*[41] a person went into a jewellers and ordered some jewellery in excess of £2,000 with which he purported to pay by cheque in the name of one Mr Bullough. He gave the address at which Mr Bullough lived and the sales assistant verified this address from a directory. 'Mr Bullough' then requested that the goods be held until such time as the cheque which he had just written

40   The '*bona fide* purchaser for value without notice' simply means a genuine purchaser who buys property at the market rate and without knowledge that any prior dealing with the property may have been dishonest.

41   [1919] 2 KB 243.

cleared; but he wanted to take a ring from the assorted jewellery to give to his wife immediately. Of course, he was not Mr Bullough but had forged the cheque. The ring was pledged for £350 to an innocent person. In resolving the dispute as to ownership of the ring, it fell to be determined whether the sales assistant intended to sell only to Mr Bullough or to the person in the store who represented himself as Mr Bullough. If it was intended to deal only with the real Mr Bullough, the contract was void *ab initio*. If it was intended to deal with the person in the store at the time of the sale, then a valid contract had been formed which would be voidable but which would be voidable too late to prevent the transfer of ownership. The court held that the sales assistant intended to deal with the person who represented himself to be Mr Bullough and not with the real Mr Bullough alone. On the facts of the case, this is a wholly reasonable judgment. The mistake as to identity was not part of the contract and therefore was not a mistake in the legal sense at all. A mistake would be selling jewels worth £5,000 for £50: this would go to the heart of the contract. The contract was one of sale and purchase. The identity of the parties was in fact a side issue. The check made as to the address was a means of checking credit-worthiness.

Compare this with *Ingrams v. Little*,[42] a case of remarkably similar facts save that the contract involved the sale of a car and it was at a private residence. The fraudster called to the seller's house and offered to buy the car for £700 odd. When he purported to pay by cheque, the deal was called off, whereupon he described himself as a businessman, one Mr Hutchinson, from a certain area. The seller then checked that the address he had been given belonged to this businessman and accepted the cheque. Needless to say, it was forged, and the car was further sold on to a *bona fide* purchaser for value without notice. In determining the ownership of the vehicle, the court had to adjudicate on the validity or otherwise of the contract. On the rationale of the earlier case, it would appear that the better view would be to say the contract was voidable but not void by virtue of mistake, because identity is not crucial to the contract in question. The court, however, held the opposite, finding that the seller intended to sell to Hutchinson and Hutchinson alone, and not any person who might represent himself as such. Identity was therefore crucial in this case.

As a result of the subsequent case of *Lewis v. Avery*,[43] the better view is that the *Ingrams* case is to be treated with some caution. On similar facts the court held that identity was not crucial and expressly doubted the validity of the earlier case. Mistake as to the identity of one party to the bargain will not be grounds for rendering the contract void unless the identity of that person is crucial to the contract. Thus, a contract to buy a person's jumper is different than a contract

---

42 [1960] 3 All ER 332.
43 [1971] 3 All ER 907; *Citibank v. Brown Shipley* [1991] 2 All ER 690 (on the basis of fraud as to the identity of a person Bank A prepared a draft in favour of Bank B. Bank B paid out on this draft, also believing in the fraudulent identity. The court left the loss with the original bank who prepared the draft).

to buy a jumper which someone who purports to be a famous film star is wearing, if the fraudster knew that the contract was made solely on the basis of the assumed identity. Such would be a mistake sufficient to render the contract void. Mistake as to the identity of the contracting parties is not a mistake in the legal sense unless such identity has become part of the core obligation of the contract. In practice, rebutting the presumption that the identity of the contracting parties is not crucial to the contract will be a difficult hurdle for any litigant.

16.07 CROSS PURPOSES

Cross purposes occur where both parties are mistaken as to the contract but it is not a shared mistake. For example, X believes that he is selling his houseboat in Florida to Y, and Y believes he is buying X's house in Florida. This is well illustrated in the case of *Megaw v. Molloy* (discussed earlier). Clearly the parties are not *ad idem*; accordingly, no contract has come into existence. Of course, the test is that of the objective third party and not the subjective belief of the contracting parties. Thus, in *Scriven v. Hindley*,[44] where the purchaser attempted to purchase tow and the seller sell hemp, the parties were deemed to have come to no conclusive contract. This was so because the facts of the case would lead an objective by-stander to hold that no agreement had been reached. Proof of such objective verification of a failure of mutual consent is difficult to attain and it is normally relatively easy for a court to hold that a contract has come into existence on certain terms, even if this was not intended by either, or indeed both, of the parties to that contract. Thus, in *Wood v. Scarth*[45] an offer by the defendant to let a pub for £65 per week subsequent to a discussion with the plaintiff's clerk was enforced, despite the fact that the discussion had mentioned that a premium of £500 would also be payable. The plaintiff was in reality unaware of this and believed that the agreement involved only the rent payable. The defendant was bound by the exact letter of offer made and which a third party would consider to contain all the relevant terms. The contract, therefore, was enforceable. Of course, even where the contract is so enforceable, relief may be granted for misrepresentation or some other ground, as explained earlier.

16.08 SUMMARY

The concept of mistake remains highly complex but may be summarised as follows:

- A mistaken belief as to an operative element of the contract which is shared

---

44   [1913] 3 KB 564; *Raffles v. Wichelhaus* (1864) 2 H&C 906 (two ships, bearing the same name (Peerless) left from the same port, but at different times. One party believed the contract to relate ship A, the other party to ship B. The court held there was no liability for refusing to honour the contract).

45   (1858) 1 F&F 293.

equally by the contracting parties will render the agreement unenforceable only if it goes to the identity, ownership or existence of the subject matter and not if it concerns an attribute or lesser consequence of the contract.[46] For all other cases where the mistake is shared, the claim is one at equity and the onus of proof to be discharged is high.[47]

- A mistaken belief as to an operative element of the contract not shared by the contracting parties and of which no party is, or should be, aware, will render the contract void only if a third party would determine that the parties never, in reality, came to an agreement.[48] This will be exceptionally difficult to prove in practice.[49]

- A mistaken belief as to an operative element of the contract not shared by the contracting parties and of which one of the parties should have been aware, will render the contract liable to be set aside at equity on such terms and conditions as the court sees fit, and, since the remedy is equitable, the exercise of such discretion is limited to that described above. Note also that relief may be available at tort where one party negligently led the other to believe in the mistake.[50]

- A mistaken belief as to an operative element of the contract not shared by the contracting parties and of which one of the parties is aware will render the contract void *ab initio*.[51] (Note that mistake as to identity is not normally an operative mistake, although this presumption may be rebutted with difficulty).[52]

- A mistaken belief will not operate to render a contract void where the parties have agreed to conscious uncertainty in the agreement, that is an adventure contract or gamble.[53]

- A mistaken belief which does not render the contract void may still operate to permit relief on some other ground such as misrepresentation, etc.[54]

---

46 *Bell v. Lever Bros*, ibid.
47 *Solle v. Butcher*, ibid.
48 *Smith v. Hughes* (1871) LR 2 QB 597 ('if whatever a man's real intention may be, he so conducts himself that a reasonable man would believe he was assenting to the terms proposed by the other and that other party upon that belief enters into a contract with him, the man thus conducting himself would be equally bound as if he has intended to agree to the other parties terms', *per* Blackburn J at 607); *Clayton Love v. B+I Transport* (1970) 104 ILTR 157.
49 *Lucey v. Laurel Construction*, unreported, High Court, 18 December 1970.
50 *McRae v. Commissioners*, ibid.
51 *Lewis v. Avery*, ibid.
52 *Wood v. Boynton*, ibid.
53 See chapter 17, ibid.
54 *Hartog v. Colin and Shields*, ibid.

17.00

Misrepresentation

17.01 INTRODUCTION

Misrepresentation concerns pre-contractual statements made by the parties to the contract which are subsequently discovered to be untrue for one reason or another. In the negotiation of any contract, there will be many claims and promises made, not all of which will become part of the final contract but which will have had a significant impact on the decision to enter the contract. It is these statements, whatever form they take, with which we are now concerned. Misrepresentation, like the concept of mistake in our legal system, has been an unruly offspring that submits to no straightforward analysis or exposition.[1] The concept incorporates many different aspects of the law of contract and it is not always easy to distinguish their applications. For example, sometimes the courts will hold the contract void for mistake yet in similar situations permit relief by way of breach of contractual term, or else use the concept of misrepresentation. Like the concepts of offer and acceptance, the practitioner of contract law must not bind himself too tightly to *ex post facto* reasoning and analysis in this area.

Moreover, in this area, lateral thinking has an important role. One's thoughts must not be confined to the narrow doctrine of misrepresentation *per se* but cover all of contract law. Further, there will be times when it is appropriate to step outside the law of contract and seek relief elsewhere. It is also true to say that decisions in other areas of law, such as tort, have had an impact on the substantive application of contract principles. In many ways misrepresentation resembles in microcosm the impact of the fusion of two legal systems that occurred in the Judicature Act.[2] Even though the two remain separate, running in the one stream but not intermingling, it is impossible to ensure such absolute division; one will impact on the other. Thus, relief for misrepresentation should be examined from all aspects, although of necessity this discourse is somewhat limited.

---

1   See Cheshire and Fifoot, op. cit., p. 267 et seq.; Clark, op. cit., p. 228 et seq.; Greig and Davis, op. cit., p. 799 et seq.; Calamari and Perillo, op. cit., p. 356 et seq.
2   See chapter 26, ibid.

17.02 THE RULE

A misrepresentation is an untrue statement of fact which does not form part of the contract but which induced the party to enter into the contract. A mere misrepresentation does not automatically give rise to a remedy. It must be of a certain type that the law deems worthy of giving a remedy. Thus, the law will not interfere simply because the seller has said an untruth. The claimant must prove that the misrepresentation falls into one of the specified categories for which relief is available and that the misrepresentation is of sufficient impact on the result of the contract to require that relief be given.

All of the following elements must be proven:

* the misrepresentation must be of fact,

* it must not form part of the contract,

* it must have induced the party into entering the contract.

Even when this has been done, it is still by no means certain that the relief will apply, for it will depend on the categorisation of the misrepresentation. Misrepresentations are classified as fraudulent, negligent, or innocent.

17.03 MISREPRESENTATION OF FACT

Statements of fact A misrepresentation must be an untruth. It is clearly not actionable if it transpires to be true. But the misrepresentation must be one of fact and not opinion or law.[3] Thus, to state that the vehicle has a mere 20,000 miles on the clock when it in fact has 120,000, is to misrepresent a fact. But to say that the vehicle is the best I have ever driven is a statement of opinion and not actionable, even if untrue. In general, it has been said that a misrepresentation implies a *factum* not a *faciendum*, that is, an existing or past fact, not a future fact.[4] This does not mean that a statement of future intention can never be a misrepresentation, for in *Edgington v. Fitzmaurice*[5] a prospectus inviting subscriptions to a company for the purposes of erecting buildings and so forth

---

3   See chapter 16, ibid, for the distinction between fact and law; note that as outlined in chapter 16, the distinction between mistake of fact and mistake of law has been questioned. It follows therefore that a distinction between fact and law in misrepresentation would also be inconsistent, but see *Doolan v. Murray*, unreported, High Court, 21 December 1993, where Keane J dealt with a misrepresentation of law as being decided in the traditional mistake of law manner; Restatement, Second, Contracts, s. 170; note that a statement of foreign law is a statement of fact: 12 Williston 1495.

4   Spencer, Bower and Turner, *Actionable Misrepresentation* (3rd ed.), p. 42; 12 Williston, s. 1491-1494.

5   (1855) 29 ChD 459; but cf. *Maddison v. Alderson* (1883) 8 App Cas 467 (a promise to do something in the future could not be a representation).

was held to be a misrepresentation where the promoters of the company (who issued the prospectus) never intended to use the money for those purposes. The statements in the prospectus, even though expressing a future intention, were a lie and could not be used to avoid liability. The case is justifiable as to result but difficult with respect to principle. It would appear that the court was impressed by the fact that the promoters never intended to carry out their intentions. Essentially they made an untrue statement of fact as to their intentions. As Bowen LJ pointed out,

The state of a man's mind is as much a statement of fact as his digestion.[6]

Bowen LJ also realised that proving such a state of mind would be difficult, but for the case at hand the onus was readily resolved. The important onus to prove is that of the person's state of mind at the time, not the end-result of his actions. A person who intends, at the time he so states it, to do something has not misrepresented a statement of fact if he or she subsequently resiles from it. But if he states an intention to do something which, at the time it is stated, he has no intention of doing, then he makes a misrepresentation. Presumably, in determining what has occurred, the court will be guided by the demeanour of the party and the surrounding actions and circumstances. It is a burden that few claimants would desire to rest their cause of action upon.

Statements of opinion   Fact will not, however, extend to cover a belief or opinion held by someone. Thus, a statement in *Bissett v. Wilkinson*[7] that in the judgment of the vendor the land was capable of supporting 2,000 sheep was held to be a statement of opinion honestly held by the vendor and not a statement of fact. Accordingly, no misrepresentation had occurred. Further to confuse the issue, however, it is possible that a statement of opinion may form a misrepresentation if the opinion is not actually held by the person, or if he should have reasonably known it to be incorrect or if he alone knew of the relevant facts from which to draw the opinion. The first rule is clearly involved where the person is lying as to his opinion, such as *Smith v. Land and House Prop. Corp.*,[8] where the tenant of a house which was for sale was described as 'a most desirable tenant'. In fact the rent was in arrears and what rent had been paid had been obtained only under pressure. However, in the ordinary way, the description of a tenant as most desirable is a statement of opinion at best. It is typical of the hyperbole that we expect to be used by sellers of items. So, we are accustomed to seeing cars being advertised as 'the best drive in town' etc. These are clearly subjective statements of opinion to which no legal significance can normally be expected to attach.[9] In the case at bar, the court held that, since the vendor knew

6   Ibid. at 483.
7   [1927] AC 177.
8   (1884) 28 Ch D 7.
9   See Keeton, 'Fraud: Misrepresenta-

tion of Opinion', 21 *Minnesota Law Review* 643; Handler, 'False and Misleading Advertising', 39 *Yale Law Journal* 22.

the real facts, his intention was to misrepresent this statement, and it granted relief on this basis. Once again the case is justifiable as to result but suspect as to rationale. If the court's view is correct, would a car manufacturer be guilty of misrepresentation if it claimed the vehicle it had manufactured could 'drive responsive to the drivers needs', when in fact it was well known within the industry as handling like two tons of dead lead?[10] *Smith's* case may be explicable on the basis that the court found that the vendor did not believe the statement of opinion; but the second point identified earlier, namely, that he should have reasonably known the representation of opinion to be false, would cover the example of the motor vehicle manufacturer just given. Indeed, in *Esso v. Mardon*[11] the opinion of the oil company that a garage could throughput up to a certain figure of petrol per month was held to be a misrepresentation of fact even though it was clearly an opinion. The court in essence decided that the oil company should have known that this was incorrect; the fact that they did not would not absolve liability. The final point where a misrepresentation of opinion will be treated as that of fact is where the opinion is based on facts known only to the person making the misrepresentation. It is unclear if this is so where the opinion is formed innocently, negligently or intentionally. Moreover, there is a clear ambiguity between the concept of a statement of opinion and the basis for liability with respect to the type of misrepresentation involved (this is discussed below). How can it be that a statement as to the throughput of a petrol station is a statement of fact, whereas to say the land is 'uncommonly rich water meadow'[12] is a statement of opinion. There is no doubt that the courts are heavily influenced by the nature of the case, the injustice done to one of the parties and the intent of the other. However, the traditional analysis of opinion–fact is unsatisfactory and incoherent and seriously mixes the concepts contained in the notion of misrepresentation.

The resolution of this problem requires us to look first, not at the mind of the person making the misrepresentation, but, at the nature of the misrepresentation. If the misrepresentation is made in a such a manner that it could objectively be read as being a statement of fact, then it may render the person liable for misrepresentation depending on the frame of mind of the person at the time the opinion was so stated (see discussion below). Where the circumstances clearly indicate that the statement is given in an opinion form, then it should not render the person so liable.[13] The question to be determined, then, is when is opinion presented as fact. A statement is delivered as one of opinion–fact when it is

10 *Pontiac v. Bradley*, 210 P 2d 348.
11 [1976] QB 801.
12 See below.
13 Making a statement of fact in the form of an opinion does not render it other than a misrepresentation of fact: *Brooke v. Rounthwaite* (1846) 5 Hare 298. However, the plaintiff will fail unless he can prove that he has actually been induced by such a misrepresentation, or that he has relied upon it.

surrounded by other details that would lead a reasonable person to conclude that it is intended to be regarded as fact.[14] Thus, a generalised statement that it is 'uncommonly rich water meadow',[15] 'it is the best car I have known' and so forth are clearly opinions. But to surround the opinion with elements that clearly aim to transmute the objective view of the opinion into that of opinion–fact, such as a person with experience in the area representing a specific throughput or detailing what earnings are anticipated to be, should give rise to liability in misrepresentation. However, it should be noted that some misrepresentations are of opinions that are not 'susceptible of knowledge';[16] so, a claim by a stockbroker that the shares will reach £25 each by the end of the year is not actionable as it is an opinion which is not possible to be stated as a fact.[17] But a claim by a petrol company as to the potential throughput of a particular station is susceptible of knowledge.[18]

The Restatement, Second, distinguishes between an opinion based on knowledge and an opinion based on judgment. An opinion based on knowledge would appear to be more than a statement of opinion *simpliciter*.[19] This is close to the reasoning outlined above, though less satisfactory, for it appears that liability under the Restatement, Second, could be avoided by virtue of a distinction which is unintelligible to the layman. Certainly, if the opinion is surrounded by detailed facts, the objective person would view the representation to be one of fact. Even an opinion not based on detailed facts, might be held to be a statement of fact, depending on the person who offered it.[20]

Statements of law   We have discussed the difficulty associated in distinguishing between fact and law. A misrepresentation of law cannot, of course, be actionable, for the doctrine of *ignorantius*, outlined in the chapter on Mistake, would clearly not allow the party to recover, even if he depended upon the legal knowledge of the other party. However, this must be treated with extreme caution. First, it seldom occurs that statements of law are used to induce people

---

14   *Reese River Silver Mining v. Smith* (1869) LR 4 HL 64 (the publishing of expert reports on the potential capacity of a mine was held to be a fact—the motive was irrelevant, the promoters were trying to exaggerate the earnings of the company).
15   *Scott v. Hanson* (1829) 1 Russ M 128.
16   *Kennedy v. FloTronics*, 143 NW 2d 827.
17   *Esso v. Marden*, ibid.
18   Ibid.
19   Restatement, Second, Contracts, s. 168.
20   See Calamari and Perillo, op. cit., p. 362 where they state the exceptions to the rule that there is no relief for reliance based upon an opinion. the exceptions are '(1) where there is a relation of trust and confidence between the parties, (2) where the representor claims to be an expert, (3) where the representor has superior access to knowledge of facts making the opinion false, (4) where the opinion is stated by a third person posing as a disinterested person, (5) where the opinion intentionally varies so far from reality that no reasonable man in the representees position could have such an opinion.' (Footnotes omitted).

into entering a contract; it is far more likely that a mix of fact and law will be involved. For example, a statement such as 'This property is not the subject of rent control legislation'[21] contains both law and fact and would lead a court to find that a misrepresentation had occurred because fact is inseparably tied up with law. Second, relief may still be available where the statement of law is contained as a term of the contract. This will often happen since the point involved with the law normally carries some significance, as in the above example. Finally, relief may also be available in tort in an action for deceit, where the law has intentionally been mis-stated, or in an action for negligence, where the law has been mis-stated negligently.

Silence   Can silence ever constitute a misrepresentation? In general no, silence can never constitute a misrepresentation, for there is no onus on a person to reveal facts to the other contracting party.[22] The doctrine of *caveat emptor* has a firm hold on our legal system. As has been said

> Simple reticence does not amount to legal fraud, however it may be viewed by the moralists.[23]

However, some notes of caution should be entered here. First, what constitutes silence may have a more narrow definition at law than in ordinary parlance. One word, one affirmative or negative grunt, removes the element of silence, as does any other body language that is capable of inferring some specific meaning, for, as the above statement continues,

> But a single word or a nod or a wink or a shake of the head or a smile . . . would be sufficient ground for a Court of Equity to refuse a decree of specific performance.[24]

---

21   *Solle v. Butcher* [1949] 2 All ER 1107.
22   *Fox v. MacKreth* (1788) 2 Cox Eq Cas 320; *Laidlaw v. Organ*, 15 US (2 Wheat) 178; in the US, contract negotiations are viewed as analogous to a poker game—disclosure of one's hand is to be avoided!; but there is a different approach in this jurisdiction, *Gill v. McDowell* [1903] 2 IR 463 (the seller should have disclosed the fact that the animal was a hermaphrodite, since this was substantially different from the sale of a cow or a bull). This case is justifiable since, if a buyer seeks to purchase a car, and makes this clear to the seller, the seller cannot refrain from disclosing that he is in fact selling a work of art made from a non-functioning car. This is better dealt with as a mistake as to a fundamental characteristic of the contract, such as to substantially alter the nature of the item contracted and render the contract unenforceable. Clark, op. cit., p. 248 suggests that it may be confined to agricultural sales, though there is nothing in the judgment to limit the principle in this manner.
23   Calamari and Perillo, op. cit., p. 365.
24   Calamari and Perillo, op. cit., p. 366.

Secondly, in certain situations silence is simply not sufficient. Where a representation has been made, it must be a full and frank disclosure. A half truth may in fact be a full lie, and the party having opened the line of enquiry, so to speak, must see it through to its conclusion. To say that the property is being sold with tenants is a misrepresentation where those tenants have given in notice. The representation is a half truth and a full lie.[25] On the other hand, if the vendor sells the property silent as to the status of those tenants, but the purchaser himself believes that the tenants will stay in the property after the transaction, it is not a misrepresentation on the part of the vendor if he fails to notify the prospective purchaser of the fact that the tenants have given notice. Moreover, a representation that was true at the time it was made but which subsequently changes and this change is known to the person who made the original representation, places an onus on that party to reveal the change in circumstance.[26]

Finally, two specific circumstances require mention at this point. Firstly, silence is never a defence in contracts of *uberrimae fides* (contracts of utmost good faith). These are normally contracts of insurance, and are specialised contracts outside the scope of this work.[27] Effectively, at common law they place an onus of full disclosure of all material facts on the person seeking the contract of insurance. This peculiar rule of insurance contracts has been rejected in other jurisdictions[28] but remains well entrenched here.[29] Secondly, where a fiduciary relationship exists between the parties there is a similar lack of silence as a defence.[30] A fiduciary relationship exists by virtue of equity; it defies exact definition but can be illustrated through example; thus, a trustee is a fiduciary, so are company directors.[31]

---

25 *Gill v. McDowell* [1903] 2 IR 463; *Dimmock v. Hallett* (1866) 2 Ch App 21; *Curtis v. Chemical Cleaning and Dyeing Co.* [1951] 1 All ER 631 (a statement concerning the extent of an exclusion clause was incomplete. The court held this to be a misrepresentation).
26 *Davies v. London and Provincial Marine Insurance Co.* (1878) 8 Ch D 469.
27 See Birds, *Law of Insurance* for further details.
28 In South Africa for example, see *Mutual and Federal Insurance Co. v. Oudtshoorn Municipality* [1985] 1 SA 400.
29 But see *Aro Road and Land Vehicles v. ICI* [1986] IR 403 where an insurance company sought to avoid paying out on a policy of insurance because the insured had failed to disclose that, 19 years earlier, he had been convicted of receiving stolen goods. In light of the harshness of the requirement of disclosure with respect to insurance contracts completed with minimal formalities, particularly contracts of insurance for travel and carriage of goods purposes, the court agreed the rules of disclosure should be relaxed, see also *Keating v. New Ireland Assurance* [1990] ILRM 110. The rule of disclosure should be viewed as reduced in severity in these cases.
30 See ibid. for a full discussion on what has been termed constructive fraud; Restatement, Second, Contracts, s. 161, Comment d.
31 See Keane, *Equity*, op. cit.

17.04 THE MISREPRESENTATION MUST NOT FORM PART OF THE CONTRACT

If the misrepresentation forms part of the contract, then the correct course of action is to sue for breach of contract, which is discussed fully in chapter 22. The remedies available for breach of contract are both more certain and more expansive than the remedies available for misrepresentation. The real difficulty lies in determining whether the misrepresentation has become part of the contract or not; we have already discussed this in detail in chapter 11 on Express Terms. In certain categories of contracts, rescission is also be available by statute where a misrepresentation forms part of the contract but is determined to be a warranty (see below).

17.05 THE MISREPRESENTATION MUST HAVE INDUCED THE PARTY INTO ENTERING THE CONTRACT

No actionable misrepresentation occurs unless the misrepresentation has in some way caused the party to enter into the contract. It does not have to be the sole reason for entering into the contract, or even the primary reason, provided it had some impact on the making of the contract. In *Smith v. Lynn*[32] two parties, X and Y, were interested in buying a certain property, which was advertised as being in good structural condition. X was successful, but two months after the purchase he decided to sell the property. He used the same advertisement that had originally been used. Y now successfully bid for the property. It was then discovered that the property was not in fact in good structural repair. Y sued X for misrepresentation in the advertisment. The claim failed. Although another analysis of the case is possible, the claim failed because the representation as to structural condition (the advertisment) did not cause Y to enter the contract.[33] Y had entered into the contract uninterested in any claim made by X for the property: Y had already decided to purchase the property earlier. It may well be that Y was induced into this desire for the property by the earlier misrepresentation, but this would ground an action for the original misrepresentation which would fail, since the contract was not completed by Y and no damage was suffered at that time. Thus, hypothetically, had the property been sold to an innocent bystander, it might well be that the advertisement would constitute a misrepresentation.

---

32 [1954] 85 ICTR 737; Restatement, Second, Contracts, s. 167.
33 *Grafton Court v. Wadson Sales* unreported, High Court, 17 February 1975 (a representation as to the quality of co-tenants in a shopping complex was not actionable, since the other units were let at the time the representation was made and the litigant had not relied upon the representation. If the tenants at the time had been of good quality, but subsequently left and were replaced by poor quality tenants, would the plaintiff have had a good cause of action?)

In *Museprime Properties v. Adhill Properties*[34] the issue was raised as to how material a misrepresentation had to be before relief could be claimed. Prior to this case, the suggested test was that of the reasonable man: would a reasonable man have been induced into entering the contract as a result of the representation? It now appears that the better view is that this goes only as to proof. If the claimant can show that a reasonable man would have been so induced, it makes it easier to prove that he was in fact induced. But if it can be shown that even though a reasonable man would have been induced into the contract by the misrepresentation, it is a defence to prove that the claimant was not so induced; this would be in accordance with the suggested reasoning behind *Smith v. Lynn*. As a corollary it must also follow that, despite the fact that a reasonable man would not have been induced into the contract on the basis of the misrepresentation, the claimant will succeed if he can show that he was in fact so induced, although the difficulties for the claimant in such a case should not be underestimated.[35]

The claimant must prove that he was induced by virtue of the misrepresentation. In *Smith v. Chadwick*[36] the claimant admitted under cross examination that, despite a misrepresentation that a particular person was a director of the company to which he was subscribing, the misrepresentation at no time influenced his decision to subscribe to the company's shares. The claim was therefore dismissed. And in *Attwood v. Small*[37] the vendors clearly exaggerated the potential of a mine they were selling, but the purchaser was permitted to have his own investigation of the mine undertaken, which he did. His investigators agreed with the vendor's report, which was in fact wrong. The claim was dismissed on the grounds that the purchaser did not in fact rely upon the misrepresentation but on his own experts.

Since the claimant must show that the misrepresentation induced him into making the contract, it is a defence to show that he was unaware of the misrepresentation or was aware of it but knew it to be false and so did not rely upon it.[38] If the claimant is unaware of the misrepresentation, then clearly it will be difficult to prove that he relied upon it.[39] Thus, in *In re Northumberland and*

34 [1990] 36 EG 114.
35 *Kendall v. Wilson*, 41 Vt 567 ('the law will afford relief even to the simple and credulous who have been duped by art or falsehood' at 571); *Chamberlain v. Fuller*, 59 Vt 247 ('No rogue should enjoy his ill gotten plunder for the simple reason that his victim is by chance a fool' at 836); Restatement, Second, Contracts, s. 164, Comment b.
36 (1884) 9 App Cas 187, 194; *Edgington v. Fitzmaurice*, op. cit.; *JEB Fastners v. Marks Bloom* [1983] 1 All ER 583.
37 (1838) 6 Cl and Fin 232; cf. *Cody v. Connolly* [1940] Ir Jur Rep 49 (a purchaser arranged an inspection of an animal by his own vet. The court held the vendor was still liable for misrepresentation. This case must be of highly doubtful authority).
38 *Jennings v. Broughton* (1854) 5 De GM&G 126.
39 But see *Sergeant v. Irish Multi Wheel* (1955) 21-2 Ir Jur Rep 42 (there is no need to inform anyone of the reliance upon the representation).

Durham District Banking Co., ex parte Bigge[40] the claimant could not succeed where misrepresentations as to the financial health of a company had been published but where he was unable to prove that he had read these misrepresentations or that they had been recounted to him by a third party. Relief will also be denied where the claimant has full and actual knowledge of the truth concerning the misrepresentation, for clearly in such a situation the claimant cannot have relied upon the misrepresentation if he knew it to be untrue. However, a certain degree of caution should be noted, since the knowledge of the claimant must be sufficiently full as not to compound the misrepresentation, and it must also be actual knowledge; constructive or implied knowledge is insufficient.[41]

17.06 THE SOURCE OF THE MISREPRESENTATION

It is true to say that the source of a misrepresentation can cause some difficulties —for example, where the misrepresentation does not come directly from one of the parties to the contract but comes from, perhaps, an agent. No difficulty arises if the misrepresentation comes directly from the defendant, and is made directly to the claimant. Even where the misrepresentation is made by way of a brochure or prospectus, this poses little difficulty. But is a defendant liable for the misrepresentations of his agent or employee? In *Lutton v. Saville Tractors*[42] the court found that the employers were liable for the misrepresentations of their employee with respect to whether or not a vehicle had been involved in an accident. Similarly, an agent can bind his principal in terms of a misrepresentation. This cannot be avoided by the insertion of a 'no liability for misrepresentations' clause within the contract.[43]

17.07 CATEGORIES OF MISREPRESENTATION

Misrepresentations can be classified as being of three types: fraudulent, negligent and innocent; each type of misrepresentation gives rise to different rules. What is important here is the intent of the person making the misrepresentation.

Fraudulent misrepresentation   An absence of honest belief is crucial to a claim for fraudulent misrepresentation. The courts in general consider a charge of fraud to be one that requires a heavy onus of proof and will not lightly come

---

40   (1858) 28 LJ Ch 50.
41   *Phelps v. White* (1881) 7 LR (Ir) 160; *Gahan v. Boland & Boland*, unreported, High Court, 20 January 1984.
42   [1986] NI 327.
43   Particularly where such misrepresentations are fraudulent: *Pearson v. Dublin Corporation* [1907] AC 351, but see *Dublin Port and Docks v. Builtame Dredging Co.* [1968] IR 136 for a different view on innocent misrepresentation.

to a conclusion of fraud being present. Thus, the test is subjective: the court will not find fraud, no matter how unreasonable the belief is, provided it is honestly held. In *Derry v. Peek*[44] the defendants misrepresented that they had the consent of the Board of Trade to use steam power on rail tracks rather than animal power. In fact, no consent had been obtained. The plaintiff subscribed to the company on the basis of the alleged Board of Trade consent. The Board of Trade subsequently refused consent, and the company went into liquidation. The plaintiff now sued to recover on the basis of fraudulent misrepresentation. The court found that the directors believed that the consent would be granted and that this was an honest belief; so, even though they knew the consent had not been approved at the time they made the representation, they were not fraudulent.

No matter how absurd the belief is, provided it is honestly held the misrepresentation is not fraudulent. Of course, there are limits to this analysis, for if the belief is too credulous it will be difficult for the defendant to convince a judge (or jury) of his honesty. Moreover, an honest belief so held due to the recklessness of the defendant will not, at law, be allowed to excuse a claim for fraud. Recklessness should be distinguished from carelessness. Carelessness is merely negligence (discussed later). But recklessness is carelessness taken to the extreme limit that it drifts over towards fraud. Recklessly to make a statement not knowing of its veracity and caring little about the issue is fraudulent. In the same way, deliberately to close one's eyes to certain facts may also constitute fraudulent misrepresentation.[45]

In determining the existence of fraud, no consideration is taken of the motive for the fraudulent misrepresentation. Thus, in *Delaney v. Keogh*[46] the conditions of sale were not changed, because the auctioneer believed, on advice from the solicitor involved with the carriage of the sale, that a claim by the landlord of the property for a higher rent would be denied by virtue of estoppel. At the court of first instance, the claim of fraudulent misrepresentation was dismissed, since the auctioneer did not make the misrepresentation for gain or with the intention of deceiving the purchaser. This was overturned on appeal, Holmes LJ holding that the auctioneer, even though he believed the advice of the solicitor, should have advised the purchaser of the landlord's intention. In not doing so he was deemed to be fraudulent, even though he lacked any *mala fides*.

It should also be noted that fraudulent misrepresentation will ground an action in tort for deceit; this is usually the cause of action the claimant is most likely to pursue, for a number of reasons.[47] For this reason, contract law has

44 (1889) 14 App Cas 337.
45 *Foster v. Charles* (1830) 6 Bing 396.
46 [1905] 2 IR 267.
47 The reason for this is the traditionally higher level of damages payable in a tort action. There is some evidence that the quantum of damages for breaches of both contractual and tortious obligations may be equilibrating, particularly when they arise from the same facts, see *Ashington Piggeries v. Hill* [1972] AC 441, see also chapter 25, ibid.

little impact in this area in practical terms, though, as we shall see, relief may be given under contract in any event.

Negligent misrepresentation A claim for negligent misrepresentation will be better pursued by way of a tort action. All non-fraudulent misrepresentation is deemed under contract law to be innocent misrepresentation (discussed fully below). However, it is important to remember that, since the case of *Hedley Byrne v. Heller*,[48] relief under tort is available for negligent mis-statement (as it is referred to in the law of tort), but only within certain guidelines. Notably there must be a special relationship between the parties, a relationship termed a 'duty of care'. The duty of care arises when one's actions can reasonably be foreseen to have an impact on the other person. This is true of representations made pursuant to the negotiations of a contract. However, it has been argued that liability cannot exist both at contract and tort arising from the one duty of care, and that, once a contract is formed, liability in tort ceases and the parties can sue only to enforce the contract; this argument has been soundly and rightly rejected. The rights of the claimant under tort and contract are co-extant. Thus, while relief at contract may not be available for an innocent, albeit negligent, misrepresentation, it may be available under the law of tort if a duty of care can be shown.

Can a remedy be available where the parties do not enter into a contract? Cheshire and Fifoot give the example of a situation where a sub-contractor gives a quote to a main contractor who uses this figure to compute a tender for construction of a building. The sub-contractor's quote is incorrect and is withdrawn just before the main contractor's tender is accepted on the basis of the incorrect figure. This is similar to the problem raised in the concept of mistake earlier.[49] It is clearly not a misrepresentation since it did not result in a completed contract; where no contract occurs, it is likely that liability under tort will in fact arise.[50]

Innocent misrepresentation All non-fraudulent misrepresentations are innocent misrepresentations. However, as we have seen, some innocent misrepresentations may be classified as negligent; for these relief may be available under the law of tort.[51] No relief is available under tort for an innocent misrepresentation which is not negligent. Relief for an innocent misrepresentation comes from the contract jurisdiction of the court, if any. While we say that

---

48 [1964] AC 465; *Securities Trust v. Hugh Moore & Alexander* [1964] IR 417; see also *Doolan v. Murray*, unreported, High Court, 21 December 1993; note that in *Finlay v. Murtagh* [1979] IR 249 the principle of concurrent liability in both tort and contract has been accepted, thus removing many of the difficulties.

49 See chapter 16, ibid.

50 But presumably, only if the main contractor's obligation cannot be set aside or rectified, otherwise the level of damages would be nominal.

51 *Hedley Byrne v. Heller* [1964] AC 465.

an innocent misrepresentation is not actionable under tort, we should also point out that the interpretation placed upon the concept of negligence has been extremely liberal, and in many cases negligence has been found to exist where the facts would more clearly admit a remedy under strict liability only.[52] Increasingly, the use of doctrines of remoteness and causation have been used to limit tortious liability rather than substantive rebuttal of the negligence issue.[53]

17.08 REMEDIES FOR MISREPRESENTATION

We must stress that we are concerned here with remedies pursuant to the law of contract; although it has been pointed out that relief may also be available in certain situations under a tort action, the full extent of such relief is better discussed in a dedicated work on tort. It must also be noted that the distinction between law and equity is once again quite crucial with respect to any remedies available in this area.

Remedies at law

Damages Damages are clearly the appropriate remedy at common law to compensate the claimant for the loss which he has suffered. Such damages are only payable for fraudulent misrepresentation, and, of course, negligent misrepresentation, but these are payable under the law of tort and are consequently valued using the tests for remoteness. Since the *Wagon Mound*[54] case, the rule has been that remoteness of damage is controlled by the concept of reasonable foreseeability; in other words, could the defendant reasonably foresee the harm caused as arising from his breach of the duty of care? This test is problematic with respect to fraudulent misrepresentations, since the reasonable foreseeability test is based on a claim of negligence. Where negligence is not the basis for liability, the correct rule for recovery of damages is governed by the standard outlined in the *In re Polemis*[55] case, that is, the direct consequence rule. The defendant is liable for all the damage arising as a direct consequence of the fraudulent misrepresentation.[56]

---

52 *Bank of Ireland v. Smith* [1966] IR 646; *Stafford v. Keane Mahoney Smith* [1980] ILRM 53; *Securities Trust v. Moore and Alexander* [1964] IR 417; *Hazylake Fashion v. Bank of Ireland* [1989] IR 601.

53 See generally, McMahon and Binchy, *Law of Torts*, 2nd ed.

54 [1961] AC 388; *MacAnarney and MacAnarney v. Hanarahan and TE Potterton* [1994] I ILRM 210 (where plaintiff was induced to enter a contract by negligent misstatement the normal measure of damages is the price paid for the land less the actual value at the time of purchase).

55 [1921] 3 KB 560.

56 *Doyle v. Olby (Ironmongers)* [1969] 2 All ER 119 ('the defendant is bound to make reparation for all the damages directly flowing from the fraudulent inducement . . . it does not lie in the mouth of the fraudulent person to say that [it] could not reasonably have been foreseen' at 122).

It follows that damages are not available at common law for fraudulent, negligent or innocent misrepresentation under a contract action,[57] but relief is available under the law of tort for fraudulent misrepresentation by an action in deceit, or for negligent misrepresentation in an action for negligent mis-statement, and damages can be paid accordingly.

Validating the contract Moreover, where the claimant pursues his action in tort, he is effectively retaining the validity of the contract, that is to say, the contract endures and the claimant is seeking damages for loss, both for the value of the subject matter of the contract and any consequential loss. Such calculation of loss may be far greater than if the party elects to avoid the contract entirely; it is a matter of legal strategy which relief should be sought so as to gain the best advantage for the claimant. It is not possible to void the contract and seek a remedy at common law on foot of the misrepresentation.

Remedies at equity

Rescission Equity has traditionally not used the concept of damages as a remedy, since it is a common law remedy. Yet is clear that equity would not sit idly by and permit a claimant to suffer as a result of a misrepresentation where the claimant did not wish the contract to remain valid or where an innocent misrepresentation had occurred. Accordingly, equity used the only weapon in its armoury to set the contract aside and to restore the parties to the position as if it had not happened. That remedy is known as 'rescission'.[58] A contract is rescinded so as to put the parties back into their pre-contractual position. The rather dramatic nature of such a remedy has somewhat limited the application of the equitable relief in situations where it would be appropriate. Moreover, it appears easier to obtain relief where the misrepresentation has been fraudulent. Thus, for example, rescission is not available where the contract has been executed, save where there has been fraud.

Rescission for innocent misrepresentation Before a court will grant an order for rescission at equity, a number of factors must be present. We will first assume that the misrepresentation has been innocent; then we will go on to discuss the approach of equity with respect to fraud.

Firstly, as stated, the contract must not be executed. Thus, in *Legge v. Croker*[59] a lease could not be rescinded once it had been executed. This doctrine has been statutorily amended in the United Kingdom, where execution of the

---

57 But see the statutory provisions detailed below.
58 See Keane, *Equity*, op. cit. for a fuller discussion. See also chapter 26 ibid.
59 (1811) 1 Ball & B 506; *Lecky v. Walter* [1914] IR 378 (bonds given were not secured over any asset, thus, when the debtor defaulted, they were worthless. Since the contract had been executed, it could not be rescinded); *Seddon v. North Eastern Salt* [1905] 1 Ch 326; but note that this concept has been judicially questioned.

contract is no longer considered a bar to rescission. The Sale of Goods and Supply of Services Act 1980 here has similar provisions (discussed below in statutory remedies), but it still remains valid with respect to contracts where the subject matter is real property or where the item in question is not a 'good' in the legal sense of the word.[60] Secondly, rescission is not possible where the claimant has affirmed the contract either expressly or by actions, provided the affirmation occurred with knowledge of the existence of the misrepresentation and full knowledge of the true state of facts.[61] Thirdly, as an equitable doctrine it is the subject of 'laches' or delay. The claimant will be denied relief, as with any equitable remedy, where it can be shown that he or she has delayed in taking the action.[62] The concept of what is a reasonable time within which to take the action is heavily influenced by the nature of the misrepresentation; if the misrepresentation is innocent then the courts will view a delay as being likely to bar the relief.[63] Finally, before rescission can be granted, no third-party rights must be infringed. It follows that if the right to rescind the contract is at equity, the contract cannot have been void *ab initio*, but rather voidable on election. Thus, if the contract has not been so voided prior to any *bona fide* purchaser for value acquiring the subject matter of the contract, then rescission will not be available.[64]

Rescission for fraudulent misrepresentation Rescission for fraudulent misrepresentation is limited in the same way as outlined for innocent misrepresentation. However, given the nature of the act, the courts have generally been more lenient in granting the remedy if fraud is present. Thus, rescission will be granted where the contract is completed on the basis of a fraudulent misrepresentation. Moreover, the operation of the doctrine of laches is more lenient for fraudulent misrepresentation: for example, in *O'Kelly v. Glenny*[65] a delay of ten years was held not to invalidate a claim of rescission on fraudulent misrepresentation, but in *Leaf v. International Galleries*[66] a delay of five years operated as a bar to the remedy where the misrepresentation had been innocent. In general, equity responds more sympathetically to a claim of fraud and is more likely to grant relief under such circumstances.

Statutory provisions and remedies S. 44 of the Sale of Goods and Supply of Services Act 1980 reads as follows:

60 See chapter 16, ibid.
61 *Lutton v. Seville Tractors* [1986] NI 327 (the contract cannot be affirmed if the party was not aware of the representation being false); *Peyman v. Lanjami* [1984] 3 All ER 703 (the party must know of the right to rescind); *Long v. Lloyd* [1958] 2 All ER 402.
62 *Clough v. London and NW Railway* (1871) LR 7 Exch 26.
63 See ibid.
64 Rescission is only available where *restitutio in integram* is possible: *Attwood v. Small* (1838) 6 Cl & Fin 232; *Spence v. Crawford*, 3 All ER 271; Keane, op. cit.
65 (1846) 9 Ir Eq R 25.
66 [1950] 1 All ER 693.

Where a person has entered into a contract after a misrepresentation has been made to him, and

(a) the misrepresentation has become a term of the contract or

(b) the contract has been performed

or both, then if otherwise he would be entitled to rescind the contract without alleging fraud, he shall be so entitled, subject to the provisions of this Part notwithstanding the matters mentioned in paragraphs (a) and (b)

and s. 43 states:

In this Part 'contract' means a contract for sale of goods, a hire purchase agreement, an agreement for the letting of goods to which section 38 applies or a contract for the supply of a service.

In effect, this means that, in certain contracts (contracts for the sale of goods, the hiring of goods and the supply of a service but excluding contracts for the sale of land or other items), rescission is still available for innocent misrepresentation where the contract is executed or where the misrepresentation has become part of the contract and would at common law be deemed to be a warranty not entitling the party to rescission. However, the section does not proceed to give an absolute right to rescission in such cases, as s. 45(2) states:

Where a person has entered into a contract after a misrepresentation has been made to him otherwise than fraudulently, and he would be entitled, by reason of the misrepresentation, to rescind the contract, then, if it is claimed in any proceedings arising out of the contract that the contract ought to be or has been rescinded, the court may declare the contract subsisting and award damages in lieu of rescission, if of the opinion that it would be equitable to do so, having regard to the nature of the misrepresentation and the loss that would be caused by it if the contract were upheld, as well as to the loss that rescission would cause the other party.

Thus, the court has power to substitute damages in lieu of rescission[67] where it feels it appropriate to do so in light of the surrounding circumstances. The remedy is only available where the right to rescission still applies, and this follows because the damages are awarded in lieu. If there is no right of recission, there is no possibility of awarding damages. Nor can damages be awarded where rescission has been awarded, as the remedies are mutually exclusive. This

---

67 The extent of the damages available under this section is open to debate. English authority is fairly well divided on the issue. It is suggested that the broadest possible view will be taken with respect to potential damages suffered and any loss incurred should not be excluded on narrow technical grounds.

section (45(1)) effectively imposes a statutory replacement for the principle of *Hedley Byrne v. Heller* when it states that:

> Where a person has entered into a contract after a misrepresentation has been made to him by another party thereto and as a result thereof he has suffered loss, then if the person making the misrepresentation would be liable to damages in respect thereof had the misrepresentation been made fraudulently, that person shall be liable notwithstanding that the misrepresentation was not made fraudulently, unless he proves that he had reasonable ground to believe and did believe up to the time the contract was made that the facts represented were true.

Thus, there are now statutory grounds for damages arising from a negligent misrepresentation.

Finally, s. 46 invalidates the effectiveness of clauses aimed at excluding liability for misrepresentation as follows:

> If any agreement (whether made before or after the commencement of this Act) contains a provision which would exclude or restrict—
> (a) any liability to which a party to a contract may be subject by reason of any misrepresentation made by him before the contract was made, or
> (b) any remedy available to another party to the contract by reason of such misrepresentation, that provision shall not be enforceable unless it is shown that it is fair and reasonable.

The legislation now permits rescission to be made available for innocent misrepresentation to the same extent that it is available for fraudulent misrepresentation (save with respect to the doctrine of laches, which presumably remains extant). It also provides for an award of damages to be made available in lieu of such rescission, and for an award of damages to be payable for negligent misrepresentation, and it also prohibits clauses excluding liability for misrepresentations, save where an exclusion is fair and reasonable.

17.09 CONSTRUCTIVE FRAUD

It is debatable to what extent the doctrine of constructive fraud can be distinguished from undue influence proven as a matter of fact or the duty to disclose facts when a fiduciary relationship exists between the parties. In constructive fraud, the parties have a relationship between them whereby a duty arises to disclose a fact which would not otherwise have to be revealed. The leading case of *Tate v. Williamson*[68] concerned a student who had run into financial difficulty

---

68   (1866) 2 Ch App 55.

and was advised by a friend that he should sell a certain asset. The student's friend offered to purchase it but did so without telling the student that the land had substantial mineral resources which significantly enhanced the value of the land. The sale was set aside when the student discovered the error. The case is only explicable as an example of the inherent jurisdiction of the court to do what is right in spite of the rules of precedent; so, it is very like 'sharp practice' discussed in the courts with respect to the remedy of rectification (see chapter 26).

17.09 SUMMARY

- A representation of fact, not opinion, which leads a person to enter a contract, but which does not become part of the contract, may give rise to a remedy if the representation is untrue. An untrue representation is a misrepresentation.

- Whether the misrepresentation is one of fact or opinion will depend on the surrounding circumstances in which the misrepresentation is made.

- A misrepresentation can be an oral or written statement, or it can be inferred from the conduct of the party, so that, in some instances, silence may be a misrepresentation.

- A misrepresentation must have induced the party into making the contract, that is, it must have in some way influenced the party when making the decision.

- The misrepresentation must have been made by the other party to the contract, or by his agents or employees unless expressly excluded from having this power to bind the party to the contract. Note contracts for the sale of goods or supply of services (discussed below).

- Relief is available for fraudulent misrepresentation, that is, where the party making the misrepresentation is aware that it is untrue, in the form of damages at common law under an action in tort for deceit or an action for rescission in equity.

- Relief is available for negligent misrepresentation, that is, where the party making the misrepresentation should have known it to be untrue but failed to exercise the due level of care. The remedy is that of damages at common law under an action for negligence, or for rescission at equity, although the contract must not have been performed if an order for rescission is to be granted.

- Relief is available for innocent misrepresentation only at equity and the only remedy is that of rescission, although the contract must not have been performed if an order for rescission is to be granted.

- However, in contracts for the sale of goods or the supply of services, rescission will be available for innocent and negligent misrepresentation after the contract has been performed and subject to the discretionary power of the court. The court is entitled to substitute an award of damages for an order of rescission.

- Clauses excluding liability for misrepresentation are unenforceable in contracts for the sale of goods or supply of services.

18.00

Duress and undue influence

18.01 INTRODUCTION

The concept of duress involves removal of the free will and consent required to make a contract. Duress normally consists of threats made against one party that remove his free will and results in his purportedly consenting to a contract when he had no desire to so do. Undue influence can be regarded, in many ways, as a case of constructive duress; that is, the person is effectively a free party to the contract, but in this case his freedom has been removed not by brute threats and force but by subtlety and guile. Undue influence also involves the abuse of a relationship or position in which the victim had placed considerable trust. It would be nice to say that the law has a well developed sense of what is a straightforward concept but alas, here, as with mistake and misrepresentation, the law's response is patchy, inconsistent and unclear. We shall, however, attempt to analyse this area as fully as possible.

18.02 DURESS

Common law We have already defined duress as being threats made against the victim with the aim of denying his or her free will to enter into a contract. But what sort of threats will suffice? Unfortunately the answer varies between common law and equity, the common law taking a very narrow view of the term 'threat'. At common law, duress can obviously be founded upon actual physical violence or force, but this rarely poses a problem, since actual force is normally dealt with by the criminal law and a convicted person is unlikely to sue on foot of such a contract. It is strange to realise that, at early common law, duress was allowed only on proof of physical violence to the person: a mere threat to do this violence was insufficient. As Blackstone pointed out,

> A fear of battery . . . is no duress, neither is the fear of having one's house burned, or one's goods taken away or destroyed . . . because in these cases should the threat be performed a man may have satisfaction by recovering equivalent damages: but no such suitable atonement can be made for the loss of life or limb[1]

1 See 1 *Blackstones Commentaries*; note the driving of a hard bargain can never be duress of its own, *Grand Motors v. Ford Motors*, 564 F Supp 34.

While this no longer represents good law as to its substantive pronouncement, the policy rationale continues unabated and it may more readily explain the attitude of the common law to the modern day concept of duress. Blackstone was at pains to point out that the remedy was only available where the duress was of such a nature that a subsequent remedy would be of no avail. Injury to goods could be remedied by a subsequent payment of damages and so forth. This policy still guides the modern application of the doctrine of duress.

The common law's amended approach to the implicit or explicit threat of such force has been chequered.[2] The threat must be to do something which is unlawful, that is, which constitutes a tort or a crime. No duress is actionable at law if it consists of threats to do something which could be done in any event; but equity may intervene, as we shall see later. Thus, to threaten the victim with imprisonment will constitute duress, unless the victim is in fact liable to go to jail (it should be noted, however, that a contract which threatened imprisonment might be set aside as a contract designed to pervert the course of justice). Thus, it will not constitute duress to threaten the victim with telling his mother that he does not go to Mass every Sunday since the relating of such information is not unlawful; but to threaten to tell one's mother that he is an embezzler and a drunkard, would be, if it were untrue, as it might constitute the tort of defamation.[3] Calamari and Perillo give four possible categories of duress:

(i)   Physical violence or threats thereof.

(ii) Imprisonment or threats thereof.

(iii) Wrongful seizing or withholding of assets or threats thereof.

(iv) Other wrongful acts.

In general, this is a clear analysis of the actionable threats for duress to succeed; only numbers (iii) and (iv) require some further discussion.

Point (iii) may give rise to some confusion. There is some argument in the United Kingdom as to whether or not relief can be granted for duress by way

---

2   *Lessee of Blackwood v. Gregg* (1831) Hayes 277 (the kidnapping of a 92-year-old man by his relatives, did not constitute automatic duress but was an issue left to the jury to decide whether this restraint constituted duress!).

3   There is another interesting point here: when the litigant claims that his free will has been overcome, does this refer to his subjective free will or an objective free will. The issue is hardly clear, *Kaplan v. Kaplan*, 182 NE 2d 706 and *Sibree v. Webber* 50 NE 555 appear to represent the prevalent view that the test is subjective, that is: was the individuals free will overcome (save perhaps in cases of economic duress, discussed below)? Moreover, if the parent of a child who has been kidnapped pays a ransom for the child's safe return, is not the payment of the ransom made with free will? Yet it would be set aside because this free will was obtained by wrongful acts: Dalzell, 'Duress by Economic Pressure', 20 *North Carolina Law Rev* 237; Eisenberg, 'The Bargain Principle and its Limits', 95 *Harvard Law Rev* 741.

of a threat to seize or withhold a person's goods or assets. Thus in *Skeate v. Beale*[4] a tenant agreed to pay £3 7s 6d immediately and the balance of £16 2s 6d within one month because if he did not the landlord threatened to levy distress[5] on the tenants goods for that amount. The tenant subsequently sued for recovery of the £16 2s. 6d. on the grounds that this amount was not in fact owing and that he had only agreed to it due to the threat of distress on his goods. The plea was dismissed. But this is inconsistent with *Astley v. Reynolds*,[6] where a pledgee (one who takes property as security for money advanced, a pawnbroker in colloquial terms) refused to surrender goods held unless a bonus, which had not been part of the earlier bargain, was paid. The court held that the excess payment could be recovered. The court went on to state:

> [The owner] might have such an immediate want of his goods, that an action in trover would not do his business.[7]

And it is from this that we can determine a reconciliation of the cases. Effectively, the policy at common law is to grant relief to a person who enters into a contract under duress, but only where failure to enter this contract would have resulted in injury that would be difficult subsequently to remedy. In *Astley's* case the court found that with pledged goods, failure to re-deliver the items at the appropriate time might be non-compensatable later, whereas in *Skeate* no such danger was pleaded or was obvious. In *Chandler v. Sanger*[8] the plaintiff entered into an agreement with the defendant to pay the defendant's claim only because the defendant had secured an order of attachment over the plaintiff's property—one ice truck, fully loaded, to which the order of attachment had been executed in the early hours of the morning. The plaintiff was advised that he could go to court and have the order of attachment removed but it would take three days, by which time the ice would have melted and his business collapsed. The court ordered that the money be repaid.

One possible alternative to the argument that recovery for duress to goods depends on the irreversible aspects of failing to heed the duress is that in both *Astley* and *Chandler* the defendant acted improperly. In other words, is the US position based on motive of the defendant? If it is, it is clearly erroneous and would mean that it does not represent good law here, for duress can only be judged by the impact it has on its victim. While there is no doubt that the fact of the cases swayed the earlier decisions of the courts, the doctrine is now well established, even where the actions of the defendant are innocent and honest.

---

4   (1840) 11 Ad & Q 983.
5   'Distress' is the legal term given to the landlord's right to sell personal property belonging to his tenant in satisfaction of arrears of rent. It does not require a court order, but due to certain limitations placed on the execution of distress, it is very rarely exercised by a landlord.
6   (1731) 2 Stra 915.
7   Ibid., 923.
8   114 Mass 364.

The true limitation on the doctrine is that only that money which is overpaid can be recovered; generally speaking, payment of the amount that is owing is non-recoverable even if obtained by such duress.

As for point (iv)—other wrongful acts—it is true to say that it is one of those general categories, admired by lawyers simply on the basis that it acts as a repository for difficult judgments. Having said that, the usefulness of such categories can seldom be denied; general categories permit growth in the law arising from changing circumstances. Thus, in *Link v. Link*[9] an agreement for the transfer of securities from a wife to her husband resulting from a threat by the husband to the wife that he would seek custody of the children if she refused, could be set aside for duress.

> The weight of modern authority supports the rule, which we here adopt, that the act done or threatened may be wrongful even though not unlawful *per se*; and that the threat to instigate legal proceedings, criminal or civil, which might be justifiable, *per se*, becomes wrongful within the meaning of this rule, if made with the corrupt intent to coerce a transaction grossly unfair to the victim and not related to the subject of such proceedings.[10]

Likewise, to terminate an employment at will unless the employee agrees to sell back stock to the employer is wrongful and can be actionable duress.[11] Further, it removes the requirement for unlawfulness to ground actionable duress. The difficulty with this category is the extent to which it crosses over into relief at equity or relief for economic duress (discussed later). Despite the fact that the courts prefer to exercise their equitable jurisdiction rather than enlarging existing common law rights, the category should, remain valid at common law.

Duress, of whatever category, should have induced the action complained of in a manner similar to that in misrepresentation. So it need not be the sole reason for entering into the agreement, but it must have had substantial impact.[12]

The effect at common law of duress being proved is unclear. Only in a very few cases will the agreement be rendered void *ab initio*,[13] such as where the

---

9   179 SE 2d 697.
10 Ibid., 705.
11 *Laemmer v. J Walter Thomspson*, 435 F 2d 680.
12 *Barton v. Armstrong* [1975] 2 All ER 465 (the onus is on the person accused of duress to show that the victim did not act on the duress in entering the contract); Pollock, *Principles of Contract*, 179; Restatement, Contracts, s. 496.
13 13 Williston s 1624, 1627; Lanham, 'Duress and Void Contracts', 29 MLR 615 who argues that they are void; *Griffith v. Griffith* [1944] IR 35 (the plaintiff sought his marriage to be declared void *ab initio* since he was forced into it by an accusation that he was the father of his 'wife's' child. In fact he was not the father of the child, the court held the marriage contract void *ab initio*; *M.K. v. McC.* [1982] ILRM 277; legal theory requires that duress at common law voids the contract as of right, but the courts have shown no desire to implement this; cf. *Barton v. Armstrong*, ibid.

claimant has signed an agreement, not taking any time to look at its contents, since there is a gun pointed at the claimant.[14] Such a situation involves the absence of consent entirely. In the more usual cases of duress, the contract is apparently voidable, save where innocent third parties have acquired rights in its subject matter.[15] In all cases, once the duress has ceased, any action on the part of the victim which appears to adopt the agreement (such as accepting benefits under the agreement and so forth) will defeat a claim of duress. Moreover, even if the victim takes no further action with respect to the agreement, a failure to make efforts to have the agreement set aside may disbar a claimant from relief.[16] Of course, this will not be so where the duress is of a continuing nature.[17] More properly, the correct remedy would be one of restitution for unjust enrichment, or in some cases the imposition of a constructive trust. Further elaboration is best pursued through a work on Restitution or Remedies.[18] Where this relief is sought, the contract remains valid, but voidable.

Equity Relief under equity for duress is far more comprehensive, partly because the courts have failed to utilise the concept of wrongful act at law outlined earlier. There are in fact three principal areas of equitable intervention which are difficult to separate. Firstly, the concept of undue influence (discussed below); secondly, the unconscionable bargain; and thirdly, the concept of constructive fraud (discussed earlier). We turn now to deal with unconscionable bargain, but we must bear in mind that the other reliefs mentioned may still be of some use in this area.

Unconscionable bargain The so-called 'unconscionable bargain' theory arose originally from imprudent arrangements made by heirs in anticipation of their succession rights; today such cases seldom arise.[19] What has been disappointing is the reluctance of the English courts to use the doctrine in the field of inequality of bargaining power. This is to be regretted and will not, it is hoped, be adopted in this jurisdiction. It has been said that unconscionability underlies the entire basis of equity; while this may go too far, it does contain some truth. Indeed, Bogart's contention, that the concept of equitable ownership of property is simply equity refusing to allow the legal owner of the property the

---

14 Restatement, Second, Contracts, s. 174.
15 *Byle v. Byle* (1990) 65 DLR (4th) 641.
16 The merger here between setting a contract aside for duress at common law and equity has become so inseparable that the argument against fusion of common law and equity may well be lost in this area.
17 *Great Southern Railway v. Robertson* (1878) 2 LR (Ir) 548; *Rogers v. Louth County Council* [1981] ILRM 143.
18 See Goff and Jones, *Restitution, Burrows, Restitution*; *Dimskal Shipping Co. v. ITWF (The Evia Luck) (No. 2)* [1991] 3 WLR 875.
19 For a modern application see *Buckley v. Irwin* [1960] NI 98.

unconscionable exercise of his legal rights,[20] may have some merit. And it is certainly true that unconscionability lies behind the equitable rules in mistake, misrepresentation and undue influence.[21]

Even at common law the concept of an unconscionable bargain does not go unrecognised for as it has been said:

> [An unconscionable agreement is one] such as no man in his senses and not under delusion would make on the one hand, and as no honest and fair man would accept on the other.[22]

Yet, as Calamari and Perillo point out, while the admission of such a doctrine at law has been rare, in practice the courts have used many other legal devices to produce a desired result where the bargain is unconscionable. But this is highly unsatisfactory, for as they go on to say:

> the conflict between what the courts said they were doing and what it was sometimes obvious they were in fact doing has had an unsettling effect on the law, giving the sensitive a feeling of lawlessness, the logician a feeling of irrationality and the average lawyer a feeling of confusion.[23]

While the courts in England have refused to deny the validity of contracts merely on the basis of the infirmity of one of the parties, Irish courts (like their Canadian counterparts)[24] have adopted a more liberal approach, and have set contracts aside on the basis of the infirmity of one of the contracting parties. The doctrine is enunciated in the English case of *Fry v. Lane*,[25] where it is said that in order to have a contract set aside for unconscionability three factors must be proven: poverty and ignorance of the plaintiff, undervalued consideration and a lack of independent advice. These requirements form part of Irish law but

---

20 Bogart, *Trusts*, 5th ed. pp. 9-10.
21 See ibid.
22 *Earl of Chesterfield v. Janssen*, 28 Eng Rep 82, 100; *Slator v. Nolan* (1876) IR 11 Eq 367 ('I take the law of the court to be that if two persons—no matter whether a confidential relation exists between them or not — stand in such a relation to each other, whether by reason of distress or recklessness or wildness or want of care and where the facts show that one party has taken undue advantage of the other by reason of circumstances I have mentioned—a transaction resting upon such unconscionable dealing will not be allowed to stand'); *Rae v. Joyce* (1892) 29 LR (Ir) 500.
23 Calamari and Perillo, op. cit., 402.
24 *Doan v. Insurance Corporation of British Columbia* (1987) 18 BCLR (2d) 286; *Harry v. Krentziger* (1978) 95 DLR (3d) 231 ('where a claim is made that a bargain is unconscionable it must be shown that there was inequality in the position of the parties due to the ignorance, need or distress of the weaker party which would leave him in the power of the stronger coupled with the proof of substantial unfairness in the bargain' at 237).
25 (1888) 40 Ch D 312.

have been more liberally construed, and the courts have been more willing to grant relief on this basis, as indeed have the Australian courts.[26] Thus, in *Cresswell v. Potter*[27] the concept of poverty and ignorance applied where the claimant came from a lower income group. Further, there has been ample evidence to suggest that the Irish courts have taken a paternalistic view with respect to old people, being quite willing to set the contract aside where there is a considerable age gap between the parties.

Of more importance is the question of whether or not the courts have a general jurisdiction to grant relief for unconscionable bargain as between facts that would more readily admit of inequality of bargaining power.[28] It is to be remembered that the courts use other devices to modify contracts made between parties of unequal bargaining status, as we have discussed earlier. In Canada, the express use of unconscionable bargain to interfere with such contracts has been evident, but it is in the United States that such a doctrine has reached general and overt acceptance. Accordingly, the UCC introduced new provisions designed to achieve two specific aims: a) to permit the courts openly to interfere in contracts where previous interference had been by covert action and b) to merge substantive issues of law and equity. Thus the UCC provision reads:

> (1) If the court as a matter of law finds the contract or any clause of the contract to have been unconscionable at the time it was made the court may refuse to enforce the contract, or it may enforce the remainder of the contract without the unconscionable clause, or it may so limit the application of any unconscionable clause as to avoid any unconscionable result.

> (2) When it is claimed or appears to the court that the contract or any clause thereof may be unconscionable the parties shall be afforded a reasonable opportunity to present evidence as to its commercial setting, purpose and effect to aid the court in making a determination.[29]

It is clear, however, that the section does not provide a definition for unconscionablity but a Comment to the provision does state:

> This section is intended to make it possible for the courts to police

---

26 *Commercial Bank of Australia v. Amadio* (1983) 151 CLR 449 (a bank manager secured a guarantee for the debts of a customer from the customer's parents, who spoke little English. The parents relied upon the bank manager for guidance, the court held the transaction was unconscionable).

27 [1978] 1 WLR 255; *Grealish v. Murphy* [1946] IR 35; *Lyndon v. Coyne* (1946) 12 Ir Jur Rep 64.

28 *O'Flanagan v. Ray-Ger*, unreported, High Court, 28 April 1983 (Costello J stated the doctrine could apply to a general commercial transaction); *McCoy v. Green and Cole*, unreported, High Court, 19 January 1984; but cf. *Bundy v. Lloyds Bank* [1975] QB 326 (it requires a fiduciary relationship before a transaction will be set aside).

29 S. 2-302.

explicitly against the contracts or clauses which they find to be unconscionable. In the past such policing has been accomplished by adverse construction of language, by manipulation of the rules of offer and acceptance or by the determinations that the clause is contrary to public policy or to the dominant purpose of the contract. This section is intended to allow the court to pass directly on the unconscionability of the contract or particular clause therein and to make a conclusion of law as to its unconscionability. The basic test is whether, in the light of the general commercial background and the commercial needs of the particular trade or case the clauses involved are so one sided as to be unconscionable under the circumstances existing at the time of the making of the contract. Subsection (2) makes it clear that it is proper for the court to hear evidence upon these questions. The principle is one of the prevention of oppression and unfair surprise and not of disturbance of allocation of risks because of superior bargaining power.[30]

As a statement of practice, this comment neatly encapsulates the current position adopted by the courts with respect to such things as exclusion clauses (discussed earlier). Indeed, the adoption of such a clear statement of overt principle should be welcomed in this jurisdiction, for, as Llewellyn said,

> Covert tools are never reliable tools.[31]

However, it is interesting to note that the Comment expressly excludes setting contracts aside or reformulating them simply on the basis of unequal bargaining power: the section is only available for the 'prevention of oppression and unfair surprise'.[32] Yet, in *Weaver v. American Oil*[33] the court said that, where a clause places hardship on the weaker of the parties to the contract in question,

> [It must be shown that] the provisions were explained to the other party and came to his knowledge and there was in fact a real and voluntary meeting of the minds and not merely an objective meeting.[34]

This would seem to suggest that the Comment, rightly, does not give power to a court to strike a contract, or part of a contract, down merely because the parties did not come to the contract equally. There must be something more than mere inequality. Moreover, the corollary is also true: relief under this provision is available even where the parties come to the contract with equality of bargaining power or indeed 'even where the oppressor is inexperienced compared to the oppressed'.[35]

30   See ibid., Comment b.
31   Llewellyn, *The Common Law Tradition*, p. 365.
32   51 NE 227.
33   276 NE 2d 144, 49 ALR 3d 306.
34   Ibid., 154.
35   *Miller v. Coffeen*, 280 SW 2d 100.

18.03 UNDUE INFLUENCE

In *Smith v. Henline* it was said that:

> Undue influence . . . is any improper or wrongful constraint, machination
> or urgency of persuasion, whereby the will of the person is overpowered,
> and he is induced to do or forbear an act which he would not do, or would
> do if left to act freely.[36]

Despite the similarity of this definition to that of duress given earlier, in reality
the question is not necessarily one of fear, but, as Calamari and Perillo point
out, euphoria which exercises the mind of the claimant.[37] While the term
'euphoria' may be a trifle exaggerated, the reality is that in undue influence the
claimant does not feel in the slightest unsafe when entering into the bargain.
The question is really one of trust, although the terminology used of dominant
and servient parties tends to obscure this. Where one of the parties is so dominant
that the other party has no free will, this, in all likelihood, will be an instance
of duress or absence of mutual assent. Undue influence means that because of
someone's position or relationship with one of the parties, a trust has developed
between them that transcends the prudent person's ability to see clearly. Most
of the cases involving undue influence concern the existence of a relationship
which has somehow been manipulated so that the servient partner to the
relationship acts to the benefit of the dominant party. Thus solicitors, doctors,
parents and guardians[38] and religious ministers[39] have often been held to
exercise such a relationship over certain people, and contracts made to benefit
such people have been set aside. However, it should be remembered that undue
influence is a limited doctrine, for, as has been said,

> Is it right and expedient to save persons from the consequences of their
> own folly?—or is it that it is right and expedient to save them from being
> victimised by other people. In my opinion the doctrine of undue influence
> is founded upon the second of these two principles. Courts of Equity have
> never set aside gifts on the ground of folly, imprudence or want of
> foresight on the part of the donor.[40]

The doctrine operates only where someone has been victimised. Thus,
someone must have exercised a controlling influence over the claimant. For this

---

36 51 NE 227, 233.
37 Op. cit., p. 352.
38 *Murphy v. O'Shea* (1845) 81 Eq R 329; *Lawless v. Mansfield* (1841) 1 Dr and War 557.
39 *White v. Meade* (1840) 2 Ir Eq R 420 (religious mentor had a special relationship).
40 *Allcard v. Skinner* (1887) 36 Ch D 145; but the courts have often set aside transactions
   of the type described, see *Grealish v. Murphy*, ibid.

to happen there must have been a special relationship like the ones referred to above. It should be noted that some relationships do not come within the concept as understood in this jurisdiction; thus the relationship of husband and wife does not presuppose the existence of undue influence.[41] Neither does that of employee-employer. This is, of course, not to say that it is a complete bar to pleading undue influence as between husband and wife, for, as Jones LJ stated,

> The presumption of undue influence may arise in two sorts of cases. The evidence may show a particular relationship for example that of solicitor and client, trustee and *cetsui que trust*, doctor and patient or religious advisor and pupil. Those cases or some of them, depending on the facts, may of themselves raise the presumption. Such examples, as regards undue influence, have much in common with the doctrine of *res ipsa locquiter* in relation to negligence. But then there is the other sort of case, the precise range of which is indeterminate, in which the whole evidence when meticulously considered, may disclose facts from which it should be inferred that a relationship is disclosed which justifies a finding that there is a presumption of undue influence. In other words the presumption enables a party to achieve justice by bridging a gap in the evidence where there is a gap because the evidence is impossible to come by.[42]

In the Californian case of *Odorizzi v. Bloomfield School District*[43] the claimant had been arrested on charges of homosexual behaviour and detained for forty hours without sleep. After being released, the charges were subsequently withdrawn, school officials visited him and persuaded him it was best to resign his post, and he executed a document to that affect. In setting aside the resignation the court went on to say

> The difference between legitimate persuasion and excessive pressure, like the difference between rape and seduction, rests to a considerable extent in the manner in which they go about their business. . . . However, over persuasion is generally accomplished by certain characteristics which tend to create a pattern. The pattern usually involves several of the following elements:
> (1) discussion of the transaction at an unusual or inappropriate time,
> (2) consummation of the transaction in an unusual place,
> (3) insistent demand that the business be finished at once,

41   *Northern Bank v. Carpenter* [1931] IR 268; *Bank of Montreal v. Stuart* [1911] AC 120; but cf. *Bank of Ireland v. Smyth* [1933] IR which adopts the 'tender wife' approach of *National Westmisinter Bank v. O'Brien* [1993 4 All ER in the CA (subsequently overturned by the House of Lords), see also Sanfey, 'Undue Influence and the Tender Wives Treatment' [1994] CLP.
42   *In re Founds Estate.*
43   246 Cal App 2d 123.

(4) extreme emphasis on untoward consequences of delay,

(5) the use of multiple persuaders by the dominant side against a single servient party,

(6) absence of third party advisors to the servient party,

(7) statements that there is no time to consult financial advisors or attorneys.

If a number of these elements are simultaneously present, the persuasion may be characterized as excessive.[44]

This is the type of rationale behind decisions in both English and Irish jurisdictions and, while the list is not complete, it is a useful starting point. In certain relationships,[45] the law deems a position of special trust has arisen between the parties, so that (in any unfair transaction between them),[46] the onus will be on the party enforcing any benefit under the contract to disprove the allegation of undue influence.[47] In the absence of a position of special trust between the parties, the onus rests with the claimant seeking to have the transaction set aside, to show that the transaction was made subject to undue influence.[48] All of this is subject to the fact that the remedy is at equity and, therefore, discretionary. A remedy will be denied if the claimant has delayed in seeking relief, following the general equitable doctrine of laches.[49]

It should be noted that where the relationship is so close as to warrant the finding of a fiduciary relationship between the parties such as between the trustees and the beneficiaries, then it may well be that the appropriate remedy is to call the trustees to account for profits had and received under the trust.[50]

Finally, there is a special type of undue influence that people exercise, namely economic influence. This is often referred to as 'economic duress'; however, the term 'duress', albeit adopted in this work, should be treated with some caution. The phrase more accurately describes situations where one party is in a position of economic dominance so as to be able to influence the decisions of the other party either by express or implied use of this dominance; to this we now turn.

---

44 Ibid., at 133-134 (note: the first sentence appears after the rest in the actual report, but it has been juxtaposed in this extract for the sake of clarity.)

45 *McMakin v. Hibernian Bank* [1905] 1 IR 296 (parent and child); *Wright v. Carter* [1903] 1 Ch 27 (solicitor and client); *Allcard v. Skinner* (1887) 36 Ch D 145 (religious minister and religious follower).

46 *National Westminster v. Morgan* [1985] AC 686.

47 *Gregg v. Kidd* [1956] IR 183.

48 *Williams v. Bayley* (1866) LR 1 HL 200; *Westminster Bank v. Morgan* [1985] AC 686.

49 In general see Hanbury and Martin, *Equity*, 14th ed.

50 Laches is the legal term for delay, see Keane, op. cit; (1983) 151 CLR 447.

18.04 ECONOMIC DURESS

It is true to say that in the United States there has been little support for the concept of a separate category of economic duress, or 'business compulsion', as they would term it,[51] yet there can be no denying the fairly consistent approach in the common law to such cases in Australia,[52] Canada[53] and England. In *Commercial Bank of Australia v. Amadio*[54] the court set aside a transaction whereby immigrant parents were persuaded to sign a mortgage note securing their son's borrowings to the bank. The bank manager had called out to the parents' home to achieve this result. Mason J went on to say,

> [I]f A having actual knowledge that B occupies a situation of special disadvantage in relation to an intended transaction, so that B cannot make a judgment as to what is in his own interests, takes unfair advantage of his (A's) superior bargaining power or position by entering into that transaction, his conduct in so doing is unconscionable. And if, instead of having actual knowledge of that situation, A is aware of the possibility that situation may exist or is aware of facts that would raise that possibility in the mind of any reasonable person, the result will be the same.[55]

And Deane J concluded:

> The jurisdiction is established as extending generally to circumstances in which (i) a party to a transaction was under a special disability in dealing with the other party with the consequence that there was an absence of any reasonable degree of equality between them and (ii) that disability was sufficiently evident to the stronger party to make it *prima facie* unfair or 'unconscientious' that he procure, or accept, the weaker party's assent to the impugned transaction in the circumstances in which he procured or accepted it. Where such circumstances are shown to have existed, an onus is cast upon the stronger party to show that the transaction was fair, just and reasonable. . . .[56]

Such views are more in accordance with Denning MR in *Lloyds Bank v. Bundy*,[57] where on similar facts he held, after having analysed the case law,

51 Dalzell, 'Duress by Economic Pressure', 20 *North Carolina Law Rev* (in two parts) at 237 and 341 respectively); Dawson, 'Economic Duress—An Essay in Perspective', 45 *Michigan Law Review* 253; effectively the US approach is to apply the concept of duress to such facts.

52 See Greig and Davis, op. cit., p. 973 et seq.; Carter and Harland, op. cit., p.

457 et seq.

53 *A & K Lick a Check v. Cordiv Enterprises* (1981) 119 DLR (3d) 440; see Fridman, *Law of Contract in Canada*, 3rd ed., p. 317.

54 (1983) 151 CLR 447.

55 Ibid at 453.

56 Ibid at 471.

57 [1974] 3 All ER 757, [1978] 3 All ER 1170.

I would suggest that through all these instances there runs a single thread. They rest on 'inequality of bargaining power'. By virtue of it English Law gives relief to one who, without independent advice, enters into a contract upon terms which are very unfair . . . when his bargaining power is grievously impaired by reason of his own needs or desires, or by his own ignorance or infirmity, coupled with undue influences or pressures brought to bear on him by or for the benefit of another. When I use the word undue, I do not mean to suggest that the principle depends on any proof of wrongdoing. The one who stipulates for an unfair advantage may be moved solely by his own self interest, unconscious of the distress he is bringing to the other. I have also avoided any reference to the will of the one being dominated or overcome by the other. One who is in extreme need may knowingly consent to a most improvident bargain, solely to relieve the straits in which he finds himself.[58]

Both these judgments indicate the existence of a general concept of inequality of bargaining power being used to set contracts aside. However, the doctrines have in fact been limited to cases involving economic duress, and it appears safe to say that the English courts will not move beyond this. Thus Denning's judgment represents good law with respect to economic duress only[59] and not any other type of duress or undue influence arising from inequality of bargaining power.[60] Indeed, it has proven remarkably difficult to win any case on the basis of economic duress in the English jurisdiction, although the courts have gone out of their way to admit its possibility of success. It is most likely that the claimant will succeed where a bank and an individual are involved.[61] Thus, in *North Ocean Shipping v. Hyundai*[62] a demand for a 10% increase in the purchase price of a ship before it would be completed was held valid, although in large part the judgment did place emphasis on the fact that suit had not been brought until nine months after the ship had been built. But to what extent would the court have found differently if the parties had been unmatched? In the light of *Williams v. Roffey*[63] discussed earlier, the question arises as to what extent can this economic duress now constitute good consideration to enforce the agreement itself?

Despite the wording used by the courts, particularly in England, economic duress can be maintained only where there is also an inequality of bargaining power, though even this can be rebutted where the dominant party takes steps

58 Ibid. at 765.
59 *Universe Tankship of Monrovia v. International Transport Workers Federation* [1982] 2 All ER 67; *Pao On v. Lau Yiu* [1979] 3 All ER 65.
60 *National Westminster Bank v. Morgan* [1985] 1 All ER 821; *Multi Service Book Binding v. Marden* [1978] 2 All ER 489.
61 *Harrison v. National Bank of Australasia* (1928) 23 Tas LR 1.
62 [1978] 3 All ER 1170.
63 [1990] 1 All ER 512.

to explain the position to the servient party in a forthright manner.[64] Where the parties are equal in the sense that they are commercial enterprises, it seems that the courts are less willing to interfere. It unfortunately raises the question as to the extent society is willing to tolerate duress and coercion in commercial transactions. In many ways the English courts may merely be recognising the reality of private enterprise at its most unregulated thereby reflecting an ethos current in the eighties and nineties. But where the equation is very unbalanced, the courts have found it harder.

18.05 SUMMARY

Duress is available at law to set aside a contract only where there has been physical violence or imprisonment or threats thereof to persons (or, to a lesser extent goods and property) and an under-used jurisdiction for wrongful acts, as distinct from unlawful acts. But it should be noted that duress can only succeed in circumstances where it would have been inappropriate to permit the threat to be carried out since in that event the payment of damages or any other remedy would be unsatisfactory.

At equity, relief is available for constructive fraud, unconscionable bargain and economic duress. Constructive fraud is dealt with elsewhere. Undue influence will occur either where by virtue of the relationship undue influence will be presumed or where acts of undue influence can be clearly shown. For economic duress, it appears that there should be an accompanying inequality of bargaining power for a claim to succeed and even then it will fail if the nature of the transaction was clearly explained to the claimant and understood by him or her.

Finally, no matter the basis of the claim or the nature of the relief sought, in all cases the claimant must show an unfair bargain. There is no right to relief for mere inequality of bargaining power or undue influence unless the transaction seeking to be impugned is also shown to be unfair and unwarranted.

---

64   *Inche Noriah v. Shaik Alie Bin Omar* [1929] AC 127.

Illegal contracts

19.01 INTRODUCTION

Public policy requires that certain contracts, even though validly formed, are so contrary to the common good that under no circumstances can they be enforceable. Sometimes the contract will be so tainted by the inclusion of certain terms that nothing of the contract can be saved and the entire contract must fall. In other situations only part of the contract infringes a public policy element so that all that is required is that the infringement be struck down and the remainder of the contract can proceed. The latter are more traditionally referred to as void contracts and are dealt with in more detail in the following chapter. It is to the former to which we now turn our attention.

19.02 ILLEGALITY AT COMMON LAW

Public policy is by nature an emphereal concept hardly capable of concise or static definition. Not only is public policy a question of subjective choice on the part of the judiciary, but it will, of necessity, vary from time to time and from place to place. At its broadest sweep in a definitional sense, public policy could be used to control and restrict the freedom of contractual bargain in a manner not unlike that operated under socialist law. If the courts were to implement the doctrine of illegal contracts at its widest, it would enable them to strike down contracts which served individual interests over those of society; thus in the wrong hands it could justify denying contracts which involved profit to one party only or it might be used to regulate the amount of profit that is 'reasonable'. It could also be used to regulate the private morals of society. The fact remains that the restrained use of this doctrine illustrates, to some extent, that despite the immense amount of power and trust that is reposed in the judiciary, it has not to date been abused.

In rendering contracts illegal at common law, a number of well established categories have been created; while the list is not exhaustive, it will only rarely occur that the courts will step outside it and use this somewhat draconian power. We turn now to analyse the different classifications.

Contracts to commit a tort or a crime It is obvious that a contract to kill someone, despite having all the other features of a contract (offer, acceptance, consideration, etc.), cannot be enforceable in a court of law. Neither can a contract to rob a bank, rape a woman and so forth.[1] To enforce such a contract would make no sense and in many ways the sort of people who enter such contracts tend not to seek remedies through the judicial process. Their remedial action is far less subtle and far more direct. Of perhaps more practical concern are contracts with a less obvious criminal or tortious element. Contracts of insurance are particularly fertile in this field, because by definition most are designed to indemnify for negligence. The difficulty is where negligence slips over the line into intentional acts which might constitute a crime. Thus, for example, convicting a motorist of manslaughter might exclude the victim's right to recovery against an insurance policy. The important point to remember is that the contract must be viewed in the abstract, not with respect to the actions complained of. In *Grey v. Barr*[2] the victim, while visiting the insured's house, was attacked by the insured and suffered injuries for which he sought compensation. The insured's house insurance covered accidents that occurred in the home, but the court held that the attack, being intentional, did not come within the scope of the insurance. While the result is harsh (it was the victim who would have benefitted, not the insured, had a claim against the insurance policy been successful), it is just. The case is, however, more pertinent to the construction of the term 'accidents in the home' rather than any principle of illegal contracts. If the contract of insurance was illegal; it would fall in its entirety, *ab initio*. There was clearly nothing illegal with the contract of insurance. The events complained of simply did not fall within the ambit of its terms. Had the insurance contract covered liability for criminally inflicted injuries, the contract might have been illegal.

In *Beresford v. Royal Insurance Co.*[3] the insured took his own life minutes before an insurance policy would have lapsed for non-payment. While the policy was worded so as to leave open the possibility of a pay-out on a suicide, the court refused to uphold a claim by the deceased's estate. The deceased's last act was criminal and it was against public policy that his heirs should benefit from such an act. The decision is not without difficulty, for the court did not treat the entire contract of insurance as illegal. If the contract of insurance can be interpreted as paying out on a suicide, then it is either illegal and void in its entirety or it is valid. It cannot be that it is only void to the extent that the act complained of is illegal. Suppose X hires Y to, *inter alia*, drive him to a particular location and supply him with a gun with which to kill Z. If the *Beresford* case is correct, seemingly only if Z is actually killed, or an attempt to do so is made, will the contract be void. But driving X to a particular location

---

1   A contract can be one which agrees to commit a crime without having to be overtly criminal, see *Namlooze Venootschap De Faam v. Dorset Manufacturing* [1949] IR 203 (the contract was illegal because it involved payment in a foreign currency; this was prohibited, without government permission, during the Second World War).

2   [1971] 2 QB 554.

3   [1937] 2 All ER 243.

might still be valid since the entire contract is not struck down, only the illegal part, and then only the illegal part with reference to the events which have occurred. In *Beresford*, presumably, the payment would have been made if the deceased had been killed in an accident. The case should really be treated with some caution, not perhaps as to the decision but as to the reasoning. Since the contract of insurance permitted payment on foot of suicide, it was illegal; the consequences of that illegality would be mitigated where the party claiming a benefit under it acted innocently (this is discussed in below). At all times the distinction between classification and consequences must be emphasised. First, the contract must be categorised as being legal or illegal. If it is illegal, this carries certain consequences, but these consequences may be alleviated in certain situations.

Some clarification of the principles involved here would be desirable. One possible way of looking at it would be as follows:

Contracts to commit a crime or a tort are unenforceable as between the parties to such a contract. Moreover, no party to such a contract should benefit from the consequences, direct or indirect, of such a contract. A contract which seeks to indemnify a person from liability arising from a crime or a tort is illegal, save where the indemnity operates only with respect to negligence on the part of the person so indemnified, or to such other actions as may be specified by statutory provision in certain circumstances. Further, no contract will be enforced where to do so would compel any of the parties to the contract to undertake certain acts which, subsequent to the contract being entered into, have become illegal. In all cases the illegality is to be determined from the contract in the abstract and not with reference to the events subsequently complained of. However, if the contract is lawful on the face of it, an innocent party may sustain an action to recover losses arising prior to knowledge of the illegality.

Contracts of sexual immorality   We are concerned here with contracts which are not illegal, but highly immoral. If the contract complained of is illegal, then it is rendered void as an illegal contract (see above). The difficulty with immorality as a legal concept is the changing nature of the offence. What is immoral today may not be so tomorrow.[4] Thus, for example, cohabitation between members of the opposite sex outside of wedlock was once highly immoral,[5] yet today it would not be regarded as such by the majority of people; certainly, few would advocate rendering a contract to lease a premises to an unmarried couple illegal on grounds that it was a contract which facilitated sexual immorality.[6] Moreover, homosexuality, currently legalised, may or may not still be classified as immoral.

4   *Andrews v. Parker* [1973] Qd R 93.
5   *Benyon v. Nettlefold* (1850) 3 Mac & G 94.
6   *Heglibiston Establishment v. Heyman* (1977) 246 Estates Gazette 567; *Tinsley v. Milligan* [1992] 2 WLR 508 (fact that relationship was that of a lesbian couple had no impact on case).

Prostitution is perhaps one of the most common examples of this rule. From the criminal point of view, it is the act of soliciting which is illegal; the contract to pay for sex is not a crime. But such a contract is 'illegal' in the civil sense, because a prostitute who provides sex on credit does so at some risk. Should her client fail to pay that which is owed, there will be no recourse to the courts of law to enforce the debt. Moreover, contracts ancillary to the act itself will also be construed as being illegal; thus, a contract of transportation provided to a prostitute is unenforceable.[7] A number of modern difficulties have arisen. Suppose the payment occurs by way of a credit card for sexual services (not unusual in the high class world of the so called 'call girl'). Can a client subsequently renounce the payment and refuse to honour the debt? Would the credit card company be at risk in such exchanges? Moreover, what is the position with respect to phone-sex services? Could a client dishonour that part of his phone bill which relates to such services? Suppose the phone service is run from another jurisdiction where these sex services are not considered immoral: whose standards of morality should apply? The answers remain uncertain. This classification of immoral contracts should be removed from our legal system.

Contracts encouraging immorality[8]   This generalised classification of the above principle suffers from the same defects mentioned. Such contracts would include gaming contracts. The rule rendering contracts encouraging immorality illegal, has no place in our legal system. Indeed, there is little doubt that the courts have tended to see only sexual immorality.

Contracts to prejudice the administration of justice
Contracts to discontinue legal proceedings   Such contracts are clearly illegal. Typically, they involve agreements which compromise legal proceedings of a criminal nature. Thus, a contract whereby one party agrees, in exchange for money, not to give evidence at a criminal hearing, is by and large unenforceable. It is wrong to suggest that such agreements could never be enforceable. Suppose X punches Y in the mouth at a football game. Y can proceed in one of two ways: a criminal action and a civil action. Suppose X offers to settle the civil action for £3,000 provided Y discontinues the criminal action. Is this an illegal contract? In *Keir v. Leeman*[9] an agreement whereby the plaintiff promised not to give evidence concerning a prosecution for riot and assault in return for a promise from the defendant to repay a debt, was held illegal. The crucial issue appears to have been the public concern in the action in question. If the agreement had merely been made with respect to the assault (a case of personal

---

7   *Pearce v. Brooks* (1866) 1 Ex 213; see *People v. Lee Morris*, 756 P 2d 843; *Commonwealth v. Davy's New Adam and Eve Bookstore*, 625 A 2d 119.
8   *Jones v. Randall* (1774) 1 Cowp 37.
9   (1846) 9 QB 371.

injury), such a compromise would have been valid but, in the words of Denman CJ,

> [i]n the present instance the offence is not confined to personal injury, but it is accompanied with riot and obstruction of a public officer in the execution of his duty. These are matters of public concern and therefore not legally the subject of a compromise.[10]

There are judicial precedents concerning offences of public concern,[11] but in recent times attention has focused on child sexual abuse; witness the publicity about Michael Jackson concerning the settlement between the singer and the person accusing him of sexual abuse. It will not always be clear when matters of public concern are involved, but in *Nolan v. Shiels*[12] a contract to halt proceedings with respect to an offence of indecent assault was held to fall outside the *Keir* exception, and thus illegal, because it involved an offence of public concern.[13]

Contracts to refrain from legal proceedings Contracts to refrain from legal proceedings are legal, since they involve no abandonment of proceedings (that is the discontinuance of an existing action before the courts). Thus, in *Rourke v. Mealy*[14] an agreement that the defendant would honour a negotiable instrument, which had been forged by a relative, in the face of a threat of prosecution against the defendant's relative, was held valid,[15] and in *Re Boyd*[16] pressure exerted to obtain a transfer of property which was based on a belief that embezzlement had occurred was also held valid because it did not involve the abandonment of a proceeding. However, it would not be unreasonable to expect that a court, in an appropriate case with sufficient public concern, would hold that such an agreement to refrain from legal proceedings was illegal. The question is whether society is well served by the enforcement of agreements to refrain from prosecution; refraining from the prosecution of crimes of sexual abuse, where it is generally regarded that such abuse is frequently recurrent, is to be regretted. Further, if the prosecution has commenced, a contract to abandon the proceedings is unenforceable: just because the wrongdoer is quicker and more legally knowledgeable in this instance, he should not be rewarded. The policy goals in these contracts are the same, whether the agreement is one to refrain from proceedings or one to abandon them.

---

10 Ibid.
11 *Parsons v. Kirk* (1853) 6 Ir Jur (NS) 168.
12 (1926) 60 ILTR 143.
13 In *Fisher v. Apollinaris* (1875) 10 Ch App 297 the compromise of an action for trademark infringement was held valid.

14 (1879) 4 LR (Ir) 166.
15 The case is even more surprising given that it has been held that it is not possible to compromise an action for fraud, due to the element of public concern: *Book v. Hook* (1871) LR 6 Exch 89.
16 (1885) 15 LR (Ir) 521.

Contracts to support legal proceedings Such contracts are commonly known as 'maintenance'. Maintenance is in fact a crime[17] and has been described as:

> [i]mproperly stirring up litigation and strife by giving aid to one party to bring or defend a claim without just cause or excuse.[18]

Contracts involving maintenance are clearly illegal, but only where the legal proceedings are without valid foundation.[19] Thus, if the claim has merit such contracts are valid. For example, suppose an environmental organisation promises to pay the legal costs of an action by the plaintiff against a chemical company; then, provided that the claim is not vexatious or frivolous, it is enforceable. This is important, for in many situations an impecunious plaintiff relies heavily upon the support of parties unconnected with the action, and to deny him this support would be to deny him access to justice. Indeed, the legal profession itself engages in a form of maintenance known as contingency fees; to this we now turn.

Contracts to profit from legal proceedings Contracts which, in exchange for money, involve a share in the outcome of a legal action are known as champerty. Champerty is also a crime.[20] Moreover, unlike maintenance, champerty arises even where the claim is soundly based and not just where it is vexatious or frivolous.[21] Such contracts are clearly illegal. The question then arises with respect to contingency fees operated by lawyers in many cases of personal injuries. Sometimes referred to as 'no foal, no fee', they operate in such a way that the lawyer will pursue a valid claim on behalf of the plaintiff but will charge no legal fees unless the plaintiff is successful. The lawyer will of course seek to be re-imbursed for any outlays incurred to third parties in pursuing the claim. Is the lawyer guilty of champerty in such a situation? We have seen that maintenance would not be the proper charge since these contingency fees only operate where the plaintiff has a good claim. But the lawyer will take a share of the outcome and might therefore be guilty of champerty.[22] The answer is no.[23] The payment made from the outcome covers the reasonable expenses

---

17 Though not in England, see Criminal Law Act 1967.
18 *In re Trepca Mines* (NZ) [1963] Ch 199 at 219.
19 But cf. *Uppington v. Bullen* (1842) 2 Dr & War 184 (of doubtful authority today); see *Fraser v. Buckle* [1994] ILRM 276.
20 But see Criminal Law Act 1967 in England which abolishes the criminal element; Tan, 'Champertous Contracts and Assignments' (1990) 106 *LQR* 656; Twomey, 'Competition, Compassion and Champerty' (1994) 4 *ISLR* 1.
21 *Littledale v. Thompson* (1878) 4 LR (Ir) 43.
22 *McElroy v. Flynn* [1991] ILRM 294 (where an agreement between the plaintiff and the defendant to recover an inheritance belonging to the defendant was held void as an illegal contract, although the case has more to do with the element of fraud on the part of the plaintiff, rather than a true case of champerty.)
23 Contingency fees are well recognised in the US although their acceptance has not been

incurred in pursuing the case and is not a speculative venture but designed to permit access to justice to the impecunious plaintiff where it would otherwise be denied him. Thus, most of the contingency fee is maintenance, which is valid provided the case is not without cause or justice. Any additional share of the outcome paid to the solicitor beyond the level of reasonable expenses is justifiable on the basis of public policy. Contingency fees must include an element whereby those cases where the plaintiff is unsuccessful are paid for by all successful plaintiffs—in essence operating almost as an insurance scheme.[24] Since such a figure is unquantifiable, it must be that contingency fees should fall within a narrow acceptable band. Contingency fees of 33%, as found in some US jurisdictions,[25] would clearly be unacceptable in this jurisdiction.[26]

Contracts to defraud the Revenue Commissioners Contracts which aim to defraud the proper collection and assessment of taxation payable to the Revenue Commissioners are clearly illegal.[27] Normally this occurs through failing to disclose payments or mis-labelling payments; thus salary may be made up of 'expenses', which for taxation purposes are not taxable. The English decision of *Tomlinson*[28] was followed in *Lewis v. Squash Ireland Ltd*,[29] where, because a portion of the income was fraudulently labelled as 'expenses' when it in fact was income, the entire contract was held illegal. Severance was not possible. Clark objects to this on the basis of potential injustice,[30] but one of the crucial features of an illegal contract is that the illegal element cannot be severed from the entire contract. Moreover, if in this situation severance were to be used, it surely would act as a floodgate for similar arrangements, because the parties would be secure in the knowledge that, if discovered, only the 'expenses' would be rendered illegal. By rendering the entire contract illegal, it places both the employer and the employee on notice as to potential loss, and certainly the

wholehearted. They first received official blessing in the 1908 ABA Canons of Ethics and see *Markarian v. Bartis*, 89 NH 370 (contingency fees can scarcely be said to offend the public conscience). Maine appears to have been the last State of the Union to repeal legislation outlawing such fees. The Canadian approach has been different, see 'Law Society of Upper Canada', *Professional Conduct Handbook* (1978) p. 26.

24 *Valentino v. Rickners Rhederei*, 417 F Supp 176 affd 552 F 2d 466.

25 See Wolfram, *Modern Legal Ethics* (1986), p. 526, s. 9.4.

26 The need for regulation of contin-gency fees is self evident, for further discussion see 33 ABA Rep 61 (1908) (contingency fees 'lead to absuses and should be under the supervision of the court') and 64 ABA J 26 (1978) Burger CJ (USA) in testimony to Law Reform Commission in England stated that 'since it is probably too late to abolish the institution of contingent fees in the US completely, the bar associations ought to take control of it and if they do not do it adequately, the courts ought to fix limits.

27 *Miller v. Karlinski* (1945) 62 TLR 85.

28 [1978] ICR 638.

29 [1983] ILRM 363.

30 Op. cit., p. 296.

employee will think hard before accepting a payment with a short term gain that could have immense repercussions for other statutory remedies.[31]

Contracts which tend to corrupt public officials In a system of public service which prides itself on its impartiality and freedom from corruption, it is hardly surprising that contracts which compromise a public official in the exercise of his or her duty are rendered illegal.[32] As it has been put,

> It is obvious that all such contracts must have a material influence to diminish the respectability, responsibility and purity of public officers, and to introduce a system of official patronage, corruption and deceit wholly at war with the public interest.[33]

Thus, contracts which seek to assign future payments from a public office are illegal, as in *Lord Mayor of Dublin v. Hayes*,[34] where the payment was made in exchange for the appointment to the public office: the agreement was held illegal.

Contracts detrimental to the national interest or national security Contracts made with enemy aliens are clearly illegal.[35] It should be noted that the term 'enemy alien' would not be confined to those nationals of a country with which the State was at war but would include all those, including neutrals and our own citizens, who are resident within the enemy State. Contracts made prior to the outbreak of hostilities are rendered illegal as and from the commencement of the war insofar as they still remain to be performed. They are not rendered illegal *ab intio*. Any rights which arise from the contract prior to the commencement of the war remain in suspense in that they cannot be enforced until such time as the war is finished.[36]

Even where no state of war exists, a contract which is detrimental to a friendly foreign government is illegal as a breach of international comity.[37] Cheshire and Fifoot give two examples—one, a contract to support revolution in the foreign State;[38] another, a contract to import goods which the foreign country prohibit (for example, contracts for the importation of liquor into the US during the prohibition era).[39]

---

31 *Napier v. National Business Agency* [1951] 2 All ER 264; *Hayden v. Quinn*, unreported, 16 December 1993.

32 As would contracts which tend to corrupt the officials of another State: *Lemenda Trading v. African Middle East Petroleum* [1988] 1 All ER 513. *A fortiori*, the corruption of European Union officials would be illegal.

33 Story, *Equity Jurisdiction*, s. 295.

34 (1876) 10 IRCL 226.

35 *Ross v. Shaw* [1917] 2 IR 367.

36 In general see chapter 5 on Capacity.

37 *Foster v. Driscoll* [1929] 1 KB 470.

38 *De Wutz v. Hendricks* (1824) 2 Bing 314.

39 *Foster v. Driscoll*, ibid.

Contracts which flow collaterally from any illegal contract   Not merely is
the illegal contract impugned; so also is any other contract which arises from
it, even if such contract would otherwise be perfectly lawful. In essence this is
an extension of the non-severability principle of illegal contracts. Just as the
illegal contract cannot be severed internally into those parts which are legal and
those illegal, neither can it be severed externally in relation to other contracts
which are a direct consequence of the illegal contract. In *Fisher v. Bridges*[40] an
illegal contract for the sale of land was then followed by the execution of a deed
to pay the balance of the purchase price. The plaintiff sued on foot of the deed
to pay, which, of itself, was not illegal. The court dismissed the claim, because
the deed was a product of the original illegal contract. The same is clearly true
if the subsequent contract is between one of the original parties and a third party
who is aware of the earlier illegality, for the latter becomes tainted by the
knowledge.[41] But where the subsequent contract arises between one of the
original parties and an innocent third party, the consequences of the illegality
will differ, as we shall see later.

19.03 STATUTORY ILLEGALITY

In addition to common law illegality, the legislature has from time to time
intervened and outlawed certain types of contract. There are numerous examples and normally the consequence of entering into such contracts is clearly
outlined in the legislation itself. In those few instances where such is not
outlined, it falls to the court to interpret the ambit of the illegality. Once a
contract is found to be illegal under the legislation, it is treated in the same
manner as if it were illegal at common law.

A statute may render any contract illegal, or it may impose a sanction on
those who engage in such contracts, or both. The mere existence of a fine would
not necessarily render the contract illegal.[42] Indeed, there is some Australian
authority which holds that if a statute creates a punishable offence (such as a
fine), it is not possible to render the contract itself illegal unless the Act
specifically makes it so.[43] If the statute is silent on the issue as to effect of the
statutory illegality on the enforcement of the contract, then the courts must
determine the issue. The test is to look at the purpose of the Act and to see if
the intention was to criminalise the contract or merely the actions of one of the
parties.[44] Pearce LJ made the point that if a person, in operating an unlicensed

---

40   (1854) 3 E&B 642
41   *Cannon v. Bryce* (1819) 3 B&Ald 185.
42   *Smith v. Mawhood* (1845) 14 M&W 452; *Shaw v. Groom* [1970] 1 All ER 702.
43   *Yango Pastoral Co. v. First Chicago Australia* (1978) 139 CLR 410.
44   The extent to which the intent of the legislature can be determined is questionable, see
     Greig and Davis, op. cit., p. 1115 et seq.; *Marrinan v. O'Haran* unreported, High Court,
     17 June 1971.

taxi is clearly acting illegally, this does not mean that the unlicensed taxi-driver can dump his passenger in the street late at night and claim the protection of being unlicensed and thereby have no legal contract to enforce.[45] The licensing of taxis is for the protection of the public and as a revenue-raising measure. At no point would the purpose of such a statute be served by failing to enforce it in the favour of an innocent party. The same may obviously not be true with respect to a party who is aware of the illegality and persists in any event—such as where the passenger knows the taxi-driver to be unlicensed but uses that taxi because it is cheaper.[46] In *St John Shipping v. Joseph Rank*[47] the court held that where one of the parties to a contract loaded a ship in excess of allowable weight, because he calculated that even if he had to pay the fine it would still be profitable for him to breach the law, this did not render the contract unlawful *per se*, because the statute was silent on the issue as to its effect on any contract. It is the purpose of the statute that is relevant.[48] This rationale is adopted by Castle J in *Hortensius and Durack v. Bishop and Ors.*,[49] whereby officials of the Trustee Savings Bank, Dublin were prohibited from entering into certain contracts. When they in fact entered into these contracts, the question arose as to whether such contracts were illegal. The true construction of the statute was held not to render the contracts illegal but to impose liability on the officials if they undertook a certain course of action. The net effect can sometimes be to act against the interests of the people that the statute sought to protect; thus, as was discussed *obiter* in *Phoenix General Insurance Co. of Greece v. Administratia Asigurarilor de Stat*,[50] a contract of insurance with a company which had not been licensed was, under the terms of the particular Act, illegal, even to the extent of 'carrying out contracts of insurance', thus making it impossible for an insured to get the insurer to pay out a claim despite the fact that the Act was designed to protect the public against unlicensed insurers.

The most commonly encountered legislatively illegal contracts are those of gaming or wagering under the Gaming and Lotteries Act 1956-86. Three distinct classifications of transactions are covered by the Acts: wagers, gaming and lotteries.

A wager is where the parties stake something of value on the outcome of some uncertain event or the truth of some past event. There must be a winner before the contract is a wager, but how many losers can there be?[51] English law would seem to favour the existence of one loser only; in other words, a wager

---

45 *Archbolds v. Spanglett* [1961] 1 All ER 417.
46 In *Jannotti v. Corsaro* (1984) 36 SASR 127 a contract, brought into existence to avoid stamp duty, was held to be valid because the purpose of the legislation was to raise revenue and not prohibit transactions.
47 [1956] 3 All ER 683.
48 *Gavin Lowe v. Field* [1942] IR 86.
49 [1989] ILRM 294.
50 [1987] 2 All ER 152, now reversed by Financial Services Act 1986, s. 132.
51 Note that the Tote (full name Totalisator) is not a wager as the Tote neither wins nor looses merely distributes the total pool of money available.

is between two people and no more;[52] in Canada there is some authority for multiparty wagers, where there would be many losers.[53] If the Canadian view is correct, it is difficult to see where the distinction lies between a wager and a lottery (discussed below).

Gaming involves playing a game for a stake where the game revolves, not around skill, but around chance. To play a football match for a prize is not gaming, since the match is won or lost on skill, although the supporters of many a losing side might well take issue with this! Gaming is now illegal,[54] whether for skill or chance only, if the chances of all players are not equal or the banker retains a portion of the total other than his share of the winnings or in specified circumstances.[55]

A lottery really involves either a wager or gaming undertaken between many people where there are a number of losers. It has been traditional for some time lawfully to authorise such lotteries, latterly in the form of the National Lottery and some private charitable lotteries, but such lotteries are strictly regulated, particularly in terms of the prize fund (although the National Lottery is not as strictly regulated).

Whether there is any benefit in distinguishing between the three classes is doubtful, in many ways the latter two are merely forms of a wager. The consequences of being such a wager, gaming or lottery are that the contract is void and no action can be maintained to recover any moneys or things due under the contract. This would seemingly include non-enforcement of a contract promising to forebear, in exchange for payment, some legal right arising from the wager. It is suggested that *O'Donnell v. O'Connell*[56] is wrongly decided. In that case a wager which was not being honoured by the defendant led to the plaintiff threatening to place the defendant's name on the credit risk register at the race track, and to avoid this the defendant executed a promissory note in favour of the plaintiff. The court enforced the note, claiming it was validly supported by consideration of forbearance; but this is fallacious since it effectively enforced an illegal contract. It is not supported in English case law[57] and should be treated with suspicion.

Money held by a stakeholder is recoverable before it has been paid out, including where the result of the wager is known but the party repudiates the wager prior to payment. If the stakeholder proceeds to pay out after the repudiation has been made, action to recover moneys had and received would seemingly be possible against the stakeholder. This follows simply from the role of the stakeholder and is not surprising. Only that sum given by the claimant to the stakeholder is recoverable; no action can be taken by the winner of the

52 *Ellesmere v. Wallace* [1929] 2 Ch 1.
53 *Breitmeier v. Batke* (1966) 56 WWR 678.
54 Gaming and Lotteries Act 1956, s. 4.
55 Such as slot machines, etc.

56 (1923) 57 ILTR 92.
57 *Hill v. William Hill* [1949] AC 530; see also *O'Donnell v. Sullivan* (1913) 47 ILTR 253.

bet to force the stakeholder to part with the loser's money. In essence, the stakeholder holds the money as 'trustee' and can be forced to return the money given by the claimant, but not money given by the other gambler.[58]

19.04 CONSEQUENCES OF ILLEGALITY

Contracts illegal from inception Contracts which are illegal from inception and where such illegality is obvious from the agreement are void.[59] Neither party can sustain an action on the basis of such a contract,[60] and, indeed, it can be used as a defence to any action. While it may seem incongruous that the defendant, who was a party to the illegality, can now plead that illegality in his defence, the purpose of the rule is to protect the interests of society as a whole and the fact that the defendant may also benefit is something that must be tolerated. It is important to remember that the entire contract is void and not merely the illegal element; thus in *Murphy & Co. v. Crean*[61] a contract which contained, *inter alia*, an illegal covenant to require transfer of a liquor licence, was declared illegal *in toto*. Moreover, it is clear that the moral culpability of the parties is irrelevant, for in *In re Mahmoud and Hispani*[62] a contract for the sale of linseed oil, which was illegal because no licence had been obtained, prevented the innocent party to the contract, who was unaware of the requirement, from suing on foot of any part of the agreement.[63]

A question arises with respect to the ownership of goods transferred under an illegal contract. Suppose the illegal contract involves the transfer of a car from X to Y: who owns the vehicle? The question of ownership is different from that of possession, for, if X still has possession of the vehicle, Y cannot maintain an action for recovery, because to do so would require him to rely upon the illegal contract. The reverse is also true: if X has given the vehicle to Y, he cannot seek legal redress, since no action is sustainable at law. The difficulty arises where an innocent third party then acquires the vehicle from either party. The other party can now attempt to assert his ownership rights against the third party, since the ownership is not tainted by the illegality. But who is the owner?

---

58 In general see *Toner v. Livingston* (1896) 30 ILTR 80.
59 But note *Saunders v. Edwards* [1987] 2 All ER 651 (an agreement to disguise portion of the purchase price in order to avoid tax liability, did not prevent the party from suing for contractual breach) and *Euro Diam v. Bathurst* [1988] 2 All ER 23 (a customs invoice, written at undervalue to avoid duty, did not prevent a claim on the insurance policy) appear to be authority that, in certain situations, the illegality can be severed from the transaction as a whole, particularly if the illegality has nothing to do with the claim at hand.
60 *Gordon v. Metropolitan Police Chief* [1910] 2 KB 1080.
61 [1915] 1 IR 111; *Macklin & McDonald v. Graecen* [1983] IR 61.
62 [1921] 2 KB 716.
63 See *Holman v. Johnson* (1775) 1 Cowp 341.

On ordinary contract principles, once agreement is reached ownership transfers to the purchaser; but here the contract is illegal and thus no ownership should transfer, because the illegality renders the contract invalid *ab initio*. Nor can the goods be said to have been transferred by delivery, since this only occurs where a gift is intended: this is not the case where a contract, albeit illegal, was what was intended.

Let us look at the permutations:

X contracts, illegally, to transfer the car to Y. If X then physically transfers the vehicle to Y, X cannot recover possession, since the contract is illegal. Y is now in possession of the vehicle and he sells it to Z, an innocent party. X now takes an action against Z, enforcing his ownership rights on the basis that Y had no title to the vehicle because the contract was illegal.

If X does not transfer the vehicle to Y but retains it, Y, even though he may have paid for the vehicle, cannot gain possession of it under the contract since it is illegal. X is now in possession of the vehicle and sells it to Z, an innocent party. Y now takes an action against Z, as Y claims to be the rightful owner of the vehicle pursuant to the contract.

In most situations, Z will be protected as a *bona fide* purchaser for value and without notice of the illegality, and therefore no action is sustainable by either X or Y against Z. But could X sue Y for conversion of his property, or *vice versa* depending on exactly whose property it is. In *Belvoir Finance v. Stapleton*[64] the court held that, despite the illegality of the contract of sale, title had in fact passed to the purchaser. Subsequent cases have tended to favour this view of transfer of title despite the illegality of the underlying contract.[65] Thus, in the above example it is Y who can sue on foot of the conversion: if the property has passed to Y, title will also have transferred. This is completely erroneous. Since the contract of sale is illegal, no transfer of title can have occurred. To transfer title would involve giving partial effect to an illegal contract. One argument in favour of the above rationale would be that if the purchaser had possession of the item but not the ownership, then anyone could seize the goods, because the purchaser could mount no defence against the third party claim. As Cheshire and Fifoot point out,[66] this is mistaken, because the purchaser, although not the owner, has a superior claim to any stranger. Moreover, since the judgments clearly distinguish between situations where the property has passed and those where it has not, the former giving title to the owner, the latter not, it is therefore being suggested that the consequence of an illegal contract will depend on how quickly the parties acted. A dishonest, legally aware, purchaser can act quickly and so gain rights that an equally dishonest but less legally aware seller cannot. Remember: since the contract is illegal on the face of it, both parties must bear an equivalent share of the blame. Yet passing of possession of the items is being suggested as being sufficient, when coupled with an illegal contract, to transfer

---

64   [1970] 3 All ER 664.
65   *Singh v. Ali* [1960] AC 167.
66   Op. cit., p. 378 et seq.

title. However, arguably, the correct view is that, in an illegal contract for sale, title cannot transfer from seller to purchaser. If possession of the subject matter of the contract transfers, then no action to recover possession can be founded against the party currently in possession, save in certain circumstances. If the subject matter of the contract is purported to be transferred to a third party, such third party will take title only if the third party is a *bona fide* purchaser for value without notice and the party in possession, who purported to make the transfer to this third party, will become liable in conversion to the true owner.

It is a well established rule of law that no action is sustainable to recover moneys paid on foot of an illegal contract;[67] this is a natural corollary of the above commentary that goods transferred as a result of an illegal contract cannot be recovered, although title remains with seller. Title does not remain with the seller with respect to money, since money transfers on delivery alone. Nor can title remain with the seller with respect to land, since to transfer land involves legal registration if the interest is to be upheld. The purchaser in such a situation has title to the land not by virtue of the illegal contract but by priority of his or her interest so registered. If the legal formalities for transfer have not been completed, any interest that the purchaser might have had would be equitable only, and if it arose from an illegal contract it would not be given effect.

It is clear that an illegal contract may give rise to enforceable rights.[68] As we saw earlier, an action for conversion could be maintained arising from possession on foot of an illegal contract; likewise, transfer of land could be secured since reliance was on registration and not the illegal contract. It follows therefore that actions to recover property may be sustained if the action does not disclose the illegality.[69] For example, conversion is sustainable since the plaintiff has to prove his original ownership, and prove that ownership is now in another, as a result of the defendants actions (there is no need to plead the illegal contract), whereas to recover possession would involve the defendant seeking an order directly based on the illegal contract. Thus, if the claim can be sustained, independent of the illegality, it will not be defeated by it. In *Mar Sing v. Clubby*[70] the plaintiff had leased land illegally to the defendant and some time afterwards wished to eject the defendant and terminate the lease. When the defendant failed to leave the property, the plaintiff sued for possession. As the lease was illegal, it was clear that for the plaintiff to rely on it would be fatal, because he would not be able to maintain an action in face of the illegality. He succeeded, however, on the basis of his registered ownership of the property, which was uncontaminated by the illegal contract.

---

67   *Taylor v. Chester* (1869) LR 4 QB 309 (the plaintiff could not recover money paid to a friend who had arranged for a session with various prostitutes; *Parkinson v. College of Ambulance and Harrison* [1925] 2 KB 1 (the plaintiff could not recover money paid in pursuit of a knighthood).

68   See *Euro Diam v. Bathurst* and *Saunders v. Edwards*, ibid.

69   *Scott v. Brown, Doering, McNab* [1892] 2 QB 724.

70   [1963] 3 All ER 499

Further, recovery is also possible where the parties are not equally culpable[71] or where the party repents before the contract is completed. If the parties are not *pari delicto*,[72] the court may allow the less culpable party to recover what has been transferred.[73] This is particularly so where the illegality arises from a statutory provision aimed at protecting a certain class of people. The protected class may, therefore, recover what has been lost as a result of the illegality. Typical examples of this include landlord and tenant legislation, employment law and so forth. Even outside statutory provisions where one party has represented the contract as legal when it is in fact illegal, the innocent party can recover moneys paid over: for example, in *Hughes v. Liverpool Victoria Legal Friendly Society*[74] an illegal contract of insurance did not prevent the insured from recovering the premiums already paid since the insurance company had represented the contract to be legal. No claim could be made under the illegal contract, but the expenditure could be recovered by the innocent party.

Where the party repents from the illegality, the court will assist him, but the repentance must have occurred prior to the performance of the contract (although it is in fact difficult to pinpoint exactly when this is). In *Kearly v. Thomson*[75] the court held that the performance, albeit partial, must be substantial before the claimant's repentence is ignored. It is difficult to see how this helps in the analysis of this area in any way, since the line between partially performed and substantially performed, is, to say the least, blurred. Arguably, the exception, that a party can repent from an illegal contract, should be abolished where the contract is clearly illegal on the face of it. The failure of any of the parties to carry through an illegal contract to completion should not act as an excuse to permit recovery of those elements of already performed.[76]

Contracts illegal in performance Here we are concerned with a contract which appears lawful on the face of it but where one of the parties intends to perform it in an illegal manner, and this is not known by the other party. The principle should be fairly clear:

the innocent party to a lawful contract should be able to maintain any and all actions on foot of the contract up to the point in time where the illegality is discovered but not thereafter. The party intending to perform it illegally is never entitled to maintain any action on foot of the contract.[77]

---

71 Blameworthy. *A fortiori*, where the party entered into the contract by virtue of distress: *Sumner v. Sumner* (1935) 69 ILTR 101.

72 Equally to blame.

73 *Smith v. Cuff* (1817) 6 M&S 160; *Atkinson v. Denby* (1862) 7 H&N 934.

74 [1916] 2 KB 482 (1890) 24 QBD 742.

75 (1890) 2 QBD 742.

76 *Bigos v. Bousted* [1951] 1 All ER 92 (there is no repentance where the contract is not fulfilled because of an external, supervening event).

77 See *Whitecross Potatoes v. Coyle* [1978] ILRM 31 (since one party alone intended to perform the contract unlawfully, the innocent party could recover).

This is well established by case law, such as *Marles v. Philip Trant & Sons (No. 2)*,[78] whereby a contract for the delivery of wheat seeds was illegal under a statutory provision that required an invoice to accompany the delivery. However, the contract specified 'spring wheat' seeds but in fact winter wheat seeds were delivered. The defendant could not hide behind the illegality of the contract and so prevent the innocent plaintiff from suing for breach of contract. Remember, because the contract was illegal, it should not have been enforceable to any extent, never mind allowing recovery for breach thereof. The court will, however, permit the innocent party to recover. But the limits of this doctrine must also be clear: it cannot enable the claimant to overturn legal rights without the assistance of the courts. Thus, in *Feret v. Hill*[79] a lease which on the face was lawful, but which was used by the tenant for a brothel, did not entitle the landlord to remove that tenant by force; and where such removal was effected, the tenant could maintain an action for recovery of possession. The proper approach would be for the landlord to seek rescission of the lease at equity. This follows from that which we spoke of earlier, namely, that a transfer of legal title of land can be revoked only by the courts.

Unlike contracts illegal on the face of them, contracts which appear lawful but which are illegally performed require the illegality to be pleaded.[80]

78   [1953] 1 All ER 651.   80   *Whitecross Potatoes v. Coyle*, ibid.
79   (1854) 15 CB 207.

20.00

Void and voidable contracts

20.01 INTRODUCTION

A court has the jurisdiction to refuse to enforce either a contract or a clause within the contract on the basis that to enforce it would offend against public policy.[1] Such offence does not render the contract illegal; accordingly, the court may sever that part of the contract which offends public policy, while retaining the remainder, which does not. There are three principal types of contracts or clauses within contracts which fall foul of the courts:

contracts, or clauses within contracts to oust the jurisdiction of the courts

contracts, or clauses within contracts prejudicial to the marriage relationship

contracts, or clauses within contracts in restraint of trade.

20.02 OUSTING THE JURISDICTION OF THE COURTS

A contractual term which purports to deny access to the judicial system has no validity.[2] The most common method of denying access to the courts is to confer on one party or an independent body the exclusive and final power to determine issues of law, matters of interpretation or questions of fact. In *Baker v. Jones*[3] a clause which vested the sole power of interpretation of an association's rules within the executive council of the association was held to be void as ousting the jurisdiction of the courts. But in *Scott v. Avery*[4] the court refused to hold void a clause which set, as a precondition to legal proceedings, reference to an arbitrator. Requiring the parties to undergo an arbitration before recourse was made to the courts is not unlawful unless in doing so the clause strikes at the access of the parties to the judicial process.[5] The impact this will have for the growing concept of alternative dispute resolution (ADR) remains unclear.

1   *Bennett v. Bennett* [1952] 1 All ER 413.
2   *Thompson v. Charnock* (1799) 8 Term Rep 139.
3   [1954] 2 All ER 553.
4   (1856) 5 HL Cas 811; adopted in

Gregg v. Fraser [1906] 2 IR 545.
5   Note the decision in *McCarthy v. JWT* [1990] ILRM where Carroll J refused to uphold an arbitration clause because it violated the Sale of Goods and Supply of Services Act 1980, s. 40.

261

Arbitrations are subject to legislative intervention and control,[6] but the newer methods of ADR, such as negotiation and mediation, may fall foul of this policy ground if the ADR method were made exclusive and final. Moreover, there may well be a constitutional right to be vindicated: not restricting access to the established courts of the land.

20.03 SUBVERTING A MARRIAGE

Contracts which prevent a person from marrying anybody are void as being contrary to public policy—as are contracts which require a person to marry one particular person and no other. And in *Lowe v. Peers*[7] an agreement where the man would pay the woman £1,000 if he married another woman instead of her was also held to be void. Further, contracts which reward those who find, arrange or broker marriage agreements are also void as contrary to public policy.

Contracts which purport to deal with future separation are also void because they weaken the marriage bond.[8] Contracts which deal with immediate separation are, of course, valid,[9] even where, as in *Caron v. Caron*,[10] the separation agreement provides for maintenance only so long as the maintained spouse has not re-married or begun cohabiting with another partner. This was held not to come within the formulation of *Lowe v. Peers*. A contract dealing with future separation between two spouses who have already separated but are now reconciled is not void since such contracts enable the restoration of the marriage and therefore do not subvert it.[11]

20.04 CONTRACTS IN RESTRAINT OF TRADE

In reality this has now become part of a more broader goal of public policy, namely, the protection of competition.[12] Certainly, the new legislation modelled closely on its European counterpart will in many instances be the more appropriate remedy and control mechanism; the reader is referred to more specialised works on competition policy where the full extent of these issues can be more fully developed.[13] Indeed, one cannot emphasise enough the extent to which competition rules now govern this entire area. All that we want to do here is to provide a brief synopsis of the common law position gleaned from the case law.

---

6   See Arbitration Act 1954.
7   (1768) 4 Burr 2225.
8   *Marquess of Westmeath v. Marquess of Salisbury* (1830) 5 Bli (NS) 339.
9   But note in *H. v. H.* (1983) 127 SJ 578 an agreement between two couples, swapping wives, which promised that the husbands would support their new wives was not upheld.

10 (1987) 38 DLR (4th) 735.
11 *McMahon v. McMahon* [1913] 1 IR 428; *Harrison v. Harrison* [1910] 1 KB 35.
12 Competition Act 1990.
13 See *Whish on Competition*; Power, *Competition Law in Ireland*; Bergeron, 'Setting the Cat among the Pigeons.' (1990-1993) 9 *JISL* 57.

It should be borne in mind that, in assessing clauses which seek to restrain freedom of trade, a court must examine the underlying purpose being protected by such a clause; that purpose, might, for example, be to prevent unfair use of corporate information obtained while in employment, stealing customer loyalty, and so forth. If the purpose of the clause is to punish or act *in terrorem* for breach of contract, it will be more properly construed as a penalty and dealt with accordingly.[14]

The *Nordenfelt*[15] case originates the modern judicial approach to contracts which seek to restrain one person from engaging in earning a living in a particular business or occupation.[16] Such clauses are not necessarily void but they may be void if there is no reasonable justification for them. This has been more clearly stated in *Esso Petroleum v. Harpers Garage (Stourport)*:[17] such a clause is unenforceable unless it can be shown that it gives

reasonable protection to the party in whose favour it is to operate and

is in the interests of the party against whom it is to operate and

is for the benefit of the public.

These tests need to be applied in the correct order. If the contract provides excessive or unreasonable protection to the person in whose favour it is to operate then it is void and no further analysis is required. The question of reasonable protection is heavily influenced by commercial practice; thus, exclusive distributorships are reasonable,[18] as are tied public houses.[19] Moving

14 It appears that the courts will, in certain instances, view the clause as falling outside the doctrine entirely: *Irish Shell v. Elm Motors* [1984] IR 200 (the court held that a conveyance of land, containing clauses restricting user, did not fall within the doctrine of restraint of trade, unless the land has been given to the lessor as part of an overall transaction designed to effect such a restriction of user. The party acquiring the lease has no freedom of trade that can be restrained (his right to trade comes from the lessor granting him the lease). The situation is different where the party acquiring the lease has transferred the land to the lessor, in return for the right to trade with the lessor's products: here the lessee had a freedom to trade (since he owned the property in the first place), and, in dealing with the lessor, he has restricted this freedom. This normally arises in solus agreements with garages, whereby the owner of property conveys land to the oil company; the oil company then build and market a petrol station, through a leaseback to the original owner. Since the original owner initially had the freedom to trade with his land, a solus agreement limiting his rights as a lessee is susceptible to the doctrine of restraint of trade. If the lessee of the garage was never the owner of the land he would have had no such freedom to begin with and therefore any restriction would be outside the doctrine of restraint of trade.
15 [1894] AC 535.
16 For a definition see *Petrofina v. Martin* [1966] Ch 146, 180.
17 [1967] 1 All ER 699.
18 *Kerry Co-Op v. Bord Bainne* [1991] ILRM 851; though subject to limits, see *McEllistrem v. Ballymacelligot Co-Op* [1919] AC 548.
19 *Murphy v. Crean* [1939] IR 457 (a term contained in a lease requiring that all supplies of alcohol be taken from one brewery was held valid by the court).

beyond this it is for the party relying on the impugned clause to show the court that the restraint offered is reasonable.[20] If the restraint is reasonable, the court must examine if it is in the interests of the affected party.[21] An exclusive dealership arrangement, for example, may benefit the affected party by virtue of the public recognition achieved from a marketing campaign.[22] If the answer is positive to this question then finally the impact of the agreement on the public is examined. The reality has been that by the time the court has answered the two earlier questions in the affirmative, it is unlikely to strike down the clause on the final ground unless the impact of the clause is entirely oppressive to the public. Modern jurisprudence has placed a premium on resolving the issue by looking at the interests of the parties and not of the public. This is clearly incorrect. In *Mallan v. May*[23] it was said that:

> The test appears to be whether the contract be prejudicial or not to the public interest, for it is on grounds of public policy alone that contracts are supported or avoided.[24]

This view was supported in the *Esso* case by a number of their Lordships and it finds expression in this jurisdiction from O'Higgins CJ in *Macken v. O'Reilly*,[25] where he said,

> The trial judge disregarded entirely the undisputed evidence as to the effect a change of policy would have on the horse breeding industry and on equestrian sport in Ireland. This ought to have been considered as a balance to the harm or inconvenience caused to the plaintiff.[26]

The balancing concept is somewhat misleading, but the thrust of the argument is valid. The order of evaluation for such clauses be reversed from that proposed by the *Esso* case. In other words, the clause should be looked at to see if it is desirable from the public interest. If it is not desirable, then it must be rendered void. If it is neutral to the public interest or in favour of the public interest, it should then be examined for reasonableness *inter partes*.

---

20 *Gargan v. Ruttle* [1931] IR 152 (court held it was reasonable to prevent solicitation of former customers); *Faccenda Chicken v. Fowler* [1985] ICR 589 (court held it was unreasonable to prevent competition merely because ex-employee would have confidential information concerning price: it required something more on the part of the ex-employee); *Dosser v. Monaghan* [1932] NI 209 (court held it was unreasonable to prevent ex-band members from playing in any of the towns in which the band used to play. The judge remarked that the case might be differently decided if the band members were 'famous': a case of the ex-band members winning the case but losing their dignity!)

21 *Kerry Co-Op v. Bord Bainne*, ibid.

22 *Continental Oil v. Moynihan* (1977) 111 ILTR 5.

23 (1843) 11 M&W 653.

24 Ibid. at 665.

25 [1979] ILRM 791.

26 Ibid. at 91.

20.05 SEVERANCE

The court can sever the offending clause,[27] and leave the remainder of the contract intact. The difficulty is that, while the court can easily sever one clause from a contract, the question that remains to be fully resolved is: can internal severance occur within the clause itself. In some instances the clause can be so phrased as to enable the blue pencil to be used to sever those elements that are repugnant.[28] But if this is not possible, the entire clause will have to be struck out, removing not merely the objectionable elements of the clause but also those, which if they been expressed more distinctly, would have survived. Thus, for example, in *Skerry's College Ireland v. Moles*[29] a clause which prohibited a teacher from working within seven miles of Dublin, Cork or Belfast was severed by removing Dublin and Cork from the clause, leaving only Belfast. In the same case the restriction was to apply for three years; the teacher contended that it should be reduced to two years, as this would be sufficient to protect the school's legitimate interest. The court was unable to do this, and accordingly, since the restraint was not excessive, it left the time limit stand.[30] It is, therefore, not like the position in the United States, where the courts tend to redraft the clause so as to give effect to its legitimate ambit, even if it expressly contradicts the agreement itself.[31] The US approach is excessivley flexible, and should not be adopted here.[32] The clause was drafted by the person who is now seeking the benefit of it, and if it now transpires that the entire clause should be struck down because severance is not possible, that is a risk that he takes and a risk that could have been avoided in the first place if the clause was confined to reasonable protection *inter partes*.[33] As *Cussen v. O'Connor*[34] illustrates, the scope of the

---

27 *Goodinson v. Goodinson* [1954] 2 All ER 255.

28 *Mulligan v. Corr* [1925] IR 169; but cf. *Baker v. Hedgecock* (1888) 39 ChD 520 (if the court struck out the words 'in any part of the whole world', it would require the substitution of a narrower wording: this would not be what the parties had agreed to and so could not be done).

29 (1907) 42 ILTR 46.

30 *Attwood v. Lamont* [1920] 3 KB 571 (the contract was indivisible and could not be severed) but cf. *Goldsoll v. Goldsman* [1915] 1 Ch 292 (where the court struck out the offending portions of the restraint). The cases appear distinguishable on the basis that certain elements could be severed without forcing the court to draft an agreement which the parties did not intend).

31 *Thomas v. Coastal Industries*, 108 SE 2d 328; note that the recent trend has been to avoid the 'blue pencil' rule and instead to limit the unreasonableness of the clause, see *Solari Industries v. Malady*, 264 A 2d 53 (an injunction to enforce a contract clause is given only to the extent that it is reasonable). This approach has been used in this jurisdiction, see *Cussen v. O'Connor* (1893) 31 LR (Ir) 330. The approach is not without difficulty.

32 Though see *ECI v. Bell* [1981] ILRM 345.

33 One of the difficulties encountered in the United States has been the insertion of very broad clauses which act *in terrorem*: the real extent of the restraint can only be tested through court action which involves cost (see Blake, 'Employee Covenants not to

remedy may be restricted without interfering with the contract itself, and the equitable remedy of the injunction need only be granted to the extent the court feels necessary to give justice to the case at hand. In this case the contract resulted in the clause of restraint being operative for seven years, but the court would only give an injunction to enforce the clause for a maximum of two years, which it felt was a reasonable period.

Compete', 73 *Harvard Law Rev* 625). In *Insurance Center v. Taylor*, 499 P 2d 1252 such a clause was struck down in its entirety. See Restatement, Second, Contracts, s. 184(2)

34   See ibid.

21.00

Performance

21.01 INTRODUCTION

A contract is discharged when the subject matter of the contract has been completed: at that stage contractual liability between the contracting parties has come to an end. In essence, performance serves as closure on the relationship, though of course it is still possible that a breach may occur at some later stage and give rise to liability under a breach of contractual term or condition, or under the law of tort. Thus, for example, if I purchase a television set from X, when X delivers the set and I have paid for it (in one amount or by agreement to pay over a number of instalments or at a future date) the contract is discharged by performance. However, the television set may subsequently fail to work: clearly, performance has occurred but a breach of the contract can also arise at some later stage. Note that payment is not a condition precedent to discharge by performance: the contract is performed even though payment is delayed. The agreement to pay the amount outstanding is, of course, a separate contract between myself and X, and it will only be discharged on completion of the terms of that contract. Care must therefore be taken to identify the exact contract which is being sought to be discharged by performance. In the above example, there were two contracts—one to purchase the television set, the other to pay a certain amount over a period of time. One has been discharged by performance, that is, the delivery of the set; the other, the payment of the amount, has not. On the other hand, if I agree with X to purchase the television set but we agree to delay delivery for one month until I have assembled the cash to pay for it, there is of course only one contract: the agreement to delay delivery merely indicates at what stage the contract must be discharged by performance. It will not always be clear when there is one or more contracts involved, but the courts will strive to interpret such contracts as fairly as possible.[1]

Having overcome the hurdle of identifying which contract has or has not been performed, it might seem that discharge by performance should be

---

1   Some contracts themselves can be construed as internally divisible, *Verolme Cork Dockyard v. Shannon Atlantic Fisheries*, unreported, High Court, 31 July 1978 (payment of part of the total price was to be payable on completion of a significant amount of the contract, the court held the contract was implicitly one of *quantum meruit* and not one of entire performance).

relatively straightforward, but that is not so. First, contracts are normally complex transactions and very often involve actions dependent upon other events having occurred first; so, the task falls to the courts to determine in which order the contractual steps should have occurred. Secondly, discharge by performance must be perfect and exact. If the performance is approximate (that is, not exact) it will not discharge the contract. If I have agreed with X to purchase a 21" television set, it is not good enough if I am supplied with a 20" set. It may be close to the desired performance, but it is not perfect in the legal sense. We turn to deal with these issues.

21.02 THE ORDER OF PERFORMANCE

The order in which a contract is to be performed is a question of construction of the contract, the nature of the contract itself and what would be reasonable in light of the prevailing commercial practices.[2] If X agrees to purchase the television set from Y, is delivery or payment to occur first? Occasionally, the contract itself will expressly deal with the matter;[3] thus, in business practice a contract for the supply of goods often states that payment is to take place within thirty days of delivery.[4] X's demand for payment on or before delivery, therefore, is a failure to perform. Where the parties have not expressly stated the position as to the order of the performance of the contract, the courts will look first to see whether any order was implied, and, failing such implied terms, the court will view the usual business practice in a transaction of that kind.[5] It may well be that both parties' obligations are simultaneous: in other words, payment and delivery, say, occur at the same time;[6] where this is so, the party claiming non-performance of the contract should show that he or she was willing to discharge his side of the contract by performance of his obligation.[7]

---

2   Sometimes the terminology used is that of conditions (both precedent, concurrent and independent) and an independent promise. For example of a condition, see *Trans Trust SPRL v. Danubian Trading Co.* [1952] 2 QB 297, for others see ibid.
3   *The Karin Vatis* [1988] 2 Lloyds Rep 330.
4   Note that the performance does not need to be demanded, save where the contract requires that a demand be made: *Walton v. Mascall*, 13 M & W 452 (a debtor must seek his creditor).
5   Both conditions might be independent, *Taylor v. Webb* [1937] 2 KB 283 (a landlord's obligation to repair premises is not dependant on his tenant's obligation to pay rent).
6   *Morton v. Lamb* (1797) 7 TR 125; *Paynter v. James* (1867) LR 2 CP 348 (in a charterparty, delivery of goods and payment for them are concurrent conditions); see also Sale of Goods Act, ibid.
7   *Stanton v. Richardson* (1872) LR 7 CP 421 (cannot sue for failure to load ship when the plaintiff himself was not in a position to accept the cargo); but note tender of performance must be reasonable and realistic: *Farquharson v. Pearl Insurance Co.* [1937] 3 All ER 124 (the tender of money involves actual production of money, insufficient to make such tender without the production), *Robinson v. Cook* (1815) 6

21.03 PERFECT PERFORMANCE

Before any contract can be discharged by performance, that performance must be perfect and fully in accordance with the terms of the contractual obligation.[8] As a general rule no deviation shall be permitted and the rule is strictly applied. This also means that payment for partially completed work on a contract is not recoverable.[9] Thus, in *Cutter v. Powell*[10] the widow of a sailor who died nineteen days before his ship docked in Liverpool could not recover any sums on foot of the contract of employment between the sailor and the master of the vessel, because the contract stipulated payment on completion of the voyage; and in *Bolton v. Mahadeva*,[11] where a central heating system was installed which, although it could be operated, was highly ineffective, the installer was denied recovery because the contract was not perfectly performed. There is considerable injustice here inasmuch as that one of the parties to the contract gains an unpaid-for reward. Thus, in *Cutter* the master of the vessel had the benefit of the sailor's labour for the bulk of the journey yet paid nothing for that. Such decisions have, therefore, been heavily criticised, and the courts have not been immune to these criticisms, as we shall see.

However, it should be borne in mind that, in some instances, this so-called unpaid-for reward may well be a quite expensive cost to the supposed beneficiary. Taking a look at the facts of *Bolton*, some might argue that the central heating system that was installed, even though it did not work properly, was an unpaid-for reward to the houseowner, but it might also be that the system was installed in such a way that to remedy the damage might be as expensive, if not more expensive, than to install a complete new system. Moreover, while one's sympathies might be with the sailor's widow in *Cutter's* case, in other cases imperfect performance should perhaps be punished, almost as a deterrent to prevent people from sloppy enforcement of their contractual obligations. The sailor presumably had no choice in his time of death, but the correct installation

Taunt 336 (the tender of money cannot put an onerous burden on a creditor, for example the tender of large sums or notes requiring change); note Decimal Currency Act 1969 limits the amount of legal tender in the form of coins that must be accepted; unreasonable time of tender may also render it void, see ibid for fuller discussion.

8   *In re Moore v. Laurauer* [1921] 2 KB 519 (tins of fruit should have been packed in cases of 30 tins, in fact some cases had as little as 24 tins. The court held that this was imperfect performance despite the total number of tins being correct); *Duke of St Albans v. Shore* (1789) 1 HyBl 270 (a vendor sold land with trees, trees were cut down by vendor before transaction completed. The court held that the vendor could not force the purchaser to proceed with the sale, since it was no longer possible to perform that which was contracted for).

9   But see the divisible contracts common in the construction and shipbuilding industries and discussed infra.

10   (1795) 6 Term Reports 320; *Sumpter v. Hedges* [1898] 1 QB 673; *Coughlan v. Moloney* (1905) 39 ILTR 153.

11   [1972] 2 All ER 1322.

of a central heating system was surely a matter of choice, or ability.[12] Leaving the policing of such bargains to the law of tort is unsatisfactory; it requires the aggrieved contracting party to prove negligence and, secondly, it may result in a damage award that the offending contracting party may be willing to bear. For example, a building contractor, if he could leave a project uncompleted in order to undertake a more lucrative contract elsewhere, may, in deciding not to complete the project according to the contract, if there were no doctrine of perfect performance, calculate the risk of an award for damages as a legitimate expense.[13]

21.04 SUBSTANTIAL PERFORMANCE

If the doctrine of perfect performance were taken to extremes, it would mean that many contracts would be unenforceable, because it is generally accepted that parties will not, for one reason or another, comply with every last detail of the agreement and that, accordingly, the other party would take full benefit of a contract which has been substantially, although not completely, performed. Again, this is most obvious in building contracts. In building a house, fairly detailed specifications are laid down as to the various materials to be used and services to be installed. Suppose the contract, *inter alia*, called for the provision of a dimmer light switch in the front room of the house, and the builder mistakenly placed an ordinary switch instead. It cannot be that, after the owner takes delivery, he could seek to have the entire contract set aside for failure to perform the contract exactly. Of course, the owner could set off the cost of installing the correct light switch against the builder's bill, but the builder is not estopped from saying that he or she has discharged the contract.[14]

A number of points need to be raised with respect to this. First, the contract itself must be construed to see whether the act complained of was a term or condition of the contract. If it is a condition, failure to complete the condition will clearly render the party unable to claim substantial performance.[15] Thus, if the contract specifies that it is a condition that the walls be made of 9" cavity block and the builder uses 6" cavity block, he cannot claim substantial perform-

---

12   *In re Hall and Baker* (1878) 9 Ch D 538 ('if a man engages to carry a box of cigars from London to Birmingham, it is an entire contract and he cannot throw the cigars out of the carriage half way there and ask for half the money' *per* Jessel MR at 545).

13   See *Brown v. Wood* (1864) 6 Ir Jur 221 (the court distinguished *Cutter v. Powell*, ibid., by holding that the contract was divisible: an implied term that payment would be made for work done, even if the entire project was not completed).

14   *Hoenig v. Isaacs* [1952] 2 All ER 176 (the plaintiff failed to finish a book case as part of some renovation work. The bookcase made up about 8% of the total renovation cost. The court held that the plaintiff was entitled to the cost); *Boone v. Eyre* (1779) 1 HyBl 273.

15   See the discussion on Conditions and Warranties, chapter 13, ibid.

ance, because the use of a particular block was a condition of the contract. If the term is not expressly stated to be a condition, it is still open for the court to hold that failure to comply with the term negates substantial performance. Suppose, in the above example, the court rules that the term '9 inch cavity block' is not a condition of the contract, no matter how unlikely that might seem. It is open for the court to hold that use of another type of block negates substantial performance. Admittedly, it is difficult to envisage circumstances where the court would find a term not to be a condition and yet hold that non-performance of that term negates substantial performance, but there is nothing in legal theory to prevent it from so doing. Moreover, some contracts are termed 'entire' or 'lump sum' contracts, that is to say, the contract price is payable only on the final completion of the contract, even though within that contract there are many terms and conditions. In contracts such as these, failure to complete the contract normally bars relief under substantial performance because the failure to complete will be looked upon as abandonment of the contract and a breach thereof. Thus, in *Kincora Builders v. Cronin*,[16] where the builder failed to complete insulation of the attic, he could not claim substantial performance. Such contracts are particularly important in the building trade, where without this sort of protection, most builders have a tradition of leaving their projects incomplete.

Secondly, non-performance of a number of terms of the contract which are not conditions will probably negate a claim of substantial performance. Suppose, for example, the court holds that only the terms of a contract which relate to the construction of the walls and roof of the house are conditions of the contract. If the builder erects solid walls and a roof in exact compliance with the terms of the contract, yet neglects to install light sockets, inner doors, and so forth, the cumulative effect would probably lead a court to say that no substantial performance has occurred. Thus, we see an open return to the punitive nature of the doctrine of perfect performance. The law punishes those who do not live up to their obligations.

Thirdly, the doctrine of substantial performance operates without any consent being necessary from the other party to the contract. Indeed, the doctrine is imposed over the head, so to speak, of the aggrieved party; in this sense it must be distinguished from accepted partial performance (discussed below). All substantial performance achieves is the right of the party to be rewarded for the work undertaken, where that work is sufficiently close to perfect performance to warrant, in the interests of equity, such part payment.

21.05 ACCEPTED PARTIAL PERFORMANCE

We have assumed at all times that the aggrieved party is unhappy with the performance tendered by the offending party; yet this is not always true. Acts

16   Unreported, High Court, 5 March 1973.

which would not be recognised under the doctrine of substantial performance may nonetheless enable the offending party to recover the value of the contract performed where the aggrieved party acts so as to accept the partially performed contract. However, before this acceptance of partial performance can negate the requirement of perfect performance, two elements must be present. First, there must be a new agreement inferred with respect to the partial performance; this will normally be evidenced by a new promise to pay, although it is of course not limited to same.[17] For example, where a lesser amount of goods is delivered than that ordered, if the purchaser accepts them, then he implicitly promises to pay for that portion received *pro rata* with the full contract for the sale of the items. Second, this acceptance must be freely given, at least to the extent that there was an option to accept or reject the partial performance.[18] If there was no opportunity to reject the partial performance, then it is still open to claim non-perfect performance, the acceptance of partial performance not being freely given. The example often given is that of an incomplete building on one's land.[19] It is not really possible to reject it as if it were an under-supply of ordered tins of corn beef. This is the reason behind the decision in *Bolton's* case. In that case the installation of the central heating system was not substantial performance, since the system did not work and the owner of the property had no option but to accept the work that was done, because it could not be removed.

21.06 PERFORMANCE PREVENTED BEFORE COMMENCEMENT

If the performance of the contractual obligation is tendered but refused, much will depend on the nature of the obligation tendered. If the obligation is the delivery of goods or services which is refused, this normally discharges the supplier's obligations, provided of course that the tender was in the correct form stipulated under the contract[20] and was made at a reasonable time with an adequate opportunity for the receiver of the goods or services to inspect them and to come to a free decision to accept or reject. In *Startup v. Macdonald*,[21] for example, a delivery of oil was contracted to occur before the end of March, payment in cash on delivery. The oil was tendered on Saturday, 31 March at 8.30 p.m. and refused due to the lateness of the hour. The jury found as a fact

---

17 *Christy v. Row* (1808) 1 Taunt 300.
18 *Munro v. Butt* (1858) 8 El & Bl 738; *St Enoch Shipping Co. v. Phosphate Mining Co.* [1916] 2 KB 624.
19 *Coughlan v. Maloney*, ibid.
20 *Morrow v. Carty* [1957] NI 174 (the payment of a deposit, offered by way of cheque—rather than cash which was the required mode of payment under the contract—was held not to be a valid tender).
21 (1843) 6 Man & G 593.

that the defendant had a reasonable opportunity to examine the oil and decide to accept or reject it; accordingly, damages were awarded to the plaintiff for breach of contract. Thus, tender of performance discharges liability, for it is treated as if performance had actually occurred; it may also give rise to liability for breach of contract.

If the tender is the payment of a debt, a refusal (even if the payment is tendered in the form required under the contract) does not discharge the debt. The debt is still actionable, although, presumably, the money would be paid into court in the event of the debt being pursued there.[22] Moreover, since payment of a debt can now occur other than by cash, by say, cheque or promissory note,[23] is the acceptance of such tender absolute or conditional?[24] If the acceptance of the tender of a cheque is absolute as to discharge of the contract, a subsequent dishonour of the cheque would be actionable only upon the dishonour, not upon the original contract: this cannot be. Acceptance of a tender to pay a debt, other than by cash, is conditional on the payment (usually a cheque, or similar instrument) being honoured.[25]

21.07 PERFORMANCE PREVENTED AFTER COMMENCEMENT

If the performance of the contractual obligation is prevented by one of the parties after performance has begun but before it has been perfectly performed, this will enable the other party to recover *quantum meruit*, that is, the amount or value of the work undertaken;[26] and it can be no defence to the party which prevented completion to say that perfect performance was not present.[27] The action is one of quasi contract (or restitution) and is well recognised. In *De Bernardy v. Harding*[28] the defendant wrongfully revoked an agreement he had with the plaintiff concerning the overseas sales of tickets to the funeral of the Duke of Wellington! It was held that the plaintiff could recover the value of the work done prior to the revocation of the agreement. This was in addition to his

---

22 *Griffith v. School Board of Ystradyfoding* (1890) 24 QBD 307 (this is self-defeating because the creditor is then liable for the costs of the debtor).

23 For charge or credit cards, the same problems do not arise. When the cardholder signs the sales slip, he makes a contract to re-imburse the card issuer, and the card issuer contracts to pay the vendor. If the card issuer defaults, there is no right to proceed against the cardholder, see *In re Charge Card Services* [1989] Ch 497.

24 *PMPS v. Moore* [1988] ILRM 526.

25 *In re Romer and Haslam* [1893] 2 QB 286 but the presumption of conditional discharge can be rebutted, see *Sard v. Rhodes* (1836) 1 M&W 153.

26 'As much as is deserved' for the work completed.

27 *Arterial Drainage Co. v. Rathangan River Drainage Board* (1880) 6 LR (Ir) 513 (the failure to complete drainage on schedule, led the defendant to terminate the contract in accordance with it's terms. However, the delay on the part of the plaintiff arose from the failure of the defendant to supply certain necessary information. The court held that the plaintiff could sue for work done).

28 (1853) 3 Exch 822.

right to sue for damages under breach of contract. Where it would be difficult to sustain an action for damages, as the case of *Planche v. Colburn*[29] proved, this *quantum meruit* action is useful. In that case an agreement with an author to edit a series of books and to be paid £100 on completion, was abandoned before the author had completed any book but after he undertaken much work in preparation. It was unlikely that the author could sue for breach of the contract by the defendants, since he himself had not performed his side of the contract, nor in the circumstances would it be in his interests to do so. But he was successful in an action for a *quantum meruit*, that is, restitution of the reasonable value of the service rendered.

21.08 TIME OF PERFORMANCE

As a general rule the time for performance of a contract is not normally of the essence, and failure to perform the contract by the specified date is not failure to perform as of right.[30] Of course, the contract can expressly make the time of performance 'of the essence'; in such a situation failure to so perform will result in breach of the contract.[31] Moreover, time can subsequently be made of the essence by serving notice on the party that performance is required within a reasonable time from the service of such notice and that 'time is of the essence'.[32] At one stage it had been thought that the delay after the time due for performance would have to be quite long before a notice to make 'time of the essence' could be served, but this now seems incorrect; any delay after the due time for performance, it seems, will enable such a notice to be served.[33]

21.09 RECOVERY OF PAYMENT MADE WHERE PERFORMANCE IS IMPERFECT

If payment has been made on foot of a contract which is subsequently imperfectly performed, there can be no claim for the return of the money so paid in

29   (1831) 8 Bing 14.
30   *Hynes v. Independent Newspapers* [1980] IR 204; *United Scientific Holdings v. Burnley Borough Council* [1977] 2 All ER 62; these cases overturn the common law position where time was of the essence (see *Parkin v. Thorold* (1852) 16 Beav 59).
31   *Hudson v. Temple* (1860) 29 Beav 536; note surrounding circumstances may also make time of the essence: *Harold Wood Bovick v. Ferris* [1935] 2 KB 198 (sale of public house), *Hare v. Nicoll* [1966] 1 All ER 285 (sale of speculative shares), key element appears to be extreme fluidity in price of item.
32   *Sepia Ltd and Opel Ltd v. Hanlon*, unreported, High Court, 23 January 1979.
33   *British and Commonwealth Holdings v. Quartex Holdings* [1989] 3 All ER 492 (need to be unreasonably late before notice could be served) but see *Behzadi v. Shaftsbury Hotels* [1991] 2 All ER 471 (unreasonable delay is any delay beyond the time due for performance: time can be made of the essence once the time for performance had passed).

advance unless there is a total failure of consideration.[34] The action in suc
case is for breach of contract (we deal with this more fully in the next chapter).[35]

---

34 *Whincup v. Hughes* (1871) LR 6 CP 78 (a master died before an apprenticeship was
complete, court held that there had not been a total failure of consideration with respect
to the apprentice); *Rowland v. Divall* [1923] 2 KB 500 (a total failure of consideration
occurred where the party had the enjoyment of a vehicle but where the title had not
passed—'vendor' did not own it—the court held that the plaintiff could recover money
paid on foot of the 'sale'); *Hayes v. Stirling* (1863) Ir CLR 277 (a contract to purchase
shares in a company that was never actually formed, the court held there was a total
failure of consideration and plaintiff could recover) but cf. *Lecky v. Walter* [1914] IR
378 (the purchase of shares which were worthless not a total failure of consideration).
35 See also chapter 26 on Alternative remedies where it is argued that the action is one of
restitution, see Birks, op. cit., p. 261 et seq.

22.00

Breach

22.01 INTRODUCTION

It follows from the preceding chapter that failure to perform the contract in its fullest sense is a breach of the terms of that contract sufficient to warrant the contract being set aside. But it is also clear that the courts will make strenuous efforts to ensure the validity of partly performed contracts through various doctrines such as 'substantial performance', 'accepted part-performance', 'refusal of tender of performance'. Thus, there will be many cases where a contract which is not perfectly performed will be held valid and subsisting even where a number of terms and conditions of that contract have been broken or breached. It is a general rule that damages are the appropriate remedy for a breach of contract. If a contract is fully discharged by breach, then it is in the interests of the offending party to commit any number of breaches, thus enabling the contract to be discharged. For example, X contracts to build a house for Y. X, no longer wishing to proceed with the contract, fails to commence building work on the specified date. Y claims that this is a breach of contract; X agrees, replying that as a result of the breach the contract is discharged. The law prevents this sort of abuse by requiring that the contract remain in existence, but that the offending party should be liable to compensate the victim for any damage arising from the failure to perform the contract to the agreed specifications.

It is equally clear, however, that, under certain conditions, the innocent party would suffer if the contract were to remain in existence and only damages were payable. In these sorts of cases, the law permits the innocent party to elect to treat the contract as discharged. It should be borne in mind that the innocent party must elect as to whether to proceed under damages or discharge; he may not have both. Moreover, the right of the innocent party (in the event of a breach of the contract) to elect either to proceed with the contract or treat the contract as discharged, is limited, arising in only two situations: repudiation and fundamental breach. Before turning to deal with these matters in detail, a few words of caution should be entered. Firstly, breach is connected with a failure to perform but not such failure that the court will find the contract discharged as in *Cutter* or *Bolton*. If the court finds failure of perfect performance, then the contract is discharged and no money is recoverable on foot of the work already undertaken, if any.[1] If the court finds that substantial performance has occurred (and therefore the contract is not discharged), then damages are the appropriate remedy unless the innocent party can claim repudiation or fundamental breach. Secondly, different rules apply to the sale of goods, for, if the seller delivers the wrong quantity of goods, this does not force the purchaser to select the correct number. The purchaser can elect to accept the goods as delivered, either in greater or lesser quantity than agreed, and pay the contract *pro rata* price—or he can reject them. He cannot take the items and then seek discharge for breach of contract, for to do so would mean that the purchaser would no longer be liable on foot of the contract and yet could retain the items without paying for them.[2]

22.02 REPUDIATION

In repudiation the innocent party is given the right to terminate a contract, either before it has actually fallen due for performance or on the date for performance, where it is made expressly or implicitly clear by the other party that he has no intention of performing the contract as agreed. The former is often referred to as anticipatory breach, for the repudiation occurs before the time for performance falls due and in anticipation of its non-performance. As Blackburn states:

> Where there is a contract to be performed in the future, if one of the parties has said to the other in effect 'if you go on and perform your side of the contract I will not perform mine', that in effect amounts to saying 'I will not perform the contract'. In that case the other party may say, 'you have given me distinct notice that you will not perform the contract, I will not wait until you have broken it, but I will treat you as having put an end to the contract, and if necessary I will sue you for damages, but at all events I will not go on with the contract.[3]

The classic case in favour of the existence of anticipatory breach is *Hochster v. De la Tour*,[4] whereby an agreement made in May for the plaintiff to commence work in 1 June was terminated by a letter sent late in the month of May. The court held that the plaintiff could sustain her action prior to 1 June, since there had been a clear breach of an existing promise, albeit an existing promise to undertake a future act. It is true to say, however, that courts are cautious when exercising relief for anticipatory breach and will normally require either express evidence of the anticipatory breach (as in the above case)

---

1   But note that the offending party may be able to rely on various doctrines, for example 'substantial performance', 'accepted part-performance' etc.

2   For a fuller analysis see Grogan, King and Donnellan, *Sale of Goods and Supply of Services, a Guide to the Legislation* and Forde, *Commercial Law in Ireland*, pp. 1-120.

3   *Mersey Steel and Iron v. Naylor Benzon* (1884) 9 App Cas 434 (in this case the court held that no repudiatory breach had occurred, the statement is, therefore, strictly *obiter*).

4   (1853) 2 El & Bl 678; *Leeson v. North British Oil and Candle* (1874) 8 IRCL 309.

or extremely strong evidence of an implicit nature.[5] In *Athlone Rural DC v. Campbell*[6] proof of the express intention of the defendant not to proceed with a contract partly underway took the form of a letter stating that the defendant (the District Council) no longer required the plaintiff to complete the work in question.

As regards repudiation where the time for performance of the contract has matured, time is not of the essence in any contract and the innocent party has no right to discharge the contract merely because performance has not started on the time agreed,[7] unless time has been made of the essence in the contract. However, failure to commence performance by the due date coupled with an express or implied intention not to commence performance made by the offending party will enable the innocent party to repudiate the contract. But it requires that notice should be given which makes time of the essence. The better view seems to be that any delay beyond the time limit set down by the contract will enable a party to make time of the essence; it is no longer required that the delay be unreasonable.[8] The party making time of the essence must give the other party a reasonable time within which to perform the contract.

It is clear, therefore, that an express intention not to perform the contract now or in the future will enable a finding of repudiation to be upheld. What constitutes express intention is easy to identify, but what constitutes implied intention not to perform the contract? It must be conduct clearly showing that one of the parties has no intention of performing his side of the bargain. Thus, sale of the goods to a third party or some other act inconsistent with the existence of the contract as agreed satisfies this criteria.[9]

It must be remembered that the express or implied conduct must repudiate the contract in its entirety and not merely arise due to a dispute as to the true construction of the contract in question. Two cases are illustrative of this: *Federal Commerce and Navigation v. Molena Alpha*[10] and *Woodar Investment Development v. Wimpey Construction*.[11] In the former, acting on legal advice that was erroneous, the defendant took steps which the plaintiffs believed

5   *Ross Smyth v. Bailey and Son* [1940] 3 All ER 60 (the burden of evidence required to show an intention to repudiate a contract is not lightly discharged).
6   (1912) 47 ILTR 142.
7   *United Scientific Holdings v. Burnley County Council* [1977] 2 All ER 62; *Hynes v. Independent Newspapers* [1980] IR 204; but note, a delay in performing a contract may discharge it by the doctrine of frustration, see chapter 24 ibid., *Universal Cargo Carriers v. Citati* [1957] 2 All ER 70.
8   *Behzadi v. Shaftsbury Hotels* [1991] 2 All ER 477 which appears to overturn *British Commonwealth Holdings v. Quadtrex Holdings* [1989] 3 All ER 492; see chapter 21, ibid.
9   *Bothe v. Amos* [1975] 2 All ER 321 (a wife left her husband, with whom she had a business partnership, the court held that she had repudiated the partnership); *Larkin v. Groeger and Eaton*, unreported, High Court, 26 April 1988.
10   [1979] 1 All ER 307.
11   [1980] 1 All ER 571.

amounted to an effective repudiation of the contract in question. Here the party genuinely thought that such rights existed under the contract; nonetheless, the House of Lords held that the acts constituted an effective repudiation. In the latter case, on similar facts, the defendants' belief as to the construction of the contract led to acts that the plaintiffs believed amounted to repudiatory breach. Again, the actions arose from a genuine but mistaken view of the law with respect to the contract. Here, however, the court held for the defendants: repudiation had not occurred. The latter case appears to be a more accurate statement of the law: but how can it be reconciled with the former? The better view is that the former case is a special decision whereby the plaintiff was entitled to treat the contract as repudiated because the effect of the breach had immediate consequences for the plaintiff and there was little time within which to react. In the latter case, the completion date of the contract was some time away and, therefore, there was sufficient time to have the issue resolved by the courts without exercising self-help remedies of repudiation of an anticipatory nature.[12]

22.03 FUNDAMENTAL BREACH

Previously we were concerned with the situation of prospective or anticipatory breach where the terms of the contract had yet to be fulfilled. But breach can also occur in the performance of the contract itself (see discharge by performance in chapter 21). We have seen, therefore, that the correct remedy for breach of performance is an action for damages and not necessarily the right to treat the contract as repudiated. However, in certain situations the non-performance of the contractual term is of such significance that an action for damages would be inappropriate. This is referred to as a 'fundamental breach' of the contract and enables the innocent party to treat the contract as repudiated.

We have already seen that certain terms of a contract are so important that a breach of them entitles the injured party to treat the contract as discharged (this is discussed fully in chapter 14 on Conditions and Warranties). Here we have another facet of the same problem. However, at this stage of the contract the court, and the law, are no longer concerned with mere classification but with the validation of the actions of one of the parties. Classification of the terms of a contract enables the parties to a contract to know, in advance, when they have

---

12 *Mersey Steel and Iron v. Naylor Benzon* (1884) 9 App Cas 434 (this case seems to support the hypothesis. The facts were that the parties had contracted to transfer 5,000 tons of steel over a period of time, payment on delivery. After delivery, but before payment, the supplier went into liquidation and the buyers refused to make payments since they had been legally advised that no payment should be made whilst the supplier was in liquidation. The suppliers deemed this a repudiation of the contract. The court disagreed).

a right to discharge the contract. Discharge by fundamental breach is pleaded by a party to the contract almost as a defence of his repudiation of the contract. The same legal criterion discussed earlier will apply; it is merely the timing which is altered. Whether a fundamental breach has occurred, enabling an injured party to treat the contract as discharged, depends on the significance of the term breached (according to the law or the parties to the contract) and the consequences of the breach.[13] Moreover, such repudiation for fundamental breach can operate where the injuring party intends to fulfil the bulk of the contract in question. In *Ellen v. Topp*,[14] for example, the defendant was apprenticed to the plaintiff in three trades: auctioneer, appraiser and corn factor. The plaintiff retired from the profession of corn factor and the defendant absented himself from the apprenticeship. The court held that the defendant had the right to repudiate the contract due to fundamental breach. He had been apprenticed in three trades, and now the plaintiff could only supply two trades. This is followed and extended in *Dundalk Shopping Centre v. Roof Spray Ltd*[15] to cover the poor performance of the contract in question. In that case, the defendants failed to make the roof of the plaintiff's property watertight. The court held that failure to do so within a reasonable time enabled the plaintiff to repudiate the contract and seek damages for consequential loss.

22.04 CONSEQUENCE OF BREACH

Discharge by breach cannot mean that all the terms of the contract are nullified. For example, if the contract is discharged by breach, is a 'jurisdiction selection' clause[16] inoperative, given that it is in the event of breach of the contract that the clause is to have effect? What of exemption clauses? In the case of *Photo-Productions*[17] the plaintiff employed the defendant's security firm to provide security. One of the defendant's employees intentionally and on his own burned

---

13   *Bentsen v. Taylor* [1893] 2 QB 274 ('there is no way of deciding that question except by looking at the contract in the light of the surrounding circumstances, and then making up one's mind whether the intention of the parties, as gathered from the instrument itself, will best be carried out by treating the promise as a warranty sounding only in damages or as a condition precedent by the failure to perform which the other party is relieved of his liability.' at 281); *Tramways Advertising Property v. Luna Park* (1938) 38 SRN SW 632 (the test is one of 'essentiality'—was the term so essential that the promisee would not have entered into the contract unless he had been assured of the strict performance of the term in question, and that the promisor was aware of this); for an application, see *Robb v. James* (1881) 15 ILTR 59 (failure to honour the obligation to pay was held by the court to be a fundamental breach).

14   (1851) 6 Exch 424.

15   Unreported, High Court, 21 March 1979; *Taylor v. Smith* [1990] ILRM 377.

16   That is a clause which states the law to be applied in the event of a dispute arising, and the courts where the action is to be heard.

17   [1980] 2 WLR 283.

down the plaintiff's property. The plaintiff now sought compensation from the defendant, who relied upon a clause in the contract which excluded liability for the actions of employees in such circumstances. Since the plaintiff had repudiated the contract and it now stood discharged, the argument went that the exclusion clause had no effect as it too had been discharged. The court rejected this approach and held that the discharge of obligations under the contract resulted not in an absolute discharge of the contract but only in a discharge of the relevant terms. There is an aspect of this which is not entirely logical, for it presupposes that the contract is only partially discharged by a breach. It should be borne in mind that we are not concerned here with the exclusion clause and its non-application in the case of certain fundamental breaches, which has been dealt with earlier (chapter 14). We are concerned with those cases where the breach is sufficient to discharge the contract but not sufficient to exclude the application of any exclusionary term of the contract. The consequence of the discharge is not to rescind the contract *ab initio*.[18] The effect of repudiation for breach of contract operates, not in the past, but in the future only: the discharge of contract cannot affect existing rights that have arisen under the contract at the time of the discharge. When viewed like this, the decision in *Photo Productions* is easily understood. The actions of the plaintiff could repudiate or discharge the contract as regards the future but not for events which had arisen prior to the discharge, and therefore, the exclusion clause remained valid. Of course, obligations that are yet to mature under the terms of a discharged contract may still be relevant in certain circumstances, such as the assessment of damages to be claimed. Thus, in *Moschi v. Lep Air Services*[19] the guarantor of a company's debts claimed that he was not liable for the instalments on the repayment of the debt that fell due after the contract had been discharged by breach. He claimed that, because the plaintiff had repudiated the contract, the balance of the payments due was no longer enforceable. To an extent this argument is justified, but it would have been a technical victory for the guarantor, since, on the breach of the contract, the plaintiff would become enabled to claim damages arising from the breach and such damages would be calculated in accordance with the amount not paid under the instalment agreement. Discharge by breach never removes the right of the injured party to seek

---

18 *Johnson v. Agnew* [1979] 1 All ER 883 (the plaintiff sued for order of specific performance against the failure of the defendant to honour the agreement to sell a property. In doing this, the plaintiff had clearly elected to uphold the contract of sale, but after the order had been obtained, the property was repossessed by the plaintiff's mortgage company. The plaintiff now sought leave to seek damages for breach of contract against the defendant. In permitting the alteration, Wilberforce LJ said: 'in the case of an accepted repudiatory breach the contract has come into existence but has been put to an end, or discharged. Whatever contrary indications may be disinterred from the old authorities, it is now quite clear, under the general law of contract that acceptance of a repudiatory breach does not bring about recission *ab initio*', at 889).

19 [1972] 2 All ER 393.

damages arising as a consequence of the breach; it merely gives a right to terminate any future performance of the contractual terms.[20]

Finally, it should be remembered that discharge of the contract is at the option of the party who is injured. It does not happen automatically. Such a party may for a variety of reasons elect not to discharge the contract but, instead, to treat it as subsisting.[21] But once an election is made, it is irrevocable.[22]

22.05 DISCHARGE BY BREACH NOT EFFECTIVE IN CERTAIN SITUATIONS

There are a number of situations where discharge by breach will not occur despite the presence of the requirements discussed earlier. Firstly, the delay between the breach and the attempted repudiation may be too long, thereby giving rise to a reasonable presumption that the breach has been effectively waived by the party who subsequently seeks to repudiate the contract. In *BIM v. Scallan*[23] the court held that the party should have discharged the contract as soon as he became aware that the breach could not be remedied. In failing to do so, he had effectively waived his right to discharge. Secondly, suppose the injured party purports to repudiate the contract for a reason which the court determines is not valid, and yet there exists another reason for which repudiation would have been available. Can the injured party now effectively change his pleading? Or should the purported repudiation be treated as invalid? The better view would appear to be that the repudiation is valid if, at the time in question, there were facts other than those claimed by the litigant which of themselves would have entitled the party to repudiate the contract.[24] However, in *Panchaud Frères v. Etablissements General Grain Co.*[25] the Court of Appeal cautioned about the manifest inconvenience of a 'liberty to blow hot and cold in commercial conduct'. The case involved the delivery of goods, which could have entitled the plaintiff to repudiate the contract for certain reasons, and their acceptance. Subsequently, the plaintiff sought to repudiate the contract on other

---

20 *The Mihalos Angelos* [1970] 3 All ER 125; *Hyundai Heavy Industries v. Papadopoulos* [1980] 2 All ER 29.

21 *Avery v. Bowden* (1855) 5 E&B 714 (the plaintiff failed to elect for discharge, events intervened amounting to frustration, the result was effectively to relieve defendants from liability); *The Simona* [1988] 2 All ER 742 (the plaintiff failed to elect for discharge for anticipatory breach, plaintiff continued with his part of the contract but was subsequently unable to perform his obligations as required by the contract when the time came. The court held that the defendants could now validly cancel the contract).

22 Provided that the election has been communicated: *Scarf v. Jardine* (1882) 7 App Cas 345.

23 Unreported, High Court, 8 May 1973.

24 *Boston Deep Sea Fishing v. Ansell* (1888) 39 ChD 339; *Universal Cargo Carriers v. Citati* [1957] 2 All ER 70.

25 [1970] 1 Lloyds Rep 53.

grounds, but those grounds were held insufficient. Three years later, he now sought to reassert his earlier right to repudiate the contract, but he was denied relief. Two factors seem to have worked against the plaintiff. Firstly, the acceptance of the goods when there was an opportunity to repudiate the contract. In some senses this must have appeared to the court as approbation of the contract as performed by the delivery; failure to repudiate for that breach seemed to waive the liability of the defendant. Presumably this of itself was not enough, for the second factor appears to have been the inordinate delay in claiming the basis for repudiation, a delay of three years. The cumulative effect of these factors forced the court to the conclusion that the ground for lawful repudiation had been waived and could no longer be reasonably relied upon by the plaintiff. In commercial transactions one needs to know where one stands.[26]

---

26 But see *Carvill v. IIB* [1968] IR 325 which questions this view, as does *Glover v. BLN* [1973] IR 388. Both cases concern employment law, and may not have a wider application. While commercial transactions require certainty, employment contracts require fairness, or even paternalistic protection, in preference to an emphasis on certainty.

23.00

Discharge by agreement

23.01 INTRODUCTION

Discharge by agreement occurs where both parties have agreed to forego the implementation of the contract; in some senses it could be viewed as a contract to nullify the original contract. Such agreements are really contracts in themselves and are the subject of the same rules as any other type of contract. The most notable requirement is the existence of consideration in order to render the discharge by agreement enforceable. Discharge by deed under seal removes the requirement of consideration and becomes enforceable of itself, but few discharges by way of agreement are made with the foresight that sealing calls for.

Where the agreement to discharge the contract is by way of an agreement not under seal, a number of points need to be clarified. First, have the parties actually agreed to the discharge? Secondly, even if they have, is sufficient consideration present to render the agreement enforceable? Where the contract remains either wholly or partly to be carried out by both parties to the contract, then consideration is probably to be found in the release of the obligations still in existence at the time of the agreement. Where, however, the contract is executed, that is to say, where all the obligations of one of the parties have been completed, then a problem may arise, since nothing remains to be done by that person which can constitute good consideration. The difference has been classified as 'bilateral discharge' for the former and 'unilateral discharge' for the latter. Finally, the issue of formalities arises with respect to certain contracts that come within the Statute of Frauds. We will examine each of these points in turn.

23.02 ACCORD

Before discharge by agreement can occur, it is implicit that the parties to the contract must have agreed to discharge it in some manner. The process of mutual agreement is often referred to as 'accord'. Ordinarily one would expect the agreement to suspend the contract to be express, and therefore to pose few, if any, difficulties. But, of course, situations arise where it is far from clear as to whether or not the parties have agreed by conduct that the contract is discharged. This will most likely occur where the contract has been abandoned by one of the parties—for example, where a contract has gone to arbitration and nothing further is heard for a number of years. Had the case been brought to court, there is usually a facility for seeking that the action be struck out for want of prosecution, but the House of Lords held in *South India Shipping Corp.*[1] that there is no inherent jurisdiction within either the arbitrator or the courts to strike out an arbitration for want of prosecution. This rather problematic ruling cannot be taken to mean that an arbitration that has gone on for years has an indefinite life-span, with the consequence that action is not resolved ('quieted' in legal terms) but left outstanding. The courts will infer, from lack of action, that the contract has been abandoned. This has been recognised in the *Hannah Blumenthal*[2] case where Lord Brandon said,

> The first way [of proving abandonment] is by showing that the conduct of each party, as evinced to the other party and acted on by him, leads necessarily to the inference of an implied agreement between them to abandon the contract. The second method is by showing that the conduct of B as evinced towards A, has been such as to lead A reasonably to believe that B has abandoned the contract, even though it has not in fact been B's intention to do so, and that A has significantly altered his position in reliance on that belief.[3]

This is unsatisfactory as to expression as distinct from result. It introduces the concept of reasonableness into striking out an action for want of prosecution; but how does this differ from the rule for a court action? Court actions follow well defined procedure with exactly established time limits. Most arbitrations are not strict as regards procedural aspects, so one has to utilise the concept of 'unreasonable delay' before dismissing the arbitratation proceedings. But the concept remains the same: in both cases the action can be dismissed even if it is not the intention of the delaying party to abandon the contract. Lord Brandon's distinction between 'mutual accord not expressed' and 'accord imposed on the grounds of reasonableness', while accurate, is perhaps a little too fulsome. The first limb is an accord taken from the express actions of both parties and poses little difficulty. The second limb of the principle, the imposed accord implied due to the actions of one of the parties being unreasonable, is what poses the most difficulty. Where the abandonment of arbitration proceedings occurs outside of formal court structures, more leeway has to be given in determining what delay is sufficient to constitute abandonment. This can only be decided on a case by case basis.

1   [1981] 1 All ER 289, the case has, however, been justly criticised.
2   [1983] 1 All ER 34, *The Splendid Sun* [1981] 2 All ER 993
3   Ibid. at 47.

23.03 SATISFACTION

'Satisfaction' is the term used to represent the presence of good consideration to make enforceable the accord to discharge the contract. The whole process is referred to as 'accord and satisfaction'. To some extent this issue was dealt with earlier when we discussed the variation of a contract, including its termination and the need for consideration and the use of promissory estoppel in certain situations.[4] Historically, however, this concept of accord and satisfaction arose before the evolution of promissory estoppel and a classification has been made as between *bilateral* and *unilateral* discharge.

Bilateral discharge occurs where the accord is satisfied by consideration being present, namely, both parties have rights under the contract that are still to be performed, and their waiving of those rights constitutes sufficient consideration to make the accord a new agreement enforceable in its own right. This is so whether the discharge seeks to terminate the contract, vary its terms[5] or substitute a new contract for it.[6] We shall see later that such accord and satisfaction may be unenforceable if there is a lack of the requisite formalities.[7]

An accord which waives a term of the contract, beneficial to only one of the parties involved, cannot be enforced due to the lack of consideration: thus, a request by the buyer of goods that the delivery date of the items be delayed because he is not yet in funds—a request which is agreed to by the seller—is not enforceable, because the buyer has provided no consideration, having obtained only a benefit with no burden. This would mean that if the seller subsequently tendered the goods on the agreed later date, the buyer could legitimately refuse them on the grounds that they were in breach of the date stipulated in the contract prior to the variation. This is, of course, unacceptable and has long been recognised as an untrue statement of the law. As Bowen LJ stated in *Birmingham and District Land Co. v. London and North Western Railway Co.*[8]

    if persons who have contractual rights against others induce by their

---

4   See chapter 7 and 8 ibid.

5   *Fenner v. Blake* [1900] 1 QB 427; *McQuaid v. Lynam* [1965] IR 564.

6   See *Morris v. Baron* [1918] AC 1 (intention is the overriding factor). In this case, a contract to deliver a certain quantity of goods was only partially completed. The supplier sued to recover amounts due under the contract, the purchaser counterclaimed for damages arising from the partial non-delivery. The action was settled by oral agreement. The oral agreement was never honoured, and the supplier revived the action. It was held that the oral agreement evidenced an intention to discharge the original contract, not merely vary it—incidentally, the oral agreement was not enforceable in any event, due to the lack of formalities); compare with *UDT v. Shoucair* [1968] 2 All ER 904 (an agreement to vary the interest rate on a secured mortgage did not evidence an intention to discharge the existing loan and replace it with a new mortgage).

7   See ibid. for a more detailed discussion of the formalities required.

8   (1888) 40 Ch D 268.

conduct those against whom they have such rights to believe that such rights will either not be enforced or will be kept in suspense or abeyance for some particular time, those persons will not be allowed by a court of equity to enforce the rights until such time has elapsed, without at all events placing the parties in the same position as they were in before.[9]

This is nothing more than a variation of the doctrine of promissory estoppel. Where there is a difficulty (in the case of bilateral discharge) of pinpointing sufficient consideration, the matter should be resolved by way of the doctrine of promissory estoppel (discussed earlier in chapter 8). It should, however, be mentioned that there are those in the judiciary who would hold that waiver of contractual terms, and the rules applicable thereto, is a doctrine distinct from that of promissory estoppel, even if the application of the doctrines would lead to identical results.[10] That view seems to be untenable in light of the development of the concept of promissory estoppel and the subjective valuation of consideration (discussed earlier).

For unilateral discharge, the contract has been executed by one of the parties. For example, where X agreed with Y to buy goods for £100 and those goods have been delivered, X now seeks Y's agreement to accept only £75 in full payment of the outstanding contract. We have already seen that in *Pinnel's* case this does not constitute good consideration and the agreement is, therefore, unenforceable. Such accord and satisfaction can be enforced in only two ways: by deed under seal (which does not require consideration) or by the payment of fresh consideration to render the agreement enforceable—for example paying £75 plus a book, or paying £75 one month before the £100 was due. It is sufficient that the consideration is promised. There is no requirement, as had been once thought, that the consideration should have been paid before the accord is enforceable, for, if one of the parties should fail to honour the consideration so promised, then he can be sued by the other party on foot of the subsequent promise, not the original contract (since the original contract is discharged from the date of the accord).[11] As Scrutton LJ said,

The consideration on each side might be an executory promise, the two mutual promises making an agreement enforceable in law, a contract. As Comyns puts it in his Digest . . .: 'An accord with mutual promises to perform is good, though the thing be not performed at the time of the action; for the party has a remedy to compel the performance,' that is to say, a cross-action on the contract of accord.[12]

9 Ibid. at 286; see also *Rickards v. Oppenheim* [1950] 1 All ER 420.
10 See judgements of Roskill and Cumming-Bruce LJJ in *Brikom Investments v. Corr* [1979] 2 All ER 753; *Commonwealth v. Verwayen* (1991) ALJR 540 (see further discussion of this area at pp. 117 et seq. ibid.).
11 *Morris v. Baron* [1918] AC 1.
12 *British and Russian Gazette v. Associated Newspapers* [1933] 2 KB 616 at 644.

One further point concerns the extent to which a unilateral discharge of this nature can be enforceable in the absence of consideration. If it comes within the scope of the doctrine of promissory estoppel as outlined, it can, we suggest, be enforceable; the net effect of this would be to abolish the distinction between unilateral and bilateral discharge of a contract. The preferred modern formulation of the doctrine of accord and satisfaction would seem to be along these lines: an accord to discharge a contract is binding when the accord is executed by way of a deed under seal, or where good consideration is present, even where such consideration is executory in nature, or where in the absence of good consideration the doctrine of promissory estoppel can be applied. The accord must also comply with any formalities that might be required.

It is to this compliance with formalities that we now turn.

23.04 FORMALITIES FOR THE ACCORD

Certain contracts must comply with specific legislative formalities; a failure to do this would render the contract unenforceable. The Statute of Frauds is the principal relevant statute. The biggest difficulty occurs where the accord to discharge the contract is not in writing but is an oral communication.

Let us suppose that a contract is governed by the Statute of Frauds, and that the accord is to discharge the existing written contract in full. Clearly, no written evidence of the accord is required under the Statute, since it is designed to render contracts enforceable and has no application over the extinguishment of rights. The accord to discharge the contract would not come within the terms of the statutory provisions. However, where the accord seeks to vary the terms of the written contract, the accord must be evidenced in writing, or else it will have no effect.[13] This is so because the parties are still seeking to enforce a transaction which comes within the Statute and because compliance with the Statute is equally important on the variation of an agreement, as it is on creation of an agreement. Moreover, the distinction between a waiver and a variation of a contractual right suggested by some is obsolete. The argument that a waiver does not extinguish a right, but simply renders it temporarily unenforceable, is fallacious. When a right under a contract is waived, then that term is varied: the right in its original form is not enforceable. Logic would dictate that a waiver is a variation of a contractual term.[14]

Where an accord involves the substitution of a new contract, this new contract may be subject to the formalities of the Statute.

13   *Jackson v. Hayes* [1939] Ir Jur Rep 59; *British and Beningtons v. NW Cachar Tea Co.*
      [1923] AC 48.
14   But cf. *McKillop v. McMullen* [1979] NI 85.

24.00

Discharge by frustration

24.01 INTRODUCTION

After the parties to a contract have settled all the terms and conditions which are to operate, other factors may arise which render the performance of such a contract impossible. These factors must be outside of the control of one or both of the parties: it cannot be, for example, that either party could seek to set aside a particular contract merely on the grounds that he has taken on so much work that it is physically impossible to complete that contract. We are concerned here with external factors which so radically alter the basic assumptions on which the contract is founded that its performance is futile or impossible. At common law the rule was well settled in *Paradine v. Jane*[1] that a contractual obligation rendered impossible to fulfil due to external factors does not of itself remove the non-compliant party from liability for damages for failure to perform. Of course, the parties to the contract could, if they so wished, make express provision excluding liability where external factors prevented performance and thereby displace the common law; but they would have to do so expressly. Failure to do so would imply that the parties did not intend to remove liability in such instances. The result of this rule may be quite harsh: in *Hills v. Sughrue*,[2] for example, a shipowner who contracted to take a certain cargo on board from a port in Africa was liable for non-compliance when he did not arrive at the port, despite the fact that the cargo was not there in any event.

The application of the rule in such an unsophisticated manner was clearly undesirable, so it was not long before the courts began to loosen the application of the principle; hence the development of the doctrine of discharge by frustration. The leading case was that of *Taylor v. Cauldwell*,[3] where the contract was rendered impossible to perform by the destruction of the venue in which it was to occur and for which neither party was responsible.[4] The court held that the contract was discharged as a result and that no liability arose from the discharged contract. It has been argued that there are at least five theories as to the rationale

---

1 (1647) Aleyn 26 (in 91 LQR 247) or 82 Eng Reprints 897; 6 Corbin s. 1322.
2 (1846) 15 M&W 253; *Leeson v. North British Oil and Candle* (1874) 8 IRCL 309.
3 (1863) 3 B& S 826.
4 See Page, 'Development of the Doctrine of Impossibility of Performance', 18 *Michigan Law Rev* 589.

behind this doctrine,[5] but this is really a matter for the philosophers. The decision in this case should not have gone any way other than the way that it went, for that would have made the supplier to a contract act as an insurer for the interests of the purchaser. In the words of Lord Radcliffe we find an explanation for if it had, the doctrine which is no less accurate by virtue of the colourful language he uses:

> By this time it might seem that the parties themselves have become so far disembodied spirits that their actual persons should be allowed to rest in peace. In their place there rises the figure of the fair and reasonable man. And the spokesman of the fair and reasonable man, who represents after all no more than the anthropomorphic conception of justice, is and must be the court itself. So perhaps it would be simpler to say at the outset that the frustration occurs whenever the law recognises that without default of either party a contractual obligation has become incapable of being performed because the circumstances in which the performance is called for would render it a thing radically different from that which was undertaken by the contract. *Non haec in foedera veni.* It is not this that I promised to do.[6]

24.02 THE DOCTRINE APPLIED

The application of the doctrine is not without difficulty. It is, of course, easily stated that the doctrine operates not where there is inconvenience or difficulty in performing the contract but only after events which so radically alter the whole nature of the contract that its performance as originally intended is no longer possible.[7]

The doctrine is well illustrated in the case of *Krell v. Henry*.[8] In that case, the contract involved the renting of a room which overlooked a planned procession of Edward VII. Both parties were aware that this was the sole reason for the contract. The procession was cancelled due to illness, and the parties sought to

5   See Sharp, 'Pacta Sunt Servanda', 41 *Columbia Law Review* 783; *National Carriers v. Panalpina* [1981] 1 All ER 161.
6   *Davis Contractors v. Fareham UDC* [1956] AC 696 at 728-9.
7   *Tsakiroglou v. Noblee and Thorl* [1961] 2 All ER 179 (there is no frustration merely because the cost of performance had risen due to the closure of the Suez Canal: the contract could still be performed by shipping the items by way of the Cape of Good Hope); *Staffordshire Area Health Authority v. South Staffordshire Waterworks* [1978] 3 All ER 769 (inflation beyond that of the expectation of the reasonable man would frustrate a contract. This case is of doubtful authority, and may be explicable instead as discharge by construction of the particular contract); *O'Cruadhlaoich v. Minister for Finance* (1934) 68 ILTR 174 (the statutory abolition of a court, to which the plaintiff had been appointed for his lifetime, discharged the contract).
8   [1903] 2 KB 740.

have the resultant position clarified. The court held that external events outside of their control or responsibility had intervened to make performance of the contract impossible in the manner in which it had been intended and accordingly the contract was discharged. However, compare this with *Herne Bay Steamboat Company v. Hutton*,[9] where the plaintiff agreed to make his ship available to the defendant to view the naval review and for a day's cruise around the fleet at Spithead. The naval review was later cancelled, although the fleet remained at the location. In holding that the contract had not been discharged by the cancellation of the review, a question must arise as to how it is to be reconciled with the earlier case of *Krell v. Henry*. Much has been made of the difference to be attached to the motive of the contract and its object as a rationalisation of the decisions, but such a distinction, if applicable, is not particularly helpful. The motive and object in both cases could be classified as different, and in both cases the object was capable of attainment: in *Krell* the room was still usable as was the cruise in *Herne Bay*. It was an attribute of that object, namely, the motive of the parties, that had been stymied by external events. In both cases a review or procession which induced the contract had been cancelled by third parties. If motive/object is to distinguish the cases, how is it that in one the object of the contract was to see the procession and not rent the room, whereas in the other the object was to rent the ship and not see the review? Both situations are identical and should have been treated as such; the correct interpretation of these cases involves treating them in an identical fashion. In *Krell* the object of the contract was to rent a room from which to see the procession; this object was impossible to perform since the procession was cancelled, and the contract was accordingly discharged. In *Herne* the object of the contract was to rent a ship to watch the naval review and cruise around the fleet; only part of the object could not be attained due to the cancellation of the review, but part of the object of the contract (to cruise around the fleet) was still attainable and, accordingly, it would have been wrong to treat the contract as discharged. Cheshire, Fifoot and Furmston[10] give the example of a contract where X is to drive Y to Epsom at a future date, a date known to both parties to be the day of the Derby. They then speculate what the outcome would be if the Derby were to be cancelled, and they conclude that it would depend on whether the court viewed the Derby as the foundation of the contract or merely a motive which induced the contract. The answer is not complex, but the question forces us to return to the earlier formulation of the contract to see what exactly was agreed. If the agreement was to drive X to Epsom to see the Derby, then the cancellation of the Derby would presumably discharge the contract, since the object of the contract was no longer attainable due to outside circumstances. If the agreement was to drive to Epsom and that included in the trip would be a visit to the Derby, then the contract is not discharged since only part of the object of the contract is

---

9   [1903] 2 KB 683.   10   Op. cit., p. 575.

impossible to attain, but X may still enjoy the drive to Epsom and the pleasure of that town. *A fortiori*, the same would be true if the agreement was merely to drive to Epsom and no mention was made of the Derby even through both parties knew it to be on that day. It would depend on whether the court would hold that the intention of the contract was clearly that of going to the races only (in which case discharge would occur) or whether the race trip was intended to be only part of the object of the contract (in which case it would not be discharged due to the cancellation of the races).[11]

Beyond this, a review of the case law, however illustrative, does little to help us draw a conclusion as to principle, for each fact pattern is different and what is considered a frustrating event in one situation may not be so considered in another.[12] Foreseeability of the frustrating event by the parties has been suggested as being irrelevant,[13] provided of course that the frustrating event is external in causation.[14] Thus, while relief has been granted for the unseen occurrence of a war, it is argued that it has also been granted where an event is assumed to happen but where for external factors it fails to occur.[15] In *Neville and Sons v. Guardian Builders*[16] the plaintiff entered into a contract with the defendant to develop a landlocked site. The problem of access was to be dealt with by the purchase of a strip of land from the local authority, but in the end, the authority simply refused to sell. The question arose as to the status of the contract as a result of this refusal to sell. It might be argued that the contract was discharged by external frustration, but it is difficult to see where the support for this argument can be found. The better view is to regard the object of the contract as one of two possibilities. Either the object was to develop the land on condition that the strip of land be acquired—in which case the failure to so acquire it led to the contract being set aside, not for frustration but for failure of a condition subsequent—or, the object was to develop the land on an implicit assumption that the contract was speculative on acquiring the access strip (in

---

11   *Ontario Deciduous Fruit Growers Association v. Cutting Fruit Packing Co.*, 134 Cal 21, and see in general Calamari and Perillo, op. cit., pp. 540-1.
12   War will normally be a frustrating event, see *Metropolitan Water Board v. Dick, Kerr and Co.* [1918] AC 119. However cf. *Finelvet AG v. Vinava Shipping Co.* [1983] 2 All ER 658 (a finding by the arbitrator that a contract is not frustrated when the war broke out, but when informed opinion believed it would be a protracted war, was held by the court not to be an error of law).
13   Smit, 'Frustration of Contract, A Comparative attempt at Consolidation', 58 *Columbia Law Review* 287; Aubrey, 'Frustration Reconsidered', 12 *ICLQ*.
14   Manners LC, in *Revell v. Hussey* (1813) 2 Ball&B 280, made the point that it can never be frustration merely because one party has encountered difficulties, or rising costs, in performing the contract, unless the causation of the intervening event can be traced to a third party.
15   *West Los Angeles Institute for Cancer Research v. Mayer*, 366 F 2d 220; it might if the events were sufficiently exceptional: *Jackson v. Union Marine Insurance* (1874) LR 10 CP·125.
16   [1990] ILRM 601.

other words, that the parties entered into a gamble and were willing to enter into the contract without conditions and run the risk that events might defeat them). We have come across similar contracts before, where the parties enter into a contract, the subject matter of which may or may not exist. There is nothing wrong with such a contract. Of course, such speculative contracts need to be expressly stated, for seldom will a court infer them. It is on this basis that the case really falls to be decided. Viewed in this light the resolution of the case becomes easily explained.

Clearly, frustration arises where the event is unforeseen by both parties.[17] Where the event is foreseen or envisaged and the parties do not expressly cater for the occurrence of such event, then the answer lies in discovering what the true construction of the contract gives by way of an object to the contract. If we return to the Epsom example and the Derby races, let us suppose that X agrees with Y to take him to Epsom for the races next Tuesday and both parties are aware that, say, due to the inclement weather the races may be postponed. If the contract fails expressly to provide for what is to occur in the event of a postponement, what is the position? The object of the contract is to take Y to the races, but both parties are now aware of a future external event that may render performance of that obligation impossible. The court must determine from all the surrounding circumstances whether the parties agreed that it should be a speculative contract; that is, that there was an element of risk assumed by the parties as to the occurrence of the event. If Y agreed to such a speculative contract, then he cannot treat the contract as discharged for frustration, for this is the very risk that he has run. The harshness of such an approach is mitigated by the fact that the courts will not readily infer such a speculative aspect into a contract; for that to happen, the speculative nature would have to be expressly stated (often it is in fact so stated). Thus in the above example, X might say to Y, 'If you book my taxi for next Tuesday and the races are cancelled you must still pay me what is owed, for I will have cancelled other work to accommodate your business'; it is clear here that the contract could be said to be speculative, for it will be enforceable whether or not its object is attainable. Indeed, where the contract is expressly made speculative in this sense, there is a great likelihood that the contract can be construed as dealing with the course of action to be followed in the event of a supervening event which renders the contract impossible to perform—and it is to this that we next turn. However, it must be stressed that while in most cases the speculative nature of a contract must be express, it is not outside the competence of a court to find the speculative nature implicit from the surrounding facts.

---

17 Where the event is foreseen by one of the parties, and the other party is not informed of it, then it is not possible to rely on the doctrine of frustration: *McGuill v. Aer Lingus and United Airlines*, unreported, 3 October 1983 (Aer Lingus took bookings on behalf of a US carrier that it knew was on strike, held that it was no defence to the plaintiff's claim that the strike frustrated the contract).

If a contract foresees events which would render the contract impossible to perform, and then proceeds to cater for such an eventuality, the better view is that the contract is not discharged by frustration when the events described occur.[18] Thus in *Mulligan v. Browne*[19] a contract of employment between a doctor and a hospital provided that if the hospital had insufficient funds it could terminate his employment by giving three months notice. The hospital ran into difficulty and gave the relevant notice. The contract could not be said to be discharged by frustration, but rather on the terms of the contract itself.[20] As will be seen in chapters 25 and 26, the basis for the breach has important consequences.

Self-induced frustration   It is possible that the frustration could be self-induced by one of the parties. In general self-induced frustration does not operate to discharge the contract.[21] In *The Super Servant Two*,[22] for example, a contract was entered into which was to be performed by one of two vessels, the *Super Servant One* or the *Super Servant Two*. There was no binding choice as to which was to be used, but the defendants themselves had intended to use *Super Servant Two*, though either vessel could have done the work. *Super Servant Two* then sank, and the defendants used *Super Servant One* for other work for which *Super Servant Two* would have been unsuitable in any event. The plaintiff sued, and were met with the reply that the contract was discharged by the sinking of *Super Servant Two* and the defendant had acted reasonably in allocating *Super Servant One* to other work for which *Super Servant Two* would have been inappropriate. In essence, the defendant were claiming the right to allocate the burden of the frustrating event to one particular person and not to others. The court rejected this view and held that the sinking of *Super Servant Two* was not the frustrating event. In fact the frustrating event was the defendant's actions in electing not to perform the contract; they could, after all, have chosen to perform the contract with the plaintiff, rather than honouring contracts they had made with other people. There is a difficulty here, since, if the court's view is correct, the defendant is not absolved of liability; it merely changes the plaintiff. Thus, if the contract were performed as requested by the plaintiff, other contracts made by the defendant would have been frustrated and they presumably would have sued. The judgment is, no doubt, based on the earlier case of *Maritime National Fish v. Ocean Trawlers*,[23] where the defendants obtained licences to operate only a certain number of vessels in their fleet and they chose to assign those licences to vessels other than the one which they had entered

18   Though it might, if the events were sufficiently exceptional: *Jackson v. Union Marine Insurance* (1874) LR 10 CP 125.

19   Unreported, Supreme Court, 23 November 1977.

20   However, the drafting of such clauses must be carefully done, see *Eastern Airlines v. McDonnell Douglas Co.*, 532 F 2d 957 (language should be particular not general).

21   *The Eugenia* [1964] 2 QB 226.

22   [1990] 1 Lloyds Rep 1.

23   [1935] AC 524.

into a contract with the plaintiff. The court held that the defendants could not rely on self- induced frustration; in other words, they could have easily assigned one of the licences to the vessel which the defendant had hired. But this case is different from the *Super Servant Two* case. That case involved Hobson's choice: no matter what the defendants did, one person's contract would not be performed; this was not so of the earlier case, where the selection would have only affected the defendants and not other innocent parties. The *Super Servant Two* decision does not seem to represent good law: where events occur which will render the performance of two or more contracts impossible, an election should be possible as to which of the contracts should be frustrated by the event, provided that the choice is reasonable and discloses no *mala fides*. The view of Treitel should be adopted in this jurisdiction: if *Super Servant Two* is adopted it means that on the same set of facts a party can successfully plead frustration where only one contract is frustrated, but where there are two or more contracts to be fulfilled an election to perform one of the contracts will remove the claim to frustration and a failure to perform any of the contracts will also exclude a claim for frustration, since the contract, or at least one of them, could be performed. This seems unduly punitive and inconsistent.[24]

Finally, the onus of proof in showing that the frustration was self-induced rests not with the party pleading the frustration but with the party alleging that it was self-induced; so, unless it can be clearly shown that the frustrating event arose out of the actions of the party, it will be assumed that the events are externally caused: in *Constantine Line v. Imperial Smelting Co.*,[25] for example, where a vessel blew up (and it could not be definitively proven that the explosion was as a result of the negligence of the owners), there were three possible explanations, of which negligence was one; therefore, the claim of frustration would succeed. On the other hand, in *Herman v. Owners of SS Vicia*[26] and *Byrne v. Limerick Steamship Co.*[27] the failure to obtain travel warrants and a war permit, respectively, were held to arise from the actions of one of the parties. Since it was self-induced, a claim for frustration was barred.[28]

24.03 EFFECT OF FRUSTRATION

The effect of discharge by frustration can be quite onerous. Such discharge operates to remove liability for any rights that may arise in the future in furtherance of the contract. But it does not discharge the contract *ab initio*:

---

24 See Treitel, op. cit., p. 805 et seq. for further argument.
25 [1942] IR 304.
26 [1946] IR 138.
27 [1941] 2 All ER.
28 Consider the question of self induced frustration arising out of negligence,

see Simon LJ in *Constantine Line*, ibid., who gives the example of an opera singer who carelessly catches a cold, and looses her voice. He was of the view that this was not self-induced frustration.

obligations that have matured prior to the discharge still remain enforceable. In *Appleby v. Myers*,[29] a contract for the installation of machinery was frustrated by the destruction of the building (as a result of a fire which was no one's fault) into which the machinery was to be installed. The installer sued the defendants for the value of the work done. Since the contractual obligation to pay for the machinery had not matured at the time the contract was discharged by frustration, no liability arose on the part of the defendants. In other words, the loss lay where it fell;[30] the installer of the machinery could not transfer it to the defendant. This might at first glance appear somewhat unfair (and there is no doubt that this appearance of unfairness led to the subsequent *Fibrosa*[31] decision) but on reflection it seems justifiable. The alternative is to transfer the loss to the defendant; but the defendant has gained no advantage and a simple application of loss transfer does not resolve the complex issues involved. The *Fibrosa* case itself relies upon a total failure of consideration arising from the frustrating event. Yet this case is further unsatisfactory since the repayment of money ordered ignored the expenditure that had been incurred in attempting to fulfil the contract, which had been frustrated by war.

The difficulties arise from the inability of the common law to apportion the loss between the parties. Loss transfer seems to be the only appropriate remedy. Yet, in reality, the very nature of a frustrating event is one which is outside of the control of both parties, and to apply a remedy such as loss transfer (which implies an element of fault) seems without merit. Loss sharing should be the order of the day. Shifting a loss that arises involves an arbitrary choice and one which will lead to injustice. The complicated Law Reform (Frustrated Contracts) Act 1943 in the UK hardly seems to be any improvement in this area, given the interpretation of it by the courts.[32] It is submitted that the American Restatement which permits the court

> to grant relief on such terms as justice requires including protection of the parties reliance interests,[33]

seems to be the better view. Under this section restitution becomes not merely the undoing of an unjust enrichment but also the sharing of the gains and losses between the parties on an equitable basis.[34]

---

29   (1867) LR 2 CP 651.
30   *Chandler v. Webster* [1904] 1 KB 493 (on facts similar to *Krell v. Henry*, ibid., the party still owed for the balance of the rental on a room he had booked to view the coronation procession. Though the contract was discharged, it was discharged only as to the future, the rent for the room had been due before the discharge arose, and, therefore, was still owed. In *Krell* the rent was due after the contract was discharged).
31   [1943] 2 All ER 12.
32   See Cheshire, Fifoot and Furmston, op. cit., pp. 587 et seq.
33   S. 272 (2) see Illustrations 1 to 6, in particular note that this may involve the insertion of a term into the contract by the court, Comment c.
34   Dawson, 'Judicial Revision of Frustrated Contracts', 64 *Boston University Law Rev* 1.

In conclusion, the effect of a discharge by frustration is to relieve the parties of any obligations arising out of the contract which had not matured at the time of the frustrating event. It does not remove liability for obligations that had already matured at the time of the frustrating event. The harshness and potential injustice of the rule has not been the subject of legislative intervention in this jurisdiction.

25.00

Damages

25.01 INTRODUCTION

At common law the basic remedy is one of damages, that is, a payment of a sum of money to compensate for any losses incurred.[1] Almost all writers make the point that the common law does not enforce the contract *per se* but merely compensates for failure to perform, though this should not necessarily be seen as unsatisfactory. There is little to be gained from forcing people to pursue a contract when the underlying mutuality of assent has broken down to the extent that they now face each other across the courtroom. This is not to say that enforcing the execution of the contract is never available as a remedy, merely that it is far more difficult to convince the court of the appropriateness of such a remedy (convincing it to use its equitable jurisdiction is not an easy matter). We will deal with equitable remedies later, but our attention at this stage is focused on the remedy of damages. In discussing damages, two clear distinctions must be made. Firstly, when a contract is breached, the consequences of that breach flow from it in an irregular pattern. In some instances, the consequences will flow freely and extensively; in others, they have fewer ramifications. The extent to which these consequences must be compensated is termed the 'remoteness' of the damage. At some point the law will hold that the damages now sought to be compensated are too remote, too far removed from the events complained of, to warrant compensation. This is not to say that the party has not suffered these damages; it simply means that the law will not make provision for them. Secondly, within the scope of those damages which are not too remote and therefore compensatable, what is the nature of the compensation to be so paid? How is it to be quantified? This is referred to as the 'measure of the loss'.

25.02 REMOTENESS OF DAMAGE

Hadley v. Baxendale[2] was the seminal case which laid down this distinction between remoteness and measure of damages. In that case, remoteness of

---

1   *Robinson v. Harman* (1848) 1 Ex 850 (the loss is calculated as that which is required to put you in the position you

would have been if the contract had been performed correctly).
2   (1845) 9 Ex 341.

damage was delineated by Alderson B as follows:

> Where two parties have made a contract which one of them has broken, the damages which the other party ought to receive in respect of such breach of contract should be such as may fairly and reasonably be considered as arising naturally, i.e., according to the usual course of things, from such breach of contract itself, or such as may reasonably be supposed to have been in the contemplation of both parties, at the time they made the contract, as the probable result of the breach of it.[3]

There are thus two aspects to the rule—normal damage that can be reasonably expected,[4] and special damages that the parties were aware would occur if a breach arose.[5] In the case at bar, the extended closure of the plaintiff's mill due to the negligent delay of the carrier of a replacement part was held not to be normal damage, since it might reasonably be assumed that the plaintiffs had a spare part in their possession while awaiting the new part; nor could it be classified as special damage, since no particular attention had been drawn to it under the contract.

In the later case of *Victoria Laundry v. Newman Industries*[6] the definition was reformulated along slightly different lines. First, remoteness was now determined on the basis of reasonable foreseeability; reasonable foreseeability was predicated on the knowledge of the parties, actual or imputed. Actual knowledge is knowledge which the parties are aware of; imputed knowledge is knowledge which the parties should have been aware of in the ordinary course of their dealings. The *Heron II*[7] made a subtle distinction in terms of reasonable foreseeability; in the *Victoria Laundry* the reasonable foreseeability *of the defendant* seems to be the point, whereas the *Heron II* termed it the reasonable foreseeability *of both parties*. The latter view seems to be correct, since contract is founded upon the parties' intentions as distinct from a normative standard.

There remains a difficulty, however, with the rationale used in remoteness of damage at contract. In *H. Parsons v. Uttley Ingham*[8] a contract called for the

---

3   Ibid. at 354-5.
4   *Stoney v. Foley* (1897) 31 ILT 165 (a diseased animal on land can be expected to infect that land); *Wilson v. Dunville* (1879) 6 LR (Ir) 210 (lead pellets in animal feed could reasonably be expected to injure the animals); *Stock v. Urey* [1955] NI 71 (customs duty that had to be paid to recover a car purchased which, unknown to the purchaser, was illegally smuggled between the North and South, was recoverable as being reasonably part of the loss incurred).

5   *Waller v. Great Western Railway* (1879) 4 LR (Ir) 326 (the loss was held not to be recoverable since the defendants had not been made aware of the particular condition of the items —some horses whose diet had been changed and but for which no damage would have occurred).
6   [1949] 1 All ER 997.
7   [1969] 1 AC 350.
8   [1978] 1 All ER 525.

installation of a storage silo for pig feed. The silo ventilator was incorrectly installed and failed to open; accordingly, the pig feed went mouldy. The pigs were fed from the silo and over 200 died from food poisoning. Under contract it was clear that the plaintiff could recover the loss of the pig feed, but it was the loss of the pigs that required to be compensated. The case is extremely interesting in its exposure of the unsatisfactory nature of this area of contract law. If *Heron II* is a correct statement of the law, then the plaintiff, to recover, must show that the events were reasonably foreseeable by the parties to the contract. But if the plaintiff must show reasonable foreseeability, why did the court permit the plaintiff to recover? If the events complained of must be reasonably foreseen by the defendant and the plaintiff (as is required under the *Heron II*), why was the plaintiff not held to be the author of his own downfall since he too must have seen the consequences of feeding the mouldy pig feed to the pigs? The court was doubtless swayed by the fact that, had the plaintiff sued in tort, he would have been governed by the rules of remoteness at tort, namely, reasonable foreseeability of the ordinary person. The court was unduly influenced by this, but there is no conceptual difficulty in imposing different levels of remoteness in damage as between contract and tort. Firstly, the relationships are radically different, the former based on consent, the latter imposed upon the parties. Thus, in contract, the remoteness of damage is set by what is agreed between the parties whereas the tort standard must be a normative standard. Secondly, in contract, liability is strict, but in tort it normally requires negligence. Again it follows that remoteness can be distinguished, since where the liability is strict it should be limited to the sort of damage envisaged by the parties, whereas where liability only arises on proof of failure to meet the requisite standard expected by society, then remoteness of damage is limited to the sort of damage envisaged not just by the parties to the contract but by society, since one of the parties has failed to achieve the standard set by society.

This may lead to certain discrepancies such as *Kemp v. Intasun Holidays*,[9] where the plaintiff's wife had suffered an asthma attack during a package holiday. The booked accommodation was not available, and the replacement rooms were in fact staff quarters and exceptionally dusty. The award for the asthma attack was set aside by the Court of Appeal as not being reasonably within the contemplation of the tour operator: asthma being a rare condition and the tour operator, not having been informed of it beforehand, could not be liable in contract.

25.03 EXTENT OF DAMAGE

After determining that the damage is not too remote, it next falls to assess the extent of the damage for which the defendant will be liable. In the above *Kemp*

9   [1987] 2 FLTR 234.

case, let us for a hypothetical example: assume that the plaintiff had informed the defendants of his wife's asthma. Under the rule of remoteness the asthma attack is now within the contemplation of both parties (under the *Heron II* test) and therefore the defendants are liable for damages arising from it. But are the defendants liable for all damages or is such liability further limited? Suppose as a result of the asthma attack, a hospital trip were necessary: could these damages be recovered? Yes. But suppose that the plaintiff's wife had died as a result of the asthma attack: would liability attach to the death in that situation? In other words, once some damage is in contemplation of both parties, is the defendant liable for the full extent of any such damage? Clearly, in the first limb of *Hadley v. Baxendale*, liability for damage arising in the ordinary course of business, it is limited to that damage which itself could have been reasonably foreseen; but where the damage arises under the second limb of the rule, that is, damage within the contemplation of both parties, what is the situation? In such a case since the defendant has been appraised of a particular risk, should he or she run the full extent of that risk? The answer would appear to be no. Liability for damage is to the extent that it would arise reasonably as a result of the specific issue of which the defendant was aware. Thus, in the above example, the defendants would be liable for the death as a result of the asthma attack only if it would be reasonable to so include it as a possible consequence of the damage. Ordinarily, asthma attacks do not bring death; therefore recovery for the full extent of the damage should be denied. If, however, the defendants had been told that the plaintiff's wife suffered from severe asthma and another attack could kill her, then the defendant would be liable for such a consequence.

Two cases illustrate this point very well. In *Hickey (No. 2)*[10] the court held that while inflation could be foreseen, it was not reasonable to foresee it for a period of six years; it therefore restricted the award. And in *Pilkington v. Wood*[11] the defendant was held not liable for the impecuniosity of the plaintiff where the plaintiff incurred unusual expenditure of alternative accommodation because he was unable to purchase an alternative property.[12]

25.04 MEASURE OF DAMAGES

General   It now falls to calculate the quantum of damages payable in the event of a breach of contract. There are a number of well defined heads of loss for

10   [1980] ILRM 107.
11   [1953] 2 All ER 810.
12   See also *Diamond v. Campbell Jones* [1960] 1 All ER 583 (the loss of potential increase in the value of property, pursuant to plans for alterations made by the plaintiff before the defendant broke the contract of sale, was held not to be recoverable); compare this with *Chaplin v. Hicks* [1911] 2 KB 786 (a promise to give the plaintiff an interview for one of twelve slots in a show—plaintiff to be one of fifty. The defendant broke his promise, the court held that the jury award could stand, even though had the plaintiff attended the interview she might not have got the position).

which a plaintiff may sue, but a word needs to be said about the purpose behind the award of damages for a breach of contract. It differs fundamentally from the role of damages in tort, which is to compensate for losses arising, that is, to place the parties as if the event had never occurred, to restore them to the original position prior to the cause of action. Since in this situation damages compensate a breach of contract, the role of damages must be to place the plaintiff in the position that he would have been had the contract been performed correctly.[13] It should be borne in mind that compensating the plaintiff to bring him to the position he would have been in had the contract been performed correctly may well internally involve *restitutio in integram*,[14] and it is this which causes some considerable confusion in both academic analysis and judicial pronouncements on this area. For example, again using the hypothetically adjusted facts of *Kemp v. Intasun* mentioned earlier, where the plaintiff had in fact informed the tour operators of the asthma condition, and where the asthma condition involved several trips to the hospital, an award of damages in contract should compensate for failure of performance and this may well involve *restitutio in integram* for all hospital expenses from the asthma attack. The remedy is still at contract, but its calculation is similar to that of tort, for the hospital visits would not have occurred if the contract had been performed correctly.

More difficult is the calculation of losses arising merely from the performance as distinct from the consequences. Suppose X promises to sell 100,000 tons of farmyard manure to Y at £1 per ton to be delivered on 31 January. The delivery day comes, and all is silence from X. Due to the lack of the manure, Y cannot plant his crops, but he has already contracted to pay five men £30 a day as and from 31 January to plant the crops. He makes alternative arrangements for the manure and it arrives on 3 February. The manure is now being purchased at £1.20 per ton from Z. The award of damages is to place Y in the position as if the contract had been performed. His labour costs, if they come under either limb of remoteness of damages, must be compensated fully from 31 January to 3 February, for these damages arise as a consequence of failure to perform the contract. Further, there are damages which arise not as a consequence of failure to perform but which arise from the non-performance *per se*. In other words, suppose in the above example Y had hired no labour; he is still entitled to compensation for non performance of the contract. Indeed, it is clear that he would be entitled to 20p per ton, since he has to arrange supplies from Z at a higher price than what was contracted for with X.

---

13   *Thomspon v. Robinson Gunmakers* [1955] 1 All ER 154 (the defendant failed to complete the purchase of a car from plaintiff, he now claimed that the plaintiff had suffered no loss since the plaintiff had given the car back to the supplier. The court ruled that the loss was the 'loss of bargain' that the plaintiff would have made if the contract had been completed); 5 Corbin, s. 992.
14   Complete restoration to one's original position.

Expectation/reliance loss This type of loss is known as the 'expectation loss'. It is a loss which affected the expectation of Y. Let us suppose that in making the contract with X, Y had paid the amount owed prior to delivery. When the delivery day comes, since the market in farm manure has risen, it is fetching a higher price per ton, X could, without the expectation loss theory, hand the original sum back because he can now sell at a higher price. This is not permissible; the courts will demand that the expectation loss be compensated as well as restitution made. It is termed 'expectation loss' because it is the loss that compensates the plaintiff for what he would have expected had the contract been performed. It is not really a loss, for in some ways the plaintiff never actually had it to lose in the first place; but the term is useful. It is sometimes suggested that expectation loss can be separated from 'reliance loss'.[15] Reliance loss is the loss that arises because the plaintiff made alternative arrangements, mostly with third parties, on the basis of the contract. In the above example, this would be the loss in extra labour charges. Really, reliance loss is a somewhat unnecessary notion, for the compensation of the loss is not to compensate the reliance but rather as a natural consequence of the rules on remoteness. Expectation loss includes therefore, in appropriate cases, reliance losses[16] (this will be discussed below). If that is so, the categorisation of the loss is not really important.

The reliance concept has been brought in from the United States, but the classification into expectation and reliance loss is used for a far different reason in that jurisdiction.[17] Under the Restatement, expectation loss is not available in the breach of a contract enforceable by virtue of promissory estoppel.[18] Reliance loss is all that is recoverable and this makes sense, because the essence of promissory estoppel is reliance. Therefore, the proper remedy is not to compensate for loss of expectation but re-imburse expenditure incurred in reliance upon the contract.

Further, a plaintiff may be in a position to claim only the reliance loss where it is impossible to calculate the expectation loss. Thus, in *Anglia Television v. Reed*[19] the plaintiff sued for reliance losses when the star of a proposed film

---

15 See Fuller and Perdue, 'The Reliance Interest in Contract Damages (1 and 2)', 46 *Yale LJ* 52 and 373.

16 *Liebermann v. Templar Motors*, 140 NE 222 (the plaintiff made car bodies for the defendant. After performance had commenced, but before completion, the defendant repudiated the contract. The court held that the plaintiff was entitled to loss of profit from the transaction and any losses incurred in producing the items in question. This was because mitigation was not possible, in other words the car bodies were wanted by no one else).

17 Calamari and Perillo op. cit., p. 591-2 make the point that there is little difference between Fuller and Perdue's formulation and the traditional view, but admit that it is gaining increasing acceptance as a tool of analysis.

18 Restatement, Second, Contracts, s. 351(3).

19 [1971] 3 All ER 690; Restatement, Second, Contracts, s. 349.

repudiated the contract, on the basis that it would have been difficult to show what profit, if any, the film would have made. In contrast in the US case of Kim Basinger, *Boxing Helena*,[20] the star repudiated the agreement to do the film on the basis of its excessive sex and nudity. The film was subsequently released with a different star but failed at the box office. The producers sued Ms Basinger and were awarded $8 million in damages. This case is difficult to justify if based in contract alone for the correct damages involve loss of profits (which in this case could not be quantified) or loss of expenditure incurred (which in this situation were minimal).

It is open to the defendant, if being sued only for reliance losses, to counterclaim that the plaintiff would have made no profit in any event from the contract and that the expenditure was wasted expenditure on the part of the plaintiff. In other words, the defendant claims that there is no expectation loss. In *Bowley Logging v. Domtar Ltd*,[21] the court accepted the defendants' view that their failure to perform fully the contract actually saved the plaintiff money, but in *CCC Films v. Impact Quadrant*[22] the onus of proof on the defendants was held to be quite high.[23] Of course, the defendants may not claim an absence of any expectation loss if the contract required expenditure to be incurred prior to the performance of the contract itself. Thus, in *Pollock v. McKenzie*[24] expenses incurred by the plaintiff in going to the seller's place of business to collect cattle which had been the subject of an earlier agreement but which the seller refused now to deliver were recoverable as reliance losses, even though it was not clear that any expectation loss arose, that is, the price of the cattle had not altered. It follows that reliance losses incurred prior to the contract being entered into are also recoverable—as was the case in *Anglia Television v. Reed*[25]—provided that they are not too remote.

Can reliance loss be claimed in addition to expectation loss? It is argued that the plaintiff cannot have both the lost profit and the outlay of expenditure incurred, because this not merely compensates the plaintiff but makes it profitable for him. Accordingly, the plaintiff must elect to chose one or the other; he is free to make whichever election is the most profitable from his point of view. This was certainly the view in *Cullinane v. British 'Rema' Manufacturing*,[26] where both Evershed MR and Jenkins LJ in effect stated that the plaintiff must elect which loss to pursue. However, as has been pointed out in Australian case law, the plaintiff's real difficulty in that case was the way in which the claim was both presented and proven. In truth, the case might have been better argued

20   The New York Times, 3 March 1994.
21   [1978] 4 WWR 105 affd (1982) 135 DLR (3d) 179.
22   [1984] 3 All ER 298.
23   See also Restatement, Second, Contracts, s. 349, Comment a; 5 Corbin, s. 1033.
24   (1866) 1 QSCR 156.
25   [1971] 3 All ER 690.
26   [1954] 1 QB 292; see *Waterford Harbour Commissioners v. British Rail Board*, unreported, Supreme Court, 18 February 1981.

on reliance loss, since the expectation loss was difficult to prove and, moreover, the plaintiff had limited it to only three years of the ten-year life-cycle of the item in question. In *Banks v. Williams*[27] the reliance loss was really a part of the expectation loss; the plaintiff had entered into a contract to supply maps to a federal province of Australia, but before the maps had been delivered the province repudiated the agreement. The plaintiff claimed for both expenditure incurred and loss of profits. The court upheld the plaintiff's claim, at least after reducing the expenditure loss by the value of the work already done and which could be sold elsewhere. It is the judgment of Cullen CJ, however, that proposes a proper solution. His reasoning was adopted in *TC Industrial Plant v. Robert's Queensland.*[28] In that case the plaintiff sought to recover loss of profits when the supplied stone crusher failed to operate correctly, and to recover, in addition, the reliance loss incurred in using the defective machinery. The defendants argued that the plaintiff had to elect. The court held that the reliance loss was part of the expectation loss and therefore no election arose. The court ruled that if the machine were supplied and it involved expending £X in order to give a return of £Y profit, then the plaintiff is entitled not merely to the £Y profit lost but also the expenditure incurred in making that profit, the £X. The Australian cases are to be preferred. To give a fuller example: suppose X agrees with Y to furnish 500 maps for £500,000, delivery two months from now. The work is half completed when Y calls the contract off. Suppose the lost profit would have been £25,000 for X. It is clear that X can recover this figure. But suppose X has hired additional cartographers at a cost of £300,000, heating and lighting of the offices over that period when work was underway came to £60,000, and rent at £100,000. The value of the work at hand to date, that is, the maps completed, is £75,000. The damages would be as follows:

Expectation loss		£25,000 (Lost profit)
Reliance loss		
Wages	£300,000	
Less value of items	£75,000	
Total		£225,000
Damages claimed		£250,000

---

27 (1910) 10 SR (NSW) 220; *Commonwealth v. Aman Aviation Pty* (1991) 174 CLR 64 ('We do not regard the language of election or the notion that alternative ways are open to a plaintiff in which to frame a claim for relief as appropriate in a discussion of the measure of damages for breach of contract. In truth . . . damages for loss of profit and damages for expenditure reasonably incurred are simply two manifestation of the general principle enunciated in *Robinson v. Harman* (1848) 1 Ex 850, 855, *per* Parke B', *per* Mason CJ at 85).

28 (1963) 37 ALJR 289.

No claim for the £60,000 heat and light or the £100,000 rent can be made, because these costs would have been incurred even if the contract had never arisen. If the plaintiff had hired the premises specially to undertake the contract, the answer might be different.

In conclusion, the traditional view is that expectation loss includes any consequential loss incurred, provided such loss is not too remote (as outlined earlier).[29] If the expectation loss is incapable of exact quantification, reliance loss may be claimed by itself. It will be a good defence, if pleaded and positively proven by the defendant, that the plaintiff would have suffered no expectation loss unless the loss was incurred prior to concluding or performing the agreement. There is some authority for the principle that expectation loss cannot be claimed in addition to reliance loss; the plaintiff must elect which head of loss to use. However, the alternative view is to be preferred: that is, expectation loss and reliance loss can both be claimed, but recovery is reduced by the value of any expenditure that remains with the plaintiff. Moreover, the expenditure must have been incurred only in expectation of the contract occurring.

Other types of damage

Punitive damages In certain cases, there may be neither expectation nor reliance losses, or they may be so small as to be virtually worthless, yet the courts may feel that the action of the defendant is so far removed from the norms expected in the conduct of contractual dealings that an award of money should be made, not to compensate the plaintiff, but to punish the defendant and so send a strong signal as to how such a breach of contract is viewed. These punitive damages are well accepted in tort actions where the plaintiff's injury is slight or indeed as in the Ford Pinto automobile case, where the motor manufacturer deliberately made an economic choice as to the costing of claims that might be made against the company for a defective car and the cost of changing the manufacturing process for the model in question. Clearly, to award normal damages in such a situation would not adequately remedy the issue. It required more than mere compensation of the plaintiff, for the defendant had already allowed for this. Instead, the court awarded punitive damages against the defendant. It is true to say that in general the courts in Ireland frown upon such awards in contract,[30] although Canadian courts have used an extension of the remoteness principle to cover additional damages that one would not normally expect in breach of contract actions.[31] Clearly an element of *mala fides* is required,[32] or at least a complete disregard for the plaintiff, for example, with

---

29 Nor may any loss be claimed that would involve double recovery to the plaintiff, in particular see Treitel, op. cit., pp. 833-4.

30 *White v. Metropolitan Merchandise Mart*, 107 A 2d 892; 11 Williston s. 1340.

31 *Brown v. Waterloo Regional Board of Commissioners of Police* (1983) 103 DLR (3d) 748.

32 *Garvey v. Ireland* (1979) 113 ILTR 61.

respect to the safety of the plaintiff.[33] Punitive damages may explain the decision in the *Boxing Helena* case, where the defendant breached the contract partly on the basis that the breach would have no significant consequence. No Irish case of such an award exists outside the specialised field of employment contracts,[34] which, as was stated earlier, are now of sufficient difference as to be treated separate from general contract law. However if an appropriate case arises, punitive damages should be available for contract breach.[35]

Unjust enrichment The plaintiff may instead of seeking any of the losses outlined above, seek to recover from the defendant any advantage gained by the defendant arising from the breach. There is certainly Irish support for this,[36] and some Canadian support,[37] but it is suggested that it is incorrectly based. A claim for unjust enrichment is not one that should be made under contract. A claim for unjust enrichment is one of the restitution remedies and best dealt with in relevant associated works.

Nominal damages The plaintiff may seek nominal damages where the injury is slight and there are insufficient grounds to raise a claim of punitive damages. For every legal wrong there is a legal remedy.[38] However, the value of nominal judgments, used primarily to establish a precedent or as a peg on which to hang costs,[39] has diminished with the emergence of the declaration[40] and the use of sums deposited into court, whereby if the plaintiff fails to achieve an award from the court in excess of such sum, costs of the action are not available to the plaintiff.[41]

---

33 *McDonald v. Sebastian* (1987) 43 DLR (4th) 636 (landlord suppressed information concerning unfit drinking water).
34 *Garvey v. Ireland*, ibid. It is open to debate that this case in fact merely proves that a breach of contract can give rise to a tort for which punitive damages can also be imposed, see *Klingbiel v. Commercial Credit*, 439 F 2d 1303 (a breach of a contract amounted to the tort of conversion which enabled punitive damages to be awarded).
35 Though it remains open to debate that the court would give a limited application and follow the majority of its American brethren and make an award of punitive damages based on breach of fiduciary relationship without an independent tort being committed as in *Brown v. Coates*, 253 F 2d 36. To be preferred is the concept of punitive damages payable on evidence of fraud, malice or such like, as in *Boise Dodge Inc v. Clark*, 453 P 2d 551.
36 *Hickey v. Roches Stores*, unreported, High Court, 14 July 1976 (contract to be breached since it was calculated that even after compensating for the breach the contract breaker would still make a profit. Finlay P seemed to suggest that damages should be increased so as to deprive the contract breaker of the additional profit earned. This is a bad statement of law, if such damages are to be awarded it must be as punitive damages, not unjust enrichment).
37 *MacIver v. American Motors* (1976) 70 DLR (3d) 473.
38 *Ashby v. White*, 92 Eng Rep 126.
39 *Stanton v. New York & E Railway*, 22 A 300.
40 See Keane, *Equity*, op. cit.
41 See RSC.

25.05 TIME FOR CALCULATING LOSSES

The correct time for assessing the damages incurred by the plaintiff is the date of the breach of contract.[42] There are, of course, exceptions to this and in limited instances, the correct date is the date of judgment[43] but it should be borne in mind that this is highly unusual and will not easily be granted by a court. It happens particularly in disputes concerning land. In *Vandeluer & Moore v. Dargan*[44] the date of assessment of the damages was the date of judgment in an action for specific performance which subsequently turned out to be unenforceable. And in *Corrigan & Corrigan v. Crofton*[45] the date was that of judgement since the plaintiff, being of limited means, could not remedy the breach at the time it was made. This case is explicable on the basis that the defendants had denied liability and the plaintiff would have had to suffer the loss if the defendants were not held liable. Finally, the vagaries of exchange rate transactions appears diminished, for in *Miliangos v. George Frank Textiles*[46] there is authority for awarding damages in a foreign currency and this has been adopted in *Cremer (Peter) Gmbh v. Co-operative Molasses Traders.*[47]

25.06 GENERAL DAMAGES FOR INCONVENIENCE, DISTRESS ETC.

Traditionally damages at contract have not permitted recovery for inconvenience, distress and so forth.[48] Such damages are normally associated with tortious actions.[49] However, in recent times there has been a tendency to view such damages as available in a contract action,[50] particularly with regard to

---

42 The rule is not applied absolutely, *C Sharpe v. Nosawa* [1917] 2 KB 814 (date was when goods of the quality required by the contract were available on the market); *The Hansa Nord* [1976] QB 44 (date is that of arrival of ship not breach); *Van den Hurk v. R. Martens* [1920] 1 KB 850 (date was when it could be reasonably be expected to open the packages, not date of delivery); *Hoenig v. Isaacs* [1952] 2 All ER 176 (in a contract for the provision of a service, relevant date is date of finding replacement).

43 [1981] ILRM 75.

44 [1985] ILRM 189.

45 [1985] ILRM 564.

46 [1975] 3 All ER 801.

47 [1985] ILRM 564; *Wroth v. Tyler* [1974] Ch 30 (date of assessing loss was to use the value of the property as at the date of the judgement not the breach).

48 *Hobbs v. LSWR* (1875) LR 10 QB 111; *Kinlen v. Ulster Bank* [1928] IR 171; though cf. *French v. West Clare Railway* (1897) 31 ILT 140; *Rolin v. Steward* (1854) 14 CB 595 (refusal to honour cheque could lead to damages for loss of reputation or creditworthiness).

49 The question of employment contracts is illustrative. Whilst English courts have tended to grant damages for mental distress arising from a breach of employment contracts, the American courts have gone the other way, see *Redgrave v. Boston Symphony Orchestra*, 557 F Supp 230.

50 *Johnson v. Longleat*, unreported, High Court, 19 May 1976 (failure to build house to correct standard, could

package holidays. With respect, there is nothing in the authorities which prevents recovery under these headings in a breach of contract action, but the rule in *Hadley v. Baxendale*[51] with respect to remoteness still applies and it is this which prevents many claimants from recovering under such headings. In *Kelly v. Crowley*[52] the plaintiff could not recover damages for emotional suffering on his discovering that a breach of contract had resulted in his obtaining a hotel, as distinct from a public, liquor licence. The rationale is clear. Ordinary business people when entering a contract can foresee that the other party to the contract has the normal commercial fortitude to be expected and that such party will not suffer compensatable distress if there is a breach of contract, such breaches to be anticipated as normal. On the other hand in *Jarvis v. Swan Tours*[53] a customer for a package holiday can be foreseen by the tour operator as suffering from distress if a breach of the contract arises. Seen in this light, it is clear that, in an appropriate case, damages for distress, inconvenience and so forth are as available in contract as they are in tort but the restricted rules of remoteness of damage in contract will limit its availability.

25.07 LIQUIDATED DAMAGES AND PENALTIES

There is nothing to prevent the parties from agreeing the amount of damages to be paid in the event of a breach and where such agreement is a reasonable attempt to quantify the amount of damages the courts will give effect to this, provided of course it does not seek to limit the amount of liability of one of the parties only, in which case it will be treated as an exclusion clause, discussed earlier. Such a clause which seeks to calculate the damage arising from a breach is one which is termed liquidated damages.[54] The clause, however, cannot be used *in terrorem* or as a penalty, that is to say that the agreement can only compensate for losses that arise and not punish the defendant for breach of contract. If a clause is construed as a penalty clause, then the equitable jurisdiction of the court will be available to set such an agreement aside.

Whether a clause is a penalty or liquidated damages is ultimately a matter of construction. Some guidance is to found from the judgment in *Dunlop Pneumatic Tyre v. New Garage & Motor Co.*[55] Firstly the sum involved must not be

---

recover loss of enjoyment); *Hotson and Hotson v. Payne* [1988] CLY 409 (failure to provide contracted wedding reception could result in damages for loss of enjoyment); *Hirst v. Elgin Metal Casket Co.*, 438 F Supp 906 (failure to correctly provide funeral services entitled damages for loss of enjoyment); McCormack, *Damages*, p. 593 et seq.

51 Ibid.
52 Unreported, High Court, March 1985.
53 [1973] 1 All ER 71.
54 *Toomey v. Murphy* [1897] 2 IR 601; *Wallis v. Smith* (1882) 21 ChD 243.
55 [1915] AC 9; *Workers Trust and Merchant Bank v. Dojap Investments* [1993] 2 WLR 702; Wallace, 'Deposit or Penalty? the Price of Greed' (1993) 44 *NILQ* 207.

excessive when compared with the greatest amount that could have been conceivably lost from a breach of the contract. In effect, the greater the amount involved, the more likely it is to be viewed as a penalty. Secondly, it flows from this that if the agreement requires payment of a sum higher than that which is owed, if the sum is not repaid under the terms of the contract, then this is a penalty clause. Thus, a clause which states that a sum of £100 must be paid if a debt of £50 is not repaid by the end of the month is a penalty clause. The same is not true of acceleration clauses under which a contract for a sum to be repaid by instalments contains a clause whereby the entire sum falls due on default of one payment. This accelerates the debt but does not increase it beyond that which is owed. Generally, a term which imposes ordinary rates of interest for late payment of a debt is not a penalty clause, but in *UDT v. Patterson*[56] the clause required repayment not merely of the capital sum advanced but of the entire interest due over the anticipated 36 months of repayment. The defendant defaulted after the first instalment. The court held that the payment of the interest over the full period of the loan even where the loan was to be repaid earlier constituted a penalty.[57] Thirdly, where a clause imposes a pre-determined liability for breach of more than one contractual term and no distinction is made between the potential consequences of the breach, such clause is more likely to be viewed as a penalty.[58] Thus in *Jobson v. Johnson*[59] a term which required the re-conveyance of shares at a fixed price for any default in repayment over a six-year period was held unenforceable because no distinction was made between a default after the first payment and a default after the second last payment.[60] In *Schiesser International (Ireland) v. Gallagher*[61] an employee's obligation to repay travelling and other expenses if he left his employer less than three years after the employment commenced was struck down since the clause imposed the same liability for the employee if he left after the first month as where he left after 2 years and eleven months.

---

56   [1975] NI 142.
57   Note however the decision of the Court of Appeal, overturned by the House of Lords, in *Bridge v. Campbell Discount* [1962] 1 All ER 385 where it was held that where the lessee of a car terminated the agreement pursuant to its terms this was not a breach of contract and so the penalty clause should apply and the *in terrorem* rules were irrelevant. This appears to be the better view, see *Export Credit Guarantee Department v. Universal Oil Products* [1983] 2 All ER 205 (penalty rules apply only to breach of contract not termination under its terms); in this jurisdiction see s. 5, Hire Purchase Act 1946.
58   See also *Ford Motor Co. v. Armstrong* (1915) 31 TLR 267 (clause was disallowed since the amount payable did not vary with the infringement but remained the same).
59   [1989] 1 All ER 621.
60   See *Irish Telephone Rentals v. ICS Building Society* [1991] ILRM 880 (clause which required payment of all instalments due under the contract for hire was held to be a penalty even where a discounting provision was in operation which discounted the amount owing in recognition of shorter maintenance period and the advantage of receiving payments up front. *Held* that these discounts were insufficient).
61   (1971) 106 ILTR 22.

It is true to say that where damages are difficult to determine, the court is more likely to accept the pre-agreed view of the parties in the matter.

Where a clause is deemed to be a penalty clause it is unenforceable. However, it is assumed that the clause will exceed the actual loss of the party involved. Where the loss exceeds the amount of the penalty, it appears that the party can elect to recover either for the actual loss or the penalty.[62]

25.08 MITIGATION

Under s. 2 of the Civil Liability Act 1961, a defence of contributory negligence is available for breach of contract actions. Thus the plaintiff's claim for damages arising from a breach of contract may be reduced by the amount by which the plaintiff carries a share of the blame for the breach.[63] It is difficult to see, however, where a breach of contract by the defendant can be said to be partly the responsibility of the plaintiff and thus, whilst technically possible in this jurisdiction, the English case law which excludes contributory negligence as reducing the plaintiff's damages[64] remains relevant.

This is in contrast to the position at common law where the plaintiff must attempt to mitigate, or reduce, his or her damages.[65] Thus in *Cullen v. Horgan*[66] it was stated that as regards the non-supply of goods, at some point in time the plaintiff had to treat the contract as broken and attempt to secure alternative supply elsewhere; failure to do so could cost the plaintiff uncompensatable damages.[67] And in *Payzu v. Saunders*[68] the court held that the breach should have been mitigated by the plaintiff continuing to deal with the defendant. There the plaintiff had agreed with the defendant to buy silk on credit. Due to late payments, the credit facility was suspended unilaterally by the defendant who then demanded cash payments. The plaintiff refused to continue dealings but no alternative source was available to purchase the silk from. The defendant

---

62 *Public Works Commissioner v. Hills* [1906] AC 368.
63 *Lyons v. Thomas* [1986] IR 666 (plaintiffs award of damages for deterioration in property between contract for sale and completion was reduced by 10% since the plaintiff was aware of the deterioration and failed to inform the vendor. A case of some dubious merit).
64 *Forsikringsaktielelskapet Vesta v. Butcher* [1988] 2 All ER 43.
65 *Brace v. Calder* [1895] 2 QB 253 (plaintiff was an employee with a five year contract, employers ceased to trade, offered another job on the same terms a couple of months later, refused. *Held* that plaintiff, in failing to take up offer was only entitled to nominal damages); *BIM v. Scallan*, unreported, High Court, 8 May 1973 (plaintiff should have repossessed boat and not waited, could not now claim damage for deterioration).
66 [1925] 2 IR 1.
67 *Malone v. Malone*, unreported, High Court, 9 June 1982 (interest could not be recouped by the plaintiff since he should have mitigated his loss by repaying the loan which he no longer required).
68 [1919] 2 KB 581.

was willing to supply the item but not on credit to the plaintiff. By refusing to take the silk the plaintiff had failed to mitigate his damage. This is not so where, as in *Lennon v. Talbot*,[69] the altered terms and conditions on offer to the plaintiff are substantially prejudicial to the plaintiff and in reality *Payzu* is perhaps better confined to its facts. The onus of mitigation rests with the defendant and it is an onerous burden to discharge.

The need to mitigate the level of damages occurs only after the breach has occurred, there is no duty to mitigate an anticipated breach of contract. In *White and Carter (Councils) Ltd. v. McGregor*[70] the respondents repudiated a contract which had not yet fallen due for performance. The appellants refused to accept the repudiation and commenced work on the basis as if the contract was to be honoured. They now sued for the expenditure incurred after they knew that the contract would not be honoured. As Lord Keith put a hypothetical proposition,

> [A] man who has contracted to go to Hong Kong at his own expense and make a report, in return for remuneration of £10,000 and who, before the date fixed for the start of the journey and perhaps before he has incurred any expense, is informed by the other contracting party that he has cancelled or repudiates the contract, is entitled to set off for Hong Kong and produce his report in order to claim in debt the stipulated sum.[71]

The House of Lords, surprisingly, in a three-two majority decision held in favour of the appellants, permitting them to recover for expenses incurred after they became aware of the anticipatory breach.

25.09 INTEREST AND TAXATION

Interest on damages cannot be awarded prior to the judgment for the liquidated damages being made.[72] Once a judgment is rendered for a specific amount of damages, then legislative provision entitles the plaintiff to recover interest on the amount of the judgment at pre-determined rates of interest.[73] Interest is not recoverable where the debt is paid prior to the judgment but long after it is due.

Damages in contract, are subject to taxation save in cases of wrongful dismissal or a breach of a contract of service.[74]

---

69   Unreported, High Court, 20 December 1985.
70   [1961] 3 All ER 1178.
71   Ibid. at 1190.
72   *London, Chatham and Dover Railway v. South Eastern Railway* [1893] AC 429; *President of India v. La Pintada*

Compania Navigacion [1985] 1 AC 104.
73   Courts Act 1981 s. 19(1), the right is not automatic, see *Mellowhide Products v. Barry Agencies* [1983] ILRM 152
74   *Hickey (No. 2)* [1980] ILRM 107.

26.00

Alternative remedies

26.01 INTRODUCTION

In many instances the concept of damages will be inappropriate as a remedy; a claimant will then seek the alternative remedies available to him in the legal system. For the purposes of contract, the principal alternative remedies to damages are rescission, rectification and restitution. Each remedy is a highly developed area of our legal system, and there are many specialised works available. What follows here is a short synopsis of the main elements of the remedies as they apply to contract law, but the reader is advised to read those more specialised works on remedies.

26.02 RESCISSION

There will be many instances when a party to a contract will require that the contract be rescinded and treated as if it is at an end. At common law this can happen by action of one of the parties who believes that the other party has so breached the tenor of the contract that he now wishes to treat it as over.[1] We have dealt with this issue to an extent in the chapter 22 on Breach and chapter 14 on Conditions and Warranties.

At equity, the court has a general discretionary power to grant rescission of many transactions, including contract transactions, on certain grounds. A transaction will be set aside if it has been entered into on the basis of a fraudulent misrepresentation, or silence where the law requires disclosure, or if the transaction is unconscionable or was made subject to duress or undue influence. If the claimant can show that the transaction is tainted by any of the above elements, the court may order the transaction rescinded. However, this remedy is subject of a number of limitations. First, *restitutio in integrum* must be possible, or at least, there must be practical justice in returning the parties to a situation identical to that which would have been if the transaction had never occured.[2] Second, the contract remains voidable and not void. It is not void automatically (or by an action of any party to the contract) and requires a court order. Third, when the court gives an order of rescission, it is void *ab initio*, that

---

1 *Robb v. James* (1881) 15 ILT 59.
2 *Enlayer v. New Sombrero Phosphate Co.* (1878) 3 App Cas 1218.

is, it is back-dated; this is unlike rescission at common law which is void *in futuro* only.[3] Finally, like all equitable remedies, the remedy is discretionary and the court may refuse to grant the remedy, despite the existence of all the necessary ingredients, if it feels that it is unnecessary to do so or that it would cause greater injustice than the harm remedied.

26.03 RECTIFICATION

Rectification is the remedy whereby a document containing incorrect terms of an agreement previously made may be corrected to reflect more accurately the true agreement. This will most likely arise in contract law in the area of mistake; reference should be made to chapter 16 on Mistake. It should be first noted that the law is only permitted to rectify documents; so the claimant must show that there is in existence a document, and that document does not represent the prior agreement; that is, there must be a discrepancy between the original agreement and the document. The prior agreement does not have to be enforceable or concluded.[4] But the mistake in the document must be shared by both parties, that is, the reduction to writing must not represent what only one party had agreed to. If both parties to the contract were of a different opinion as to what had been agreed upon, then, save in rare circumstances, no rescission will be available. In *Irish Life Assurance Co v. Dublin Lands Securities*[5] a contract for the sale of lands mistakenly included certain land which the vendor did not intend to include. The purchaser was unaware of this, but the contract was for a parcel of ground rents. Keane J in the High Court refused to order rectification of the contract so as to remove the land included by mistake. He classified the issue as one of unilateral mistake and therefore, there having been no fraud or sharp practice on the part of the purchaser, no order for rescission was available. This has been followed in *Ferguson v. Merchant Banking*,[6] where on similar facts the court held that the agreement for sale was that of various bits and pieces of property; however, the court could not determine the common intention of the parties as to what constituted those bits and pieces, and it refused an order for rectification.

So if the claimant seeks an order for rectification he must show the true

3   *Johnson v. Agnew* [1980] AC 367.
4   *Monaghan County Council v. Vaughan* [1948] IR 306 (a letter of acceptance of tender sent by County Council, mistakenly stated who should receive the money, the court held that the document could be rectified despite the fact that the prior agreement was unenforceable due to lack of formalities. This proposition has not been entirely without criticism, for it means that a prior agreement which of its own could not be enforced, takes priority over a subsequent contract which can).
5   [1986] IR 332, on appeal to Supreme Court decided on diferent isssue, see [1989] IR 253.
6   [1993] ILRM 136.

common intention of the parties as to the transaction—a relatively difficult onus to discharge. A document will not be rectified merely because one of the parties was mistaken as to the nature of the agreement. It will only be rectified if it does not reflect the common intention of both parties.

26.04 RESTITUTION

Once a contract is formed, any breach of it gives rise to a remedy in damages, not restitution. However, restitution is still an important remedy where the parties are at the pre-contractual stage, such as the payment of a deposit.[7] Further, restitution is also an appropriate remedy where there has been a total failure of consideration,[8] but the failure must be total and no benefit taken under the contract. In *Rowland v. Duvall*[9] the plaintiff used a car purchased from the defendant. On discovering that the title was defective, the car had to be returned. Was the use of the car receipt of a benefit under the contract, since it was collateral to the main benefit? The court held that it was not a benefit. A benefit has to be a partial receipt of what was promised under the contract.

Restitution may also be used as a remedy where a contract has been performed but has for one reason or another been vitiated. The law has developed certain rules with respect to this sort of restitution.

Restitution for work undertaken[10] If the plaintiff has undertaken work for the defendant on the basis of a contract that was felt to exist but which in fact did not exist, then it is possible to recover for the value of the work undertaken.[11] Where the contract did exist but has been discharged by the defendant's action, then a claim will also succeed.[12] There is a difference between the two claims, however. In the former (where no contract exists) the claim can only succeed where the defendant has received a benefit, for it is this unwarranted benefit that must be restored to the plaintiff; but if the defendant has not benefitted from

---

7 *Chillingworth v. Esche* [1974] 1 Ch 97.
8 *Hunt v. Silk* (1804) 5 East 449.
9 [1923] 2 KB 500.
10 Though see *Folens v. Minister of Education* [1984] ILRM 265 (preparatory work undertaken for a contract which was never concluded could be recovered, *Brewer Sreet Investments v. Barclays Woollen Co.* [1953] 3 WLR 869. However, the case is better analysed as two contracts: the primary conract which was not concluded, and a preliminary contract where the Department of Education promised implicitly to compensate the plaintiff for the costs of any expenditure incurred if the primary contract were not completed).
11 *Henehan v. Courney & Hanley* (1966) 101 ILTR 25; *Devaney v. Reidy*, unreported, High Court, 10 May 1974.
12 *Rover International v. Cannon Film Sales* [1989] 3 All ER 423 (this case seems to suggest that damages should not be limited, the issue remains to be finally adjudged. By permitting recovery greater than would have been allowable under the contract, there is a breach of legal theory and consistency).

the actions of the plaintiff, it is difficult to see how the plaintiff can recover for any expenditure incurred.[13] Where the contract is discharged by the fault of the defendant, then the plaintiff should be able to recover the expenditure incurred. The amount that can be recovered is the value of the benefit received, and, where appropriate, the expenditure incurred.[14] The question of whether this amount can exceed the total envisaged under the contract is debatable.[15] The quantum is what is reasonable.[16]

Where a contract exists but has been terminated according to its terms, the situation is governed by the terms of the contract and not by restitution.[17] Where the plaintiff has not completed his side of the bargain, an action for restitution is unlikely to succeed.[18]

Restitution to the plaintiff of money given to the defendant This includes not merely money paid by the plaintiff to the defendant but also money paid to a third party on behalf of the defendant and money received by the defendant, on behalf of the plaintiff.

Money paid on the defendant's behalf Money expended by the plaintiff in discharging an obligation of the defendant[19] is normally recoverable where the plaintiff can show that he was constrained to expend the money[20] and the defendant was legally obligated to pursue the expenditure.[21]

Money received on the plaintiff's behalf There is authority to enable the plaintiff to recover the sums so received[22] but the issue is relatively complex and should be left to specialised works on restitution.[23]

Money paid by mistake If the mistake is one of fact, the money so paid is generally recoverable,[24] but not if the error is one of law.[25]

13 *British Steel v. Cleveland Bridge and Engineering* [1984] 1 All ER 504.
14 *Travers Construction v. Lismore Homes*, unreported, High Court, 9 March 1990.
15 Sometimes misleadingly known as *quantum meruit*.
16 See chapter 21 on Discharge by Performance; *Beresford v. Kennedy* (1887)21 ILTR 17.
17 For example, *Macclesfield Corp v. Great Central Railway* [1911] 2 KB 528 (the plaintiff repaired a bridge that the defendant was legally obligated to repair. The plaintiff now claimed to have the cost paid to him by the defendant. In that case the claim failed, see below); *Beresford v. Kennedy* (1887) 21 ILR 17.
18 *Exall v. Partridge* (1779) 8 Term Rep 308. The law does not assist a volunteer but see *Schneider v. Eisovitch* [1960] 2 All ER 169.
19 *Brooks Wharf v. Goodman Bros.* [1956] 2 All ER 809.
20 See Ibid.
21 *Shamia v. Joory* [1958] 1 All ER 111.
22 *Kelly v. Solari* (1841) 9 M&W 54; *National Bank v. O'Connor and Bowmaker* (1966) 103 ILR 73.
23 *Jackson v. Stopford* [1923] 2 IR 1; see chapter 16 on Mistake for a fuller discussion.
24 See chapter 19 on Illegal Contracts and chapter 20 on Void and Voidable Contracts for a fuller discussion
25 See in particular Keane, *Equity*, op. cit.

Money paid for an ineffective contract   Money paid by the plaintiff for an ineffective contract is generally not recoverable unless there has been a total failure of consideration or where the contract is void on grounds of public policy.[26]

26.05 SPECIFIC PERFORMANCE AND INJUNCTIONS

In some situations, the aggrieved party may seek to have the contract specifically performed in accordance with its terms. This is particularly so with respect to contracts for the sale of land. In such situations, the claimant will seek an order of specific performance of the contract of sale for land or a mandatory injunction in all other cases. To obtain these remedies it must be shown that damages are inappropriate as a remedy, and, since both specific performance and the injunction are equitable reliefs, they are granted only at the discretion of the court. The role of these remedies is so specialised that they are best dealt with in dedicated works such as Keane, *Equity and Trusts in the Republic of Ireland* and Fry on *Specific Performance*.

26   See Goff and Jones, *Law of Restitution* and Burrows, *Restitution*.

27.00

Assignment of contractual rights

27.01 INTRODUCTION

Pursuant to the doctrine of privity (which has been criticised earlier and which restricts the ability to sue to enforce a contract to those persons who were a party to the contract in the sense that they provided some consideration to the agreement) it of necessity follows that assignment of a contractual right cannot be enforced. By 'assignment' we merely mean transfer of the contract.[1] Thus, if X has entered into a contract with Y whereby Y will pay X £100, a contract made between X and Z to assign this right to receive the £100 will not give Z any right to enforce X's contract with Y; otherwise it would circumvent the doctrine of privity. Of course, Z could sue to enforce the rights accruing under the assignment, but his action lies against X only, and not Y. However, by Z suing X to enforce the assignment, Y becomes legally liable, but this involves a tripartite action where one of the parties, X, is present only for the sake of form rather than substance. Moreover, Z cannot force X to take an action against Y to comply with the contract. If X does not wish to sue Y for performance, then at law he need not do so, though, of course, Z could then sustain an action for breach of the contract of assignment against X. This rather absurd position would be unnecessary if the courts in this jurisdiction were to take the enlightened view on privity as outlined earlier (see chapter 9), because Z, being an intended beneficiary of the contract, albeit *ex post facto*, should have a right to sue in his own name. At the very least, for consistency to be observed, it should be that there is a complete bar on the assignment of contractual rights, but this is in fact not the case.

First, since the logical consequence of such a bar to assignment of contractual rights is extremely cumbersome, certain statutory provisions have been enacted to permit assignment of such rights and to allow direct enforcement by the assignee. Most notably, policies of insurance (both marine and life), negotiable instruments and shares are now capable of assignment by virtue of statutory provisions, although in many cases this merely represents a statutory codification of existing legal exceptions to the general rule on assignment. Second, even

---

1   Bailey, 'Assignments of debts in England from the Twelfth to Twentieth Centuries', 47 *LQR* 516, 48 *LQR* 547.

where the legislature has failed to act, the assignee may, on taking out the assignment, obtain from the assignor a power of attorney with respect to the enforcement of the right.[2] Thus, the assignee may sue to enforce the right without further recourse to the assignor, although technically speaking the assignee then enforces the action as the assignor and not in his own name or right.[2] However, it is a useful device which can often be utilised. Finally, the courts of equity would permit enforcement of an assignment in limited situations; it is to these we now turn.

27.02 THE EQUITABLE PRINCIPLES

In general, courts of equity permit the assignee to enforce an assignment in his own name, but, since equity follows the law, this enforcement of the assignment in his own name can only arise in certain situations. First, the assignment must have clearly intended to transfer the property right of the contract to the assignee. This is all that is required at equity. There is no requirement, in general, for notice to be given to the other party to the contract or indeed for the assignment to be in writing or to take any particular form. The intention must, however, be clear, although not necessarily express. Both parties must intend to transfer property, that is, the right to sue to enforce the contract, referred to in law as a 'chose in action'.[3] Provided such intention is present, the effect of such assignment will take the following form:

Assignment of a legal chose in action Since equity follows the law, the assignor must be a party to any action to enforce the assignment of a legal chose in action. What then is a legal chose in action? It is a chose in action which, prior to the Judicature Acts, would be enforced only in a common Law court—for example, a debt due under a contract. Equity would interfere only to the extent that it would force the assignor to become a party to the action either as plaintiff or as co-defendant in an action taken by the assignee. Equity can do this because it still follows the law and merely forces the assignor to join the action in order to perfect the equitable transfer of title. It is, however, unsatisfactory and cumbersome and remains an anomaly that should not have survived the Judicature Acts. The rationale behind such machinations is clear when there were two distinct courts, but today in a unified structure, the difference between the enforcement of a legal and equitable assignment should not exist. Since it is the assignment which is being enforced in equity, rather than the chose in action, similar rules should apply to both types of chose in action. In England, this was given statutory recognition by the Law of Property Act 1925.

2   If the assignor dies, so too does the right to sue: *Porter v. Turner*, 124 ER 7.
3   Intangible property.

Assignment of an equitable chose in action An equitable chose in action is one which, prior to the Judicature Acts, would have been enforced in the Courts of Equity. Chancery jurisdiction in this issue would be mostly concerned with property interests such as trust property and legacies. If the chose in action is equitable, then it will depend on the nature of the assignment. We have already said that the equitable assignment of a chose in action, legal or equitable, occurs by the intention of the parties involved. But the question remains, does the assignment cover the entire interest or only part of it? If the assignment is absolute then the assignee may bring suit to enforce the equitable chose in action in his own name. No joinder of the assignor is either necessary or desirable because all the rights under the transaction have been transferred, the assignee now stands in the shoes of the assignor for all aspects of the transaction. A judgment given in such an action is complete and final and not open to any competing interest or party to further pursue the debtor. Where, however, the assignment is partial, or not absolute, joinder of the assignor is necessary in order for the judgment to resolve the entire consequence of the case and not open the other party to the contract to competing and conflicting judgments.

What then constitutes an absolute assignment?[4] The entire interest of the assignor must be transferred to the assignee for the time being, unconditionally and completely under the control of the assignee. Note, therefore, that the assignment need only be for a limited duration and need not be a permanent assignment which deprives the assignor of all rights forever.

Absolute assignments must be distinguished from conditional assignments, assignments by way of charge and assignments of part of a debt. A conditional assignment either operates or terminates on the happening of a certain event so that in *Durham Bros v. Robertson*[5] an assignment which contained the term 'we hereby assign our interest in the above mentioned sum until the money with added interest be repaid to you.' was held to be a conditional assignment since the assignment was valid only to the extent necessary to satisfy a particular amount. An assignment operating by way of a charge is illustrated by the case of *Jones v. Humphreys*[6] where the assignment over the person's salary to the extent of any indebtedness past, present or future was held to constitute a particular fund that the creditor could have recourse to the extent of the indebtedness and not an absolute assignment of the salary. Assignment of part of a debt has been regarded as not being an absolute assignment, though the rationale for this is more difficult to justify.

27.03 SOME ADDITIONAL REQUIREMENTS

Whilst it is true to say that for assignment at equity to be effective it merely must have been the intention of the parties to assign the contractual right in an

4   See Corbin, 'Assignment of Contrac-   5   Ibid. at 526.
     tual Rights', 74 *Univ of Penn LR* 207.   6   [1902] 2 KB 10.

absolute manner, certain other activities also impact upon the successful nature of the assignment or otherwise and we deal with now. They do not affect such an assignment's validity but merely its application.

Notice We have already seen that to effect an equitable assignment of a chose in action all that is required is intention between the assignor and the assignee and that, in general, no notice need be given to the other party to the contract. However, failure to give such notice will prejudice the assignee in certain instances. First, where no notice has been given the assignee runs the risk of being bound by any payments made by the other party to the assignor. Those payments must have been made whilst the other party was unaware of the assignment, otherwise the assignee will not be so bound. Secondly, and perhaps more importantly, as a result of *Dearle v. Hall*[7] the giving of notice operates to give priority over an earlier assignment which has not been notified, provided of course that the later assignee was unaware of the earlier assignment at the time he or she entered into the assignment. Knowledge of the earlier assignment after the assignment has been entered into but before notice is given will not invalidate the priority. If the later assignee was aware of the earlier assignment prior to the actual assignment, then notice to the other party will not operate to give priority.

The notice need take no particular form, save with respect to those required under the Statute of Frauds, i.e. land and interests therein but it must be clear and unambiguous that an assignment has occurred. For example, in *James Talcott v. John Lewis and North American Dress Co.*[8] notice to pay the amounts outstanding to an agent was held to indicate a matter of convenience and not notice that an assignment had taken place.

Assignment subject to the equities In *Roxburghe v. Cox*[9] an assignment occurred of a sales commission of £3,000. The commission was paid directly into a bank account of the assignor before the assignee notified the defendant of the assignment. Unfortunately, the assignor owed the bank the sum of £647 which was set off against the incoming £3,000. The assignee sued the defendant but the court rejected the claim since the assignee took the assignment subject to any equities that occurred prior to the notification. Thus if the assignee had notified the defendant prior to the transfer of funds, he would have been protected. As James LJ stated,

> Now an assignee of a chose in action . . . takes subject to all rights of set off and other defences which were available against the assignor, subject only to this exception, that after notice of an assignment of a chose in action the debtor cannot by payment or otherwise do anything to take away

7   (1828) 3 Russ. 1.
8   [1945] 1 All ER 247.
9   (1881) 17 ChD 520.

or diminish the rights of the assignee as they stood at the time of the notice. That is the sole exception.[10]

27.04 ASSIGNMENT OF LIABILITIES

At law and equity it is not possible to assign contractual liabilities unless the consent of all the parties is obtained, in effect a novation.[11] In *Tolhurst v. Associated Portland Cement Manufacturers (1900) Ltd*[12] Collins MR said,

> It is I think quite clear that neither at law or equity could the burden of a contract be shifted off the shoulders of a contractor on to those of another without the consent of the contractee. A debtor cannot relieve himself of his liability to his creditor by assigning the burden of the obligation to someone else; this can only be brought about by the consent of all three, and involves the release of the original debtor.[13]

In this sense an assignment of a liability is not possible for in reality what happens in novation is the extinguishment of the original liability and the replacement of it by a new liability.

This prohibition on assignment of contractual liabilities does not of course prevent the use of sub-contractors but only where such use is expressly or impliedly consented to by the parties to the contract. Moreover, such sub-contracting does not remove the liability of the original contractor to the other party. Thus if X contracts with Y to build an office block, it is accepted construction practice that X will sub-contract various elements of the work to other people, such as Z. There are, therefore, two contracts, that between X and Y and that between X and Z. No assignment has taken place. If X fails to honour his contract because of Z's actions, Y cannot sue Z directly, his cause of action being against X. Note also that the service that is being sub-contracted must not be of a personal nature where substitution of the parties would be inappropriate — as was said in *Davies v. Collins*[14] by Greene LJ:

> Whether or not in any given contract performance can properly be carried out by the employment of a sub-contractor, must depend on the proper inference to be drawn from the contract itself, the subject matter of it and other material surrounding circumstances.[15]

The amount of trust reposed in the party given the nature and skill of the operation will also likely affect the courts attitude in such cases.

---

10   Ibid. 526.
11   *Mallory v. Lane*, 79 Eng Rep 292.
12   [1902] 2 KB 660

13   Ibid. at 668.
14   [1945] 1 All ER 247.
15   Ibid. at 250

27.05 CERTAIN RIGHTS INCAPABLE OF ASSIGNMENT

In a few situations certain contractual rights cannot be assigned. Thus alimony payable to an ex-wife, pensions and salaries from the public purse and so forth are not capable of assignment. In like fashion, assignment of some contractual rights of a personal nature are also ineffective, thus in *Kemp v. Baerselman*[16] a contract whereby the defendant agreed to supply eggs to the plaintiff could not be assigned to a third party. The reason appears to have revolved around a clause whereby the plaintiff was prevented from taking eggs from another source, a clause which would have been of no value to the defendant if assignment were envisaged in the contract. However, an assignment over future property not yet in existence is possible, as in *Glegg v. Bromley*[17] where a wife pledged the proceeds of a claim against a third party to her husband, the case not having been settled at the time. The assignment was held valid.

Finally, it is of course open to the parties to deal expressly with the issue of assignment within the contract itself, either permitting it or prohibiting or requiring consent. Many financial arrangements on credit are organised so that the lessor of a car may not assign the contract and so forth. The wording of such clauses should be specific and unambiguous.[18]

27.06 SUMMARY

In summary the following can be held with respect to voluntary assignment.

- A legal assignment of a chose in action (a contractual right) is not possible, save where permitted by statutory provision or a provision within the contract itself;

- A legal or equitable assignment of a contractual liability is not possible save where permitted by the express, clear and unambiguous terms of the contract itself;

- An equitable assignment of a chose in action at law is not effective and the assignor must be a party to the action;

---

16   [1906] 2 KB 604.
17   [1912] 3 KB 474.
18   *Linden Gardens v. Lenesta Sludge* [1993] 3 All ER 417 (the assignment made of a contract, together with chose in action, was not permitted under the original contract (JCT Clause 17) save with the written consent of the other party. An assignment was made, the question was whether or not it was effective. The trial judge ruled that it was not, but this was overturned by the Court of Appeal. The Appeal to the House of Lords resulted in the assignment being rendered ineffective. There were other complicating factors to the case).

- An equitable assignment of an equitable chose in action is effective only if the assignment is absolute and in such cases the assignor need not be a party to the action because the assignee can sustain an action in his own name;

- Where the equitable assignment of the equitable chose in action is not absolute then the assignor must be a party to the action;

- Equity will force the assignor to be a party to the action in an equitable assignment;

- Intention is all that is required to complete an equitable assignment but the assignment will take affect subject to the equities[19] and the doctrine of notice will operate to determine priorities between assignments;

- Some contractual rights are inherently incapable of assignment.

19 That is, subject to whatever rights third parties have acquired over the property.

Bibliography

Anson, W.R., *Principles of the English Law of Contract*, 26th. ed., Oxford University Press, 1989.

Atiyah, P.S., *Sale of Goods*, 8th ed., Pitman, London, 1990.

Atiyah, P.S., *Consideration in Contracts: A fundamental restatement*, (1971).

Atiyah, P.S., *The Rise and Fall of Freedom of Contract*, Oxford University Press, 1985.

Aubrey, G., 'Frustration Reconsidered', 12 *International and Comparative Law Quarterly*.

Bailey, H., 'Assignments of Debts in England from the Twelfth to Twentieth Century', 47 *Law Quarterly Review* 516 and 48 *Law Quarterly Review* 547.

Baker, J.A., 'The Future of Equity' (1977) 93 *Law Quartely Review* 529.

Baker, J.A., *An Introduction to English Legal History*, 3rd ed., Butterworths, London, 1990.

Ballantines, J.A., *Law Dictionary*, Lawyers Co-Operative Publishing, Rochester, 1969.

Barndt, T., 'The Possible Words of promise', 45 *Texas Law Review* 44.

Benjamin on *Sale of Goods*, Sweet and Maxwell, London, 1990.

Bently, M. and Coughlan, P., 'Proprietary Estoppel and Part Performance' (1988) 23 *Irish Jurist* 38.

Bergeron, T., 'Setting the Cat among the Pigeons', (1990-1993) 9 *JISL* 57.

Bianca, C.M., (ed.), 'Commentary on International Sales Law', *Transnational Juris Publications*, 1980.

Binchy, W., *Irish Conflict of Law*, Butterworths, Dublin, 1988.

Birds, J., *Law of Insurance*, 3rd ed., Sweet and Maxwell, London, 1993.

Blake, R., 'Employee Covenants not to Compete', 73 *Harvard Law Review* 625.

Bogert, G., *Trusts*, 6th ed., West Publishing, Minnesota, 1994.

Braucher, R., 'Freedom of Contract and the Second Restatement', 78 *Yale Law Journal* 598.

Buckland, W. and McNair, A.D., *Roman Law and Common Law*, 2nd ed., William Gaunt and Sons, New York (1994 reprinted from 1936).

Burrows, A., *Restitution*, Butterworths, London (1993)

Byrne, R., and McCutcheon, J.P., *The Irish Legal System*, 2nd ed., Butterworths, Dublin (1990).

Calamari, J.D., and Perillo, J.M., *Contracts*, 3rd ed., West Publishing, Minnesota, 1994.

Calamari, J.D., 'The Check Cashing Rule', 1 *New York Continuing Legal Education No. 2*.

Cantoma, *The Italian Legal System*, Butterworths, London, 1985.

Caraballo, W., 'The Tender Trap: UCC s. 1-207 and its applicability to an attempted accord and satisfaction by tendering a check in a dispute arising from a sale of goods', 11 *Seton Hall Law Review* 445 (1981)

Carter, J.W., and Harland, D.J., *Contract Law in Australia*, 2nd. ed., Butterworths, Sydney, 1991.

Casey, J., *Constitutional Law in Ireland*, Sweet and Maxwell, London, 1993.

Cheshire, G., Fifoot, C.and Furmston, M., *The Law of Contract*, 12th ed., Butterworths, London (1993)

Chitty on *Contract*, Sweet and Maxwell, London.

Chloros, A., 'Comparative aspects of the intention to create legal relations in contract', 33 *Tulane Law Review* 607

Christie, R., *Law of Contract in South Africa*, Professional Publishers, South Africa, 1981.

Clark, R., 'Restatement of the Law of Contracts', 42 *Yale Law Journal* 643.

Coaker J.F., *Willie and Millin's, Mercantile Law of South Africa*, 18th ed., Juta Publications, South Africa, 1984.

Coleman, J., *Risks and Wrongs*, Cambridge University Press, 1993.

Collins, H., *Law of Contract*, 2nd ed., Butterworths, London, 1993.

Corbin, A.L., *Contracts*, West Publishing, Minnesota (1952)

Corbin, A.L., 'Assignment of Contractual Rights', 74 *University of Pennsylvania Law Review* 207.

Corbin, A.L., 'The Interpretation of Words and the Parol Evidence Rule', 50 *Cornell Law Quarterly* 161.

Corbin, A.L., 'Offer and Acceptance and some of the Resulting Legal Relations', 26 *Yale Law Journal* 169.

Coughlan, P., 'Swords, Shields and Estoppel Licences' (1993) *Dublin University Law Journal* 188.

Cunningham, R.A., 'A proposal to repeal section 2-201: the Statute of Frauds Section of Article 2', 85 *Com LJ* 361.

Dalzell, T., 'Duress by Economic Pressure', 20 *North Carolina Law Review* (in two parts) at 237 and 341 respectively).

Date-Bah, G., 'Enforcement of third party contractual rights in Ghana', 8 *University of Ghana Law Journal*.

Dawson, J., 'Judicial Revision of Frustrated Contracts', 64 *Boston University Law Review* 1.

Dawson, J., 'Economic Duress—An Essay in Perspective', 45 *Michigan Law Review* 253.

Dias, A., 'The Unenforceable Duty', 33 *Tulane Law Review* 473.

Dole, R., ' Merchant and Consumer Protection: The Uniform Deceptive Trade Practices Act', 76 *Yale Law Journal* 485.

Dwyer, M., 'Subject to Contract—a controversy unresolved?' (1993) 3 *Irish Student Law Review* 16.

Eisenberg, M., 'The Bargain Principle and its Limits', 95 *Harvard Law Review* 741.

Eisenberg, M., 'Donative Promises', 47 *University of Chicago Law Review* 1.

Farnsworth, E.A., *Contract*, 2nd ed., Little Brown and Company, Boston, 1990.

Fennell C., and Lynch, I., *Labour Law in Ireland*, Sweet and Maxwell, London, 1993.

Forde, M., *Constitutional Law in Ireland*, Mercier Press, Cork, 1987.

Foulke, R., 'Mistake in the Formation and Performance of a Contract', 11 *Columbia Law Review* 197.

Fridman, G.H., *Law of Contract in Canada*, 3rd. ed., Carswell, Toronto, 1994.

Fridman, G.H., 'Joinder of Documents to form a memorandum', 22 *Conveyancer and Property Law (ns)* 275.

Fried, C., *Contract as Promise*, Harvard University Press, Boston, 1981)

Friel, R.J., and Donegan, D., 'Disclaimers on Intestacy', *Irish Tax Review*, March 1992.

Fuller, L. and Perdue, J., 'The Reliance Interest in Contract Damages (1 and 2)', 46 *Yale Law Journal* 52 and 373.

Goff, R., and Jones, G., *Restitution*, Sweet and Maxwell, London, 1993.

Grieg, D.W., and Davis, J.L.R., *Law of Contract*, Law Book Company, Sydney, 1987 with cumulative supplement (1993)

Grogan, V., King, T. and Donnellan, E., *Sale of Goods and Supply of Services, a Guide to the Legislation*, Incorporated Law Society of Ireland (1983)

Gutteridge, H., and Megrah, M., *The Law of Bankers Commercial Credits*, 7th ed., Europa Publications, Brussels, 1987.

Hamson, N., 'The reform of consideration' (1938) 54 *Law Quarterly Review* 233.

Handler, G., 'False and Misleading Advertising', 39 *Yale Law Journal* 22

Hays, R., 'Formal Contracts and Consideration: A Legislative Program', 41 *Columbia Law Rev* 849.

Hazeltine, H.D., 'The Formal Contract of Early English Law', 10 *Columbia Law Review* 608.

Henderson, J., 'Promises Grounded in the Past: The idea of unjust enrichment and the law of contract', 57 *Virginia Law Review* 11151A.

Holmes, O.W., *The Common Law*, Little, Brown and Company, Boston, 1881.

Honnold, J., 'Uniform Law for International Sales', 2nd. ed., Kluwer, Deventer, 1991.

Horn, N., *German Private and Commercial Law*, Clarendon Press, Oxford, (1982.

Horwitz, A., 'The Historical Foundations of Modern Contract Law', 87 *Harvard Law Review* 929.

Keane, R., *Company Law in the Republic of Ireland*, 2nd ed., Butterworths, Dublin, 1992.

Keane, R., *Equity and Trusts in the Republic of Ireland*, Butterworths, Dublin, 1988.

Keeton, W.P., 'Fraud: Misrepresentation of Opinion', 21 *Minnesota Law Review* 643

Kelly, J., *The Irish Constitution*, Professional Books, Dublin, 1980.

Kronman A., & Posner, R.A., *The Economics of Contract Law*, Little Brown and Company, Boston, 1979.

Lanham, T., 'Duress and Void Contracts', 29 *Modern Law Review* 615.

Law Society of Upper Canada, *Professional Conduct Handbook* (1978).

Llewellyn, K., *The Common Law Tradition*, Little Brown and Company, Boston, 1960.

Macauley, F., 'Non Contractual Relations in Business: A preliminary study' 28 *American Sociological Review* 55.

MacNeil, I., *The New Social Contract*, Yale University Press, New Haven, 1981.

Maine, H., *Ancient Law*, University of Arizona Press, Phoenix, 1986.

McBaine, G., 'The rule against disturbing plain meanings of writings', 31 *California Law Review* 145.

McCormack on *Damages*, Sweet and Maxwell, London.

McGovern, G., 'Contract in Medieval England: The necessity for quid pro quo and a sum certain', 13 *American Journal of Legal History*.

McMahon, B. and Binchy, W., *Irish Law of Torts*, 2nd ed., Butterworths, Dublin, 1990.

Meaghar, R.P., Gummow W.M. and Lehane, J.R., *Equity: Doctrines and Remedies*, 3rd. ed., Butterworths, Sydney, 1992.

Mee, J. 'Taking Precedent Seriously', (1993) 11 *Irish Law Times* 55.

Mooney, J. 'Old Kontract Principles and Karls New Kode', 11 *Villanova Law Rev* 213.

Murdoch, H., *Dictionary of Irish Law*, Topaz Publications, Dublin, 1988.

Nichols, B., *French Law of Contract*, 2nd ed., Clarendon Press, Oxford, 1993.

O'Dell, E., 'Principle against Unjust Enrichment', (1993) 15 *Dublin University Law Journal* 27.

O'Dell, E., 'Estoppel and Ultra Vires Contracts', (1992) 14 *Dublin University Law Journal* 123.

Oliphant, H., 'Duration and Termination of an Offer', 18 *Michigan Law Review* 201.

Page, F., 'Development of the Doctrine of Impossibility of Performance', 18 *Michigan Law Review* 589.

Patterson, H., 'Equitable Relief for Unilateral Mistake', 28 *Columbia Law Review* 859.

Posner, R.A., *Economic Analysis of Law*, 3rd ed.

Riddell, A., 'The Mystery of Seal', 4 *Canadian Bar Review* 156.

Rosenthal, I., 'Discord and Dissatisfaction: Section 1-207 of the UCC', 78 *Columbia Law Review* 48 (1978).

Sabbath, H., 'Effect of Mistake in Contract: A Study in Comparative Law', 13 *International and Comparative Law Quarterly* 798

Sanfey, R., 'Undue Influence and the Tender Wives Treatment', *Commercial Law Practitioner* (1994).

Sharp, A., 'Pacta Sunt Servanda', 41 *Columbia Law Review* 783.

Simpson, A., 'The Horowitz Thesis and the History of Contracts', 46 *University of Chicago Law Rev* 533.

Simpson, A.W.B., *History of Assumpsit and the Law of Contract*, Oxford University Press (1987)

Smit, J., 'Frustration of Contract, A Comparative attempt at Consolidation', 58 *Columbia Law Review* 287.

Smith, A., *An Inquiry into the Nature and Causes of the Wealth of Nations*, University of Chicago Press, 1976).

Snell, E.H.T., *Principles of Equity*, 28th ed., Sweet and Maxwell, London, 1982.

Tan, H., 'Champertous Contracts and Assignments', (1990) 106 *Law Quarterly Review* 656.

Treitel, G.H., *The Law of Contract*, 8th ed. Sweet and Maxwell, London, 1991.

Twomey, K., 'Competition, Compassion and Champerty', (1994) 4 *Irish Student Law Review* 1.

Unger, G., 'The Critical Legal Studies Movement', 89 *Harvard Law Review* 1685.

Wagner, R., 'How and by Whom may an offer be accepted', 11 *Villanova Law Review* 95.

Wallace, H., 'Deposit or Penalty? the Price of Greed', (1993) 44 *Northern Ireland Law Quarterly* 207.

Waltons, N., *Introduction to French Law*, Clarendon Press, Oxford, 1966.

Whish, R., *Competition Law*, 3rd ed., Butterworths, London, 1993.

Whittier, F., 'The Restatement of Contracts and Mutual Assent' 17 *California Law Review* 441.

Williston, S., *Mutual Assent in the Formation of Contracts in Selected Readings On the Law of Contracts* (1931)

Wolfram, C.W., *Modern Legal Ethics*, West Publishing, Minnesota, 1986.

Wylie, J.C.W., *Irish Land Law*, 2nd ed., Professional Books, Dublin, 1988.

Index